ALONG A RIVER
The First French-Canadian Women

French-Canadian explorers, traders, and soldiers feature prominently in this country's storytelling, but little has been written about their female counterparts. In *Along a River*, award-winning historian Jan Noel shines a light on the lives of remarkable French-Canadian women – immigrant brides, nuns, tradeswomen, farmers, governors' wives, and even smugglers – during the period between the settlement of the St Lawrence Lowlands and the Victorian era.

Along a River builds the case that inside the cabins that stretched for miles along the shoreline, most early French-Canadian women retained old fashioned forms of economic production and customary rights over land ownership. Noel demonstrates how this continued even as the world changed around them by comparing their lives with those of their contemporaries in France, England, and New England. Exploring how the daughters and granddaughters of the *filles du roi* adapted to their terrain, turned their hands to trade, and even acquired surprising influence at the French court, *Along a River* is an innovative and engagingly written history.

JAN NOEL is an associate professor in the Department of History at the University of Toronto.

JAN NOEL

Along a River

The First French-Canadian Women

UNIVERSITY OF TORONTO PRESS
Toronto Buffalo London

© University of Toronto Press 2013
Toronto Buffalo London
www.utppublishing.com
Printed in the U.S.A.

ISBN 978-1-4426-4396-3 (cloth)
ISBN 978-1-4426-1238-9 (paper)

Printed on acid-free paper

Library and Archives Canada Cataloguing in Publication

Noel, Janet
Along a river : the first French-Canadian women / Jan Noel.

Includes bibliographical references.
ISBN 978-1-4426-4396-3 (bound)   ISBN 978-1-4426-1238-9 (pbk.)

1. Women – Saint Lawrence River Valley – History.   2. Women – Saint Lawrence River
Valley – Social conditions.   3. Women – Saint Lawrence River Valley – Economic
conditions.   4. Human ecology – Saint Lawrence River Valley – History.   5. Saint
Lawrence River Valley – Colonization.   6. Saint Lawrence River Valley – Social
conditions.   7. Saint Lawrence River Valley – Economic conditions.   I. Title.

HQ1459.Q8N63 2013   305.40971409032   C2012-901931-3

University of Toronto Press acknowledges the financial assistance to its publishing
program of the Canada Council for the Arts and the Ontario Arts Council.

 Canada Council   Conseil des Arts
for the Arts   du Canada

 ONTARIO ARTS COUNCIL
CONSEIL DES ARTS DE L'ONTARIO
50 YEARS OF ONTARIO GOVERNMENT SUPPORT OF THE ARTS
50 ANS DE SOUTIEN DU GOUVERNEMENT DE L'ONTARIO AUX ARTS

University of Toronto Press acknowledges the financial support of the Government of
Canada through the Canada Book Fund for its publishing activities.

This book has been published with the help of a grant from the Canadian Federation
for the Humanities and Social Sciences, through the Awards to Scholarly Publications
Program, using funds provided by the Social Sciences and Humanities Research Council
of Canada. The author acknowledges a Standard Research Grant from SSHRC.

Contents

ALONG A RIVER
The First French-Canadian Women

Introduction

This book is a study in human ecology. It examines the many ways women whose ancestors were born in France responded to conditions in the St Lawrence Valley between the 1630s and the 1830s. We take for our boundaries the densely settled part of New France that lay along the St Lawrence River and its tributaries. That region was commonly called Canada during the period of French rule there, from the early seventeenth century until 1760, subsequently becoming the British colony of Quebec. Our subjects lived in or around the thousand-kilometre river basin that stretched from the Gulf of St Lawrence to Lake Ontario. Back from the river lay the northern forests, just past the thin rows of cleared fields where each family was ordered to put up posts to keep rudimentary trails from disappearing under blankets of snow. Much of this book explores interactions of people with the wide river and its uplands. And yet each ship that arrived in port carried across the Atlantic an infusion of ideational and material culture from the mother country. Since those aspects of life interest us too, our book embraces the interplay of culture *and* nature, particularly in the world of daily work. Readers may wonder why this study covers such an unusually long period of time. It is because, through the many and various changes of two hundred years, there was a surprising continuity in the way gender was perceived and performed among the region's French-Canadian majority.

Though the book spans two centuries, it concentrates mainly on just one sex. While full appreciation of the gender order requires covering the spectrum, there has been very little scholarship relating to masculinity in early French Canada. For that reason this book concentrates on the considerably larger body of gender research that relates to women. Yet the goal is a little broader than a monograph on ways that working the land transformed women from France. While the book chiefly describes female colonists, their fathers, brothers, husbands, and sons do also stride across these pages, since we cannot hope for any deep understanding of a society without examining the basic relationships of life. In particular, male codes of honour among the officer class, about which family histories offer many clues, are explored in some depth. The aim of the book is a synthesis that offers not only specialized material for scholars but other material that will interest students and more general readers. With the goal of creating such a work, my own archival research is frequently supplemented with important findings by others. I have taken particular care to incorporate key French-language scholarship that has been unavailable to English-language readers.

Although this book will take account of metropolitan influences as well as environmental ones, it perhaps tips the balance a bit back towards the environment as a field of analysis. To some extent the purpose is simply to *restore* balance, since the environment received rather short shrift in that impressive body of late-twentieth-century work drawing its inspiration from metropolitan French historiography. As we shall see, the leading Canadian frontier history was written earlier, just before the rise of Women's History, in the 1960s when it was still acceptable to write even a 'social history' of a people that was focused overwhelmingly on its masculine half.[1] Part of our task is to examine environmental influences simply because the last generation of historians to take the environment seriously were poor matchmakers. They paired their larger-than-life fur trader with two dolls – lovely, speechless Pocahontas, and Stay-at-home Wife, minding home fires while the hero donned his buckskins and slipped off in his canoe. Ethnohistorians have already brought the native 'doll' to life. This book strives to do the same for her French-Canadian counterpart. We would like to show that her work involved much more than might have been imagined, as she awaited birchbark missives from Jean-Baptiste. She too traded furs; she manufactured the buckskins and the canoe; often enough she tilled the family fields. She, and even more certainly her daughter, did not remain a French peasant in clogs gazing wistfully down the river towards France: she, like her husband, embraced the woods. She proceeded to reinvent herself as a *canadienne*.

Mapping Transatlantic Women's History

Before we narrow our lens to the 'Laurentian' colony (proximate to the St Lawrence River), it is important to understand something about the history of women in France, England, and the American colonies. Our first section, 'Mapping Transatlantic Women's History,' serves that function. France and England were, of course, the colony's two successive mother countries, as they in turn assumed control of lands that had already been inhabited for thousands of years by aboriginal peoples. After Samuel de Champlain established his outpost at Quebec in 1608, French settlers began to concentrate along the north and south shores of the St Lawrence River and its tributaries. After Britain conquered the colony in 1760, she proceeded to rule over the French majority and did so until a much-expanded 'Canada' emerged as a dominion in 1867. Thus, the histories of women in France and Britain are obvious points of reference for understanding *canadiennes*. The book begins with a sketch of relevant themes in their history that allow us to situate the Canadian story within its crucial transatlantic context.

The bordering American colonies are the third reference point. They were at numerous times between 1608 and 1840 characterized as 'the enemy,' although during much of the period they were also trading partners who welcomed illegal furs that were spirited across the border from New France to New York and New England. In both England's colonies to the south and France's colony to the north, immigrants encountered a novel environment. Besides sharing the New World's rich resources and social possibilities, both Canada and the adjacent English colonies experienced 'heroic' beginnings (less glorious from a native standpoint) as religious experiments directed by small bands of Catholic or Protestant zealots. Did the fresh start bestow opportunities and liberties on women that echoed those that some men experienced? Or did women encounter exclusions more like those facing the non-white minorities of both regions? On this and other questions, the Americans are there for comparison, and they help us identify what was distinctive about their French-speaking neighbours. With its rapidly growing population and vigorous urban and commercial development, Anglo-America always seemed more dynamic than French America, save in one regard: the frail northern colony made a remarkable thrust into the interior of the continent, forming military and trading alliances that allowed France to lay claim to three-quarters of the continent by the early eighteenth century. Appreciating the vast geographic reach of the Franco-Amerindian network is essential to understanding women's occupations in the colony.

To advance our goal of situating Canada's colonial women within the broader history of women on both sides of the Atlantic, chapters 1 and

5 will present relevant information about economic, political, and legal developments in the seventeenth and eighteenth century 'pacesetter' jurisdictions of France, England, and the northern American colonies. Aware of trends there, we can discern what was distinctive about Canada. The comparison allows us to perceive that the colony retained ancien régime (old order) gender practices for an unusually long time. Our *tour d'horizon* of the history of women in France, England, and America reviews the period 1600 to 1800. If it stops short of 1840, the terminal date for our study of Canada, this is because the situations that transformed ancien régime gender codes had already occurred in the three other jurisdictions by 1800. By then the three great eighteenth-century revolutions – American, French, and Industrial – had all made their mark, and the new gender values that attended them were clearly in evidence. Gender historians have identified these new values as 'fraternal' ones replacing older 'patriarchal' ones; and many have followed Joan Landes, Lynn Hunt, and James McMillan in seeing such a development as a largely negative one for women.[2] Only slowly would that new gender order, with its decidedly mixed blessings for women, permeate the Laurentian colony. In many ways (as our concluding chapter 8 will indicate) Lower Canada would remain an ancien régime colony as late as 1830, forty years after the old order had been toppled in France and a full seventy years after the British Conquest. Our comparison of French, English, American, and Canadian political trajectories and legal codes will indicate how tardy the growing gender restrictiveness in the other jurisdictions was in reaching Canada. Thus the chapters devoted to the history of women in other jurisdictions serve to situate the Canadian case in transatlantic perspective.

Most of the book deals more exclusively with Canada. Part Two, 'Along a River,' introduces the female missionaries and immigrants who first came to live in the looming forests and their interactions with the First Nations who had lived there for centuries. Then it looks at various ways the colonists and their descendants made a living from the New World's resources, focusing on those engaged in trade. Part Three, 'Transatlantic Codes,' moves on to the legal and social frameworks that did so much to shape the economic activities of noblewomen in the manors and in the convents that stood out from the humbler houses along the river. Two underlying themes will guide us whenever our discussion turns to Canada. The first is the way in which the Canadian environment shaped the lives of the female colonists. The second is the influence exerted by hierarchical French social values that continued to exert a pull, especially on the upper classes. Let us look more closely at these twin themes that are central to the book.

'Frontier' and Metropolis in the History of New France

The impact of the Canadian environment, as well as interaction with First Nations who held first claim to the land and its resources, is a major part of the analysis here. How did the presence of aboriginal peoples, as well as the extensive waterways and rich natural resources of their land, affect the history of colonial women? The question requires us to review a classic scholarly debate about the impact of the environment and the aboriginal peoples on the colony's development. We turn first to key proponents of the 'frontier' thesis, then to the opposing 'metropolitan' school of thought.

The 'frontierists' made some choice observations about women, both aboriginal and French: 'The attraction of the fur trade for so many inhabitants is not easily explained.... Perhaps the complete independence which a man found in the forest, not to mention the charms of willing Indian girls, was compensation enough for many discomforts. Canadians ... were men of broad horizons ... were a wife to nag too constantly, some of them at least could hire out as voyageurs for the west.'[3]

Anyone who has navigated boiling rapids or slept under northern lights cannot help but admire those men. More open than any other group we know to what First Nations had to teach, they shook the peasant dirt from their feet, savoured maple and tobacco, and ventured thousands of kilometres in frail vessels and on foot. As a French observer recorded in the 1750s, *canadiens* were the best possible guardians of the colony. They were not crippled by the cold as French troops were. Indeed, 'they alone can go in canoes in summer, on snowshoes in winter, subsist on a bit of flour, lard and suet, make forced marches through the woods for three to six months at time, withstanding the rigours of winter, living from the mouth of their musket, that is to say by hunting and fishing alone.'[4]

It is not the goal of this book to diminish this iconic figure in any way. Without cramping his style, we would still like to know a little more about this travelling man's 'significant others.' Did they too transform themselves in response to the bracing New World and wide open spaces? Fortunately historians of fur trade marriages have already shown the complex motivations of Indian 'girls' who formed alliances with fur traders for a variety of reasons, economic and otherwise.[5] However, historians have tended to leave the French-Canadian wife out in the cold. If there is *any* popular image of her, it is perhaps the one C.W. Jeffreys sketched, standing on the banks of the St Lawrence in clogs and Breton headdress, staring down the river towards France – an essentially 'metropolitan' interpretation. Her relation to the 'frontier' escaped scrutiny because gender became a major category of historical analysis at precisely the time frontier interpretations were going out of fashion, when in the 1970s Canadian 'frontierists' W.J. Eccles and R.C. Harris acknowledged they had somewhat overestimated the New World influences on New France. Nonetheless, some of their constructs were of enduring value. Because readers will encounter at several points in this book the argument that the natural environment and the First Nations peoples profoundly shaped the history of colonial women, let us briefly revisit the subject of the frontier in New France.

It is not necessary to accept nineteenth-century American historian Frederick Jackson Turner's full-blown thesis about the creation of a new man on an egalitarian frontier to realize that wilderness conditions affected any who settled there. The forest and its peoples occupied an enormous place in the history of New France. Between 1604 and 1760, France laid claim to vast tracts that would extend from the east coast of today's Canada to the Saskatchewan River system on the western prairies, and down the Mississippi valley to New Orleans. The most thoroughly colonized part of this sweeping domain lay along the St Lawrence River and its tributaries. This heartland of New France was then known as Canada – the name that would one day be applied to a whole nation. That was fitting, for woodsmen from the strip farms of the little riverside Canada of the seventeenth century were no strangers to expansion. Coming from a small cluster of population surrounded on all sides by forests, they seemed (as successive officials from France complained) much freer than the more sedentary, heavily taxed peasants of France. It was because of colonists who ranged so far into the woods and forged such close alliances with the native peoples that several mid-twentieth-century Canadian historians decided to adapt the American frontier thesis to New France. The numerous young men who headed to the woods and lived beyond the rule of law among the Indians seemed to qualify for what Turner had identified as the new man who left eastern institutions behind to forge a less-constrained, more democratic society farther west.[6] Eccles and Harris used this model to explain the men of New France who pushed ever westward, emulated the freedom of the natives, and escaped authorities' attempts to regulate their lives and their trade.

After 1970, frontier historians of Canada began to be reined in by the 'metropolitans.' They suggested it was time to trash the frontier stage-set. This group, well schooled in *Annales* renditions of the history of France, offered cogent reasons for regarding the colony along the St Lawrence not so much as a new society but, on the contrary, a microcosm of the old country. Metropolitan historians pointed out that the colony never developed the egalitarian society that was supposed to appear on frontiers. Instead, it rather faithfully reproduced the French hierarchy of nobles, clergy, bourgeoisie, artisans, labourers, and farm folk (the last known in Canada as *habitants*). Elites jealously guarded various ceremonial privileges, and they usually intermarried with their own group. People carefully dressed to show their status (nobles in feathered hats and richly coloured fabrics trimmed with gold, embroidery, and lace; business-minded bourgeoisie in black; commoners in caps and garments of homespun or deerskin). Further countering any notion of frontier egalitarianism, some historians of the metropolitan school also portrayed a Canadian peasantry exploited by overlords in ways reminiscent of the situation in France. Though they did not have to face the same crushing taxes levied in France, *habitants* often disputed the modest feudal dues claimed by priest and seigneur, which suggests they found them burdensome.[7]

Moreover, as the metropolitan school pointed out, Canadians never abandoned traditional institutions the way frontiersmen are supposed to do. The colony adhered to the Custom of Paris as its legal code. Government positions and councils were modelled on those of French provinces. Parish institutions, schools, hospitals, poor relief, apprenticeship systems, and ecclesiastical and military bureaucracies were all based on French models. The way pioneers in the clearings lobbied (sometimes even rioted) to have a church and school nearby suggests that getting away from traditional institutions was the furthest thing from their minds. At Quebec where the uncongealing river allowed French ships to arrive each May, the wealthy faithfully followed Parisian fashions, necessarily one season behind since there was a kind of news white-out between November and April. Visitors commented that Canadian towns looked like those in northern France. Far from glorying in the great quantities of land available, most colonists settled closely together. The metropolitan historians explained why: the forest was not a gateway to freedom but a daunting barrier, full of trees so gigantic it was exhausting to clear even one. Clearly the colony did not develop on entirely original lines. In fact, well into the nineteenth century European visitors continued to exclaim how much it reminded them of old, pre-Revolutionary France.

Trade and war also obeyed the dictates of France, rather than imperatives of the frontier. Frontierist notions of the fur trade as a way young
men could escape the toils of settled life met with evidence that by the
eighteenth century, as the trade moved ever farther west, it fell into the
hands of family companies that kept a supply of trained men in their regular employ. Although covert trading makes precise counts impossible,
it seems clear that running off to the woods to trade was an opportunity
open to an ever-shrinking percentage of the expanding population. In
addition, as Louise Dechene observed, most of the profits accrued to
enterprises that were centred on the ports of La Rochelle and Bordeaux,
not to the colonists themselves. France's long arm not only snatched
back profits but also dictated key policies, such as that of keeping un-
profitable posts open for purely imperial ends. Indeed Dale Miquelon,
even W.J. Eccles himself,[8] uncovered an array of evidence that French
economic and military goals closely shaped colonial existence. When
France went to war, the colony went to war. Far from having a frontier
independence, the colony was like a puppet on a string, Little France
controlled by Big France. With all this evidence in hand, the 'metropolitan' historians were able to challenge interpretations based on the
frontier and the continental interior. They turned their faces to the Atlantic, presenting the ocean as a connector rather than a chasm, and
recasting the habitants as run-of-the mill French peasants. Scrutinizing
the colony through *Annales* binoculars, they invited us to perceive the
endless woods looming at the edge of every clearing not as a golden
opportunity for adventurous spirits but rather as a barrier that gave conventional peasants extra work to do.

One does wonder, though, just how far to go in regarding early Canada as Little-France-on-the-St-Lawrence. France in 1700 was a densely
populated country of twenty million people. It had a diverse economy
where sumptuous wealth contrasted with desperate poverty (and thousands roamed in search of work). There were varied fields and vineyards
that had been cultivated in customary ways for centuries, ancient market towns and villages connected by well-travelled roads. Canada in 1700
was a settlement of twenty thousand (1 per cent of that of France), with
two small towns (Quebec and Montreal), a village (Trois-Rivières), and
so few roads that the river remained the best highway. Even that was
blocked by freeze-up nearly half of every year, cutting off communica-
tion with France. Summer did permit a voyage from Quebec down to
the sea of six hundred kilometres, and then thousands more across to
France; but only a fraction of the populace ever made the trip. Except

for those living near the two towns, the tiny French population until the 1740s had fairly limited contact with domestic markets. Many families had a large degree of self-sufficiency in food, clothing, shelter, furniture, tools, and transport. The colony was surrounded by vast tracts of forest, its people heavily outnumbered by First Nations. One cannot ignore these physical facts.

There were other differences too. It seems unwise to ignore the repeated letters from colonial officials observing what they clearly perceived – in dozens of dispatches from a variety of different governors, intendants, and others – about the relatively unconstrained behaviour they found in the colony. They attributed it to various factors including indulgent childrearing, the influence of the Indians, and the free life of the fur trade. Though the frontier historians may have stressed such evidence unduly, weight needs to be given to those comments, as well as to *habitant* resistance to living in supervised old-world village structures. And indeed historians by the turn of the twenty-first century did begin to swing back somewhat towards somewhat fuller acknowledgment that both the French models *and* the forest played their part in shaping the distinctive French-Canadian people who emerged by the eighteenth century. As Thomas Wien responded in regard to Louise Dechene's reference to 'medieval' qualities of the fur trade, 'Don't mistake the continent. The immediate ancestor of this system of exchanges is the longstanding aboriginal trade of North-Eastern America.' Wien aptly commented that work in the metropolitan vein stresses what is familiar from a European perspective but sometimes takes for granted the (colonists') adaptation to the new.[9]

Women and Environments in Early French Canada

To understand how colonists adapted, our three-chapter section entitled 'Along a River' will track, first of all, the arrival of female immigrants at the colonial ports. Then it will begin to trace the colony's exportable natural resources down inland waterways and across the ocean to Europe, taking a tour of posts, farms, towns, and ports to identify women who were involved in the commerce of the frontier. Because the term *frontier* is freighted with connotations of egalitarianism and innovation that (the metropolitans have convinced us) are of somewhat limited applicability in an ancien régime colony, our discussion will revolve around a more neutral concept, that of the environment. The environmental historian's concern with the interaction of human beings and nature brings fresh understanding to many features of colonial life: the ideas of wilderness the first immigrants brought with them, the technology they used to transform natural resources, and the seasonal and weather patterns that determined their routines. (We leave largely for another day how these activities in turn *altered* the environment, though our discussions of missionaries and fur traders briefly note impacts on First Nations and their habitat.) The primary focus is on this question: How did the natural environment affect women's participation in commerce? The term *environment* can be defined as external conditions affecting plant and animal life, and as the area surrounding a place.[10] The first definition – conditions affecting plant and animal life – relates to climate, air, water, and other natural resources. We shall see, in chapter 2, how the external conditions of clean water and air and good growing conditions had a salubrious effect on the *filles du roi* and other immigrants. Those external conditions also included a forested natural environment that would cause furs, timber, birchbark, and other woodland staples to remain a vital part of the populace's economic life throughout the colonial period.

Let us move on to the second definition, 'the area surrounding a place.' In terms of their surroundings, the colonists who dwelt along the banks of the St Lawrence or its tributaries looked out to a vast hinterland. It included the fur-trading country bordering the Upper Great Lakes that was known as the *pays d'en haut*, from which myriad rivers led into ever more distant trade hinterlands. To the south lay the colony of New York, to which Canadians smuggled furs in large number. They also had an eastern hinterland that stretched seaward from their own local markets in villages and towns, on down the river towards the fisheries and ports of Gaspé and Louisbourg, and on across the ocean whose waves eventually lapped the shores of western France. We shall discuss women working in all these locales. Their ventures spanned the fur and timber trades, local manufactures and markets, the fisheries, and the transatlantic trade.

As the book moves beyond its initial historiographic section, the environmental influences come to the fore in chapter 2, when the discussion begins to focus on Canada. The reader will be introduced to key immigrant groups, will learn the attractions of the New World environment for both the female missionaries known as *dévotes* and the immigrant brides known as *filles du roi*. Chapters 3 and 4 in their turn also stress environmental influences. They document the hundreds of women involved in the trade of natural resources that were the colony's essential export commodities – an assemblage of data that owes much to several years of able assistance by Université de Montréal researcher Molly Richter. The immense geographic distances covered in culling and shipping these resources elicited participation by whole families along the vast chain of commerce that extended from Bordeaux to the Saskatchewan River.

Cultural Spaces

After those central chapters that analyse women's place in the resource economy, the next three-chapter section, 'Transatlantic Codes,' represents a shift towards the second strand of interpretation, in which French culture exerted a stronger pull. Some aspects of female experience closely replicated cultural patterns of the mother country. Chapter 5 discusses a variety of legal codes before narrowing the discussion to the Custom of Paris, the code Canadians shared with their compatriots living in and around the French capital. It explains the legal underpinnings that allowed women to inherit property and use it. This right was, like all European women's rights in this period, restricted in comparison to the entitlements men enjoyed. By sketching what was happening in other jurisdictions, though, chapter 5 will show that Canadian women did possess significant property rights, certainly in comparison to women in common law jurisdictions.

The rest of the section on 'Transatlantic Codes' turns to colonial nobles, first to secular gentlewomen and then to religious ones who engaged in various public or profitable enterprises. Their actions seem more responsive to cultural imperatives generated in the mother country than to the natural environment. In examining those upper echelons, one becomes aware of elaborate hierarchies, codes of honour, clientage networks, and battles of slander and wit more redolent of Versailles than of the frontier. One enters into the life of the colonial 'big house' (admittedly not too big) to capture the mentality of leading families in which female members were publicly active. Since female elites supposedly led a life of leisure, one might ask why they bothered to work as hard as some evidently did. What induced them to start manufactories, join trade factions, or go to France to lobby the court for benefits? Chapter 6, while not ignoring environmental factors, indicates how noblewomen's choices were affected by the martial and caste-like values of the French *noblesse*.

Chapter 7 follows women in some of the same families into the convents. There too aristocratic values and clientage systems that extended all the way to the French court were surprisingly strong. We shall see that nuns served as political agents carrying out Crown policy, particularly during wartime. They were always economic agents, undertaking milling, farming, building, craft production, even provisioning shipyard workers and garrisons in faraway forts. The discussion of issues of 'caste and clientage' among the nobility are in basic accord with the theories of Louise Dechene and other scholars who endorsed the vision of a colony that increasingly conformed to French models. It is no accident that the key examples in this section of the book are drawn from the eighteenth century when 'normal' French stratification was clearly reasserting itself, particularly among the ranks of society that had most to gain from it.

What else will the book show, beyond metropolitan and environmental influences? The chapters we have described, and indeed the study as a whole, will nuance an assertion made in historian Peter Moogk's richly researched cultural history *La Nouvelle France* that New France was a land of 'the patriarchal family' and 'a male-dominated society' in which 'family interests took precedence over individual rights and the *père de famille* defined those interests.'[11] These notions are not without foundation, for laws and a number of formal institutions did privilege men over women. But a categorical judgment that 'father ruled' misrepresents a fluid situation. It ignores the unusual status of upper-class women in ancien régime France, and it overlooks the widely acknowledged hardening of gender ideology that occurred in the Western world well *after* the colony took shape. It closes the door to understanding the shifting degrees of feminine agency. To do so obscures a distinctive feature that our book reveals: the Canadian situation in several ways remained more open than the one that emerged in Georgian England, post-Revolutionary France, and the American colonies.

Ignoring the ways gender history evolved between the seventeenth and nineteenth centuries leads to errors such as labelling colonial women 'dependents.'[12] Historians of pre-industrial societies have long recognized that family farms and artisanal shops depended on the work of both sexes, evident in the way widows or wives supervised when husbands were absent – which could not be done by someone ignorant of the work. Family farms were, as the name implies, based on interdependence of males and females, young and old. This study will present hundreds of women who went well beyond the vital economic production seen in virtually every pre-industrial economy – that is, beyond farming, working with livestock, and fabricating clothing and other items for family use, sale, or barter (not to mention birthing and rearing a labour force). Our discussion of noblewomen and nuns will show how they daily exerted diverse economic agency within colonial towns and seigneuries. It will show women from the highest classes to the lowest engaged in a wide range of market activities relating to the international staples trade. Even after the French period ended in 1760, this legacy would remain, allowing Canada under British rule to continue offering positive alternatives to gender restrictions arising elsewhere. It is misleading to portray the 'patriarchal family' as a constant from New France to the Duplessis era, as is done in *La Nouvelle France*. In fact, most French-Canadian fathers awaited the middle decades of the nineteenth century to experience any significant expansion of their powers, when the combined influence of British common law and customs, Enlightenment philosophy, and Napoleonic French law led to curtailment of female civil rights and economic activity. Moogk is on firmer ground in conceding that, while he believes New France's patriarchal family was sanctioned by law, it could be compromised in practice.[13]

This book also questions the value of the 'deputy husband' concept elaborated by New England historian Laurel Ulrich and later seen as relevant for New France. As we shall see in chapter 1, this is a term with which there is little evidence American colonists were familiar. I hope the countless, and to all appearances self-directed, economic and political activities not only of wives but also of widows, nuns, and other unmarried women described by myself and other historians will send this concept back to the bookshelf of quaint terms where it belongs, at least as far as Canada is concerned. Perhaps not all scholars would agree; the work of Josette Brun, for example, stresses female legal subjection and the apparent overriding of some wifely legal rights in urban New France. One could concede that *some* wives and widows may never have performed any business transactions without invoking Jean-Baptiste's instructions, his supposed wishes, or his sacred memory. But many made major decisions when their putative lord and master was thousands of kilometres away, his likelihood of return a complete question mark. Researchers are aware too that innumerable transactions by women and men alike occurred without aid of legal documents, sometimes to cover illicit activity, sometimes just to save money. Moreover, many surviving letters, petitions, and notarial records suggest a wife was taking an initiative (as the work of Katherine Young amply showed),[14] many making little or no reference to a husband as they did so. For widows, nuns, and other single women, this was even more obviously true. Like Moogk's 'patriarchy,' the 'deputy husband' is a blunt term, a smothering blanket cast over a vibrant and varied reality.

River of Memory

Section Four, 'River of Memory,' closes the book with a one-chapter sketch of continuities in British Quebec. It shows how much the place remained an ancien régime colony in the early nineteenth century. Although the towns slowly began to transform themselves from 1760 onward, well into the 1830s the rural majority remained largely immune to the revolution in gender values that had occurred elsewhere. Country occupations, lifestyles, and legal practices changed very slowly. France's Canadian colony persisted in *its* 'pre-Revolutionary' period for nearly a half century after 1789, as pride was expressed about avoiding the guillotine, the Terror, and the closing of convents and churches that devastated the old order in France. Indeed France's erstwhile colony experienced no profound political upheaval until 1837.[15] Thus the entity we describe as ancien régime Canada began with the colony's founding in 1608 and survived into the 1830s. This is not to deny the onset of agrarian problems as well as the growth of rural villages and small industries, and the gradual rise of political discontent. Still, outside of the modest urban centres of the period, the evidence of major transformation of rural lifestyles, especially those of women (who seldom played an active part in *patriote* agitation even where it existed) seems slight compared to the evidence of continuity with tradition.

Chapter 8 builds that case by surveying key developments in both town and country in the three-quarters of a century after the British Conquest of 1760. Both cultural and environmental explanations come into play. Political and cultural isolation from revolutionary and Napoleonic France allowed old regime practices to persist well into the nineteenth century, harbouring what Lord Durham would term 'an old ... society in a progressive world.'[16] Environmental factors – not least, simple geography and persistence of near-subsistence farming – compounded that isolation. Not only were the two successive mother countries far away, but within the colony itself much of the French population lived on seigneuries that insulated them from daily contact with English-speaking newcomers. Historian Maurice Seguin argued that this was fortuitous for the preservation of French-Canadian culture, and it might also be seen as fortuitous on the gender front. Ignorance of new transnational beliefs about the essentially different natures of men and women had its advantages. It helped buffer *canadiennes* from various restrictive laws and practices emerging in Britain, France, and America. Our closing chapter thus provides a sketch of the early-nineteenth-century socio-economic landscape in which codes that were elsewhere obsolete continued to operate. Yet the chapter does also show the beginnings of change. By the 1830s females began to disappear from political agitations, the franchise was officially withdrawn, and property rights that had been exercised for two hundred years came under attack.

To sum up, this book has three basic thrusts. One is to compare the gender history in early Canada with that of seventeenth- and eighteenth-century France, England, and the bordering American colonies, which establishes the thesis that restrictive new gender ideologies did arise but were slow to reach the colony. The book also deals with two other interpretive strands, the metropolitan and the environmental: in what ways did the culture of old France shape women's working lives in the colony (and did it affect some groups more than others)? Then there is the corollary: in what ways did the St Lawrence valley shape the daily work of *canadiennes* between 1608 and the 1830s, and which groups did it affect the most?

Be it noted that the weight we place on the natural environment should not be mistaken for some sort of feminist frontier thesis. We do not see old institutions shunned, nor do we perceive a radically new, egalitarian society arising in the Canadian settlements. The interplay between a new territory and an old culture was quite complex. Still, the New World setting – the interaction with native peoples, the natural resources, the vast geographical expanse – did place a particular stamp on the history of women. Since this topic eluded the masculinist gaze of the earlier generation of 'frontier' historians, we take particular care to include it here, noting how often our subject wears moccasins, ventures past the clearings, knows Indian words, sells furs. The unfolding chapters will take stock of how the environment affected colonial women at four different stages. Initially, the Canadian setting with its forest peoples attracted several very unusual female religious leaders from France when the colony was being founded, women who dealt daily with First Nations and organized the colony's first systems of health care and public education with them in mind. Secondly, when hundreds of marriageable young women began to arrive in the 1660s, they benefited both from the healthful rural environment and from institutions created by the religious women. Thirdly, after the sons of those immigrant brides extended the fur trade into the continental interior, literally hundreds of women got involved in operating and supplying this long-distance trade. A final way the environment exerted major influence was that the geographic isolation and persistence of a pre-industrial resource economy helped buffer the colony from new, rigidly gendered lifestyles developing in eighteenth-century France, Britain, and America.

Still, French social and gender hierarchies always existed in Canada; one might bend them but could not break them. French influences remained so important that we cannot claim an entirely new man *or* new woman was created on the Canadian frontier, however influential were its First Nations and its resource-rich environment. Still, this book will show that indigenous peoples, the terrain they roamed, the flora and fauna found there – the Canadian setting in general – did have a major influence on women from all walks of life. Under French rule in Canada (1608–1760), there emerged a distinct people that only slowly transformed itself in the eight decades after the British conquered them. That post-Conquest society deserves a full study of its own. Nonetheless, our closing chapter will suggest how and why this ancien régime gender order persisted for so long.

PART ONE

Mapping Transatlantic Women's History

Chapter One

Transatlantic Trends 1600–1800

In discussing seventeenth- and eighteenth-century women, one needs to be aware of what has been called the 'master narrative' of women's history. Understanding this narrative, and its relation to the histories of France, England, and colonial America, is a foundation of our work on women in early Canada. One theme of the current study is that ancien régime Canada would for decades remain figuratively 'frozen in time,' largely impervious to the various gender upheavals and erosions across the Atlantic and in the English colonies next door. New restrictive practices that began to prevail elsewhere by the eighteenth century did not become widespread north of the St Lawrence until after 1830.

The colony provided rather poor soil for exotic ideas. Though it has not been unanimously accepted by historians (and at one point generated vigorous debate), there is nothing particularly startling about the view that early Canada tended to be more of a backwater than a pacesetter. It was widely portrayed that way by eighteenth- and nineteenth-century travellers under both French and British rule. A succession of visitors commented on how customs and material culture were either primitive (as befitted a land of forests and savages) or archaic, reminding them of bygone times in Europe. We have already discussed the 'metropolitan' view of a colony that was more derivative from French models than innovative. It is also seen as a poorly funded derivative. As Louise Dechene observed in her highly influential *Habitants et marchands de Montréal au XVIIé siècle*, seventeenth- and eighteenth-century Canada was lacking 'long-term inducements to entice merchant capital to the land,' which placed 'brakes on both production and social development.'[1] In some ways – certainly in comparison to the American Colonies – Canada did tend to display a fairly sluggish and undiversified economy, with upper echelons in that beleaguered colony tending to replicate a rather

old-fashioned military *noblesse*. There were few echoes of either the renowned intellectual climate of eighteenth-century France or the political
innovations of eighteenth-century America. It should be noted, though,
that usually even the poor found enough to eat in the colony,[2] which was
more than could be said of ancien régime France.

If the reader accepts at least to some extent Dechene's characteriza-
tion of the colony as an 'isolated and underpopulated,' one with a rural
majority that reproduced 'generation upon generation, static communities that more or less resembled those that emerged soon after their
arrival,'[3] we may proceed to our second proposition. In the context of
seventeenth- and eighteenth-century gender history, isolation and un-
derdevelopment were in some ways a blessing for women. The closing
chapter of this book will enumerate various merits of remaining outside
the new, more androcentric civic order that established itself in various
metropolitan centres before 1800. Supporting the proposition that there
was benefit in being behind the times is the 'master narrative' articulated
by leading historians of women over the course of the twentieth century.
However, the issue is complicated by the fact that the master narrative
itself is no longer accepted without question. A brief *tour d'horizon* of the
historiography of women in France, England, and early America will summarize key themes and search for what consensus can be found about the
shape and direction of gender change between 1600 and 1800.

This brings us to one grand designer who has been the subject of so
much public discussion and private inspiration across the decades that
we might take the liberty of calling her by her first name, Alice. Those
who are aware of how her work was a godsend for a new generation of
historians of women in the 1970s and 1980s might even call her Saint
Alice. Even those who consider her theories more suited for burial than
for the firmament can acknowledge Alice Clark as a pioneer of the archival research and sustained analysis that came to characterize twentieth-
century professional work in women's history.

If Clio is the muse of history, Alice is the muse of women's history.
How many scholars framed a debate that held centre stage for nearly
a century? 'Even today,' Amy Erickson wrote in her introduction to the
1992 re-edition of Clark's book, *Working Life of Women in the Seventeenth
Century*, 'her findings are as regularly confirmed as they are disputed.'
In 1998 another historian observed that 'the early modern period is still
dominated by Clark's *Working Life of Women in the Seventeenth Century*.'[4]
Clark published it in 1919, with the aid or inspiration of a small group of
feminists including Olive Schreiner, Dorothy George, and Mrs George

Bernard Shaw. It enjoyed a second life when it was re-issued in 1968, just in time to fascinate a whole new generation of feminist scholars. In 1919 and in 1968, most historians still left women out of their purview, on the theory that their role was relatively unchanging and/or relatively insignificant. How heartening, and how valid, was Clark's assertion that, far from being too simple to warrant scholarly attention, precisely the opposite was true: 'Owing to the greater complexity of a woman's life her productive capacity must be classified on different lines from those which are generally followed in dealing with the economic life of men.' Clark's assertion sprang from some impressive historical discoveries. She had scoured the archives and combed the literature in a way that allowed her book to overturn assumptions about what was 'traditional' for women. She discovered seventeenth-century farmwives as well as aristocratic, professional, and artisanal wives who managed enterprises and oversaw workers of both sexes. Her findings countered assumptions about subordination and assumptions about confinement inside the house: 'In agriculture the entire management of the milch cows, the dairy, poultry, pigs, orchard and garden, was undertaken by the women ... the mistress employed in her department men as well as women servants ... [also] women and girls were largely employed in field work.'[5]

The book established English women's essential place as producers in early modern times. Guild records from the fourteenth through the seventeenth centuries for carpenters, armourers, upholsterers, apothecaries, goldsmiths, and merchants referred to both 'brothers and sisters' in these trades and exhorted apprentices to obey their 'masters and mistresses.' Other documents identified women managing estates, owning patents, planning orchards and gardens, working as healers and midwives, and engaging in all sorts of trades, ranging from substantial shippers to humble pedlars carrying packs over long distances. Refreshingly, Clark gave equal weight to women's unpaid work. She pointed out that everywhere women produced (not just cooked) a large proportion of the family's food. Wives, she added, 'can hardly have been regarded as mere dependants on their husbands when the clothing of the whole family was spun by their hands.'[6]

However, the picture grew darker over time. Clark noted the extension of large-scale capitalist organization to textile production in the second half of the seventeenth century. Poverty, she believed, compelled certain women to begin accepting the low wages the new industrialists offered. As this system expanded, it greatly reduced wifely productive capacity because 'far from being able to feed and clothe her family, her

wages were barely adequate to feed herself,' diverting 'a large proportion of the produce of a woman's labour ... from her family to the profit
of the capitalist or the consumer.'[7] The erosion of wifely status was compounded by the Reformation suppression of convents as independent
centres of learning, by influential new theorizations of female exclusion
from affairs of state. There was also exclusion from the scientific training that was increasingly requisite for medical occupations, as the elite
began turning to 'male midwives.' Wives' influence over their husbands
also declined as men began more commonly to find work and associates
away from home. In the long run, Clark argued, the changes worked to
relegate women's 'productive capacity to ... household drudgery or to
the lowest ranks of unskilled labour.'[8]

While providing us with a master narrative so influential that even
today's reader may find it familiar, Clark's book had its shortcomings.
Modern demographers have proven false her notion of large seventeenth-century families. Her chapter on women running estates suffers
from a paucity of examples. Clark also conceded that 'in the skilled and
semi-skilled trades ... the extent to which married women were engaged
... must always remain largely a matter of conjecture, and unfortunately
it is precisely this point which is most interesting.'[9] Moreover, though
Clark presented the seventeenth century as pivotal, her discussion
ranged confusingly across the centuries; indeed her conclusion stated,
'This depreciation of women's productive value to her family did not
greatly influence her position in the seventeenth century, because it was
then only visible in the class of wage-earners'[10] – a group of quite modest
proportions in an England that was still 83 per cent rural in 1700. Our
Muse made mistakes, no question. But was she on the right track?

Certainly Clark adumbrated, though she did not name, a powerful
underlying force that allowed a seemingly neutral economic transformation towards capitalist production to affect women so adversely: 'These
far reaching changes ... may not have been a necessary consequence....
They may have arisen from some deep-lying cause, some tendency in human evolution which was merely hastened by the economic cataclysm.'[11]

The next wave of feminist historians would say the word out loud. Towards the end of the twentieth century, the concept of 'patriarchy' began
to appear in some historical texts as one of the major forces in history,
which indeed it is, but one that, like the male sexual organ, was generally too sacrosanct for the public gaze. Though she did not pronounce
either of these *P* words, Alice was there, eyes wide open, in 1919. Her
contribution was to provide what even her detractors concede is a master

narrative of women's history, a Marxist-tinged theory that women's loss of control over economic production accompanied the rise of a loosely defined 'capitalism' and lowered their status. One need not be a Marxist to appreciate this point. Being a producer does not automatically translate into high status (certainly not, for example, in the case of a slave). However, barring an unusually tyrannical union, a spouse who produces much of the family's livelihood is likely to have a certain leverage. Clark's view – that women were marginalized for their loss of a direct role in household production that was concurrent with ideological change – had a tremendous influence on women's history on both sides of the Atlantic during the field's great expansion after 1968.[12] Clark established the idea that economic marginalization of women originated in the early modern period, sometime after 1600. Critics sometimes label this the 'golden age' theory; but since that term presumes its error, we shall refer to it more neutrally as 'marginalization' theory. The concept spilled over to other periods of history, creating a general tendency in women's history to counter Whiggish or 'progressive' histories with 'regressive' ones. To better understand the historiography of women 1600–1800, we have discussed the source and direction of this early Light.

Patriarchy has been defined as 'a system of society or government in which men hold the power and women are largely excluded from it.'[13] Many historians now accept the acquisition and maintenance of male hegemony as one of the great shaping forces in history. Generally, though not invariably, historical records reveal governing elites, dominant institutions and legal codes upholding masculine authority and interests, and assigning less public authority and lower economic status to females. Yet the degree varies. Patriarchy ebbs and flows; its phases and intensity are not always and everywhere the same. Gender has a dynamic quality, and it interacts with other elemental dividing lines such as class, ethnicity, and 'race' in countless ways. As we venture to compare women's role in the economies of several early modern societies, we shall begin with the broad question of whether the intensity of patriarchy was increasing (as Alice Clark's work implies) in the seventeenth and eighteenth centuries. While this question cannot always yield unequivocal answers, so many gender historians have addressed it that it supplies a solid framework for transnational comparisons. Since those comparisons will allow us to place our discussion of French Canada in context, this chapter briefly describes how the master narrative of female marginalization plays out in the historiography of seventeenth- and eighteenth-century France, England, and English America.

Economic Trends 1600–1800

Before discussing socio-economic trajectories, we must acknowledge a complication: the fact that wealthy women, unlike wealthy men, often had little control over their wealth. The dilemma of whether a wealthy woman in a patriarchal society is victimized is summed up in the witticism, 'Did Lady Astor oppress her footman, or did her footman oppress Lady Astor?' Certainly in England of 1870, Lady Astor had fewer political rights and possibilities for paid career than her footman did, but she enjoyed vastly more material comfort, at least so long as she remained in the good graces of Lord Astor. In regard to women's situation in a hierarchical society, such complications inevitably arise. Do we want to know whether at least some women were eligible for rights and opportunities (for example, education, occupational choice, political voice, and property rights)? Or do we focus on more purely material questions about the average standard of living of the average woman? As we shall see, the answer to the question of whether things were getting better or worse between 1600 and 1800 will vary according to which kind of question we ask. Chapter 1 turns first to material standards of living and range of occupations; then it weighs women's political rights in comparison to men's, looking at what we might call the citizenship scale in France, England, and English America. Later, chapter 5 of the book will take a close look at property rights in those three jurisdictions.

Discussions of the English Economy

A number of historians of English women have shared Alice Clark's view that marginalization became pronounced sometime during the course of the seventeenth and eighteenth centuries. Bridget Hill's *Women, Work and Sexual Politics in Eighteenth Century England* focused on the latter century, when enclosures and other agricultural transformations combined with industrialization to undermine spinning, a traditional source of female livelihood. Dairywomen too lost ground to commercial operations that hired men exclusively.[14] It became less common for farm wives to supervise market and the domestic gardening, the poultry and pigs, even the farm's account books. When a woman moved to piecework or factory work, she lost her former decision-making power about what to grow, how to process it, when to sell it, and at what price. Further down the social ladder, it became more difficult for wives and widows to live on cottage plots and use common lands.[15] Hill documented changes Clark had seen first emerging the century before: herbalists, midwives, and healers were further disqualified as they were formally or informally barred from training in new techniques. Women's presence in mining and trade sectors decreased. A number of studies support the contention that new forms of piecework did not typically generate enough income to feed and clothe the family as effectively as woman's contribution to the older agrarian economy had done.[16] Robert Allen, for example, argued that, on balance, new opportunities in proto-industry failed to compensate for agrarian setbacks: 'There can be little doubt that the employment opportunities of women were brighter in 1676 than in 1831.'[17]

As gender lines hardened in the new occupations, they also hardened in the old. In Surrey, for example, girls in the eighteenth century lost access to apprenticeships in bricklaying, carpentry, blacksmithing, milling, pistol-making, ironmongering, skinning, and fishing; they were directed instead towards millinery, mantua-making, seamstressing, and a variety of household tasks. Domestic service became a female ghetto: though the two sexes had served in roughly equal numbers in 1688, the occupation was 76 per cent female by 1851. Declining opportunity to meet male fellow servants further dimmed the job's attractions.

As some historians were documenting eighteenth-century marginalization of working-class women, a brilliant exposition of the same trend among the middle class appeared. Leonore Davidoff and Catherine Hall's *Family Fortunes, Men and Women of the English Middle Class, 1780–1850* was a methodological breakthrough. The authors marshalled records of three successive generations of the same families to show how family and community life gradually evolved to reduce commercial activity by middle-class women. Setting Alice Clark's template down on a little corner of English society (Quakers and evangelicals of Essex/Sussex counties and Birmingham), Davidoff and Hall discovered a perfect fit for middle-class women at that later date. The 1780 generation of women worked in family businesses, helping, for example, to ship cocoa, brew ale, or manufacture buttons. The second generation, in 1800 or thereafter, moved the children out to the suburbs or away from the shop, as development of limited liability companies and more formal financing arrangements began to redefine business as masculine rather than familial. The third generation of women not only eschewed trade but became wholly immersed in nurturing their families, and their option to engage in business disappeared. In 1839 one leading author of advice books for Victorian ladies, Mrs Ellis, stipulated the caste-like avoidance of trade that had come to seem necessary: 'Gentlemen may employ their hours of business in almost any degrading occupation ... [and] be a gentleman still; ... if a lady but touch any article, no matter how delicate, in the way of trade, she loses caste, and ceases to be a lady.'[18]

The Protestant groups that *Family Fortunes* examined were important because their star was on the rise, even in British colonies as far away as Canada (as chapter 8 discusses). The book affirmed the theory of female economic marginalization, and it established the end of the eighteenth century as the period when England's influential middle classes began to experience it.

Challenges to the 'Master Narrative'

The mainstream interpretation of Clark and her followers has not won universal acceptance.[19] Judith Bennett questioned the idea of rising separate spheres in the seventeenth and eighteenth centuries, noting that ever since medieval times work had been largely segregated. Bennett made the much quoted remark that 'no matter what the actual occupations of women, they tended to work in low-skilled, low-status, low-paid jobs, and they also tended to be intermittent workers, jumping from job to job or juggling several tasks at once. This was true in 1300, and it remained true in 1700.'[20]

Bennett wished to show that women, 'eternal amateurs' in the labour force, were always handicapped in patriarchal societies, and that Clark's view of earlier happier times was rose-coloured. In a study of brewing she noted that men replaced women at the point when operation became large-scale and commercial; before that, it was 'a classic sector of women's work characterized by low status, low skill, and low remuneration.'[21]

Remembering the single women who are often forgotten (and who ranged up to one-quarter of the female population), Bennett completed the negative picture of late medieval times by observing that in 'neither 1381 nor 1700 were single women able to find employment in long-distance trade, in professional occupations, in civil service.'[22]

Bennett's statements seem rather sweeping; one thinks, for example, of a number of single ladies of courts who were 'civil servants' by early modern standards, of nuns who were pharmacists, hospital and school administrators, and so on. Her concepts of status and pay also run the risk of situating women's activities 'within male definitions of work, while important ideas about women's work were derived from their positions within the household.'[23] Bennett did, however, raise doubts about the marginalization narrative. She was soon joined by others.

In a famous article appearing in the *Historical Journal* in 1993, Amanda Vickery waved a red flag in the face of feminist historians. She supported Bennett's point that the spheres had *always* been largely separate. In sixteenth-century Norfolk, for example, men 'unless old, feeble, or simple, ... rarely did jobs like weeding or picking over corn ... any more than women built houses, hewed timber, ploughed, harrowed, threshed, carted hay and corn, dug ditches or cut hedges.' All too many historians, she admonished, 'follow Engels by presenting women as valued and productive on page one of their study, but then ultimately devalued and redundant by the conclusion, usually fifty years later.' It is 'extremely difficult to sustain ... the argument that sometime between 1650 and 1850 the public/private distinction was constituted or radically reconstituted in a way that transformed relations between the sexes.'[24]

The dogma of decline, Vickery charged, led to absurdities such as Susan Amussen's work on seventeenth-century Norfolk and Davidoff and Hall's work on early-nineteenth-century Suffolk, each claiming to have located (very different) turning points of marginalization. 'Are we to believe,' Vickery asked, 'that women were driven out of a public sphere of production and power in one district in the seventeenth century, while just over the county border the same development was delayed by well over a hundred years? Surely uneven development of this magnitude would have raised some contemporary comment, or at the very least female migration.'[25]

Vickery also raised the question of whether economic involvement in production and trade actually *would* enhance women's status. She contended that even gentry wives who no longer engaged in household production did not necessarily lose authority, for they were vital to supervising the manor and its servants, writing letters that smoothed their children's way in life, furnishing and supplying the household (especially since husbands were often away on missions of business, politics, or pleasure).[26] Vickery also made the excellent point that acquisition of household consumer goods can be regarded as skilled work rather than frivolous leisure.

Though it offered useful cautions about the 'master narrative' of marginalization, Vickery's work had its blind spots. She asserted that since ladies read widely, involved themselves in charity, conversed about politics, and also attended theatre, public events, and assizes, 'it is deeply questionable whether genteel women's mental horizons were any more hidebound than men's.' This seems rather naive in light of her own concession that their 'economic and political power was obviously much

more circumscribed,' including a 'virtually non-existent career structure
and exclusion from the major institutions of the state.'[27] It does wonders
for the 'mental horizons' to have access to careers and major institutions
of state, not to mention higher education. Vickery also falls into unsup-
ported assumptions about the old family economy, that 'it is not clear
that a woman's industrial work was any more agreeable when directed
by a husband, rather than a formal employer.'[28] *Did* the husband direct?
Or did men and women work as a team? Or did they each direct their
own tasks? Will we ever have enough data to really know which of these
scenarios was most common?

Peter Earle's study[29] of the female labour market in London 1695–
1725 sought to penetrate that mystery. Earle concentrated on London
church courts, which dealt with issues such as defamation, marriage,
and divorce and heard female testimony, including by what means they
were maintained or employed. Earle compiled a list of 851 respondents
that was 'somewhat biased towards the poorer women of London' but
included all classes.[30] He found that, in contrast to the 28 per cent of
women reporting paid employment in 1851 London, 57 per cent of the
1695–1725 group did so, indicating that 'contemporaries do not seem
to have had any moral objection to women working for their living,
quite the opposite.'[31] Earle also noted that in the earlier centuries the
occupational range was somewhat wider than in 1851; the seventeenth-
and eighteenth-century occupations included butcher, tallow-chandler,
linen draper, wholesale stocking dealer, goldsmith, stone engraver,
chair-caner, tobacco pipe deliverer, water seller, pawnbroker, and 'hard
labourers, day labourers.' There were women who made fans, bellows,
bricks, flasks, pipes, pottery, sacks, and sieves. Other categories included
teacher, professional letter writer, parish clerk, vestrywoman, singer and
singing teacher, mistress of a company of comedians, upholsterer, sailor,
discounter of sailors' wage tickets, errand-runner for prisoners, turnkey
in a prison, and a widow who did searches for others in the Fleet Registry.
There were also midwives, specialists in treating cancer and pox, and all
manner of victuallers and shopkeepers.

Debate continued. The cover of Robert Shoemaker's 1998 *Gender in
English Society, 1650–1850: The Emergence of Separate Spheres?* announced
that the book would contest 'the prevailing view that women had significantly greater economic and political opportunities in pre-industrial
England.'[32] He conceded that female medicine, midwifery, and agricultural activities too, declined (indicated in an 1800 commentator's remark that a farm wife would 'faint at the idea of attending at market,

like her mother and grandmother, with a basket of butter, pork, roast-ing pigs, or poultry, on her arm.')[33] Yet other doors opened during the eighteenth century. Demand for nurses, teachers, and governesses grew, as did work in arts, crafts, and literature. There was new employment, perhaps even a net gain in female jobs, due to industrialization, with piecework making up for the decline in spinning. Debate will no doubt persist well past 2019, when Clark's book reaches its centenary.

What conclusion should we draw from this discussion of women's work in seventeenth- and eighteenth-century England? It seems to me that the weight of evidence still supports the thesis of marginalization, but clearly it was not so stark and unilinear as Clark thought. In agriculture and textiles, as well as a range of traditionally non-gendered occupations, women did seem to lose ground, and domestic service did become a low-status female ghetto. Taking agriculture, hand-spinning, and service together, it is credible that a majority was affected by deterioration in these areas. Still, new opportunities clearly presented themselves in con-nection with industrial production, including opportunities for single women, who had a tenuous place in the older economy. Middle-class women found more chances to teach or publish. It is also true that the wealth generated by industrialization, if it did not on the whole advance equality between the sexes, did encourage the luxury trades where many women were employed. It also offered an array of new consumer goods conducive to comfort and leisure at a time when control of the means of production, or self-directed employment, was decreasing.

The American Colonies

Did America's course follow that of its mother country? The colonial pe-riod began with the founding of Jamestown in 1607 and ended with the winning of independence in 1784. One of the most influential historians of New England women, Laurel Thatcher Ulrich, deliberately skirted the question of marginalization that looms so large in the history of English women. Other historians, though, did address this issue. We shall first discuss Ulrich's portrayal of women of the New England and then see how other historians situate themselves on marginalization. Our focus is primarily New England and New York because they neighboured the Canadian colony on the St Lawrence.

Coming to history with a background in literature, Laurel Ulrich was not particularly interested in the evolution of the 'status of women' or questions of power in general. In *Good Wives: Image and Reality in the Lives of Women in Northern New England 1650–1750*, she wrote, 'The story of female experience in America is not to be found in a linear progression from darkness into light, from constricted to expanding opportunities … (or vice versa), but in a convoluted and sometimes tangled embroidery of loss and gain, accommodation and resistance…. [S]tatus is … so complex. To enlarge the role of deputy husband [i.e., 'male' activities assumed by wives] might mean to contract the often highly cherished roles of housekeeper and mother.'[34]

Ulrich eschewed the battle between one camp of historians who saw the colonial era as one of wide opportunity for the women who worked as blacksmiths, tinsmiths, gunsmiths, printers, and shipwrights, and another camp that saw women as narrowly confined to domestic concerns (such as the Loyalist women Mary Beth Norton studied who were unable to describe their family assets). Ulrich dismissed this as merely the difference between 'what was permissible and what was probable.' She did declare colonial women 'by definition basically domestic.'[35] With a husband whose decisions were expected to reflect his wife's opinions and interests, domesticity was not confining but enobling. Wifely skills included butchering pigs, making candles, and of course the eternal spinning at the wheel. Woman's chief monument was her progeny, and her mothering extended to the whole neighbourhood and to several generations. Yet in an age that did not yet associate women with innocence and virtue, there were pithy marital battles and outspoken women who came to life in Ulrich's book, women who inspired Puritan sayings such as 'He who wooeth a widow must go stiff before.'[36]

The most contentious aspect of *Good Wives* is Ulrich's concept of 'deputy husband.' Women who performed what the nineteenth century would label as 'male' roles, such as managing farms or businesses, were never perceived by Ulrich to do it in an independent or equal capacity. She asserted that the notion of womanly independence was alien to this family-centred culture: 'Almost any task was suitable for a woman as long as it furthered the good of her family and was acceptable to her husband.' True, 'a wife with a talent for business might become a kind of double for her husband,' but most wives, Ulrich reminded the reader, 'had other things to do.'[37] Since this concept has also been utilized in reference to early French-Canadian women, it merits closer scrutiny.

There are problems with the deputy husband concept. The term appears in the book's extensive primary quotes only once, one single prescriptive reference in Thomas Fuller's 1642 *The Holy and Profane State*.[38] The 'deputy husband' is thus an abstraction, with no evidence that it was ever part of common parlance. While conceivably it could capture the outlook of many wives, it begs entirely the question of what guided single women and widows. Is it really true that Ann Brackett, a woman captured by natives who took the initiative to repair a canoe that allowed her husband, herself, and two other members of their household to escape, saw herself as someone's 'deputy'? Who 'deputized' Hannah Durston, kidnapped a week after giving birth, who recruited her maid and a boy to help her slay and scalp her ten captors? Indeed it seems indicative of the very different values of the seventeenth century that Durston was a hero to the Puritans, but in the nineteenth century was portrayed as a hag. As Mary Beth Norton noted, 'Unruly and undeferential wives abounded' in Anglo-America. Presenting any female activity outside the domestic as 'deputized' may capture an aspect of New England patriarchy, but it seems too small a box to hold the region's prophetesses, frontierswomen, witches, its many outspoken wives and widows. One can almost hear them kicking to get out![39]

Some historians dealt directly with the question of change over time. Gloria Main asserted that conditions improved for northern women. After the seventeenth century, when men and women often toiled outdoors together, demand grew for skilled non-farm labour of both sexes. Accompanied by rising school attendance by country girls, 'the growing ability of women to earn money and conduct business at the local store can be viewed as a positive good, giving them greater control over their own lives.'[40]

Other historians saw the trajectory as a negative one. Elaine Foreman Crane argued that although New England women's wages were perennially lower than men's, such considerations were less important in the barter economy of the early colonial period, when women traded their cloth and produce for other goods. She found widows and married women featured prominently in seventeenth-century account books, less so later on. In neighbouring New York, there was also a pattern of decline. Carol Berkin noted forty-six female traders in Albany just after 1650 but none in 1700, while New York City also saw them diminishing in merchant ranks and disappearing altogether as tapsters, brewers, launderers, and bakers.[41] Deborah Rosen, too, affirmed that the number of female merchants, shopkeepers, and artisans dropped over the course of the English colonial period and attributed it to the decline of Dutch law and custom. Increased use of debt instruments during the eighteenth-century consumer revolution further handicapped women, who could not sign enforceable contracts.[42]

Were things getting better or worse for female colonists in America? As in English history, the dearth of economic data on domestic production and the diverse ways of measuring economic well-being allow only tentative conclusions. But since the seaboard economies developed so dramatically between the early seventeenth century and the end of the eighteenth, it seems reasonable to accept Gloria Main's contention that northern colonial living standards were, on the whole, improving and women's lives were getting easier. As for the question of equality between the sexes, even an optimist such as Main notes that male and female wages had been closer to parity in earlier stages of settlement when male and female tasks tended to overlap.[43] Thus, regarding the economy of the northern colonies, we might reasonably postulate that in 1800 women of America were more affluent, but less equal, than they had been in the early decades of settlement. Our study of French Canada will show equality persisting to a greater extent for a longer time.

Women and the Economy in France

France, like Canada, had a population that was close to 80 per cent rural. In *The Prospect before Her: A History of Women in Western Europe*, Olwen Hufton described farm women in France and elsewhere: 'For the majority of Europeans … living from the land the most usual designation of a married woman was that of "farmer's wife" and this term covered a vast social spectrum…. the farmer's wife generally tended livestock, particularly chickens and pigs … grew vegetables, did dairy work, kept bees, preserved and pickled, helped prepare goods for sale and perhaps took them to market, lent a hand at harvest and during haymaking.'[44]

These were working wives. A seigneuress or lady of the manor managed the household and sometimes certain domestic manufactures, along with garden and orchard. She played a crucial role in hospitality and in negotiating the marriages that lay at the heart of French dynastic alliances. Like the Englishwomen discussed by Alice Clark, a capable lady might at times direct the entire estate, levying rents, arranging sale of produce and maintenance of the property while her husband was away for purposes of business, sociability, war, or politics. She might be godmother to village girls, for whom she was expected to provide job references, while dispensing poor relief, medicine, and advice to tenants or local villagers.[45] Farther down the ladder, the farm wife looked after livestock and did the dairy work that produced much of the household's fat and protein. Her spinning and sewing, gardening, gleaning, barter, and paid work all contributed to the family livelihood.

Though there were regional variations, agriculture was less prosperous in France than in England, with a distinct impact on living standards. English wheat yields between 1660 and 1730 soared to almost double those of France. In France, 'a far greater proportion of the rural poor clung tenaciously to a small plot, an extended garden and commons use rights.'[46] Subdivision tended to allow French peasants to remain on their plots, making them less prone than the English to emigration or proletarianization. The poverty of the French peasant promoted the 'economy of makeshifts,' the combining of any available kinds of work, exchange, and poor relief to make ends meet. The phenomenon occurred in both England and France, as did long treks in search of livelihood; but in France it involved many more people. Itinerancy was more common among males, leaving many wives in charge of farm, herd, or fishery for part of the year. Such a division of labour required a high degree of complementarity, and clearly women were able to carry out a wide range of tasks. When intrepid traveller Arthur Young reached Auvergne in the 1780s, he marvelled to see only women doing farm work, a predominance not unknown in Canada.[47]

Demographics tell the same story. It is a sign of the poverty of the French peasant that while in the second half of the eighteenth century on average she bore one more child than her English counterpart, she lost it as the result of a higher infant mortality rate.[48] Pointing in the same direction is the rising age of marriage, leaving ever more Frenchwomen as spinsters. Lower marriage ages are indicators of 'easier employment situations, better wages ... availability of farmsteads.'[49] In Britain up to 1750 the average age of marriage was above twenty-six, but it fell to twenty-three by 1800. In France the age oscillated between twenty-two and twenty-four during the seventeenth century but rose by the Revolutionary era to twenty-six. French agriculture saw improvements in the eighteenth century, though progress was fairly modest before 1760.[50]

Two aspects of French society helped offset its relatively lacklustre economic growth. The first was kin networks, which were apparently closer than in rural England. The young remained more likely to marry a neighbour and settle in the vicinity.[51] In those densely populated villages there were no doubt family feuds and importuning cousins; but the important social and political instrument of female speech also had scope to operate. Relatives might offer employment, marriage prospects, and help in time of need, be it a failed harvest or a violent husband. In town too, a study of Nantes showed, collateral relatives often stepped in to support the legal interests of widows and other kinswomen.[52]

A second element gave some relief to the relatively stagnant picture in France. Since this institution would also play an essential role in Canada, we will spend a little time examining the French teaching and nursing sisterhoods. In the renewed Catholic zeal that swept seventeenth-century France, women at all levels of society women joined the drive to Christianize the populace, combat heresy, and administer to the needy. Cloistered groups such as the Augustinians and the Ursulines expanded spectacularly, with the result that some towns began to have more girls than boys in primary classes. In the following century, Ursulines were at work in three hundred French urban areas. In Paris alone there were forty-three different convent schools run by various orders. By 1700 – in sharp contrast to 1600 – there was a general expectation that urban French girls would go to school.[53]

Seventeenth-century France also saw an upsurge of uncloistered *filles séculaires* similar to the group Marguerite Bourgeoys would establish in Montreal. They took simple, annually renewable vows, lived in houses rather than convents, and spent most of their day not in prayer but in serving the local populace. They set up small schools in the countryside and they often staffed the local Hôtel-Dieu for the sick or the Crown-subsidized Hôpital Général, which was an all-purpose reformatory and refuge. Though historians debate whether penal or benevolent aspects predominated, demographer Jacques Dupaquier concluded that care in such institutions improved whenever the sisters ran them, partly because they typically allocated 20 per cent of their budget to nourish the inmates.

French lay sisters exercised a certain autonomy. Protected by contracts with municipalities that were drawn up at the orders' headquarters in Paris, they kept control over their pharmacies. They could often hold their own in conflicts with physicians: 'The sisters would ... make an annual audit ... account for the drugs, perhaps look after the bakery, laundry, and livestock or ... supervise the work of the orphans.... [T] heir individual dress allowances (about eighty *livres* in the 1780s) were guaranteed; they were assured of absolute control over the servants ... and the right of deciding who could be admitted as a patient.... The superior of the Congrégation de la Mission ... would use his influence at Versailles to defend the sisters against local attempts to whittle down their rights.'[54]

These efforts bore fruit. Hufton noted that the French Sisters of Charity provided France with the best nursing services in Europe. On the eve of the Revolution, an astonishing hundred thousand people in France were in hospitals and hospices, compared to three thousand in England. Mary Astell and other English observers admired the French system, and in 1789 French émigré sisters would be shocked to see the conditions in British institutions. (In New France, as we shall see, General Wolfe's British forces would seek out French rather than English care.) The French institutions became part of the economy of makeshifts to which the poor might look for assistance. Revolutionary-era attempts to suppress them would cause such an outcry that nursing orders would be exempted from the ban on religious communities.[55]

Such communities offered an alternative to marriage all along the social scale. They protected Catholic countries from the narrow prospects Mary Astell counted on the fingers of one hand for single Protestant gentlewomen in England: governess, housekeeper, lady's companion, mantua-maker. Likewise, lower-class daughters found an alternative to farming, domestic service, and needlework by becoming *filles séculaires*. The option was particularly important, since some 10–15 per cent – in some cases rising to 25 per cent – of the Northwestern European population remained single.[56] There were eighty thousand members of cloistered female orders in France in the 1660s. They were still fifty-three thousand strong in the more secular France of 1789, heavily outnumbering the *filles séculaires*. Revolutionary repression caused a sharp drop in the cloistered orders, and there were only twelve thousand nuns in France in 1800.[57] But in the seventeenth century, when they went out to construct a colony in the wilderness, Canada's female founders went armed with French traditions of single women providing practical service to the public, and doing so with significant independence and institutional support.

For the purposes of our historiographic survey, the evolution of women's place in the French economy between 1600 and 1800 resists easy judgment. Hufton, whose work focused primarily on France, long ago made the acerbic observation that the location of this *bon vieux temps* 'has proved remarkably elusive.' Wiesner and Simonton, who studied European women's work, agree that any sharp dividing point is hard to document.[58] The latter two writers concur, though, that although work had always been gendered, male and female work gradually became more segregated in a way that was inevitably hierarchical. Wiesner made the assessment in terms of the two variables of class and gender: 'For the very poor, social class was probably more important than gender.... For the nobility and bourgeoisie however, the early modern period appears to be a time when ... "the perception of women as marginalized by gender became stronger than the perception of women as divided by class."[59]

Let us try putting the French components together. First, there was the stricter gender bar. Add to this an economy that saw rural France fall behind rural England. Then there are the telling indicators of delayed marriages and high infant mortality. Taken together, do they not suggest that eighteenth-century Frenchwomen were experiencing economic decline relative to French men, and also relative to their English and American sisters? Where the peasant way of life persisted, complementarity of tasks would have endured; but the growing gender segregation in other employments was considerably more ominous than in the more prosperous settings of England and America. The branches of these families who departed for Canada in the seventeenth century were likely to face less gender discrimination, as we shall see.

Summarizing Economic Change

How can we summarize our transatlantic investigation of early modern women? Does it bear out the notion of marginalization beginning during the seventeenth century and spreading to various classes in the following century? It does seem that by 1800 in all three settings – English, French, and American – sharper lines were drawn between male and female labour than had existed two hundred years earlier, a segregation that usually privileged males over females. However, in eighteenth-century England and America, the growing affluence makes it hard to say that women's economic position was declining. The efficiencies of the agrarian and industrial revolutions had perhaps begun to enhance living standards in England and had certainly supplied new work opportunities to a number of women. America, where colonial life had been primitive at the beginning of the seventeenth century, offers the clearest case of rising affluence and comfort by the close of our period. Frenchwomen were doing least well on the 'affluence scale,' contending like the others with segregation *and* with a less dynamic economy. But when we turn, in our next section, to the 'citizenship scale,' the tables will turn in favour of the French.

Political Trends 1600–1800

The theory of marginalization seems valid when one considers the political position of women between 1600 and 1800. They lost weight on the 'citizenship scale.' Decline occurred first in England and America. In France, there was a golden age and a glorious Revolutionary sunset before female political participation was curtailed at the very end of the eighteenth century. Before attempting comparisons, we shall take some care to define the term *politics* in a way that is relevant to feminine experience. In a book that will soon turn to Canada, this chapter offers points of comparison regarding women in politics in other pacesetting jurisdictions.

Meaningful discussion of seventeenth- and eighteenth-century women in 'politics' invites one to define the term rather broadly, to include any behaviour that suggests a woman who saw herself as a citizen entitled to a voice in the decisions or activities of the state. The literature on early modern women has taught us to consider their tongues as instruments to sway political action, at least action by village elders and local magistrates. This makes sense in settings full of illiterate people, and it is in line with the longstanding acceptance of female rioting as political *desiderata*. Incendiary gossip would seem to deserve the sort of attention historians give to more formal petitions and protests, though it is harder to trace.

Literates engaged in other sorts of politics. In Jürgen Habermas's notion of a sphere of public opinion that served as the cultural backdrop for law and politics, many articulate women had a role to play. Among them were courtesans, or to use a less loaded term, women of the court. This group received a salacious press from the bourgeois males who toppled the ancien régime, but historians of women have discovered a number of court ladies who, whatever their bedtime stories, had an impact on policy in a period that predated a professionally trained civil service. This discussion will outline the impressive political activism of certain women in seventeenth-century England, France, and America, then discuss theories of why such voices grew fainter. The chapter closes with the revolutions in America and France, when Frenchwomen far outshone their American sisters.

Seventeenth-century crises brought women to the fore.[60] In England, political energies were electrified by the regicide of Charles I and the ensuing religious civil war and Interregnum of 1642–60. Female prophets during that period outnumbered male ones, and they often addressed the social and political issues of the day. Women petitioners seeking release of jailed leaders asserted their public rights in their petitions to Parliament, asking rhetorically if they did not possess 'equal unto men ... a proportionable share in the Freedoms of this Commonwealth ... an equal interest with the men of this Nation, in ... Laws of this Land?'[61]

Across the seas in Massachusetts, the same mid-seventeenth-century years of the English Civil War and the French Fronde saw a small but significant suggestion that American women were members of the polity too. In the largest recorded gathering of female petitioners before the American Revolution, over 30 per cent of the women of Boston and nearby Dorchester in 1649–50 organized a petition for the release of Boston-area midwife Alice Tilly. Tilly had been jailed on complaints of malpractice. True, Tilly's supporters bowed to the prejudices of the lawmakers in admitting their heroine showed 'ouer-much selfe conceitedness,' and calling themselves 'poore and trembling petitioners' speaking with 'humility and childlike boldness.' Still, this was identified by Mary Beth Norton as 'American women's first collective political action.' Like their sisters in the English Civil War, they too identified themselves with the public domain, declaring. 'Wee shall remaine (though weake yet) true hearted in the Freedoms of this commonwealth ... equal well wishers, & endeavourers of the publick good of those churchs & Comon wealth God has cast us in.'[62] The Massachusetts court bowed to the wishes of the 'women's childbirth community' and released Tilly.

In a more general way, Norton argued that seventeenth-century notions of authority were based on honouring parents: 'Not by co-incidence did many of the most contentious incidents in the seventeenth-century colonies revolve around high-status or fictive widows.... Under the theory of unified power, such gentlewomen as [religious leader] Mistress Anne Hutchinson and [Lord Baltimore's attorney and agent] Mistress Margaret Brent [represent] ... a conceptualization of power that on the one hand glorified the power of fathers and on the other offered mothers, symbolic and real, unparalleled access to the wielding of legitimate authority.'[63]

For example, Lady Margaret Brent, who helped quell a rebellion by selling Lord Baltimore's cattle to pay the troops, was a fit leader according to the Maryland Assembly, since, they observed, 'It was better for the colony's safety at that time than in any man's [hands] ... for the Soldiers would never have treated any other with that ... civility and respect.'[64] Thus, seventeenth-century England and America saw occasional assertions of female political authority. The English Civil War even inspired claims to citizenship equal to that of males.

The record becomes considerably more impressive when we turn to the country that was to exert the greatest influence on early Canada.

In France, despite exclusion from the throne under the Salic Law and a gradual erosion of courtly powers after the fifteenth century, French-women retained an unusually strong civic position. A number of studies have demonstrated that 'women manipulated Old Regime structures and found in the courts, the armies, the churches and the salons sources of power.'[65] They participated in royal cabals and governing clienteles and were an acknowledged part of the intelligentsia. The Regent Anne of Austria in the early seventeenth century was involved in statecraft and surrounded herself with learned women, just as her predecessor Marie de Medici had done. Counter-Reformation piety moved Anne and other wealthy court ladies to sponsor colonization. Hefty funding was supplied, for example, by Cardinal Richelieu's niece Madame d'Aiguillon and others for female missionary founders of New France. In an age when the courtly rich were often devout, French mystics such as Madame Acarie attracted a circle of male and female *dévots*, presaging the later salons. A way was opened for female learning, as a spectacular mural in Cardinal Mazarin's palace attested: the 'muses' surrounding Apollo were said to be portraits of the Parisian '*précieuses*' or learned women.[66] This hospitable climate saw François Poullain de La Barre publish his *De l'égalité des sexes* (1673), a major event in the history of feminist thought.

In the same mid-seventeenth-century years that Englishwomen were prophesying and petitioning during the English Civil War, French women played a considerably more dramatic role, politically and militarily, during the noble uprising known as the Fronde. A coterie of military leaders signalled that the tradition of Jeanne d'Arc was alive and well. Madame de Montpensier, 'La Grande Mademoiselle,' led troops against the faction supporting her cousin, the future Louis XIV. She rode into battle in male costume 'with her big feathered hat adding to her already impressive stature,' and she was borne in triumph into Orleans. Her compatriot, the Princess of Condé, marched on Bordeaux and persuaded the citizens to support the Frondeurs against the King. The duchesse de Chatillon was also active in combat. For a brief period 'some women ruled in France during major events; those who entered into negotiations with them, princes or members of *parlements*, recognizing their authority as legitimate.'[67] For example, Anne of Cleves negotiated treaties that brought warring factions together. The duchesse de Longueville, wife of a Norman governor and sister of two royal princes, helped recruit her brothers to the cause. Author of a major Fronde pamphlet, she was accused of high treason. She supported the Paris and Rouen *parlements* in their resistance to Anne of Austria and Cardinal Mazarin. She plotted military strategy with other nobles and gave her protection to the radical Ormée movement in Bordeaux. It should be noted that throughout their remarkable adventures, though, these aristocrats made no assertion of women's collective rights. That would await the great upheaval of 1789.

Order was eventually restored under Louis XIV, who ruled with increasing authority from 1643 to 1715. The Sun King tamed the nobility and subjected it to the elaborate court rituals of Versailles. He set a model for the courts of Europe in recruiting both sexes to create a pageantry of unprecedented brilliance and authority. Under the Sun King's very personal style of rule, a royal confessor or a determined mistress could be as politically influential as a Crown minister.[68] The King appreciated intelligent women, and his jealous control of decision-making sometimes made it easier for him to accept counsel from them than from males.

Under this regime two royal favourites, the Princess of Ursins and Madame de Maintenon, rose to considerable power. Ursins directly influenced the King's policy and appointments relating to Spain. As for Madame de Maintenon, the King conducted many Cabinet meetings in her rooms, sometimes asking her opinion during the process. Her political influence lay not so much in policymaking as in selection of Crown ministers and ecclesiastics.

Louis's successors were less interested in politics, and the women of their courts tended to win prominence for loyalty or beauty, not political savvy. Still, in the mid-eighteenth century Madame de Pompadour was identified by both Voltaire and the Minister de Bernis as the de facto prime minister of the indolent Louis XV, important for adopting as her protégé the talented Duc de Choiseul.[69] Royal mistresses such as Madame de Pompadour and Madame du Barry did have associations with policies and ministers, but this raised a public outcry not seen in Madame de Maintenon's time. With Louis XVI's wife Marie Antoinette, criticism of womanly political intervention (by that time more illusory than real) took the form of outrageous pornography that vilified the Queen as a sexual predator too voracious to spare even her own young son.[70]

France was not the only place things were going downhill. Turning back to the English-speaking world, a number of historians on both sides of the Atlantic have detected a relative decline in women's participation in the polity sometime between 1600 and 1800. 'Why,' ask Mendelson and Crawford in their *Women in Early Modern England*, 'did certain women manage to assert formal civil and political rights at the beginning of our period, and why did these rights deteriorate or disappear over the course of the seventeenth century, at the very moment when non-elite men were making larger claims for their inclusion in the political nation?'[71] The substantive power wielded by Queens Elizabeth and Mary Tudor contrasts with the later, lesser control of the Stuart queens and other court ladies (who also had less education).

A decline also affected women further down the social scale. During the mid-seventeenth-century Civil War and Interregnum, as we have seen, women were still involved. A parliamentary order to administer an oath of allegiance to 'all adult inhabitants' had caused some jurisdictions either to include women as oath takers or at least name women who refused. Some single women had voted in seventeenth-century parliamentary elections; and there were female churchwardens and overseers of the poor. However, Mendelson and Crawford conclude, 'by the eighteenth century, the weight of legal opinion had shifted to the view that women should be excluded entirely from civic duties, which were now deemed "inappropriate" to their sex.'[72]

New trends emerged. Scientific writers in the seventeenth century increasingly rejected the one-sex model of the body (female sexual organs considered as inverted male ones) and began to emphasize difference instead.[73] In the realm of political theory, the revered philosopher John Locke, brought before the tribunal of gender, has been found wanting. The move from a hierarchical state (with the family mirroring and buttressing the monarchy) to a contractual state was in some ways progressive; but unfortunately Locke and other influential theorists managed to largely excise women from the ranks of those who could make contracts.[74] Middle-class men came to dominate civic life through new voluntary associations as well as public institutions.[75] Colonial America, too, witnessed a growing exclusion of influential women from civic life that paralleled the one in England.[76]

While eloquent female voices did resound in the Habermasian public sphere of eighteenth-century literate culture, debating societies, Loyalist and anti-slavery campaigns,[77] English bluestockings never achieved the prominence of the French *salonnières*. While feminists such as Mary Wollenstonecraft and Catherine Macaulay broadcast feminist seeds far and wide, these failed to germinate, having apparently fallen on barren ground.

In contrast, there was nothing barren about the French salon. Salons are a stellar example of women's insertion into a Habermasian public sphere of ideas and opinions. Salons are credited with giving many of the philosophes a platform, as they united nobility and bourgeoisie, and women and men, in a common intellectual and political endeavour. The French prided themselves on living in a country where 'the fair sex was not ... cloistered ... [but rather] allowed to frequent the other sex in "respectable freedom."'[78] Salons began with Madame Rambouillet's famous *chambre bleu* in the 1620s and flourished up through the Revolutionary period. At salons, according to James McMillan, 'the business of the Enlightenment got done.' A *salonnière* needed considerable organizational skill to make the weekly or twice-weekly sessions successful, conversation being 'not haphazard but structured, with the hostess setting the agenda.'[79] The British philosopher David Hume was astonished to find that in France 'the females enter into all transactions and all management of church and state.... [N]o man can expect success, who takes not care to obtain their good graces.' Even Napoleon, not a noted connoisseur of female authority, was still being diplomatic about it when he declared in 1795 that only in France 'do women deserve to wield such influence. A woman, in order to know ... what power she has, must live in Paris for six months.'[80] Ministerial appointments were also strongly influenced by the backing of powerful *salonnières*, who 'could make or break careers and often provided havens for new political philosophies and the new political opposition to the monarchy.'[81]

Apart from the Marquis de Condorcet, mathematician and future revolutionary who steadfastly promoted female education and citizenship, the many philosophers who found an essential forum at salons did little to advance the rights of women. They championed the rights of commoners, citizens, slaves, Jews, Indians, and children, but not of women.[82] Indeed the philosophy of Rousseau asserted that to please men was the essential goal of female education. Rousseau's heroine Julie was told, 'Julie! Incomparable woman! You exercise in the simplicity of private life a despotic empire of wisdom and goodness' (which elicited an ironic rejoinder from *salonnière* Madame de Stael: 'It is not for an empire but for equality that women must do battle'). Madame Roland continued to conduct a salon during the Revolution, but the form went into decline during the Napoleonic years. Disempowering too was the denial of formal training that excluded women from the increasingly professionalized fields of science and philosophy, music and art.[83] Court painter Elisabeth Vigée-Lebrun characterized the eighteenth century as a time when 'women ruled' until 'the Revolution dethroned them.' Revolutionary Olympe de Gouges summed up the dilemma before and after the upheaval: 'Women are now respected and excluded, under the Old Regime they were despised and powerful.'[84] Neither case represents gender utopia. Still, where else were numbers of women, among the aristocracy and in the salons, so close to the political pulse as in France? The truly unusual influence of French women of the courts and salons provides a context for a handful of Canadian women who attained influence in governing circles, who will appear in subsequent chapters.

Women and Two Revolutions

Discussion of colonial and ancien régime women in politics naturally concludes with the two great eighteenth-century revolutions. We begin with the 1776–84 war of independence in America, and afterwards turn to the more dramatic upheaval in France. An idea prevalent around the time of the 1976 bicentennial of American 'exceptionalism' – an innovative revolution that assigned novel and ennobling tasks to women – faded to less positive assessments. Reforms of primogeniture and divorce laws are no longer thought to have affected many women. Women petitioned, boycotted, and spied, but why did they not use the occasion to assert their citizenship, as English women did during their civil war and Frenchwomen would do during their Revolution? The dearth of public discussion of women's rights during the Revolutionary and early Republican periods is striking. Though the writings of English feminists Mary Wollenstonecraft and Catherine Macaulay appeared in numerous American libraries, their ideas stirred little public debate, and the advanced views of various American women of the Adams clan also fell on deaf ears. An absence of institutions such as salons stifled the small numbers of well-read feminists.[85] Moreover, the unusually high literacy rate of Americans made them all the more susceptible to sentimental novels and advice literature extolling the submissive and domesticated 'true womanhood' that washed over the Atlantic world in such a way to leave few feminists standing. To see women acting revolutionary during a Revolution, we must turn to France.

Female citizenship was a live issue in France, which would transmit new notions of citizenship across the Western Hemisphere. We have already seen the importance of elite women during the Fronde, at Versailles, and in the salons. Other roots of activism appeared in peasant quarters. Female participation in ancien régime bread riots and other protests was commonplace. Frequent spinning bees during the winter evenings gave rural women a forum to discuss local affairs in the presence of courting youths and other men who dropped in. The bees could serve as organs of local, unofficial popular justice, which the women evidently considered their business.[86] Women's defamation and praise would later affect the fortunes of Revolutionary factions, and the majority of people crowding around the guillotine to affirm its lethal verdict would be women. Considered well within woman's province of feeding her family, the food riot also became a vehicle for Revolutionary activity.

Female activism was widespread in the French provinces at the end of the eighteenth century.[87] Women contributed to the *cahiers* of grievances that heralded the Revolution, calling for legal and educational equality, marriage reforms, even for political representation. It is now known that there were at least fifty-six women's clubs between 1789 and 1793, and historians are still counting. Often these were affiliates of male clubs, and they concerned themselves with philanthropy, monitoring food supplies and prices, outfitting soldiers, and organizing patriotic celebrations. Some went further. The Besancon *Amies de la Liberté et L'Egalité* lived up to their name in 1793 by demanding the female franchise from the National Assembly. A working-class widow, 'Jeanne Nègre,' in the Carcassonne region led about a thousand men and women who took over the town and killed an official in their quest for grain that was being shipped away. Other provincial women rallied the troops for patriotic mobilization in 1792. Some, appealing to ancient Gallic precedents, were among several dozens known to have served in the Revolutionary armies, until forbidden to do so in 1793.[88] Others acted as counter-revolutionaries, sheltering priests and nuns and opposing Revolutionary cults. Women's voices and the tramp of women's feet accompanied the Revolution from beginning to end.

Around Paris, such activism at several crucial times affected the course of the Revolution. In 1789 some six thousand women went to Versailles exhorting the King to reduce bread prices. At a time of stalemate between the King and the National Assembly, they helped obtain the former's assent to limits on his royal sovereignty as well as his agreement to leave Versailles and move to Paris. Their part in these 'October days' was assessed thus by Michelet: 'The men took the Bastille, the women took the King.'[89] August of 1792 saw women fighting in the insurrection at Tuileries palace that overthrew the monarchy.

In the later, more radical phases of the Revolution, several female clubs formed. The Société Républicaine Révolutionnaire was a militant working-class group that donned red pantaloons and red liberty caps, its 170 members typically older married women without small children. This club had a fundamental role in 'ushering in the Terror; it was considered as one of the principal forces of the revolutionary movement during the summer of 1793 by ... the police, the other clubs, and the revolutionary authorities.'[90] They were instigators of the insurrection of 31 May that year.

Others, too, went where none had gone before. In 1792, three hundred Parisiennes petitioned the Assembly, claiming citizenship and requesting arms. Historians H. Applewhite and D. Levy equate their ground-breaking assertion of their rights to defence of self and country with feminine citizenship.[91] Manon Roland led a patriotic salon and covertly guided the work of her husband who was minister of the interior. Louise de Karalio edited a patriotic journal, and playwright Olympe de Gouges published her declaration of women's right to citizenship – an assertion echoed by several other groups of women addressing the National Assembly. Théroigne de Méricourt dressed as an Amazon and called for a legion to join her. Two of more than thirteen hundred women rounded up as suspects during the Terror, Roland and de Gouges fell victim to the guillotine.[92] As James McMillan wrote, by 'identifying with the Rights of Man and the Constitution of 1793, and by publicly advertising their commitment to the Revolution by word, deed and even dress [including guillotine earrings] ... women effectively made themselves into active citizens, whatever the law might say.'[93] Despite the casualties, these were exhilarating times that saw women push open a number of doors.

Powerful winds slammed them shut again. There was the centuries-old force of patriarchy, ever ready to reassert itself. It appeared in the misogynist literature directed against Marie Antoinette and assertive *citoyennes* alike. There was also Rousseau's new doctrine of sexual determinism. 'Saint Jean-Jacques' attracted both male and female devotees among the bourgeoisie with his calls for free choice of spouse. They accepted his condemnation of the public licentiousness of court ladies. They heeded his honeyed calls to a new, but very private idealism for wives and mothers whose service was so very sacred they must not leave the home in any significant capacity. Here was a new cloister indeed, each unit supervised by a male head. The mission did endow mothers with a new sense of dignity and purpose.[94] But Rousseau's doctrines were all the more insidious since they gave inequality a new lease on life in progressive circles, recasting womanly 'difference' as a dictate of a benevolent Nature rather than of a discredited Divinity. Another Revolutionary legacy was a new 'fraternalism' that began to bond men even as they rejected older forms of patriarchalism. Revolutionaries commonly characterized republican virtues and culture as explicitly male. The combination of old and new forms of misogyny left little place for political women. One by one, the doors closed. The Société Républicaine Révolutionnaire was dissolved on 20 October 1793. Ten days later the Convention banned all female political clubs, now considered incompatible with a woman's natural vocation to nurture her family. In May 1795 the Convention decreed that, lest women disturb the peace, they must remain at home, with gatherings of five or more subject to dispersal by force.

To a degree far surpassing anything seen during the American Revolution, Frenchwomen had reached exhilarating heights as direct participants in their country's great political upheaval. They actually raised the question of their citizenship, again and again. However, the seemingly boundless possibilities of the early Revolutionary years disappeared between 1793 and the century's end. The banning of the political clubs, the disarming of female soldiers, the disgrace of leaders, and the enthroning of Rousseauian maternalist ideology effectively dispelled the breathtaking vista that opened up for a few heady years of Revolution in France. As James McMillan wrote, 'The period from the late eighteenth century through to the First World War was remarkable for the degree to which a particular vision of woman as a domestically oriented being came to be accepted.... It had not always been thus.'[95]

Conclusion

What conclusions emerge from our transatlantic comparisons of seventeenth- and eighteenth-century women's history? When we follow political trajectories, we see that England's reactionary Restoration period narrowed women's direct political participation in elections and local offices, in the decisions of church and state; and by the eighteenth century the American colonies followed suit. If one wishes to define the public sphere very broadly, one can be optimistic about women's growing presence in literary and philanthropic aspects of eighteenth-century public life. This did not prevent their political rights from receding. France, on the other hand, remained exceptional. For the better part of the two centuries in question, that country produced one of the most astonishing periods known to the history of women. The seventeenth and eighteenth centuries saw considerable feminine influence at courts, in the arts and sciences, and in the salons, culminating in an impressive degree of activism from all classes during the Revolution. As the period ended, though, maternalist ideology attained the same chilling grip in France as in England and America. By 1800, relative to what had gone before, a most unseemly torpor had descended upon the *citoyennes* of France, as they slipped into line with their sisters in England and America. All these groups also faced increased economic inequality and more occupational segregation.

This chapter has demonstrated myriad ways that the domestic ideology gripped England, America, and eventually France, by 1800 and manifested itself in narrowing work options and shrinking civic participation. Women in the remote colony of Canada would emulate neither the courtly glories nor the Revolutionary exploits of their French sisters. However, they would also avoid the repressive currents that followed in the wake of various upheavals we have discussed in France, England, and America. Women on the St Lawrence lived a long distance from the metropolitan centres of Europe and America, and it was not their clothing alone that lagged behind the latest fashions. They would perpetuate older forms of family work, family governance, and family-oriented law well into the nineteenth century, as this book will show. Our study now takes us to French Canada.

PART TWO

Along a River

Chapter Two

River of Promise

Our attention now turns to Canada, and we open the subject by introducing the most significant groups of female immigrants, who arrived
in the years between 1639 and 1673. It is the second, third, and fourth
generations of women in New France whom we will analyse in depth in
this book. Their seventeenth-century forebears, the first large generation of *canadiennes*, deserve at least an introduction. Their history brings
us back to the observation at the opening of the book that women were
never properly considered in 'frontierist' works that weighed the social
impact of the environment. Though they received scant attention in
those works, the environment was decisive for both major categories of
female pioneers. They consisted of two separate groups, quite distinctive in class, outlook, and numbers. What did they have in common?
The people and resources they encountered along the St Lawrence
River profoundly shaped the experience of both. Before 1650, it was
the human occupants of the forests who were the chief source of attraction for the influential group of missionaries known as *dévotes*. Three
of the *dévotes* would capture a place in French Canada's pantheon that
patriarchal societies almost always reserve for men: founders of a nation. Later, for hundreds of immigrant brides known as *filles du roi*, it
was other aspects of the environment – wide open spaces, arable land,
clean air and water, ample fish and game – that changed the course of
their young lives. The environment is the common thread we shall use
to stitch their different stories together, incorporating what is most useful from French- and English-language scholarship, before we move into
deeper analysis of eighteenth-century French-Canadian women in the
rest of the book.

The *Dévotes*

In a dream God took her to a vast country full of mountains, Valleys, and heavy fogs. Later the Lord said to her explicitly 'It was Canada that I showed you, you must go there and build a house for Jesus and Mary.'[1]

Fog is an environmental phenomenon. It can occur when warm air makes contact with a cold body of water, causing condensation that obscures navigation. Marie Guyart was a thirty-four-year-old widow in the French town of Tours when the fogbound land of Canada loomed up in her dreams. As a child she had stood on chairs and preached her own version of the sermons she'd heard in church. She was married at seventeen. Her husband died two years later and she was left alone with an infant. She went on to manage her brother-in-law's transport company alongside the Loire River, eventually supervising thirty workmen. Later, ignoring the tears of her eleven-year-old son Claude, she placed him in the custody of relatives and became a nun in the local Ursuline convent, taking as her name in religion Marie de l'Incarnation. Accustomed to penitential practices such as wearing thorns next to her chest and rising at night to flagellate herself, she won a reputation as an unusually devout nun. She was, as well, a craftswoman known for her fine embroidery. She was also a mystical writer (beatified by Rome in 1980), whose meditations are still studied today. To read them is to experience many dark nights of the soul and ecstasies of divine love. One might say the fog in her dream sprang from the collision of heavenly visions with real stories of the northern woods and their inhabitants. They were known as '*sauvages,*' a term that in seventeenth-century French signified people who lived in the woods (from the Latin root *silvaticus*) and did not have the same negative connotations it would later acquire. They figured prominently in the enthusiastic conversion stories sent to France by Jesuit missionaries in Canada, stories not yet permeated with torture and martyrdom. Indeed the nuns would soon encounter women so much at home in the forests that they clad their infants in beaver skins stitched together with moose tendons, and could navigate the St Lawrence astride mere logs if they lacked a canoe.[2] What the fog obscured was the minimal interest these people had in converting to Catholicism, a European faith enmeshed in wealth and political power, great monasteries and cathedrals, libraries full of theological treatises, a male God, an elaborate hierarchy, and rigid doctrines about sexuality. All these features were incongruent with the classless society, the non-patriarchal religion, the sexual freedom and relative sexual equality, and the comparatively mobile lifestyles of the Montagnais, Algonkian, and Iroquoian-speaking peoples of North America.

In the climate of Catholic revival then penetrating the wealthiest circles of the wealthiest country in Europe, any such difficulties were minimized. Far from being repellent, *les sauvages* exerted a magnetic pull on the purses of aging philanthropists. They were equally magnetic for some brilliant people in their twenties and thirties – even one sixteen-year-old nun – who quite simply offered their whole lives. Jesuit priests had already worked for a century among the peoples of China, India, and Brazil before coming to Canada, and they operated on the rule that it was improper for them to teach members of the other sex. For that reason, their annual *Relation* from Canada in 1634 posed a question: 'Is there not ... some good virtuous woman who would wish to come to this country to ... gather up the blood of Jesus Christ by instructing these savage little girls?'[3] The question seems to have sent a shiver down the spine of hundreds of women in Catholic France. For the first time, they were being invited to go abroad to spread the word of God. Applications flooded in from both nuns and laywomen desiring (Jesuit *Relations* of the following years reported) 'to come finish life in a small cabin dedicated to serving little savages who run without restraint through the great forest,' 'to endure the rigours of a much colder climate and labours which would daunt even men.'

Though the notion of female proselytizers remained controversial in France, these missionaries took sail for the explicit purpose of converting new peoples.[4] To the great joy of the saintly Marie de l'Incarnation, she and five others were chosen to go. This would give the Ursuline leader a wider field of action, placing her at considerable remove from the kind of clerical censorship that could befall outspoken female mystics in France.[5] Though the Jesuit priests had not anticipated so many volunteers, they decided that having both a school to teach Indian girls French ways and a hospital to care for the sick would encourage the natives to settle among the French, laying the basis for a sedentary Christian society where these converts would intermarry with Europeans. That first group consisted of the hospital sisters Saint-Ignace and Saint-Bonaventure de Jésus and Saint-Bernard, as well as Ursuline sisters Marie de l'Incarnation and Marie de Saint-Joseph and their lay patron Madame de la Peltrie.

Remarkably, these women were not lost to history. Their activities were not dismissed by nineteenth- and twentieth-century historians as unworthy of notice. Nor did these forceful characters meet the fate of seventeenth-century New England heroine Hannah Durston, who was initially considered heroic for slaying her family's captors but who by the nineteenth century was labelled a 'hag.' The Catholic tradition of honouring its saints served the missionaries well. From the time of seventeenth-century Sulpician Dollier de Casson onward, priests recorded these women's stories, sometimes with an eye to canonization. Aware of their own potential for sainthood, conscious of posterity,[6] *dévotes* likewise recorded their own stories and those of colleagues they esteemed. The convent tradition of writing annals provided additional documentation. In accounts laced with visions, miracles, and deliberate cloaking of benefactors who sought anonymity, it is sometimes difficult to pinpoint 'what happened.' But at least we know what they *thought* happened, because they wrote it down (a decidedly European perspective on things, as we shall later discuss). In a subsequent era, the intense Catholicism that characterized French Canada for more than a century following a major religious revival in 1840 encouraged preservation and publication of these old documents. In the twentieth century, alongside edifying works for pupils and parishioners, there appeared scholarly works by Claire Daveluy, Dom Guy Oury,[7] and others that skilfully analysed and annotated the documentary evidence relating to the early missions.

It is unusual for nuns to number among the first recorders of a national history, but it happened in Canada. Marie de l'Incarnation's letters, like those of the Jesuits, are an essential source on the early colony, and they reveal activities and perspectives of French and native women that do not appear in the Jesuit *Relations*.[8] Montreal Hôtel-Dieu sister Marie Morin, who entered the convent in 1662 at age thirteen, incorporated much of the town's story into her chronicle of the hospital, making her the first historian born in the colony. In the eighteenth century the Quebec Hôtel-Dieu produced another pair of historians, Jeanne-Françoise Juchereau de la Ferté and the witty and cultured Marie-Andrée Regnard Duplessis. Their collective work on *Annales of the Hôtel-Dieu* from 1636 to 1716 is yet another valuable encapsulation of colonial history. They allow us to view a country's founding through feminine eyes.

In sum, French Canada was established at a rare moment of seventeenth-century female religious activism, and it preserved and cherished the stories of its 'founding mothers.' It embraced them not with reverence alone, but also with a strong tradition of historical scholarship dating from the mid-nineteenth century. Historians have the documentary evidence to tell and retell this story, trying to make sense of it to audienc-

es that change with the passing decades, as Catholics, nationalists, ethnohistorians, feminists, and postmodernists bring their different questions
to the study of the past.[9]

Marie de l'Incarnation

Marie de l'Incarnation, and two other women whom we shall soon meet,
were to play an exceptional role in building foundations for a Christian
utopia on the St Lawrence. Things would not, however, turn out as they
expected. The missionaries imagined winning thousands of natives for
Christ along the river's misty shores. Had they been able to see more
clearly, they might never have come.

Certainly *most* French people did not want to come. Ever since Samuel
de Champlain had set up a trading post at Quebec in 1608, his countrymen had proved resistant to any calls for colonization. The Crown, finding the pelts of the northern woods a poor substitute for the gold and
silver in the Spanish colonies, also showed scant interest. The trading
companies that initially ran the colony had little incentive to sponsor
settlers, for the natives required no assistance in trapping the furs and
bringing them down to the posts. In 1641 there were only about two
hundred French settlers, mostly at Quebec, a few more at the Tadoussac
post farther east. It did not help that Champlain had formed a military
alliance with the Wyandot (Hurons) against the Haudenosaunee (Iroquois), incurring the enmity of some of the most renowned warriors on
the continent. Stories of torture and martyrdom would soon add further
chill to the colony's reputation.

Though fog is typically a hindrance to seeing clearly, it facilitated
the mission of Marie de l'Incarnation in 1639, her one-way trip to the
wilderness to save *les sauvages*. Oblivious to the troubles ahead, the tall
Ursuline, after a special audience with the Queen of France, joined a
handful of female companions in finalizing travel arrangements and
bidding adieu to tearful relatives. In those same years, women were going to New England and Virginia as wives, slaves, or indentured servants.
By contrast, Canada received an indomitable group of educated single
women questing for pagan peoples in the mists. When they set sail in
early May 1639, Marie de l'Incarnation felt 'I was entering paradise ...
risking my life for love of Him who had given it to me.'[10] They thought
the end had come when their ship nearly hit an iceberg that loomed up
suddenly in a fog so thick they could not see from one side of the ship to
the other.[11] However, they arrived safe and sound on the first day of Au-

gust at the little port of Quebec. It seemed 'almost a dream,' a bystander
reported, for 'from a floating prison were seen issuing these virgins con-
secrated to God, as fresh and as rosy as when they had departed from
their homes.'[12] Touching shore, they knelt and kissed the soil. Marie de
l'Incarnation later recalled her first impressions: 'Now that I was in this
country and able to observe it, I recognized that it was what Our Lord
had shown me…. The huge mountains, the vast spaces … Now I saw the
very same thing except there was less fog…. [T]here were only five or
six little houses at the most. The whole country was a great forest full of
thickets…. [W]e were surrounded by savages – both men and women –
naked to the waist.'[13]

At the beginning, hopes were high. The fur trade governor Charles
de Montmagny treated the newcomers royally, firing a cannonade to
celebrate their arrival and inviting them to dine at his table. The very
next day he escorted the three hospital sisters (all young women in their
twenties), to meet the natives at the Sillery mission near Quebec. Their
benefactor, the Duchesse d'Aiguillon (niece of the powerful Cardinal
Richelieu) wished to fund a hospital in a cabin right in the Indian settlement, and the sisters hastened to comply. The nuns would balk at leaving their cabin, even when settlers were being killed twenty kilometres
away, and reports arrived of Iroquois plans to abduct the sisters; they
stalled, even though the governor and his council asked them to return
to town. After all, there were pressing duties in their little wooden hospital. Over one hundred native patients arrived in the first year, many with
smallpox. It was too early, everything still too new, for them to realize
that the plagues were due to North American lack of immunity to European microbes.[14] 'I prefer being here,' Mother Saint-Ignace, their superior, declared, 'to being Empress of the whole world,' and she laughed
for joy when she herself was later diagnosed with a terminal illness. Exhausted with overwork, the sisters had their own share of sickness. But
they caught tantalizing glimpses of what was originally conceptualized as
an interracial Christian community, with the nuns educating aboriginal
brides for French husbands. Some native women worked in the hospital, carrying and helping patients and preparing food, and they seemed
to embrace the new religion wholeheartedly. Their little girls played a
game based on a picture of the Duchesse d'Aiguillon, kneeling beside
a crucifix. One would say, 'She is on her knees,' and they all knelt; 'her
hands are folded,' and they all folded theirs. The sisters' highest hopes
were fulfilled when the people of the forest walked into the wards and
asked to be taught how to pray, undertook self-flagellations surpassing

even those of French *dévotes*. The dying Mother Saint-Ignace asked to be carried into the ward to expire among the new converts.

Meanwhile, Marie de l'Incarnation and her companions similarly set to work in a temporary two-room wooden convent in Quebec that was soon surrounded by the wigwams of native families. Modifying the cloistered lifestyle of Ursulines in France, they welcomed up to eight hundred visitors a year in their parlour, feeding visiting chiefs and native families who stopped in for *sagamité*, a native corn stew the sisters learned to prepare. Marie de l'Incarnation's descriptions suggest a perhaps less than completely successful resolve to triumph over bourgeois fastidiousness:

> The filth of the savage children, who were not yet used to the cleanliness of the French, sometimes led us to find a shoe in a cooking pot. And every day we discovered hair and charcoal which, however, did not disgust us. People who came to visit and to whom we told these stories for amusement could not understand how we could adjust to this. Still less did they understand how we could embrace these little orphans, holding them on our laps, when their bodies were heavily smeared with grease and covered only by a small greasy rag, giving them a terrible odor. For us all this was an unimaginable happiness. Once they had grown accustomed to this, we tried to clean them up over a period of a few days…. Then we gave them some underwear and a little tunic to protect them from the vermin that covered them when they first came to us.[15]

In her first decade in Quebec, Marie de l'Incarnation's letters focused so exclusively on the 'savages' that one would scarcely know French settlers lived there too. They taught Indian girls at their school, adopting several whose parents had died. They remade their own scarce linen into children's clothing and decked their boarders out in French hairstyles and in little red robes that were said to delight the natives who saw them. The nuns were moved to tears when they first heard their converts' childish voices singing Christian hymns in aboriginal languages.[16]

Marie de l'Incarnation turned her mind to native language and culture. Her school became a multilingual institution, with instruction offered in Algonquin, Montagnais, Huron, and French. She eventually was able to write catechisms and dictionaries in Huron and Algonquin. In the early years, there were signs that even girls who stayed with the sisters only briefly were carrying the new religion back to their wandering bands in the woods. Marie de l'Incarnation was also fascinated by Iroquois clan mothers. She recorded that they had women chiefs 'who are women of

rank ... who have a deliberative voice in the councils and reach conclusions as the men do.... [I]t was they who delegated the first ambassadors
(in 1654) to treat for peace.'[17] One such matron who encountered the
Ursuline superior later sent her gifts and arranged for other aboriginal
women to go from Montreal to Quebec to meet such a rare woman of
power among the French.

The work of the nuns was integral to the tiny French outpost. Jesuit
Superior Paul LeJeune listed the Jesuit school for boys, the Ursuline
school for girls, and the hospital as the three pillars of the mission to
Christianize the natives around Quebec. Female diplomacy, seldom discussed by historians, was also part of the colonizing effort. In 1658 Marie
de l'Incarnation noted the diplomatic importance of keeping Iroquois
(Haudenosaunee) girls at the convent, since exchange of children or
kin was a key element, but 'there is no way to keep men or boys.'[18] Acting in close consultation with the governor, the Ursulines carried out his
Indian policy, which also required ceremonial hospitality.

In other ways too, the *dévotes* made themselves indispensable to the
French enterprise. Both the Augustinian hospital sisters and the Ursulines brought vital funds to the isolated outpost. They used their French
endowments to bring over skilled workmen, the Ursulines employing
ten in 1644. As superior, Marie de l'Incarnation supervised the seigneurie where they grew provisions, as well as construction of a three-story
stone convent, which was, at the time, the most impressive building in
the nascent town. She also wrote an estimated three thousand letters (of
which about three hundred survive)[19] to well-placed citizens in France to
publicize the settlement and keep the donations coming. In that regard,
and in teaching the Gospel to both sexes when aboriginal men crowded
into the parlour, Marie de l'Incarnation broke with tradition.[20]

Jeanne Mance

That is not the end of the story of the female founders; it takes stranger
turns still. Even Quebec visionaries such as Marie de l'Incarnation were
appalled by a plan to penetrate three hundred kilometres westward into
the wilderness and set up a new mission astride the trade routes of the
dreaded Iroquois. *La folle entreprise,* the foolish enterprise, Quebeckers
dubbed the project of the Company of Notre Dame. True, the site would
allow easy river access to missions even further inland,[21] for those whose
dreams of conversion were as boundless as the continent itself. A famous
portrait of Jeanne Mance, one of the administrators of this company,

portrays her as a beautiful young woman with doe-like eyes and flowing hair. Whether or not she looked the part, certainly within that breast beat the heart of a romantic. In May 1642, two small barques brought her and the other foolish enterprisers to the Montreal island, where they pitched tents and began living in the woods. Enthralled by the spring wildflowers, Mance and friends decked out a rustic altar on Montreal's mountain, netting fireflies to light the service, and praying for the enemy people who might be rustling in the woods around them. Fifty-five colonists (including ten women) decided to remain on the island as winter fell. Mance stayed, and her hospital, like the one in Quebec, quickly attracted the ailing among natives allied with the French. They became catechumens as well as patients of this useful mystic who possessed her own lancets, syringes, mortar, and other medical and pharmacological instruments.[22] Not until 1659 would she manage to recruit three French hospital sisters to help. In the first years, Mance found that some beds had to be reserved for French settlers wounded by tomahawks of the Haudenosaunee,[23] who naturally enough wished to protect their trade routes from colonists who were allied to their Wyandot rivals. Things were so dangerous that when Quebeckers later sent a vessel to check on the new island colony, the crew was told not to land unless they could catch sight of survivors moving around on the misty shores.

With Jeanne Mance, even more than in the case of Marie de l'Incarnation, we encounter a woman at the very centre of the founding of a permanent French settlement – today the second-largest French-speaking city in the world. Mance, whose father was an attorney, displayed managerial skills akin to those of Marie de l'Incarnation. The difference was that, rather than heading a convent, she co-directed a group that was primarily masculine. Her Montreal venture was connected to the controversial and secretive Compagnie de Saint-Sacrement, which shrouded it in such a veil of intrigues that the whole story will never be known. She was, as a contemporary noted, an eloquent woman. Mance had been a late addition to the group that was preparing to sail from La Rochelle for *la folle entreprise* when she joined them in 1641. She convinced the dreamy crowd to write a prospectus of their project and send it to Madame de Bullion and other wealthy Parisian ladies and gentlemen of her acquaintance. In consequence the Company of Montreal expanded from eight members to thirty-eight,[24] including nine women, and donations more than doubled. We know that Mance, at that stage of her life an ascetic who lived on bread and water, paid four successive visits to the lavish mansion of the biggest single donor of the venture, Angelique de

Bullion (widow of a French finance minister) to win her support. Trusting Mance to found the hospital she wished to endow, Madame de Buillon made contributions amounting to 74,000 *livres* across the decades.[25]

The role of Jeanne Mance as co-founder of Montreal is clearly acknowledged in the founding documents. The colonizing company's 1643 document *Les Véritables Motifs de Messieurs et Dames de la Société de Nostre Dame de Montréal pour la Conversion des Sauvages de la Nouvelle France* went to some lengths to note that Christ had accepted help from women in his travels on earth. There was clearly a desire to justify their prominence in this new work to establish the church 'in a country hitherto abandoned to demons.'[26] The document notes that the French founders of the company 'had often begged God for people to direct and lead this, His new family they were sending to the ... island, and God sent them two leaders at different times and of different sex, station and place of origin.' Mance's contemporary Dollier de Casson likewise described a woman and a man, Jeanne Mance and Paul Chomeday de Maisonneuve, as co-founders of Montreal. Mance was the official treasurer, director of supplies, and hospital director of the colony. The Company of Montreal sent the pope a document that also specified that Montreal was the creation of 'high-ranking people of both sexes.'[27]

A guiding hand of the enterprise, Mance is seen by some as more effective than her colleague Governor Maisonneuve. She took it upon herself to sail back across the Atlantic in 1649, where she revived waning French support. Most importantly, it was Mance's idea to use her hospital's endowment to recruit more men to protect the town. After the Haudenosaunee destroyed the outlying Jesuit mission of Saint-Marie-among-the-Hurons in 1649, Montreal suddenly became the front line in the Franco-Iroquois conflict. After more than a third of the colonists were slain, fear drove the survivors to abandon their houses and live in the fort. By mid-1651 there were only seventeen militia to face the onslaught of two hundred enemy warriors. 'Everyone was reduced to extremities,' Mance wrote. 'One spoke of nothing but leaving the country.' Reflecting on this, she decided it was 'better to sacrifice part lest the whole perish.' As Dollier de Casson wrote, 'Finally, as we were diminishing each day and our enemies encouraged by their great numbers; everyone saw quite clearly that if powerful help did not arrive soon from France, all would be lost. Mademoiselle Mance, considering and weighing this, told Monsieur de Maisonneuve that she advised him to go to France, that the benefactress having given her 22,000 *livres* for the hospital ... she would give it to him in order to get help.'[28]

Governor Maisonneuve agreed, and he went off to France on this quest, warning her he would not come back at all if he failed to get reinforcements. Mance advised him to interview Madame de Bullion. That latter approved the suggested diversion of her donation in order to raise troops, and she added 20,000 *livres* more, money Maisonneuve used to secure armed men for the beleaguered settlement. The year 1653 emerged in Montreal history as 'the year of the hundred men.' Dollier de Casson said Mance's actions to raise troops saved the town. Other seventeenth-century observers shared the view that raising those troops was crucial. In 1687 Governor Denonville wrote that, 'with the consent of the founder [Madame de Bullion], 22,000 livres were borrowed from the Company of Montreal to raise a hundred men to protect the Island from Iroquois attacks. These men saved it, in effect, as well as all of Canada.'[29]

It is conceivable that the Quebec settlement might have survived without Mance's action, leaving a French foothold in Canada. But as for Montreal, without the donors Mance secured and the funds she transferred at the critical hour, it does seem likely that the *folle* project of a settlement in enemy territory would have collapsed.

Marguerite Bourgeoys

The third of our trio of Canadian 'Founding Mothers' was rather different from the others. In her own day, she was an oddity. Marie de l'Incarnation and Jeanne Mance stayed true to their respectable background by communicating with court ladies and administering the large donations that ensued. Marguerite Bourgeoys, though drawn like the other two from the bourgeoisie,[30] not only lacked court ties but stooped to one of the lowliest jobs around: she reimbursed her passage to Canada by doing Governor Maisonneuve's laundry for him. Moreover, her methods as an administrator were, as we shall see, unorthodox. She did have in common with Marie de l'Incarnation a proclivity to visions, for at the age of thirty-three she was summoned to New France by the Virgin Mary. Bourgeoys wrote, 'One morning when I was fully awake I saw a tall woman dressed in a white, serge-like robe, who said to me distinctly, "Go, I will not abandon you," and I knew it was the Blessed Virgin even though I could not make out her face. That reassured me for the trip and gave me ample courage, and I found no further difficulty.'[31]

What was singular about Marguerite Bourgeoys is that she was so radical, a person who went right to the root of things in seeking change. She was considered a saint even in her lifetime because she was so unworldly.

Did Heaven tell her to carry the Gospel to the Indians? Well then, she would put herself in Heaven's hands, simply ignoring the question of any food, clothing, or money she might need for an overseas trip. She set out on her own for the port of Saint-Nazaire at a time when it was so unconventional for a respectable woman to travel alone that people assumed she was anything *but* pious. She was refused lodgings by a respectable landlady and had to barricade herself into the coach to protect herself from men who also had the wrong idea.[32] Besides sailing off to a place well known for massacres, Bourgeoys packed for this new life as though she were going on a camping trip, with just one bag that she carried herself. This was customary with her. On a later voyage she again set out without any money, sleeping on a coil of rope on the deck. Much later, at the age of sixty-nine, when her bishop summoned her from Montreal to Quebec, it was reported that she simply got up and started walking there through the February snow and slush, following her own maxim that the sisters were ready 'to go anywhere they are sent in this Country.' When the community's house burned down, she commented, 'I was more joyful than sad about that fire.' She used the occasion of rebuilding to have her followers vow 'we will not rebuild except to be more fruitful than we have in the past.'

Understandably, others could not be quite so oblivious to physical needs. After Bourgeoys had recruited three other single women from France to help with her school, she annoyed them by inviting seventeen female immigrants to lodge with them in one of their two little houses. Bourgeoys later confessed, 'I believe I did not please the sisters and that I failed to give them the necessary instructions.'[33] She actually turned down some donations as being more than they needed. Her followers were chagrined by her delay in building larger quarters (she decided a chapel was more important). Some may have had doubts too, about dining together with male servants, and about catechizing New England male captives. In any case, Bourgeoy's spirit of dedication that knew no bounds would continue to guide her followers in the next century, when it was not unusual for half of the twenty teachers working at country missions to be at the infirmary recovering from exhaustion.[34]

In 1657 Marguerite Bourgeoys began turning her visions into realities. Given a stable in which to start her school, she taught both Indian and French children, initially taking pupils of both sexes. Then she and the companions she recruited from France, likely clad in simple black dresses with woollen belts and headdresses, opened a cabin school for native girls at the Mountain mission run by the Sulpician Fathers. Soon this school had some forty students who dressed, spoke, and did needle-work in the manner of French girls.[35] Like the other *dévotes*, Bourgeoys believed the dream was coming true when she saw young converts going out to teach their own people. Moreover, the first two native members of female religious orders in North America north of Mexico belonged to the Congregation of Notre Dame, which Bourgeoys founded in Mon-treal. They were Wyandot Marie-Thérèse Gannensagouas and Haudeno-saunee Marie-Barbe Atontinon, both apparently working as teachers at the Mountain mission. In 1683 the Intendant De Meulles indicated that the Congregation of Notre Dame was markedly more successful than the Ursulines in teaching French ways to native peoples. It would seem that of the three 'Founding Mothers,' Marguerite Bourgeoys came closest to reaching the goal they all shared. The church placed her at the forefront by canonizing her in 1982.

A Mystic Invasion

What but the power of illusion could cause the Ursuline mystic to declare in 1645, 'We are on the verge of seeing the Kingdom of God extending over all the unbelievers of our America.' That statement alone signals to a contemporary reader that this narrative can hardly be presented as a simple story of accomplishment by three 'great women in history.' Any such agenda has been shelved as a result of post-1950 scholarship by eth-nohistorians and increased attention to aboriginal viewpoints. Together these led to widespread recognition that the missionary project was of dubious value to the human figures standing on that misty landscape. It was part of the larger colonial assault on aboriginal territory, culture, often life itself. Many of the 'conversions' that thrilled the missionaries were products of native syncretism – selective incorporation of aspects of other religions into their own. Inducements provided in food, clothing, shelter, arms, and gifts also raise questions about the depth of many of the conversions.

Contemporary readers may find it hard to comprehend what seem arrogant or misguided compulsions of these Founding Mothers, their visions and their obsession to convert indigenous nations. What forces impelled them? A 'mystic invasion' in seventeenth-century France had forced the church to admit a greater number of women into its inner life of prayer than the ecclesiastics at the Council of Trent had envis-aged, partly because it was necessary to use female catechists to stem the inroads of Protestantism among women. Their raptures, demonologies, and self-flagellation conform to a pattern of ecstatic religion seen in many cultures of the world across the centuries. Possible explanations are as varied as those one finds for outbreaks of 'witchcraft.' Some regard the altered mental state of the mystic as pathological. Some see it as the product of semi-hypnotic effects of private meditation or group prayer, or something chemically induced.[36] Those who favour psychosociological interpretations may perceive female psychosomatizations or 'negative mysticism' as a response to inability the translate inner 'bold new visions of freedom" into changes in the patriarchal world around them. Spiritual modelling of a transformed world can in the long run be more influential in the long run than a more direct approach.

The Canadian *dévotes*, as University of Montreal historian Dominique Deslandres pointed out, were in very unusual circumstances. They were financially independent, thanks to other women. They 'modelled themselves on the apostles, ancient and modern, and that made them hope to obtain the same miraculous results.' There was the notion that God was acting through them, and 'since all must yield to divine *dictats* ... This rhetoric, common to both sexes, turns into an extremely powerful tool for feminine socio-religious promotion.' Consciously or not, the missionary mystic could become a powerful figure.[37]

One clear sign that Canadian mystics were pushing the envelope in terms of womanly initiative came in the 1660s when one of the Jesuit priests made a covert attempt to chastise Marie de l'Incarnation. During convent recreation hour a curiously folded note arrived, and Marie de l'Incarnation began reading it aloud to the Ursulines, amid some amusement as the letter turned out to be an exhortation to mortify her self-love and submit to those over her. Scholars believe that the letter was not the work, as purported, of a young boy Marie de l'Incarnation had befriended and who had subsequently gone to live with the Jesuits. The phraseology, and the familiarity with the writing of Saint-Francis de Sales evident in the missive, strongly suggest that the anonymous sender was a Jesuit.[38] Apparently she was perceived as transgressing; but the Ursuline mystic had sufficient prestige that her critic evidently felt a need to attack covertly. Even the imperious Bishop Laval backed off and waited until after her death to force the changes he wanted in the convent's constitution. Several scholars have documented Jesuit attempts to inculcate submission in native women. Such prejudices extended to the nuns too, seen, for example, in Father Barthemy Vimont's statement that convent successes must come from heaven, since a mission to the natives had 'no attraction that pleases the senses' without which 'their sex does not possess such constancy' to persist in the effort. Unburdened with such notions of womanly inferiority, the natives referred to the convent foundresses as 'daughters of Captains,'[39] apparently perceiving something strong there.

It seems there was. *Dévotes* won powerful political allies in struggles with bishops who wished to impose cloister, boosting their ability to thwart several ecclesiastics who wished them to lead more secluded, less active lives. Bishop Laval, for example, engaged in jurisdictional battles with both Marie de l'Incarnation and Marguerite Bourgeoys (at one point forbidding the latter to recruit more sisters). He also attempted to curb an expansion of Jeanne Mance's work. Fortunately the Sulpician priests of Montreal usually supported the local *dévotes*, as did the lay authorities. Sometimes bishops did prevail; sometimes, after locking horns with the women, they backed down.[40] A century after the nuns stepped ashore, some officials would express outrage at the 'spirit of independence and liberty' the nuns showed, their 'rebelliousness' in refusing to be saddled with lay administrators as French convents were, to hand over patients wanted for questioning, to open their books for the intendant's inspection. Authorities suspected this unwonted behaviour sprang from the early establishment of convents, pre-dating both bishopric and royal government.[41]

When *dévotes* had sufficient force to tackle traditional hierarchies, why did their missionary goals elude them? A major blow was struck, of course, when the most promising group, the relatively sedentary Wyandot nation, which entrusted some of its girls to Quebec convents, was destroyed by the Haudenosaunee in 1649. Moreover, some aboriginal women numbered among the strongest opponents of the missionaries, as did the Montagnais who warned her people, 'Do you not see that we all are dying since they told us to pray to God? Where are your relatives? Where are mine? Most of them are dead. It is no longer a time to believe.'[42] Apart from associating the missionaries with the dreaded smallpox, measles, and diphtheria, First Nations heard from the missionaries unaccustomed, patriarchal maxims about female chastity and submission. Still, scholars continue to puzzle over the precise impact of missions on native women. Anthropologist Roland Viau, for example, believes powers of Iroquoian women at missions actually increased, since the men were increasingly absent for colonial trade and warfare. Some, such as the Mohawk saint Kateri Tekakwitha, were clearly attracted by Catholicism and believed in it deeply while at the same time adapting it to their needs.[43] The story of missionary–aboriginal contact is complex and defies easy judgments.

In time even the missionaries confessed to bitter disappointments. All too soon their hard-won converts, such as the Wyandot child prodigy who impressed convent visitors by speaking and singing in French, died a victim of European diseases. So too died the little Iroquois named Louise, baptised at six, gone at seven, laid out in a coffin in a white robe with a crown of flowers.[44] For Marie de l'Incarnation it took nearly twenty years for the fog to lift, for her to see that the surviving converts were pathetically few. It has been pointed out that she had a practical side: despite being 'constantly in conversation with her God, this didn't prevent her from closely supervising construction of her new convent, mounting ladders and platforms and counselling the architect and the masons.'[45] Her realistic side prevailed when in 1668 the tall Ursuline finally stooped to the humiliating admission that its was 'difficult if not impossible' to adapt Indians to French customs. 'We have more experience with it than anyone else,' she wrote, and 'of a hundred girls who have passed through our hands, we have scarcely civilized one.' She observed, 'We find them docile and bright, but when one least expects it they climb over our cloister walls and go roam in the woods with their families, where they find more pleasure than in all the amenities of our French dwellings.'[46]

Though there were still seventy to eighty Wyandot day pupils in the early 1660s, recognition was dawning that the Christian utopia was not to be. Dispatches from the intendant began to confirm the Ursuline failure to turn native girls into French ones. They dropped the vow to teach Indian girls around 1720, closing down the last native class a few years later. Surviving records indicate only thirty-three church-sanctioned French–Indian marriages in the seventeenth century, twenty-nine of them involving a native bride.[47] Marie de l'Incarnation in her heart of hearts never really gave up. She singled out native girls for the prized front row at her deathbed in 1672. Surrounded by them, she whispered at the end, 'Everything is for the Savages.' In Montreal the dream, or at least some practical manifestations of it, lasted longer: the Hôtel-Dieu wards continued to include a number of native patients, and the Congregation of Notre Dame was still teaching native girls to work with wool late in the French regime.

Dévotes and Colonists

Turning from the questionable goals of missionizing, we can move onto surer ground in assessing service to the growing numbers of French colonists in the St Lawrence valley. Their compatriots benefited when the *dévotes* sponsored immigrants, and then boarded and nursed those in need. At least in that context, they did more good than harm. It was a boon to the infant colony when Mance and Bourgeoys made several voyages to France to recruit settlers, including a dozen teachers. Male colonists quickly married the single women they shepherded across in 1650, 1653, and 1659, and who were initially housed at the Congréga-tion's farm. As we saw, Marie de l'Incarnation and Jeanne Mance also sponsored badly needed workers to help build their establishments, staff their wards, or work the farms that all the convents acquired.

They ran hospitals and hospices. By 1681 the Hôtel-Dieu of Quebec had grown to a sizeable establishment staffed by twenty-six sisters and twenty-four male and female domestics, with others working its sei-gneurie. The hospitals in Quebec and Montreal (joined later by one in Trois-Rivières), after their initial years in cold, ramshackle little build-ings gradually grew into three- or four-story institutions with thirty to forty beds. They were much praised for standards of cleanliness and care (which promoted a surprisingly high survival rate of 92 per cent among Quebec patients). Nothing, the authorities averred in the unhealthy year of 1687, 'is more important for the well being of the country than to sustain the two hospitals at Quebec and Montreal, without which the populace and the soldiers would be terribly deprived of assistance.'[48] They cared for colonists regardless of ability to pay, proximity making townspeople the most common beneficiaries.[49] *Hôpitaux généraux* (hos-pices) were also created at Quebec and at Montreal (where the Charon Brothers initially ran it) to house and control the homeless, orphaned, insane, elderly and handicapped, prostitutes, and other needy or 'disor-derly' persons. The convents typically also housed a few wealthy old pen-sioners. Like the YWCAs of a later era, they also gave travelling women a place to stay. The value of the work of the sisters is a recurrent theme in the reports of governors and intendants during the entire history of New France, reverberating even in reports of nineteenth-century British governors.

Particularly responsive to the Canadian setting were the schools of Marguerite Bourgeoys and her associates, the Congregation of Notre Dame. As we have seen, there was lay teaching along similar lines in France; and Bourgeoys had been influenced by the carefully organized classrooms and mild discipline of French educator Pierre Fourier. The Canadian schools benefited from Bourgeoys's own particularly radical vision. In an era where there was a strong class system, even in convents, Bourgeoys insisted there would *not* be two classes of sisters, that the roles of superior and cook should be interchangeable. There was to be no dowry requirement, the founder preferring to 'carry on her shoulders a woman who could not even afford to clothe herself, but had goodness and a true vocation.'[50] Lacking the capital that dowries or fees could have provided, Bourgeoys and her followers often capped a day of teaching with cleaning, ironing, sewing, and knitting far into the night in order to support the cost of their schools.[51] 'Wanderers and not cloistered,' these first members in the 1660s walked, rode horseback, or went by canoe to reach settlers along the river, relying on local hospitality. In pairs they went to set up schools in the country parishes. They did not charge tuition, though they did ask those who could to pay for French and Latin texts and bring their own slates and firewood. The first sisters were as impoverished as the settlers they served, often lacking basic supplies.

Sometimes Notre Dame sisters received a hostile reception when they first appeared in a community. Two who arrived at Quebec in November 1685 lightly dressed were 'asked where our beds and equipment were; we were ridiculed and humiliated in every way. Some said we would die of hunger ... and that we had been sent to look for husbands.'[52] They proceeded to the Ile d'Orléans where they were lodged some distance from school. When she set out in a snowstorm one winter day, twenty-two-year-old future Superior Marie Barbier fell into in a ditch and would have perished had not farmers come out to search for their cattle and spotted the dark-clad figure amid the drifts. They apparently did not value her, for after pulling her out they left her on the ground instead of taking her inside to warm up. Was this a reflection of what one historian called the lack of 'civilized moral standards' in the early days? Other early sisters too were ridiculed, humiliated, accused of looking for husbands.

Those who benefited most from their services were people of the humbler ranks, especially women. They would not normally have attended school in France, much less in a remote colony in the middle of the woods. At a time when women needed to manufacture much of the family clothing, the sisters instructed them in spinning, knitting, and dressmaking as well as other necessities of household organization. They also ran a special needlework school in Montreal. Some of their schools had supplementary free classes for servants and other mature students who wanted to get some education. Many schools eventually added boarding facilities so girls living further away could attend. The founder specified that any chastisement of pupils must be moderate.[53] The efforts made by country parishes to secure their services, and the many donations from ordinary people, attest to growing appreciation for the Congregation of Notre Dame.

By 1707 there were forty sisters and ten different schools for girls. At least fifteen different schools were eventually established at various locations in Canada during the French regime. They included the Indian mission on Montreal mountain as well as the boarding, day, and vocational schools in the town below. Others existed at various times at Trois-Rivières, Lachine, Pointe-aux-Trembles, Boucherville, Champlain, Prairie-de-la-Madeleine, Saint Laurent, Quebec, Chateau Richer, Beaupré, and at Saint Famille on the Ile d'Orléans. At the Montreal and Quebec schools, attendance reached one hundred or more.[54]

Their value was recognized. Time and again governors and intendants upheld the sisters' desire to remain uncloistered so that they could work freely among the settlers. Eighteenth-century officials praised the Congregation of Notre Dame as a model that should be followed in any efforts to improve boys' education in the colony.[55] Notre Dame schools, along with resident or travelling curés, would consolidate Catholic practice in the Laurentian heartland where, one eighteenth-century visitor avowed, even habitants in remote areas were better instructed in their religion than was common in France. One is not surprised to see a such a populace become active in religious confraternities, taking care to have masses said for the dead, or displaying sacred relics at the head of religious processions organized to pray for rain. The sisters' success among the common people led educational historian Roger Magnuson to conclude that in Canada 'the notion of popular education found its first true expression in the Congregation of Notre Dame.'[56]

The teaching orders did what they could to instil basic education in at least some of the settlements that stretched out across hundreds of miles of riverfront. While habitant daughters attended the Congregation of Notre Dame schools, bourgeois and noble families in the towns were more apt to send their daughters to the Ursulines or the little pensions that the hospitals ran. Here too the curriculum was heavily oriented towards religion, reading and writing, needlework, and other domestic skills; but at the Ursulines' they also practised arithmetic with little counters and benefited from a longer stay than was typical at the country schools, though even there it seldom extended beyond a few years, when a girl was somewhere between the ages of six and sixteen.[57] Even the Quebec Ursulines, who put some of their energies into educating the daughters of the elite, were cited by the authorities as 'useful to the public, instructing for free all the young children of the town and environs and teaching them to work.'[58] In a turn away from evangelism towards ancien régime 'normalcy,' the 2,000-*livre* Crown subsidy for educating native girls was redirected towards needy young French gentlewomen in 1712.

Did all this effort produce *savantes* in the bush? Questions of literacy and gender are somewhat confounded by a common French custom of teaching girls to read but not write, so that a reader might not be able to sign her name. According to Magnuson, the Congregation of Notre Dame made rural schooling more common among girls than among boys. They did teach some writing, too. This resulted in some unusual situations in which females showed more ability to write their names than males did, though samples from the end of the French regime show rural men about 1 to 2 per cent more likely to sign than women. In the towns, where many of the men came from France, males were substantially more likely to be able to sign their names (56.0 per cent versus 43.8 per cent in a late-seventeenth-century sample from Quebec and Montreal). Lower rates for both sexes in the countryside pulled the average for the population as a whole down to the 25 per cent range. Just as women in France were less literate than their English counterparts, those in New France were less literate than their New England counterparts. However, the French colony saw a much smaller gap *between* the sexes; the fifteen-to-thirty-point spread between women and men that prevailed in seventeenth- and eighteenth-century France and New England was reduced to less than a ten-point gap in Canadian towns, and to virtually nothing in the countryside where three-quarters of the population lived. In short, New France did not have a very literate population, but the gender gap was smaller than usual.[59]

The sisters fostered upward mobility in some of the young women they taught, according to French military engineer Louis Franquet, who toured the colony in the 1750s. Admitting the usefulness of such schooling, he nevertheless perceived it as 'a slow poison which leads to a depopulation of the countryside, given that an educated girl ... puts on airs, wants to set herself up in the city, sets her sights on a merchant and looks upon the circumstances of her birth as beneath her.'[60]

Thus, as they gradually relinquished the goal of proselytizing native peoples, the founders increasingly contributed to the lives of colonial women. Besides providing rudimentary schooling and medical care, they created a welcoming climate for members of their own sex, even housing a key group of female immigrants, to whom we shall soon turn.

Unlike the male orders, the female ones were popular enough to renew their ranks from the rising generations of Canadians. The largest, the Congregation of Notre Dame, had by 1681 attracted nine Canadian postulants. That convent must have overflowed with youthful enthusiasm, since over half its members were in their teens or twenties.[61] In 1718 (when its numbers were capped) the Congregation had eighty sisters. Founders and other illustrious members of all the convents became the subject of many stories, legends, and an unusual number of portraits (unflattering likenesses from an era when beauty and smiles were not female requirements).

As communities with varied resources and occupations, they apparently offered fulfilling career paths to a growing number of French Canadians. At the Quebec Hôtel-Dieu, postulants typically joined at age fifteen. Records of the combined hospital and school the Ursulines ran at Trois-Rivières indicate that the sisters studied botany and had their own chemistry laboratory. They prepared medicines and the dyes used in needlework and painting, Ursuline specialties.[62] Such institutions allowed talented women to work as artists and artisans, teachers, administrators, pharmacists, and ward supervisors. As nurse-practitioners, they filled an important gap in a colony that had only four professional physicians between 1608 and 1760, leaving the public in the hands of barber-surgeons who lacked academic training. Sisters who had access both to mentors and to convent medical libraries may have been more skilful. At the Montreal Hôtel-Dieu Sister Judith Bresoles, renowned for her remedies, assumed responsibilities similar to a physician's.[63] Still other sisters busied themselves with masonry or fieldwork.

Gradually the mystical founders passed away and the convents began to replace legendary figures with more down-to-earth Canadian recruits. By the end of the French regime Canada would have 225 sisters at the hospices and hospitals, Ursuline and Congregation of Notre Dame schools;[64] adding the *converses* or lay sisters would bring the figure closer to 300. The frequency of vocations suggests the sisters served as role models for many Catholic girls. As one historian wrote, 'Any reader of the annals of religious congregations will know that although their members practiced personal humility, they made up for it in esprit de corps. The pride religious women were required to deny in themselves was transferred to their communities – therefore, by way of a sort of code, to their sex.'[65] Is it a sign in their favour that a number of hostages captured in raids on New England and lodged in convents refused to return when their relatives ransomed them? Esther Wheelwright, who eventually became mother superior of the Quebec Ursulines, was one of several who decided to take the veil.[66]

The convents' material assets bolstered their authority. As we shall see in a later chapter, various French endowments, the lands they possessed, and the goods and services they produced fostered a degree of independence that some lay and clerical authorities (as we shall see in chapter 7) would find overweening. While none of the orders lived lavishly, each had important financial assets. A sampling of accounts from the early eighteenth century indicated female religious orders received subsidies from the Crown amounting to between 77 and 87 per cent of those granted to the male orders (the Jesuits, Sulpicians, and Recollets). In a society where the church owned one-quarter of the seigneuries, all of the convents had seigneuries, and the Ursulines ranked among the larger clerical landholders.[67] Members of various orders sold food and medicine to townspeople, made altar cloths, statues, and decor for churches, and produced handicrafts and embroidery prized by elites. At the Montreal Hôtel-Dieu founded by Jeanne Mance, the sisters' own work and resources provided as much as 82 per cent of the annual income.[68]

All told, female missionaries played a vital role in providing funding, bringing over immigrant workers, and offering social services that were sorely needed in a new colony. Their contributions were crucial from the 1630s to the 1660s when retention of the colony was in doubt. Their value endured: the Quebec and Montreal Hôtels-Dieu, the Ursuline school, and the Congregation of Notre Dame continue to serve the Canadian populace to this day.

For better or for worse, the leaders we have discussed marched at the very forefront of an imperial project, not only serving it but also shaping it. They wrote many of its first records. They conversed with French royalty and colonial governors, with bishops and aboriginal chiefs. Particularly remarkable, because it thrust a woman into such a statesman-like role, is Jeanne Mance's role as a co-founder of Montreal, as well as her offer of her own hospital's endowment to raise troops to prevent its abandonment. Canada survived a half-century of royal neglect until it was at last made into a Crown colony in 1663 and given a regiment for its protection. The Catholic zeal of the first decades eventually cooled, but after it did, the colony retained several female-run institutions and a recorded history of female founders who had supplied leadership at a crucial time. Women may have done this in other times and places, but is there another case so well documented? In contrast to the usual anonymous 'founding mothers' of nations who made the essential contribution of producing babies, food, and raiment, these single women became public figures whose names were written into the history of a new people. On the gender front, Canada presents a rarity in the founding story of nations.

The *Filles du roi*

Religious women represented only a handful of the immigrants who arrived during the seventeenth century. We turn now to more ordinary female migrants who landed by the hundreds on Canada's forested shores. Unlike the *dévotes*, this group was not at all attracted by the thought of savages. They grew up at a time when stories of the Iroquois were used to threaten misbehaving children. In the words of one historian, most seventeenth-century settlers were less interested in wilderness adventures than in working hard 'to make the country habitable, build up a family holding, and recreate a familiar lifestyle, hoping that their labour and the practice of a tried routine would bring them security.'[69]

In 1663, the year the French government at length undertook to set up the mechanisms of state and transform the struggling mission colony into a Crown colony, it commissioned the services of a gentleman, Louis Gaudais-Dupont. He was told to go to each dwelling and take count of how many lived there, their occupations, and the size of their fields. Aware of the scant farming being done and the attacks on isolated settlements, the Crown urged him to work to bring the settlers closer together so they could help one another in time of need. Had it also dawned that the nuns and the handful of aging women there were not going to produce much in the way of babies? Gaudais-Dupont was told to observe 'whether there lacked in that country women and girls, in order to send there the necessary number next year.'[70] There was sympathy for the sufferings of the straggling colonists besieged by hostile Haudenosaunee (who were waging their own battle for survival). The French were also anxious about the English colonists to the south who so vastly outnumbered Canadians. The officials worried that the men who flocked to the woods in search of furs would never settle on farms and feed the colony. Certainly they would not do so without wives. In both the French countryside and the North American clearings, agriculture was an arduous business that succeeded best with the personal motivation and the many hands that were typically supplied by a married couple and their children.

The 1663 directive to take inventory of colonial women is an early document relating to the ancestors of millions of French Canadians, the *filles du roi* or 'king's daughters. They are the forerunners of all the many immigrant groups who have stepped ashore in Canada since their day. Some 850 women were sent from France in the ensuing decade, and we have records for 770 of them who definitely survived the passage and settled in the colony. They have always been associated with the French Crown, which helped recruit many of them, usually paid their transportation, and frequently provided dowries – often doing all three.[71] Later, once the population was established, the Crown would turn to the cheaper expedient of giving dowries to women born in the colony, in a practice that continued into the eighteenth century.[72] The decision to send the *filles* created the first large pool of colonial women. They were not of course the very first to come. We have already seen the arrival of female missionaries that began in 1639. Even they were not the very first, for a trickle of women had arrived since 1617, adding up to 400,[73] before the *filles* began to come in the 1660s. However, the *filles du roi* of 1663–73 are by far the single most important group, representing half of all the French female immigrants who settled permanently in the colony. Sent out to be brides for single men (who were some six times more numerous than single women),[74] they kindled new hope that the French would begin to flourish on the St Lawrence.

Natalist policies, designed to encourage a population to reproduce, have a long history in French Canada. Even in the twenty-first century, the Quebec government has provided baby bonuses to encourage large families. During the nineteenth and twentieth centuries, Catholic clergymen condemned mothers suspected of trying to limit the number of children they bore. Especially in rural districts, a high birth rate characterized the French-speaking population, and their anticipated assimilation did not occur. Still, pressures to produce a big family could be very taxing to mothers. The tax began early, when natalist policies made their debut along the St Lawrence in the 1660s.

To modern sensibilities, the natalism of the seventeenth century has a certain cattle-like quality. Today, people who advertise for a partner usually take care to tout their individual attributes. At the beginning of the twentieth century, even the 'picture brides' who came from Japan to British Columbia exchanged preliminary photographs with their intended. In the seventeenth century, people were less individualistic.[75] Only one adjective appeared on the entire the bill of lading the French minister of marine [the colonial minister] J-B Colbert sent to Quebec in 1667 regarding '400 good men, 50 *filles*, 12 mares, 2 stallions.'

French immigrant brides, about whom historians actually know very little, have been portrayed in various ways over the centuries. Their name has been plagued by an association with prostitution. This link appeared – by way of denial – as early as 1640 in the *Journal des Jesuites*, and there was another denial from colonist Pierre Boucher in 1664 to the charge that women of ill repute had migrated to Canada. The traveller Baron de Lahontan on the other hand, fanned the rumour, joking about the 'viciousness' and 'sins' of female immigrants. Lahontan also quipped that fat *filles* were the most popular, best able to endure Canada's winter and least able to run away! Gustave Lanctôt's 1952 *Filles de joie ou filles du roi* argued fairly persuasively that sexual innuendo arose from confusing the *filles* with a number of emigrants to Louisiana and the Caribbean who had been recruited from sex workers.[76] Yves Landry consolidated the case by showing that there were fewer children born out of wedlock in seventeenth-century Canada than in seventeenth-century France; indeed the rate for the *filles* was even lower than the Canadian average. Not everyone, of course, was as pure as the driven snow. Two of the *filles*, for example, would one day became prostitutes in the district where men came off the ships in Quebec City; two others committed bigamy.

Apart from the question of their 'virtue,' debates over the years also revolved around how well educated the *filles* were. Optimistic assessments were based on knowledge that the Parisian Hôpital Général aimed to teach students literacy and a trade, and on a comment one year by the superior of the Quebec Hôtel-Dieu that the group of them she had encountered was well educated. However, Landry's discovery that only 23 per cent[77] of the *filles* signed their name to marriage registers and other documents seems to suggest fairly undistinguished backgrounds, neither their early lives nor their residency at the Hôpital Général offering opportunity to learn to write. On the whole they can be characterized as a group that was *démuni* – deprived.

On the other hand, about 12 per cent of the *filles* were drawn from the bourgeoisie and the minor nobility. The majority of this group could write. They were apparently willing to go to the colony because of family losses – of a father or a fortune – that made it difficult for them to marry well in France. Some received from the King dowries as large as 600 *livres*, though most of them had to make do with the same 50-*livre* gift (often in household goods) the commoners received.

All in all, the *filles du roi* were quite a mixed group. Ages ranged from the early teens to a few who were middle-aged, the average age being twenty-four. About 20 per cent of the group were widows. Although the majority were urban, some peasants jostled with Parisiennes.[78] There was even a sprinkling originating from Morocco, Portugal, and other Mediterranean countries. Letters written by Intendant Jean Talon indicate what he had in mind. Recruits were to be healthy and capable of farm work. In 1670 he stipulated that they 'be not in any way deformed by nature, they have nothing repellent about their appearance; that they have some skill at handiwork.'[79]

How were the brides found? Recruiters were offered a commission. A Canadian friend of Marie de l'Incarnation, Madame Bourdon, stepped forward to collect and chaperone some, while in Paris a 'demoiselle Estrienne' recruited others. Both concentrated on the Hôpital Général. Priests from the parish of Saint-Sulpice, on the other hand, helped assemble women from a wider area of the Ile de France. While those agents worked around Paris, the archbishop of Rouen and several merchants helped recruit peasant women from northwestern France. We know so little of the individual stories of the *filles du roi* that we cannot accurately estimate how often the trip was their own decision, and how often the result of being strong-armed by guardians or government officials. There are divergent scraps of evidence. Intendant Talon, the official most closely concerned with the venture, wrote in March 1673 to alert officials that if the King wanted more of them that year, the directors of the Pitié (a wing of the Hôpital Général) must send him a list (*estat*) of women of the *hôpital* 'disposed to come to Canada.'[80] This raises the possibility that the candidates may have had some say in the decision. So does Colbert's request to the archbishop of Rouen to find robust young villagers '*bien aisées*' to go to Canada '*pour estre mariées et s'y establir*,' adding that he wanted people to go voluntarily.[81] Migration was plausibly a matter of choice for the small minority who presented themselves at the ports and asked for passage (probably fewer than a hundred). On the other hand, a sense of conscription arises from the rare account of one *fille* who later testified in a lawsuit. This is how she recalled her last glimpse of the Seine when her journey from the Hôpital Général to the New World began: 'At the beginning of May 1670, having been named along with many other *filles* of the *hôpital* to go to Canada by order of the King, they were conducted as far as the Red Bridge (Pont Rouge) by the said clergy and by Auber the hospice's surgeon, [and] by Madame de Houssy, the Superintendent.'[82]

In any event, the recruits must have known the idea was for them to marry and stay forever in Canada, where bachelors abounded. Some of the *filles* came with assets, but many had little besides what they were wearing and the contents of long wooden boxes called *coffres*. We have record of the clothes one seventeenth-century immigrant brought in that box, contents which historians believe were typical. She had head coverings and handkerchiefs. She had a camisole, a ribbed wool house-dress, and two tattered petticoats (one listed as green and very tattered). She must have heard about the cold, for the rest was outerwear: two coats, one jacket, a muff, and sheepskin gloves. For many like her, daily life was perhaps sufficiently grim to encourage taking a leap in the dark. Passing long winter nights with a husband on a farm offered at least a chance of a secure livelihood, even of happiness.

The voyage, which typically lasted between six and nine weeks, cannot have been pleasant. In contrast to most immigrants to seventeenth-century New France, only 10 per cent of the *filles* had the comfort of travelling with relatives.[83] Seasickness and storms at sea were common. The *demoiselles* on one ship had a hungry voyage, thanks to a dishonest captain and a guardian who stole half their provisions. It is left to the imagination what lay behind the complaint of a chaperone in 1669 that some of that lot had been 'very gross and difficult to handle.'[84] Add to this the smell of death: shipboard fevers were common in this period, and on average 10 per cent of passengers died. To keep things in perspective, these were not the horrors of the Middle Passage, the transport of shackled slaves from Africa to the Virginia colony that lay to the south. In any event, eager eyes must have scanned the shore as the towering cliff of Quebec came in sight and the ship sailed in to the row of wharves, taverns, and storehouses tucked beneath it.

What kind of welcome awaited the travellers? Clearly, some had a rough time of it. In 1669, a year when most came from the Hôpital Gé-néral, there was report of the newcomers not being robust enough to withstand the harsh climate and heavy farmwork. There were misunderstandings about dowries; some who had been promised several hundred *livres* received only a portion of it. Crammed into a little house beside the Ursuline convent, these inexperienced pioneers several times nearly burned it down. One who was caught at the wrong place and time on the Ile d'Orléans lived out a bad dream (one the *dévotes* would have embraced) when she was kidnapped by the Iroquois.[85]

Still, the typical scenario seems a rather brighter one, in which the women exerted some agency. The colonial officials were particularly solicitous of the very youngest immigrants, the fourteen-, fifteen-, and sixteen-year-olds. Probably because of such intervention, the teenag-

ers waited longer to marry than the others, and the officials stayed on
hand to witness their marriage contracts. Farmers, contract labourers,
soldiers, and officers flocked to Quebec when word went out that a ship
of brides had arrived, or as soon as their indentured or seasonal work
in field or forest permitted. To the extent that it was possible, the brides
took care in selecting a life partner. They were reported eager to dis-
cover whether a suitor had a *habitation*; that is, was he a drifter or land-
less labourer, or was he in possession of a real home? Eleven per cent
of the *filles*, apparently realizing they had accepted someone too hastily,
broke off their first engagement to make another.[86] In that action we
hear a faint voice, and it is not submissive. Admittedly it bears little re-
semblance to the heaven-obsessed determination of the *dévotes*. Here instead were orphans and charity cases daring to say, 'Packed and shipped
we may have been, but here on these new shores, *we have discovered we
have some choices in life.*' The rest of this book will explore diverse ways
female descendants of the *filles* responded to the choices the New World
had to offer.

We have discussed whether the brides were there voluntarily, and the
same question might be asked of the grooms. Again, indications vary.
Bachelors of marriageable age faced Quebec Sovereign Council decrees
of 1670 and 1671 that required them to marry fifteen days after the arrival of the ships carrying the *filles*, under pain of losing the right to hunt,
fish, and trade with the Indians. Military officers who took a bride were
offered a bonus. Some men actively wanted to marry; Talon reported
in 1667 that many of the soldiers recently sent out from France were
requesting a wife and a place to live in the colony.[87] 'Canada is a poor
country' was a steady refrain of newly arrived officials. In an impoverished colony, peopled with new immigrants, the dowry provided by the
King must have added to the bride's allure.

Eighty per cent of the *filles* married within six months, typically in the
autumn of their first summer ashore. In 1667 Marie de l'Incarnation
reported couples were being married in groups of thirty. The entire 150
who arrived in summer 1669 were married or engaged by November.[88]
Over 80 per cent of these new couples went to rural areas, most to the Ile
d'Orléans or other river settlements near Quebec. Since there were few
roads, many would have gone in boats, stepping ashore into a scarlet and
yellow autumn landscape, straining for the first glimpse of her husband's
cabin. Her dowry could provide for the first improvements, a few farm
animals, and perhaps eight months' worth of supplies of staples such as
wheat, peas, and lard.[89]

By their first wedding anniversary, many of these new couples fulfilled the fondest hopes of colonial officials. Reports reached the King that his 'daughters' were fertile, some giving birth nearly every year. Intendant Jean Talon reported 600 to 700 births in 1671 alone.[90] It was noted that year, too, that the isolated settlements were developing into a line of French dwellings extending all the way from Montreal Island to lands east of Quebec. Babies would by then be crawling across the dirt floors of the cabins. The brides would by now have learned to haul water from the river, beat the wash in a cauldron, and ward off the chill with endless stoking of fires and shovelling of ashes. They would have learned to turn a spit to roast a deer shot by their husbands, at the same time rocking the cradle with their foot. They would step out to tend to farm animals and vegetables when time permitted. Those whose husbands were traders would soon enough have to run the whole farm for part of the summer. Wives would doubtless relish the occasional encounter with other *filles* at a church service or at one of the outdoor ovens where bread was baked. Proud of all the signs of life and growth, Intendant Talon at last felt confident in making a prediction to the French court. 'This country,' he wrote in 1671, 'will become something great.' In 1685 Governor Denonville reiterated Talon's assessment, declaring, 'The large number of infants makes me hopeful; one sees in the Canadians the promise of a great people.'[91]

Demographic studies show that the optimism was well founded. The new brides seemed to grow more fertile as each year passed, particularly when they reached their thirties. They bore an average of 7.4 children.[92] The numbers who died in childbirth were lower than in France, eight per thousand versus ten to twenty per thousand. The average age of death was sixty-two, the median sixty-six. *Filles* who reached age forty could expect to go on to about seventy. Yves Landry's research revealed they outlived various other contemporary groups, rivalled only by the ruling families of Geneva. Even British peers did not live to such an old age as they did. The population of France itself did not attain the same longevity until two hundred years later, in the second half of the nineteenth century. This is particularly striking, since many of the brides sprang from parents who had died early.[93]

Why did this deprived group become so healthy and prolific? As with many immigrant populations, selectivity was at work. Government agents had been instructed to choose those of childbearing age. By the late 1660s they were urged to select those who were strong or, as Marie de l'Incarnation wrote in 1668, to find country girls 'able to work like the men.' It is also plausible that those put forward by themselves or others to undertake the journey were particularly energetic souls. The estimated 10 per cent of shipboard deaths would have further weeded out the frail. There are two confirmations that this 'selection' factor was important. The first is that the *filles du roi* outlived their husbands by more years than was common in France. This may be partly due to the more dangerous occupations of colonial men, but it also suggests the women's basic strength. The second indicator that selectivity was important is the fact that *filles* lived on average a year longer than other Canadian women who had arrived before 1680, even though both groups would have encountered similar occupational structures and environmental conditions.[94]

The Canadian environment, beyond a doubt, was another component of this success story. As Intendant Jacques De Meulles observed in 1683 of the Canadians, 'One lives very easily, fish and other food is abundant for all.'[95] In an early eighteenth-century report, Attorney General Ruette d'Auteuil was more specific about the blessings of the new land. Canada's virtues included a salubrious climate, and a cold, cleansing air that he believed kept epidemics from spreading. There was wood everywhere to provide fuel. Grain and fruit were abundant, he pointed out, while fishing and hunting supplied the other ingredients of a healthful diet.[96] This catalogue of resources stands in contrast to the bread diet so common in France, especially at institutions such as the Hôpital Général. It is true that epidemics occasionally stalked the land. In the deadly year of 1687 measles, purpura, and lung infections killed 500 colonists. However, 500 babies were baptized that same year. Fifty years later an official would note that Canada had an unusually healthy population, which had shown itself capable of withstanding fatigue and war, of traversing its great waterways, of producing numerous offspring.[97] Canada's resources had allowed the immigrants to rise above the sickness, poor diet, and bleak institutions of their youth.

Several findings add to the evidence that the environment played a vital role in the health and fertility of these women. The first relates to the settlement's vast open spaces. It was salubrious to be away from the port of Quebec (and to a lesser extent, Montreal) where disease often came in on the arriving ships. The 82 per cent of the *filles* who settled in the countryside lived on average two years longer than the urbanites. A second environmental indicator is the fact that there was a delayed effect; it took a few years of living in the new land before these women became truly fertile. As noted, it was after age thirty that their fertility began strongly to surpass that of French women and to match that of other seventeenth-century Canadian women.[98] This suggests a greater debt to environmental influences than to being a select group of immigrants right from the start. Healthy and well fed, they conceived more readily and brought more children to term. The population shot up from approximately three thousand to nearly nine thousand in the decade between 1667 and 1677. Growing up amid fields of wheat and vegetable gardens, with game and fish in nearby woods and streams, their children would never know the cramped lives and malnutrition of the French poor.

Conclusion

To sum up, in our introduction to the seventeenth-century pioneers, we have seen that the forested environment was an essential element in the experience of Canada's first female colonists. It affected both the *dévotes* who came in the 1630s through the 1650s, and the *filles du roi* who followed in the 1660s and 1670s. The religious women made their improbable journey into the fogs of the St Lawrence for one reason: to convert the woodland peoples along its shores. Forest peoples who were ignorant of the Christian God were a magnet to them and their aristocratic patrons. They serve as our first example of a feminine colonial experience that was profoundly shaped by the environment of the New World. Despite their best efforts, the mists lifted and the natives fled the clearings. It was with considerable regret that they gradually transformed themselves from converters of *les sauvages* into more ordinary teachers and nurses of their French compatriots.

The *filles du roi* stand in contrast to the missionaries. Everything we know about them suggests the brides who came from France after 1663 did not see the forest as an attractive entity but a fearsome one. And yet it was they who benefited most from it. Unlike the *dévotes*, who usually remained in the colony's relatively insalubrious port towns, the vast majority of the brides married and dispersed with their husbands to clear and cultivate the stump farms along the St Lawrence. That was hard labour, but it repaid them with notably better nutrition and health than that of their relatives who stayed in France. To the *dévotes*, Canadian woodlands offered the prospect of fresh converts. To the *filles*, the woods delivered a healthy new life.

Chapter Three

Women and the St Lawrence Fur Trade

Once the seventeenth-century immigrants established themselves along the banks of the St Lawrence, how did they and their descendants make a living? Most subsisted on the plant and animal products of their habitant farms and the nearby woods and waters, with only occasional market transactions. As we strive to see how women participated in these activities, we encounter a limited pool of scholarship, including lack of any comprehensive study of the role played by women in business in New France.[1] Attempting to uncover single-handedly *all* the remunerative activities that engaged female colonists in town and country would be overwhelming. So we have made a choice. Because the economy revolved around such staples as fur, fish, timber, and agricultural produce, it seems reasonable to concentrate our attention on the exchange of natural resources. Studying marketable colonial goods has the advantage that, in comparison to subsistence activity, they were more likely to leave some trace in the colonial records. Here as we begin our central chapters, which focus on the market economy, the goal is to produce at least a rough sketch of the productive resource work that occupied so many female colonists, from the most ordinary *habitante* to the most exceptional noblewoman. Before we turn to certain public figures who were truly extraordinary, in chapter 6, two chapters will explore several hundred women of all classes who were involved in supplying various natural resources to local or international markets, and another will probe the laws that regulated such activity. Here in chapter 3 we begin by tracing the range of female involvement in the fur trade, and then situating Canadian activities within broader patterns of pre-industrial work. Chapter 4 follows up with many more instances of women involved with a number of other marketable natural resources that were drawn from forests, farms, and fisheries.

The geographic distance covered in order to cull and ship colonial resources was immense, and it elicited participation of whole families along the long chain of commerce that extended from Bordeaux to the Saskatchewan River. We direct our attention primarily to the core and the immediate hinterland of Laurentian 'Canada' rather than the larger New France that included Louisbourg and New Orleans, though we do branch out to certain regions that drew their traders from the central colony. For those dwelling along the banks of the St Lawrence, the hinterland extended in several directions. They could look westward towards the fur-trading country bordering upon the upper Great Lakes that was known as the *pays d'en haut*, from which myriad rivers led into ever more distant fur-trading regions. Or they might turn southward towards neighbouring New York, where fine timber grew and where Anglo-Dutch colonists constituted an eager market for smuggled furs. Alternately, they could gaze eastward down the river, which stretched past their own local markets in villages and towns, then on towards the fisheries and ports of Gaspé, Labrador, and Louisbourg, from whence goods traversed the seas to the West Indies or more frequently, the ports of western France.

This chapter will demonstrate that women had a major involvement in the trade in furs in the St Lawrence valley and its hinterland. As well as supplying examples of elite women in that trade, it shows very ordinary ones participating in all sorts of ways. How can we make sense of all these data? The findings call for a re-examination of various interpretations of women in New France, including my own earlier work. European scholarship of recent decades, to which we return at the very end of this chapter, confirms that female economic production and exchange was in no way exceptional in pre-industrial societies. The economically active women in New France we discuss here were, in large degree, simply part of a transatlantic norm. However, we shall see that there was some variation in the patterns, with Canada clinging to some older models of women's work after other parts of the Atlantic world began to change.

The fur trade is a logical place to begin the discussion. By far the leading export from New France was the furs and hides of animals.[2] Many came from the *pays d'en haut* around the Great Lakes and (as the French regime progressed) further west; others from the Mississippi valley. Besides beaver, the hides of moose, deer, bear, wolf, and marten were exported. Seal and other marine pelts were taken from the Tadoussac and Labrador posts. The trade also included many spin-off activities such as servicing the forts – places where military and trade functions were inseparable. As we shall see, men, women, and children all worked along the lengthy trade lines that connected the most distant posts along the

Saskatchewan and Mississippi Rivers to the St Lawrence and over the ocean to France. Since our discussion of commerce will often involve discussing amounts of *livres*, the reader can put its value in context by knowing that the best-paid workers around 1740 might earn as much as 3 *livres* a day. Around the same time a stone house at Quebec averaged 4,000 *livres* in value, a wooden one in Montreal 2,000 or less.[3]

Training a keen eye on the cash, and accompanying us on our travels, will be the 'Nagging Wife.' Who is she? We hope this exploration of the fur trade will improve upon the perfunctory characterizations of women typical of so much of the writing on New France. The important body of work on the Canadian frontier, for example, did not bother much with women. As we noted earlier in regard to leading writers of the 'frontier' school, while R.C. Harris portrayed young aboriginal women as a *pull* factor that drew *habitants* into the fur-trade regions, W.J. Eccles envisioned women as the *push* factor: 'Canadians ... were men of broad horizons ... were a wife to nag too constantly, some of them at least could hire out as voyageurs for the west.'[4] Thanks to several decades of deconstruction of the ever-so-willing Indian maiden by fur-trade historians, we now know that her motivations went beyond sexual gratification.[5] The European wife on the St Lawrence (who also participated in the fur trade) remains ripe for reconstruction. In this chapter we note more than fifty elite examples, then more plebeian cases, followed by another coterie who conducted shadowy operations outside the bounds of the law whose true extent remains forever in the shadows. After introducing the reader to various individuals and groups, the analysis will then turn to consider underlying reasons for their activity.

Involvement of Elites

Some nobles busied their hands at trading counters. One could find substantial dealers at certain forts and missions. Madeleine de Roybon d'Allonne was one of the *filles du roi* drawn from the lesser nobility. Daughter of the carver-general at the French Court, she arrived in Canada in 1671 at age twenty-five. About a decade later she was granted seigneurial land near Fort Cataraqui. She made improvements to that holding and acquired four other properties. She set up trade with native allies before enduring captivity among the Iroquois. A biographer speculates that D'Allonne may have been romantically linked with the explorer de La Salle, but colonial records reveal a more businesslike motive for lending him 2,141 *livres* in 1681: he was to supply her with 800 *livres* worth of beaver plus assorted fur trade merchandise.[6] She was implicated in the trade of the fort in 1700 and expressly forbidden to trade brandy in a 1708 decree. In 1717 she petitioned the Marine Council on behalf of herself and a group of others to be allowed to continue the Cataraqui trade. At that time Governor Vaudreuil advised the Crown that commerce had always been the petitioners' main interest.[7]

Wives of military officers formed a significant group of traders. At Fort Detroit, Commander Alphonse de Tonty made himself unpopular by charging exorbitant prices for goods and services. His first wife had in 1707 been accused of usurping trading privileges. There was, after all, the usual cramped salary and copious family (Wife Number One gave birth to the last of thirteen infants before expiring in 1713). After Tonty's death, his second wife, Marie-Anne La Marque, would petition for Crown assistance, asserting, 'I have worked all my life.' It seems she had. She had borne fifteen children by a first husband. Later, as 'Veuve La Pipardière,' she had been caught red-handed in Montreal with forbidden English trade cloth, bribing a native to claim that it was his. Authorities seized two English blankets stashed under her son's bed, and a neighbour claimed another dozen had been tossed out the window. She fought back by accusing Montreal Governor de Ramezay, his son, and sister-in-law of smuggling and attempted murder. Later given permission to marry Tonty and manage his household, Marie-Anne La Marque found much to do. After long service both in Detroit and in Montreal (where she served as Tonty's financial *procuratrice*), she informed the Crown she had exhausted her own assets in support of the western post, where the obligations of the command included keeping up the commander's house, maintaining the native alliances, and sustaining the fort's defences.[8] The records indicate that each of Tonty's two successive wives turned her hand to economic transactions, which was common enough for women connected with post commanders. At Fort Niagara, Madame Celeron traded, and we know she branched out into grain, shipping some of it to Quebec. The fur-trade accounts of Rouen/Canada agents Havy and Lefebvre also indicate substantial business with Mesdames Guy (Jeanne Trouillier), Brunet and Moquin, and Mlles Auger, De Joncaire and Texier,[9] some of whom had male relatives at the French posts.

Two military families merged when Marguerite Legardeur de Repentigny, at age nineteen, married thirty-six-year-old Jean-Baptiste Saint-Ours Deschaillons. While he served at successive western posts, she served as his *procuratrice*, buying merchandise and shipping it to him. She also signed the deed that created a business partnership between her spouse and another man to outfit canoes and conduct trade in the *pays d'en haut.* She administered the family's Saint-Ours seigneurie, too. A document of 1740 shows Marguerite acting as the family's agent even when her husband was in town, just as her entrepreneurial mother had done before her.[10]

The successive wives of officer François-Marie Picote de Belestre also involved themselves in their husband's western diplomacy and trade. The first, Anne Nivard Sainte-Dizier, appeared on the list of Crown expenses for furnishing at Fort St Joseph (near Niles, Michigan) a horse for transport from the fort to the village of the Sakis, and supplying two pigs to make a feast for the natives at the fort. The second wife, Marie-Anne Magnan, stayed in the colony but received power of attorney for her husband when he departed for the west. It was she who dealt with merchant Louis Saint-Ange Charly for trade goods, and she was still paying western accounts after the Conquest.[11]

Family interests in fur ventures could survive the death of a husband. The rank of Louise Chartier de Lotbinière, daughter of a Quebec government official, is indicated by having as godfather Governor Frontenac and godmother the lovely Elisabeth de Joybert, wife of a future governor. At eighteen, Louise married thirty-four-year-old Louis Denys de la Ronde. Procurations of 1734 empowered her to administer her husband's business affairs, for he was in present-day Wisconsin pursuing his unsuccessful copper mining venture near Lake Superior. When Louis died, he left the family heavily in debt.[12] Their son took over the father's former command at the post of Chagouamigon (near Ashland, Wisconsin). Louise, for her part, hastened east to the French court, to lobby for permission for the family to retain the post. A 1748 colonial dispatch reported that Mme Denys de la Ronde's 'commissioner' (presumably no longer the son) had gone to the post to pursue his activities and that the Crown wished one-third of the post's returns to go to the widow. She succeeded and reaped profits for years.[13]

A brother-in-law of the failed copper miner Pierre D'Ailleboust Desmusseaux D'Argenteuil wasn't much of a businessman either. At twenty-eight he married sixteen-year-old Marie Louise Denys de la Ronde Delatrinité, and the couple produced eight children. She eventually asked for a separation of goods from her husband on grounds of his mismanagement of their affairs. Living more than three decades after his 1711 demise, Louise Denys de la Ronde conducted a long and eventually successful legal dispute with the Sulpicians over claims to the Argenteuil seigneurie at the west end of Montreal island. The location was ideal for intercepting furs illegally. Both the Sulpicians and Governor Vaudreuil accused her of this activity, pointing out the lack of clearing and the fact that her children had learned more about fur and Indian languages than about agriculture. The notarial documents seem to confirm their suspicions. In 1717 Louise Denys de la Ronde commissioned a voyageur to journey to Michilimackinac for furs; a few years later she entered business with tanner Louis Mallet on the understanding it was she who would supply the animal skins. When she died her assets totalled over 46,000 *livres*.[14]

Other well-heeled widows also stepped up to the counter. In the 1740s a widow may have managed the trade of Fort St Joseph; so it would seem from the conduct of the *Veuve* Monfort. In 1742 she came to Quebec to purchase some 11,000 *livres'* worth of cloth, guns and shot, kettles, and axes to take back with her.[15] Catherine Thierry (widow of Charles Le Moyne de Longueuil) was a seventeenth-century partner of French merchant Antoine Pascaud; they supplied merchandise to the Compagnie du Nord.[16] Widow Soumande (Anne-Marie Chapoux), from a well-known colonial trading family, was cashing in twenty-three packets of moose and deer hides, bales of lynx and bearskins in Quebec in 1725, and buying 7,000 *livres'* worth of goods such as wine, brandy, and salt, amounting to one-third of an ocean-going vessel's cargo.[17]

It was not necessary, however, to await a man's death to get involved. Montreal, as a jumping off point for the *pays d'en haut*, was a hub of activity for women with living husbands or other male relatives in the west. Mesdames Benoist, Baby, and Saint-Anges Charly were active members of merchant families who provisioned the trade. During widowhood, the last supplied private traders and also the Crown, which sent her orders worth more than 1,000 *livres* each.[18] Mlle Soumande, plus the widows Soumande and Lafond, and Marie-Louise Monière all placed their signatures alongside those of other merchants a 1716 petition against the special privileges the fur trade monopoly had granted to merchants Leclerc and Pascaud. Mme Daneau de Muy dealt in castor gras. Receiving bills of exchange for beaver (which was sometimes used as currency) at the offices of fur monopolists Néret and Gayot were Mlle de Repentigny and Thèrese Petit, as well as Mesdames Biron, Chambalon, Des Muceaux, Fournier, Pascaud, and Vaudreuil. Included on a 1722 list of officers and voyageurs shipping brandy westward were Mesdames de Lorimer and Latour, while Dame Hertel sold trade porcelain.[19]

Some embraced new opportunities that came along. When hides began to outperform beaver in the export markets, Louise Denys de la

Ronde and other women with sufficient funds capitalized on the opportunity, setting up operations to tan hides that arrived from the trading posts. There were two other Montreal participants to whom we will return later in our book: Agathe Saint-Père experimented with native dying and tanning processes, and persuaded townspeople to wear skin clothing, which they apparently found more appealing after she had it dyed green or brown. The Montreal governor's daughter Louise de Ramezay established tanneries too.[20]

Further east at Quebec, one found other upper-class participants. Seventeenth-century Quebecker Éléanore de Grandmaision was a member of a fur venture formed to trade in the Ottawa country.[21] A later Quebec region landowner, Charlotte Françoise Juchereau de Saint-Denys (Madame de la Forest) was identified by Governor Vaudreuil as one his 'most cruel enemies,' and he accused her of being in a cabal with such luminaries as Cadillac, Aubert, even Montreal Governor Claude de Ramezay himself. We will not go into that tangled history; suffice it to say there were fur-trading activities that included dealings with Lamothe Cadillac, a partnership with Alphonse de Tonty, loans to various traders, and service as financial *procuratrice* for François de la Forest (before and during their marriage), which included shipping goods to him in the Illinois country.[22] Her sister-in-law Thérèse Migeon also made loans to fur traders, and she appealed all the way up to the minister of marine to quash calumnies about her husband's illicit fur-trading.[23]

Turning to posts northeast of Quebec, well known are the activities of Labrador and Tadoussac trader Marie-Anne Barbel (Madame Fornel). Accustomed to managing the Quebec end of the business while her husband supplied Labrador posts, she expanded the fur and marine-oil business after being left a widow with five children aged six to nineteen. Over forty men and boys worked for the Veuve Fornel et Compagnie that she formed in conjunction with merchants Havy and Lefevre. By 1750 she was harvesting pelts and marine oils at five eastern posts.[24] Also trading on the Labrador coast was Marie-Charlotte Charest (Madame Courtemanche), a wife who actively promoted the trade and then continued to do so as a widow with three daughters. Since their activities extended beyond furs, we will revisit these two in our next chapter.

Though the many widows and daughters who received fur trade permits (*congés*) as emoluments from the Crown often transferred them to a professional trader right away, what did it mean when in 1718 Mlle Desforest, Widow Rudepalais, and the Catalogne sisters did not? How many of the recipients maintained a financial interest in the trade? We do not know all the answers. But clearly there were a multitude of ways – marginal or major, fleeting or lifelong – in which women of the bourgeois and officer classes might involve themselves in the colonial fur trade.

Transatlantic Traders

Many women functioned as part of family trading teams, a custom well established in France. Certainly, as historian John Bosher wrote, the 'family is the key to the work of the eighteenth century merchant network,'[25] which could station cousins, nephews, aunts, and spouses on bases in Bordeaux, La Rochelle, Louisbourg, and Quebec to cover the whole operation. As Kathryn Young discovered, eighteenth-century Canadian ports housed several important female transatlantic traders, some of whom we have already encountered as traders in fur. Looking at documents relating to the one or more shiploads of furs and hides annually bound for France, Young found that 'Widows D'Argenteuil, Fornel and Pascaud assumed control of the family *comptoir* when their husbands died. On their own, they continued to outfit vessels, to underwrite insurance, and to make investments ... [while] training their sons.'[26] Marie-Anne Busquet of La Rochelle (a relative of the Charly family) married colonial merchant Jean-Jacques Catignon in 1714. For the next dozen years Mme Catignon and her unmarried sister-in-law were at Quebec, handling correspondence on colonial fur shipments and working as Quebec agents for the La Rochelle concern. Madame Catignon was knowledgeable, suggesting to her Montreal trading partner Madame Argenteuil ways to minimize shipping risks and share insurance costs. The pair of them, Young concludes, had extensive business interests that made them 'serious and competent players in the transatlantic trade.'[27] Mesdames Charly, Pascaud, and Soumande likewise played 'a significant role in the French colonial trade.' There was also a long list of people operating in less prominent ways. Young counted thirty female entrepreneurs, many of them involved in one way or another with the fur staple that was shipped abroad.

Marguerite Bouat (Madame Pascaud) stood near the apex. She operated the most prominent La Rochelle company involved in the Canada trade for a decade after the 1717 death of her husband Antoine. Coming from a Montreal mercantile family, Marguerite Bouat was no stranger to working a ledger book to her own advantage, charging what Governor Beauharnois would later call 'interest on interest.' She had the advantage of being part of Governor Vaudreuil's powerful network. It was he who recommended her appointment as a commissioner at La Rochelle to regulate the excessive prices of the merchants there. She served as a lobbyist, too, trying to soften up the French court with lovely Canadiana such as small deer and birchbark canoes. She passed along astute summaries of Canadian views and practices, accurately pointing out that monopoly would inevitably drive Canadians into illegal trade with the English.[28]

'Small Fry' in the Trade

Toiling away in anonymity were many petty traders and provisioners of the fur trade who were drawn from the humbler classes of society. In the forests stretching back from the Great Lakes, native and Metis women who trapped and traded are not easy to trace.[29] At and around the French posts, the 'small fry,' probably often of mixed blood, sometimes do step into the light. At Detroit, for example, many women were recorded supplying goods and services to the Jesuit mission or to the Crown. Madame Goyau began laundering and baking for the mission to the Hurons in 1743 at a salary of 100 *livres* per annum. Evidently happy with trade goods in lieu of cash, she received from her employers shirts, blankets, pairs of *mitasses* or leggings, brandy and peas, deer and beaver skins, and gunpowder. Likewise Madame L'Oeil Eraillé must have envisioned trading the beads and vermillion, the multiple shirts and pairs of footwear she received from the mission. There were other Detroit traders too. Madame Saint-Martin was supplied with trade goods, forty-six Siamese knives, and twenty-four woodcutters' knives. The missionary said he 'gave to Gambille's wife 40 branches of porcelaine, to sell for me ... [and] 3 large cloth blankets, one of which is trimmed and half scarlet, and [16] ... pairs of *mitasses*, 13 shirts, large, medium-sized, and small [and] ... 7 half-*livres* of vermillion.' Madame Gambille had various irons in the fire. She conveyed to the Jesuits, for example, the 144 *livres* Charles Courtois owed them for wheat. She also proffered stockings and iron for a mattock that another woman, 'Cecile,' had made. Another woman, Madame Cuillerier, stipulated that fixing the exact price on the barrel of powder and fifty pounds of ammunition she bought from the Jesuits would await her husband's return; but husbandly intervention is not mentioned in the other accounts we cite here from the Detroit Journal of the Jesuits. 'Caron's wife' was another active trader, paid by the mission for '62 brasses of deerskin thongs,' five hundred nails, and porcelain beads she sold, plus 'ten pistoles for the purchase of a farm.' Mademoiselle Royale and Madame Skotache also traded with the mission, goods such as knives, steel for striking fire, beads and vermillion. Madame Delile sold the Jesuits meat and Madame Pilette did some grinding.[30] Madame Mallet sold brandy and Madame Senneville sold corn. Madame Barrois earned money by making plain and fancy *capots* (hooded capes), mittens, hoods, footwear, trade shirts, travelling bags, and tents that were ordered by officer Baron de Longueuil for various chiefs and tribes proceeding to Montreal or to Fort St Joseph.[31] Marie-Madeleine de Colon de Villiers presented M. Debreuil with a bill for 655 *livres* that gives some idea of the range of her business:

    4 sacks of wheat
    13 pieces of meat
    Firewood
    Brandy
    Bread
    Deerskin
    Tobacco
    Men's trade shirts
    3-point blankets
    Cloth[32]

Similar activity was recorded around the Great Lakes lying farther west. At the large trading station of Michilimackinac, Manon Lavoine (*Veuve* Chevalier) fed the natives who had accompanied the French officer LaCorne from Montreal and also supplied a 140-*livre* canoe and a horse for a feast. Marie Laplante Bourassa provided a hundred pounds of grease ordered by Commander LaCorne as well as lodging for a French envoy to the natives at a tense time. Demoiselle Blondeau collected twenty-six *livres* for the *capot* she contributed to French diplomatic efforts. Native and Metis women were also active traders.[33]

In other cases, women profited when aboriginal peoples brought their furs down to the colonial towns. In 1742 the Crown paid Montrealer Marguerite Launay, for example, to lodge thirty-eight Potawatami and other Indians for two weeks, also rewarding 'Suzanne' and another woman, as well as two others who supplied food and firewood.[34] *Veuve* Laprairie ran a cabaret that sold visiting Indians beer. The generally small amounts involved in such transactions signal an important point: petty trading was an everyday activity by ordinary people. It may have been a sideline, but it helped support families and individuals. All these small businesspeople signal Detroit, Michilimackinac, and Montreal as local exchange economies that fully integrated female traders and workers. They would continue to trade long after the Conquest, all along the Mississippi valley where, as historian Jay Gitlin wrote of the Franco-American traders who played leading roles there until 1840, 'more often than not, partnerships were family affairs.'[35]

There were three significant groups of female suppliers whose size remains a mystery. In the 1750s French engineer Louis Franquet visited a Trois-Rivières dockyard that was said to produce the best birchbark canoes in the colony. These were hefty cargo and military craft bound for the *pays d'en haut.* He reported, 'They were building an eight-man one; it was thirty-three feet long five feet wide, two and a half high, with a price a three hundred *livres*.... [They make] so many that they bill the Crown for more than six thousand *livres* per year; it is women and girls who build them; they are completely made of birchbark with rounded flooring of cedar or fir ... the seams, covered with resin, are waterproof, but one must avoid rocks.'[36] Franquet does not enlighten us about whether these women and girls who were making big canoes were aboriginal, Canadian, or some mixture of the two – but they were certainly using an aboriginal skill, in which women made the cladding of canoes after men made the frames.

Another group was the many women who made cloth and clothes for sale or barter. This was an activity of growing importance, partly in response to strong fur-trade demand for these items. In November 1685 Governor Denonville noted of Canadian girls and women that 'les menus ouvrages de capots et de chemises de trait les occupent un peu pendant l'hiver.'[37] Toques were another trade good that was most likely knitted by *canadiennes*. Peter Kalm reported that young women at Montreal continually picked up their needles when they were not performing other duties. We know some of them sewed for the trade, since Madame Benoist, wife of the commander at Oka, oversaw a Montreal operation making shirts and petticoats for that purpose around the time of the Conquest.[38] Others, as we shall see in our next chapter, sewed trade shirts, *capots*, and other items French officers used to consolidate native alliances.

Another group of women was employed to make the posts run smoothly. Missionary Father Claude Godefroi Coquart at the King's Domain discussed the three daughters of Joseph Dufour. The 'eldest girl is at the head of the farm,' the missionary reported. For modest wages she and her two sisters were 'occupied in raising the calves and lambs ... besides, the housekeeping is considerable. They have to churn the milk two or three times a week; to do them justice, it can be said that they are busy all day, even going beyond their strength.'[39] Even in the 1740s when efforts were made to reduce the numbers of women maintained at the posts, Intendant Hocquart noted that some women were necessary to the garrisons, including bakers, laundresses, seamstresses, keepers of livestock, and other domestics. We do not know how many in total worked at the forts, but records do provide information about Marianne and Marie Texier, who were paid for such duties at Fort Saint-Fréderic. Marianne was variously paid for baking, sewing, tending livestock, and cleaning, showing a versatility typical of pre-industrial wage-earners. Madame Courval at Fort Fréderic earned, for some reason, 645 *livres*. Marie-Joseph Baudria baked and laundered at Fort Frontenac, while Angelique Le Pailleur sewed diverse items 'for the King's trade' at Niagara.[40] Clearly a number of women farmed, milked, baked, laundered, and sewed to keep the posts running. We turn from them to one last fur-trade group, individuals who preferred to stay in the shadows.

Smuggling to New York: Transcultural Trade

The discussion of the illicit fur trade – which at times may have rivalled the legitimate trade in volume[41] – invites us to widen our purview slightly, to discuss neighbouring peoples just south of French Canada who colluded with *canadiennes* in cross-border smuggling. Colonial women who came from more northerly regions of France and the Low Countries possessed greater property rights than Anglo-American women did, a topic to be discussed in chapter 5.[42] A number worked as traders.

Even the relatively liberal construction of female rights the Dutch and French enjoyed was far overshadowed by the position of women among the Haudenosaunee (Iroquois), a third group that was involved in smuggling. In effect, when furs were smuggled across the frontier between New France and New York they often passed through two patriarchal cultures (French and Dutch) in which women were modestly empowered – and one remarkable culture that was not patriarchal at all. Various French agents, officers, and missionaries have left a trove of information about the unusual authority of Iroquois women. One of the most knowledgeable of these was the early-eighteenth-century Jesuit missionary Joseph-François Lafitau. Lafitau lived for five years among the Haudenosaunee just southwest of Montreal Island at Sault Saint Louis (now Kahnawake). This group was, of course, no longer in its pre-contact state. Still, Europeanization had made rather limited inroads, and the mission Iroquois were noted for their independence from French authorities, who were compelled to treat them as allies rather than subjects, refraining from prosecuting the domiciled Iroquois even for crimes as serious as rape and murder.[43] Lafitau supplemented his own ethnographic data with observations from earlier missionaries, and he consciously sought information about pre-contact practices too. Lafitau's startling assertion of female hegemony included claims that they possessed 'all real authority,' that the fields and harvest belonged to them, that they were in charge of tribal wealth, the 'souls of the Councils,' the 'arbiters of peace and war,'[44] with names and titles also passing down through the female line.

Though Father Lafitau makes the strongest and most detailed statement about women's unusual powers, he was certainly not alone. Other observers, particularly among the missionaries, recorded female chiefs. Marie de l'Incarnation, Ursuline superior at Quebec (whom we have already encountered, a woman of considerable authority of her own) was particularly intrigued by the 'capitainesses' with 'a deliberative voice at the councils' who selected the mid-seventeenth-century peace ambassadors sent to the French. Father Claude Dablon recorded later in that century that the matrons 'are greatly respected; they hold council, and the Elders decide no important affair of consequence without their opinion.'[45] Twenty-first century-monographs, while stopping short of Father Lafitau's assessment of a 'gynocracy' (or matriarchy), have to a considerable extent reaffirmed early views of the high status of Haudenosaunee women.[46] Haudenosaunee women and men seem to have been relatively free agents, clearly able to traverse woodland trails and waterways on missions of their own devising.

Spiriting furs out of Canada through northern New York and down to Albany was advantageous on several counts. French and native traders found that Albany paid better prices for pelts than did the monopoly Compagnie des Indes. Albany merchants could supply quality English goods relatively cheaply, including luxuries such as oysters, white sugar, and lace, as well as supplies of wampum and English strouds (woollens). Aboriginal buyers coveted English scarlet blankets with a black stripe near the border, though they were willing to pay Compagnie des Indes prices for lovely Montpellier blues.[47] Running the goods brought commissions to aboriginal carriers, some of whom had French Christian names and are thought to have been attached to the missions near Montreal. The risk was not excessive, since the French were wary of alienating their native allies. Colonial women, too, could sometimes evade the full force of law, benefiting from complaisant officials or relatives on the Superior Council who were willing to wink at their misdeeds.[48]

As with most illicit activities, the records are slim, but we have three rich sources to help us piece together the story. Decades ago Canadian scholar Jean Lunn used the mid-eighteenth-century account book of Albany merchant Robert Sanders to uncover some of the secrets of this trade. Lunn's scholarly detective work matched up events mentioned in Canadian officials' complaints about smuggling with events noted in the 1750s account book of Sanders. The New Yorker protected his French-Canadian trading partners by sending them parcels using coded symbols such as pipes and roosters. The French records reveal the way the aboriginal traders spirited the contraband past French forts in the St Lawrence and Richelieu valleys. They would sometimes stop and divert officials with the paltry pack in their canoe while their friends hustled a much heavier pack through nearby woods. They were also known to send the same lightly loaded canoe past a fort many times, fooling the commander into thinking a big haul was just a series of small permissible bundles of fur trapped by individual Indians. At other times they got through by brandishing weapons or extracting a pass from the governor himself under threat of resettling in the English colonies. Thus, behind thin veils, the trade flourished, to the extent (Intendant Hocquart estimated in 1737) that as much as one-third of the beaver exports flowed illegally.[49] Correspondence of Canadian officials to the French court has supplied another source of information. We can now piece together even more of the story with the help of a newly translated and annotated version of a considerably earlier Albany account book kept by Evert Wendell and his family.[50] Three hundred and twenty-five Indians were recorded opening accounts with siblings Evert, Harmonius, and Hester Wendell during the period 1695–1726. About 70 per cent of them were Haudenosaunee (most often Mohawk or Seneca, along with some Onondaga and Cayuga).

Together these sources allow us to reconstruct the silhouettes of the participants. In the Wendell records of 1695–1726 female traders were extremely common (having an active role as at least one of the participants in 49.6 per cent of accounts). They assumed similar responsibilities, such as bringing in comrades to meet the Wendells or standing as surety for them. About 10 per cent of the aboriginal traders were from Canada, including women named Ohonsaioenthaa, Okaajthie, Anna, and Quanakaraghto. Most commonly females were identified simply as wives, sisters, mothers of a named male, or by some personal characteristic. For example, a pockmarked 'female Mohawk ... from Canada' arrived to trade just after Christmas in 1705, bearing 'greetings from the priest.' She purchased red duffel stockings and nine bars of lead, promising to return later with five martens to pay for them. Her boy bought a coat. She reappeared to pawn an axe in March, then came again with beaver pelts to settle her account in May. She, her son, and various other family members traded with the Wendells for several years, exchanging their martens and beavers for items such as stockings, blue blankets, coats, and a red stroud blanket. She introduced another trader, an elderly Oneida woman, to the Wendells. The relationship continued on a happy note with Evert Wendell noting in 1706, 'The boy and his mother have paid everything,' and, perhaps in gratitude, he had 'given for her son for free a piece of strouds.'[51]

In another case, 'a limping female savage' first came down from Canada in 1697. Over the years Evert Wendell sold her a kettle, shirts, and rum in exchange for hides of bear, deer, elk, and marten; at one point she served as a guarantor for another woman trader. Limp or no limp, in 1700 she pledged to bring the merchant eight beavers if he gave her 'a French canoe … with which she went to Canada.' She returned to Albany the next year, beavers in hand.[52] She, her husband, and their daughter were still trading with the Wendells in 1709.

In the mid-eighteenth century, among six regular carriers Robert Sanders employed, there were four men: Togaira, Caingoton, Joseph Harris, and Conaquasse. There were two women, Agnesse and Marie-Magdeleine (whom he described as having an impediment in one eye).[53] Clearly not confined to the village clearings, these women, like those in the earlier Wendell account, made a business of travelling the 210-mile route between Montreal and Albany. Agnesse did it at least three times between May and July 1753. Canoes loaded with barrels of oysters or 130-pound shipments of beaver were typical. Marie-Magdeleine's remarks to Sanders that she knew one Montreal merchant whom she was supplying 'perfectly well' and another one 'well'[54] suggest these women were integrated into the French network too. The carriers had some control over their terms, helping themselves to a commission from the goods. Colonial women were also part of the network. Sanders explained to one of his French clients that he was sending her cloth in exchange for her furs and would have included some beautiful lace, but because the carrier siphoned lace off for sale to friends, Sanders dared send no more.[55] Waiting at Kahnawake for nice things to arrive from Albany were three Canadian sisters, to whom we shall soon return after a brief introduction to Dutch collusionists who lived south of the St Lawrence.

Defiance of authorities was commonplace among Dutch women who traded furs with their Iroquoian neighbours around Albany and Schenectady. When they sold alcohol or evaded trade taxes, authorities caught some of them. Because reports of these incidents that reached magistrates may offer insight into similar attitudes on the Canadian side, they are worth perusing. In 1680 Albany Sheriff Prichard Pretty searched the Schenectady house of the Borsboons. Grietje, the mother of the house, 'threatened to pull his hair' when he spied a beaver pelt sticking out between the bed boards and tried to seize it. She also tried to bribe him into silence with two beavers. This brush with the law apparently did not faze Grietje Borsboon, for the following year Sheriff Pretty saw her and her son travelling into Albany. Suspecting that they were concealing illegal furs under their clothing, he undertook to search them. Court records indicate that mother and son 'refused to let them make a search and ... resisted ... grabbing him by the throat and collar and calling him a rascal, etc.' Grietje and her son were fined twenty-five guilders. Another woman arrested by an Albany sheriff screamed at him, 'Run, get out of the house, you interfere with my bargaining. If I must give you money, let me make enough to do so.'[56]

It was not uncommon for these petty traders to run family businesses, recruiting their children as workers. Dennis Sullivan's account of official efforts to end this trade reveal considerable female involvement. For example, in August 1677 'nine defendants were charged with being near the Indian houses ... five of whom were listed as the daughters of Albany burghers.' Similarly next summer four of five defendants found to 'incessantly, contrary to ordinance ... go themselves or to send their children to the Indian houses on the hill' were female. Women of Albany's Hoogeboom family, young and old, were charged with numerous illicit exchanges of trinkets, knives, paints, and other goods.[57]

Aware that the woods between Montreal and New Albany were alive with complicit women, let us turn back to New France, where a notorious female smuggling ring flourished for many years. It centred on a trio of single women from Montreal. The colony's highest officials, Intendant Gilles Hocquart and Governor General Charles Beauharnois, sent a series of letters to the French minister of marine in the 1740s. Hocquart wrote in October 1744, 'My suspicions would fall on the Demoiselles Desauniers, although I have not been able to detect any proof nor to catch them in *flagrante delicto*.'[58] That same year his co-ruler, the governor general, asked the minister himself for permission to remove them if suspicions were confirmed. Marguerite, Marie-Anne, and Magdeleine

Desauniers, the correspondence revealed, had begun modestly enough, merely supplying clothing to the Indians. They were not under the authority of any father or husband but operated on their own as '*filles majeures / non-mariées*.' Soon enough the store they had built began to carry a good deal more than clothes, offering a wide variety of provisions at cheaper prices than in Montreal. Still later, their buildings were found to contain supplies used for the western fur trade. It was said that native women colluded in the business by hauling furs from Montreal hidden in baskets.[59] A functionary of the French West Indies Company alerted government officials that the sisters would naturally have received some furs from the Indians in payment for merchandise in their store. Why, then, did they never bring any furs into the company's office, through which all exports to France were supposed to pass? The sisters protested their innocence. After a good deal of direct and indirect investigation, officials had sufficient evidence to order the Desauniers to close shop. After that, why did the trio nonetheless opt to stay at the mission without visible means of support, rather than return to what was said to be a handsome house they owned back in Montreal? Officials suspected that they were not in fact complying with the order to cease trade.

One would like to know more about the culture of women such as these three, who seem to have blithely operated outside the law. As historian Richard White demonstrated, some cultural intermediaries around the Upper Great Lakes basically 'went native' in the fashion of the buckskinned frontiersman, and we know that people of mixed blood selectively adopted European technology, customs, and dress.[60] These Montreal-based intermediaries cultivated both the council fire *and* the drawing room. The sisters had the advantage of being fluent in the native tongue. Being female may have been an advantage too since, according to Lafitau, the Iroquoian women at the mission tended to be in charge, the men being away in pursuit of furs September to February, away some other times on war parties. The Desauniers were reported to be charitable to the sick and poor, in another practice that squared with native custom.[61] Fuller knowledge of the Desauniers' social mores would be fascinating. Did they make sexual choices with the same freedom with which they told lies, for example? Many *Canadiennes*, after all, were evidently influenced by Amerindian costume, alarming a European visitor with their short skirts 'halfway up the leg,' native style. The autonomy and unconventionality of certain fur-trade participants may reveal a degree of 'going native' sufficient to justify what Natalie Davis called 'an enquiry about the history of European women that ... [makes] use of

Iroquois tropes and frames.' The history of – shall we call them rogue females? – on those eastern frontiers remains full of mysteries, including smokescreens they themselves created to conceal their activities.

However effectively the Desauniers inserted themselves into native culture, it appears they also showed well in French parlours. Since officials never commented on their attire, one suspects Marguerite, Marie-Anne, and Magdeleine Desauniers retained the conventional long dark gowns of the French bourgeoisie. Their network included their many relatives among Montreal merchants. When the governor and intendant finally mustered the resolve to eject them from the mission, army officers and clergymen responded with petitions on their behalf. Prominent traders attested that the Desauniers sisters had conducted business in Montreal and the mission village for about twenty-four years 'with all the rectitude and probity suitable to merchants, and they have always conducted themselves with honour and distinction in their business.'[62] Receiving this petition at Versailles, how could the minister of marine know that one of the signators, Monier, was the same name that appeared in Albany merchant Robert Sanders's letter book as one of the leading Montreal smugglers?

As the words continued to fly, Marguerite, Marie-Anne, and Magdeleine Desauniers ignored the directive to close down. In 1750, native informants told the governor the sisters were trading with the English via Orange and Chouaguen posts; their aboriginal collusionists went there first, then paddled stocked-up canoes of ill-gotten English goods to friendly voyageurs at points farther west.[63] Governor General La Jonquière was aghast at what appeared to be 25 per cent markups and returns, rivalling the most profitable of businesses in Europe. The exasperated governor, in a letter to the minister in 1751, maintained that the sisters were 'very adroit, very fertile with fine talk, unparalleled in presenting lies and truth with equal conviction.'[64] He eventually felt he had enough evidence to order eight soldiers to eject the sisters. However, La Jonquière died in 1752, and the trio took advantage of the naivety of his interim successor to secure permission to go to the mission for twenty-four hours to collect debts the Indians still purportedly owed them. Months later, a newly arrived governor general found them still there and ordered their removal. When first ejected from their business, the Desauniers had crossed the sea to present their case to the French court. It seems part of a long pattern that they returned to Canada claiming that the King himself had given them permission to resume business. But why, when asked, could they produce no document to prove it?

Not until 1752 did the Desauniers sisters finally close their business for good. How were unmarried sisters able to defy the express orders of the highest officials in New France for a whole decade? One factor was that French authorities only half-wanted to shut down smuggling, since key native allies insisted on receiving English goods. In particular the French were not prepared to quarrel with the Desauniers' trading partners, the formidable 'praying Iroquois' who had moved northward to settle at the Jesuit mission. That group had been deemed in 1735 'the most warlike in North America.'[65] Eight years later, on the eve of the War of Austrian Succession, when there was renewed threat of attack from the English to the south, the colony's rulers were still wary lest the warriors there might turn on the French colonists and attack them. Governor General La Jonquière wrote of the Desauniers sisters, 'I am only too certain of the sway they have gained over the Iroquois of the Sault, the sentiments of independence, even rebellion, they hasten to suggest to them.'[66] The Desauniers knew how to play on French fear of what, one official wrote, was practically an independent republic. Even in New France's last decade in the 1750s, the military engineer Louis Franquet recorded the sisters dissuading the Indians from letting the government build fortifications around the mission. Self-appointed ambassadors to the 'republic,' the Desauniers colluded with the Haudenosaunee to keep officials at bay.[67]

The Desauniers' defiance of a series of colonial rulers is the most remarkable female smuggling operation on record, but it was not the only one. Around the time they finally closed down, the Sanders letterbook mentions sending contraband to a Madame Desmurseaux / de Mousseaux, likely the wife of M. de Merceau/Desmurceaux (there are a variety of spellings in both the French and the English sources). He was the commander at Fort Sault Saint Louis, and the family lived just a stone's throw away from the Desauniers sisters' storehouse.[68] Had his wife simply taken over the sisters' work – with or without their blessing? A hundred and fifty miles south, at Fort Saint Frederic (Crown Point, NY), Magdeleine Bouat, wife of the genteel Commander Paul Dazemard de Lusignan, ran a store with all sorts of merchandise, including contraband smuggled in from the south by the Indians in exchange for her brandy, while her husband enforced her monopoly.[69] This kind of activity spanned the French regime. At Trois-Rivières, Jeanne Enard (*Veuve Crevier*) had expanded her mid-seventeenth-century brandy trade into a broader operation, eventually organizing trade expeditions to Cap-de-la Madeleine that were the despair of Jesuit missionaries there. *Fille du roi* Madeleine d'Allonne, as we saw, was accused of selling fiery liquids at Fort Cataraqui on Lake Ontario. In the eighteenth century, Madame Couagne was a wealthy Montreal receiver of Albany contraband; Madame Pipardière was a modest one, caught red-handed with a few illegal English trade blankets. An impressive twenty-six packets of beaver were seized from Dame Vinet at Longue-Pointe. 'A woman named Lafleur'[70] was implicated more than once as Montreal receiver of illegal furs shipped from Fort Frontenac, perhaps the same Madame Lafleur who apprenticed her eight-year-old daughter to serve the Desauniers sisters. In Quebec, Madame de la Forest attempted to evade regulations by unloading fur shipments from the upper country at night.[71]

Many a husband and wife, many a mother and child must have been involved in illegal activities. The records mention groups such as the inhabitants of Lachine, Bout de l'Ile, Chateauguay, Saint-Lambert, Boucherville, and other locales whom in 1726 the authorities placed under suspicion of illicit activity in 1726 because they kept more than fifty *livres* of beaver in their houses.[72] Alcohol was often involved; for example, as summer was turning to fall in 1735, one unlucky pair, Marguerite Lemoine and Pierre Liegeois, was marched into Montreal marketplace. Each was decked out with a sign that announced the crime, *Traiteur/Traîteuse d'eau de vie aux Sauvages*, among whom their illegal brandy had fuelled a violent uproar.[73] They represented a common phenomenon: a French-Canadian couple working together to advance the family fortunes. French law itself (to be discussed in chapter 5) conceived marriage as an economic community. How many enterprising women, most of whose names we will never know, were scattered around the cabins, posts, missions, back alleys, and backwoods, involved in daily dealings related to the fur trade? They drew strength from laws that allowed a woman to amass assets, from cultures that accepted their public activity and their unchaperoned travel (all the safer since Iroquoian nations seldom committed rape). Indeed, all parties to the flourishing illegal trade drew strength from the powerful Iroquois presence in the Mohawk-Richelieu corridor.

If women of French, Dutch, and aboriginal cultures traded as often as all this evidence suggests, how could anything so commonplace escape notice? As Kees-Jan Waterman discovered in his close analysis of the Wendell records, although nearly fifty per cent of the accounts they opened with aboriginal traders involved women, they were not usually named, while men were almost always named. Indeed, 93 per cent of the individual native traders (as in 'the limping female savage from Canada') who could not be identified by name were women. This work allows us to see, for the first time, how women were written out of the record at the trade counter itself. (Also written out was trade known to have been conducted by one or more female members of the Wendell family, which was either unsigned or later lost.) It is no wonder historians have subsequently failed to perceive their presence. White or indigenous, the fur trader entered the cultural imagination as a masculine figure: the trapper in buckskins, the muscular voyageur, or the managerial gentleman in a top hat. His female relatives carrying furs, commissioning canoes, settling accounts, hoodwinking officials, and escorting other women to meet the dealer fell into oblivion.[74] As Kees-Jan Waterman observed, 'In general, participation by women in the fur trade in the Northeast has not been described in the literature.'[75]

Our findings in the French records support the idea of frequent involvement. It is surprising to see how many women are revealed in our own careful combing of just one series of colonial correspondence and a scattering of other records. The count can only grow as other researchers explore the enormous database of notarial records that my research has only touched, as they look beyond the C11A series of colonial correspondence that was examined year by year for this book. Moreover, we think that *all* the names that will ever be found in written records are just the tip of the iceberg, a fraction of the women who had some involvement in the collection, production, processing, or exchange of fur and other marketable natural resources, especially when one adds agricultural products to furs (as the next chapter will do). Truly, we can never count all the instances in which women pocketed something in exchange for some colonial resource. Doing so was simply part of living. Is there some less laborious way of reaching the truth than by endlessly piling up individual cases? Is there some larger pattern to the many and varied instances of female trade that have been found by myself and others?

Re-conceiving Pre-industrial Women

How can we characterize women's place in the resource economy of New France? Allan Greer referred to a mere 'several' female entrepreneurs, and Peter Moogkt termed wives 'dependents.' Noting trade partnerships and correspondence between women of Montreal, Quebec, and the French ports, Kathryn Young raised the possibility of a professional and personal 'network' among female traders. My own early work argued that women in New France seemed 'favoured' in this regard, relative to the Victorian women who came after them and perhaps even to their contemporaries in other countries and colonies.[76]

While all these assertions contain some truth, they tend to direct attention away from the ordinary, everyday experience of women engaged in commerce. It was both smaller *and* larger than those of us who have written about it have suggested. It was *smaller* in the sense that those involved were most often of humble station, and they tended to participate on intermittently, not as part of a chosen 'career.' On the other hand, it was a *larger* role than the literature suggests because, far from the female trader being some kind of exceptional or unrepresentative figure, large numbers, likely even the *majority* of women in the colony, were involved in commercial exchange. This was, as struck many a colonial official arriving there, a poor colony, with even its noble families dependent on fur-trading and Crown subsidies.[77] Eking out a livelihood involved the active participation of both sexes throughout the history of the colony. Beyond subsistence farming, a significant part of the search for livelihood related in one way or another to the colony's leading 'cash crop,' which was fur.

Scholarship in recent decades on the history of women in Europe allows us to appreciate how ubiquitous and varied such work was. Our opening chapter noted how Olwen Hufton's *The Prospect before Her: A History of Women in Europe 1500–1800* documented gainful employments that permeated daily activities of farmwomen from France and elsewhere on the continent. The seigneuress and the peasant managed household and perhaps domestic production on widely varying scales; urban and rural women spun, and made lace and pins and various other wares.[78]

It was England that led the way towards a narrower conception of women's work. Bridget Hill found that female supervision of production and work in skilled trades ranging from healing to mining declined during the eighteenth century.[79] The study by Peter Earle cited in our opening chapter provided evidence that female employment shrank over time, from 57 per cent in pre-industrial London to 28 per cent in 1851. Early-eighteenth-century women were expected to work, the author concluded, and there was no indication of the idea that woman's place was 'in the home.'[80] The material showed that female breadwinners were once common across a broad class spectrum.

Peter Kalm, that most helpful of travellers, confirmed that not long after that time, Anglo-America stepped into the vanguard of gender change. Travelling from his native Sweden to England in the mid-eighteenth century, he was startled to see the narrowing range of female work in England. He noted shrinking activities in the city. Outside London in 1748 he was struck that 'it was very rare to see any women at work in the meadows.' After touring the countryside, he reported that English women kept clothes, dishes, and floors very clean and did very precise sewing. However, they turned to local bakers for bread and had started purchasing things they had formerly spun and woven themselves. And men milked! Kalm wrote, 'I confess I rubbed my eyes several times to make them clear, because I could not believe I saw aright, when I first came here ... and saw the farmers' houses full of young women, while the men, on the contrary, went out both morning and evening to where the cattle were, milk-pail in hand, sat down to milk.... In short, when one enters a house and has seen the women cooking, washing floors, plates and dishes, darning a stocking or sewing a chemise, he has, in fact, seen all their economy.... Nearly all the evening occupations which our women in Sweden perform are neglected by them.'[81]

Kalm added, 'It is true that the common servant-girls have to have somewhat more work in them. But still this ... seldom goes beyond what is reckoned up above.' He contrasted this to Sweden, where 'the wife, no less than the husband, is obliged in every way to bestir herself and keep her wits with her,' while 'to help to win the bare necessities of life, an English wife would not seem to be particularly well-suited.' These more prosperous farmwives also redefined their relationship to the market and ceased bringing their own butter and piglets to town to sell.[82] Kalm noted what was an indispensable catalyst for the changes: the affluence and ready circulation of cash in England. Women became more apt to rely on the production and the market activities of others. The same affluence greeted him when he went to America, where the women also spent much of the day confined to indoor work while the men toiled outdoors.

Entering Canada, though, the traveller again saw patterns familiar to him in pre-industrial Sweden. Kalm did criticize the lack of domestic cleanliness, noting the women wore dirty jackets and sprinkled the dirt floors with water to congeal the dust. Little did they care, for they were busy *out*-of-doors. 'The women in Canada on the contrary do not spare themselves, especially among the common people, who are always in the fields, meadows, stables, etc, and do not dislike any work whatsoever.... [T]hey are not averse to taking part in all the business of housekeeping... [T]hey also carry their sewing with them, even the governor's daughters.' Kalm added, 'The common people in the country seem to be very poor. They are content with meals of dry bread and water, bringing all other provisions, such as butter, cheese, meat, poultry, eggs, etc to town, in order to get money for them, for which they buy clothes and brandy for themselves and finery for their women.' Lest one think the women stayed home, Kalm clarified that 'the daughters of all ranks, without exception, go to market.'[83] Families further from town, colonial documents tell us, went to smaller markets. In short, this was the kind of traditional, pre-industrial market economy that tourists encounter in some peasant economies to this day: primitive housing and hygiene, with both sexes doing all kinds of fieldwork, and hawking their wares in open-air markets. Almost everywhere in the Atlantic world, women's work *did* eventually change, in the direction of less outdoor work, fewer home manufactures, less economic production and exchange, generally less visibility in public. In eighteenth-century Canada, *it had not changed yet*.

Conclusion

We have seen in this chapter a wide variety of female participants in the Canadian fur trade. They ranged from officers' wives and widows in Montreal who forwarded goods to active traders and provisioners residing in and around the posts themselves. They included tanners of hides gleaned in the trade and makers of canoes bound for the west. They numbered illegal traders such as the Desauniers sisters and transatlantic shippers based at Quebec or even La Rochelle. They accord with indications from pre-industrial Europe that economic production and exchange was common to women of all classes. Referring generally to women in New France as a group alive to market opportunities is not an exaggeration that conflates a small minority with the majority. Women customarily took responsibility for some of the family's livelihood. It is anachronistic to carry around in one's head an image of some other, 'ordinary' female confined inside some cosy cottage, too sweet to think of money, just cooking, cleaning, and singing nursery rhymes. Would any able-bodied person spend any more time than necessary in that most common form of housing there, a cramped, dirt-floored cabin? Nineteenth-century 'separate sphere' theorizations of men as breadwinners and women as homemakers do not fit pre-industrial regions, particularly regions that depended so fundamentally on selling fur and other natural resources to towns and distant markets.

This was a poor colony, as many an official noted. The colonists made do with what the land offered them. Frequently enough harvests failed, throwing farm families onto any other available resource. It is time to

stop applying anachronistic notions of female domesticity to pre-industrial economies based on family production. Even *habitant* women, it
was noted, possessed a few pieces of imported finery. The little cash that
families could scrape together for such items had to come mainly from
the trade in natural resources, and there was no reason for a *canadienne*
to eschew such opportunities. She was not a 'dependent,' and she was
not doing something 'exceptional' in swapping some toques she had
knitted for a beaver pelt when a native woman passed the cabin, when
she sewed a trade shirt, or persuaded a relative to include some lard
she had prepared into the cargo of one of the big voyageur canoes as it
skimmed upstream toward the Great Lakes. As she rushed to get things
ready on time, or counted up the proceeds, she was perhaps too busy to
be anybody's 'nagging wife.'

Chapter Four

Water, Woods, Earth: Making a Living

At the time the *filles du roi* and other French settlers crossed the Atlantic, a family-based economy was the norm. Indeed colonial officials specified the need for female immigrants who were strong, country girls who were, as Marie de l'Incarnation wrote in 1668, 'able to work like the men.' Though wilderness farms may have required particular strength, the hardworking farmwife was nothing new. Studies of both countryside and metropolis in early modern Europe indicate that there, too, both sexes earned their bread. In our last chapter we saw how women of various classes participated in the fur trade in Canada. It is now time to broaden our horizons to a whole range of other marketable natural resources the colony offered.

There were a number of options. Some women took from the rivers and the ocean a variety of marine oils and fish. Others engaged in manufacturing such items as baskets and boxes, and making textiles and clothing at home and in workshops. Some used the soil beneath their feet to manufacture building materials such as bricks and tiles. Others turned to the forests for bounty that included ginseng for the Chinese market, dyewoods for textiles, and plants used as pharmaceuticals. Some hired men to harvest oak for timber operations. Allied to timbering was shipbuilding, an activity that generated income for a surprising array of women, including nuns. Other women supplied the Crown with assorted provisions, especially in time of war. A few profited from land development and sales, while many thousands derived some income from products generated on farms. This chapter will examine each of those many and varied activities.

Fisheries and Marine Oils

From the chilly northern waters, women or their agents harvested fish and marine products. This activity supported individuals and religious orders too. In Marie de l'Incarnation's day, the Quebec Ursulines controlled the St Lawrence fishery around Cape Diamond and the Quebec Quay.[1] Also exploiting the bounty of the waters were Marie Anne Charest (Madame Courtemanche) and Marie-Anne Barbel (Madame Fornel), whom we introduced in our discussion of furs. They both traded in the oils of the marine animals they harvested on the lower St Lawrence and in Labrador.

Marie-Anne Barbel was a particularly ambitious trader. Her husband gave her full power of attorney to look after their interests in Quebec while he was in Labrador. After she was left a widow with young children, she ran the family firm herself. As historian Dale Miquelon noted, she being 'a typical merchant's wife of her time, was well versed in business affairs.'[2]

The Labrador trade was not for the faint-of-heart. It required understanding native trade practices and the needs of different posts, arranging shelter for men and supplies, investing in boats, and financing and shipping merchandise to that remote coast from France and Canada. A year after getting started in 1749, the Widow Fornel was shocked to learn that Intendant Bigot deemed her operation insufficiently profitable and intended to transfer her permit to another party. Barbel fought back. She vigorously defended her contractual rights and demanded hundreds of thousands of *livres* compensation if the remaining five years of her six-year contract were cancelled. She wrote a letter to the minister of marine detailing the expenses and risks involved. She had spent 25,000 *livres* outfitting and arming a ship in autumn 1749, only to have an early freeze-up immobilize it. Eventually it did bring back furs, notably 400 marten pelts collected by her employees. No native hunters, however, had shown up to trade during an unusually harsh winter that cost many of them their lives. Marie-Anne Barbel penned seven pages (still preserved in reports sent to Versailles) itemizing expenses and returns. The former included over 4,000 *livres* worth of food, barrels of beef, flour, prunes, peas, and lard for the posts. There were tools and other supplies and furnishings. There was the cost of a schooner and smaller craft. The widow had paid seven thousand *livres* for the permit to farm her five posts at Ile Jérémie, Rivière Moisie, Tadoussac, Chicoutimi, and Malbaie, and expended 86,000 *livres* on rental of ships or buildings, plus another 4,000 for travel costs. There were wages and food for ships' crews plus hats, *capots*, and other supplies to present to the natives. There were 14,000 *livres* in wages to coopers, blacksmiths, arms makers, traders, clerks, *engagés*, ship's captain and crew, bursar, fort master, hunters, servants, and day labourers – over forty men and boys. The 50,000 *livres'* worth of marine oils, beaver, lynx, young bear, red fox, marten, wolverine, otter, and mink her company had harvested did not cover all the expenses. She explained that on top of its being an unusually bad year, there were the heavy startup costs.[3] Despite her troubles the widow did take care to tithe the church with two out of eleven barrels of oil and 7 out of 131 martens. Blessings evidently flowed, and things improved in years to come.

Marie-Charlotte Charest was another 'masterful woman who had her say in the affairs of the post.'[4] She too could recount chapter and verse to the French court (which she did a number of times) about the family's trading operations on the Labrador coast and the ways they coincided with Crown interests. She was conversant with the best fishing stations, the dangers, the funds, employees, and arms needed to protect all the French fishing, fur, and marine oil operations in Labrador. The Charests were a mercantile family in Quebec, Her first husband was inducted into the business by his teenaged bride and her family. Still a minor when he died, she married his business partner, Augustin Legardeur de Courtemanche. Despite her tender years, notarial records from the time she was eighteen show her repeatedly entering into business contracts that involved leasing property, acting in her husband's absence to arrange supplies and equip a ship, and hiring voyageurs, traders, and servants for the Labrador operation. She also inducted her son and daughters into the business. Thus they all had concessions in Labrador, and son François Martel de Brouague while still in his twenties replaced his stepfather as commander in charge of protecting all French fishing stations and posts in Labrador. That represented a triumph for the lobbying in which Marie-Charlotte was so active, allowing the family to outmanoeuvre the powerful Governor Vaudreuil, who preferred a protégé of his own for that post. Good management evidently played a part too, judging by the fact that thirty-four ship captains who fished the Labrador waters appealed to have the concession remain in the hands of the Courtmanche-Charest family. The widow's appeal to have the family concessions enlarged was also granted by the Council of Marine in 1722.

This was a life full of adventure. Marie-Charlotte Charest lived for more than fifteen years on the Labrador coast, mostly in what is today Brador Bay. Traders at the scattered outposts faced the ravages of starva-

tion, sickness, and wild animals. Furthermore, there were alarms day and
night on account of the Inuit. They were retaliating for depredations by
Europeans by killing colonial traders and pillaging posts as well as ships,
which they burned to secure precious iron nails. Twice Charest played
a key role in saving her family's life. In 1719 a large group of Inuit surrounded their post and threatened to kill them. In an effort to make
peace, the family had released a young Inuit woman named Acoutsina
who had been their captive. Interrogated long and eagerly by her tribes-
women about her experiences in the Charest's household, Acoutsina was
asked by her people's captain, 'Did the men in the fort offer you insult?'
Acoutsina's reply was, 'No, she was always around Madame, who was like
my *anana* (which means mother), and if any domestics wanted to try
anything she would have beaten them.'[5] This testimony, and the gifts
and food Charest distributed to Acoutsina and the other Inuit women,
did not prevent the Inuit captain from threatening to kill the Canadian
family; but Acoutsina's tears finally stayed his hand. Shortly afterwards,
when Charest was in her forty-seventh year, their fort was destroyed by a
fire someone set in the middle of the night. Awakened by a native who
called to her from outside her room, she leapt out the window to confirm the report, then climbed back inside to rescue her three daughters
sleeping in the same room. Because it was too close to winter to secure
timber from Quebec to rebuild the fort, they headed to France instead.
There Marie-Charlotte Charest and her three daughters got caught in an
epidemic in Provence! They lived to tell the tale, and the younger generation was still pursuing profits in Labrador at the end of the French
regime.

The Acoutsina story, which of course comes to us through a French
filter (the account of François Martel de Brouague) is instructive in a
number of ways. Its suggests the sparse resources of that coast, for the Inuit whom Madame Charest-Courtemanche fed were described as being
famished. The story also permits a glimpse of the oft-noted aboriginal
avoidance of harshness toward the young. One wonders if the alleged
arson represented a covert attempt to carry out the death sentence that
Acoutsina's tears had temporarily stayed. There is a glimpse too of aboriginal reactions to missionary work, including Acoutsina's attempt to
act out elements of the Mass for her curious Inuit kinswomen. On another topic, the reference to the beating of servants counters what may be a
too-anodyne view of servitude in the sparse literature on servants in New
France. As at sea, no mutiny could be brooked in a remote post under
siege. The situation stands in contrast though, to nineteenth-century fur-

trade and seafaring accounts of brutal punishments, because the brutal administrator here seems to be a woman, not the 'man of the house' or a male overseer. Is this a variant of the occasional female warrior in New France, cases in which status took precedence over gender in an emergency need to defend a fort – and here to discipline underlings? We shall return to the theme of servants in chapter 6.

There were a number of other French colonial women besides Mesdames Fornel and Courtemanche who harvested the seas. Family operations may have been particularly characteristic of Labrador, for Versailles also proposed offering the Constantine family a supply contract there. In other maritime trade, a widow and an unmarried lady of the Pommereau family are cited in colonial correspondence between 1743 and 1747, noting a ship sailing out of Quebec with oil of the loup marine 'belonging to Widow Pommereau and coming from Labrador,' and receiving Crown bills of exchange for expenses relating to Ile Royale and the port of Rochefort. Françoise Boucher (widow Pommereau) was the daughter of a prominent early settler. She brought her husband into the business and then carried it on after his death.[6] Though we know less about them, Madame de Portneuf and Mlle Duchesné were two other parties compensated under an account for shipments of 'iron, tar and fish oil' shipped to Rochefort.[7] Thus, we can see that a number of women harvested the waters, some very actively.

Manufactures

In contrast to the custom in France and many other parts of Europe, small manufacturing in the colony was open to non-guild members. It was a relatively informal system, also involving less specialization. There was an element of unpredictability, with wide disparities in earnings. Much of the work involved women and children, which was natural when artisanal enterprises were conducted in small family dwellings. According to historian Jacques Mathieu, family systems of transmitting skills were quite important in Canada and some trades 'such as clothier, tailor, dressmaker, wigmaker and shoemaker ... butcher, baker, pastry maker and innkeeper, were in fact family enterprises in which the man, woman and children participated.'[8]

Most importantly, women made many of the fabrics and clothes worn by most of the population of that cold country. In Europe, women had been so integrally associated with the manufacture of cloth and clothing that the word *wife* derives from the word *weave*. 'Spinsters' are unmarried women, for those unburdened with children were freer to spend long hours at the wheel spinning yarn and thread. How deeply were *cana-diennes* involved? For an unregulated cottage industry that served both domestic and commercial needs it is difficult to estimate production. However, we can piece together some of the elements of the story. In the colony's early days in the 1670s and 1680s, as the *filles du roi* and their families were settling the land, a series of officials complained about their lack of skills and asked that weavers be sent over from France, and that schools for girls be encouraged to teach the arts of the needle such as spinning, weaving, sewing, and knitting. We know there were both male and female weavers during the French regime. Later, in the Lower Canada of 1833[9] it was reported there were thirteen thousand weavers in the colony, and that the majority of them were female. What trends characterized those decades between 1670 and 1833?

Certainly there was a real shortage of cloth at first, which led some colonists to wear buckskin and other hides. Early urban dwellers might select for daily wear the coarse drugget and other blends, or the dyed green jackets produced in Montreal by Agathe Saint-Père, or the cloth from a Quebec manufactory established in 1674 by Intendant Talon. Early production was probably rather limited, though. Members of the bourgeoisie were more likely to wear finer, imported cloth, typically of a dark hue, while nobles could exercise their prerogative to wear satin, brocade, and other richly coloured luxury fabrics. In the eighteenth century, the *habitant* population of the countryside was reported to dress up on Sundays in imported fabrics, which sometimes included lace, but on weekdays to revert to homespun. For society as a whole, French cloth remained a staple; indeed textiles for settlers and Amerindians were the single largest import item.[10]

Gradually, it is clear, families did learn to make apparel from scratch. In 1668 Marie de l'Incarnation reported that the Ursulines had been provided with supplies to teach both French and native students how to spin. We know that in the mid-1680s Governor Denonville said Canadian girls and women produced shirts and *capots* for the fur trade during the winter.[11] It was he who complained that their activity was limited by a shortage of cloth, and he urged further measures such as teaching *cana-diennes* to spin, to make hemp cloth and thread. He wanted the Sisters of the Congregation to distribute hemp seeds and hoped to oblige rural families to keep a few sheep. In a further call for hemp and flax farming a year later, he noted there was some production at Beaupré, which may have been under the sisters' tutelage.[12]

Cloth became more abundant after Agathe Saint-Père and the Sisters of the Congregation introduced instruction in weaving (to a workforce that included both sexes) early in the eighteenth century, providing Montrealers with much-needed *chemises* and *surtouts*. Not long afterwards, Madame de Vaudreuil reported that the inhabitants 'spin incessantly whatever fibres this land gives.' In 1737 Intendant Hocquart wrote of 'les habitans des campagnes' that 'plusieurs sont Tisserons, font de grosses toiles, et des Etoffes qu'ils appellent droguet' that they used to clothe themselves and their families. (Since he used the masculine form, we gather not all of them were female, but given the nuns' teaching of the skill we assume that some were.) Though a love of French cloth was said to induce people to buy it when they could afford it, many made do with the domestic product. Growth of the industry is indicated by the Crown purchase of over a thousand livres' worth of 'toile de Montreal' in 1747. Although soldiers' uniforms were often imported from France, some were fabricated in Montreal by the 1740s.[13] By that time, the majority of country dwellers were said to be using their own wool for homespun cloth and stockings. Clearly many colonial households produced their own fabrics for everyday wear.[14]

Did women have any connections with heavier kinds of manufacturing? Several had some involvement with the iron-forging operation at Trois-Rivières, mainly in the capacity of suppliers. Charlotte Le Boulanger married a forge partner, J-B Gastineau Duplessis. Colonial correspondence mentions her having possession of business books and papers that were left in her hands by her son-in-law, Pierre-François Olivier de Vezin, when he was a directing partner at the forges. Her alacrity to secure artillery recovered from a shipwreck suggests Madame Duplessis was no sleeping partner but seized the day. Another member of the family, Mademoiselle Duplessis, ran a store that supplied fodder and foodstuffs to the forges. The family stayed involved, for Intendant François Bigot later enforced a payment of nearly three thousand *livres* owing to Charlotte Duplessis for goods she had sold to ironworks employees. In her thirties, Thérèse de Couagne (Madame de Francheville) became a partner in this operation after her husband's 1733 death. She advanced loans and supplies to several merchants. It was Thérèse de Couagne's unhappy slave Marie-Angelique who set the fire that burned much of Montreal in 1734.[15] (Angelique was hanged for this deed, though her mistress went unpunished for *her* own form of outlawry, receiving smuggled goods from Albany.) Mademoiselle Cressy and Madame Mather were two others mentioned on forge payrolls. Though it never lived up to the high hopes for it, the colonial ironworks can be credited with supplying the stoves that kept eighteenth-century *habitant* houses warm.[16] We can see the operation lined some feminine pockets too.

Women also manufactured building materials from the local clays. Such activity expanded in the eighteenth century in response to devastating fires, which increased the demand for non-flammable urban housing. Madame Charlotte de Ramezay and her daughter Louise ran brick- and tile-making operations in Montreal.[17] Marie-Anne Barbel, whose Labrador activities we have already discussed, had a pottery operation in Quebec that employed three men. They made a product good enough to be mistaken for the French one, which was in short supply during wartime in the 1740s.

Convents too were centres of light manufacturing. Along with crafts of various kinds and shirts for the fur trade, they supplied other products. When the Montreal Hôtel-Dieu burned down in 1734, not only did it lose heavy equipment in the bakery and laundry. Also going up in the flames was a shoemaking shop full of six hundred pairs of shoes worth four *livres* a pair, as well as all the tools for making them.[18] Sisters with pharmaceutical training made remedies not just for their patients but for sale outside the hospitals, being shipped as far away as Forts Chambly, Frontenac, Niagara, and Detroit. Certified by Dr Sarrazin, some were also sent to country priests to distribute to needy habitants.[19] The Grey sisters in Montreal at various times ran a brewery on their site, made military uniforms and tents, produced attractive items for the fur trade, retailed tobacco and lime, and ran a printing operation. These supplemented more conventional sisterly manufactures such as church statuary, communion bread, candles, artificial flowers, and fine sewing and gilding.[20] The sisters worked with the unwed mothers, sex-trade workers, orphans, and disabled and elderly folks within their walls to produce this array of consumer goods.

Forest Products

The looming forests, so daunting to settlers who had to clear them to start a farm, were also alive with possibilities. It was presumably native women who manufactured some or all of the first winter gear for which Governor Courcelles billed the Crown in 1666: a large order of 4,500 *livres'* worth of wilderness footwear, mittens, and other necessities for his soldiers and the people of the country, plus 1,500 *livres'* worth of bark canoes used in the King's service.[21] Catherine Jérémie, whose male relatives worked as Chicoutimi and Tadoussac fur-trade clerks and interpreters, had a sister-in-law who was Montagnais, probably facilitating Jérémie's long study of the secrets of Amerindian medicine. She had mothered ten children and reached the ripe age of seventy-six by the time her knowledge of naturopathy brought her to the attention of Intendant Hocquart. He shipped off to Versailles, along with her instructions on how to transplant them, a parcel of herbs and roots she had collected to brew up for sufferers of bloody flux, childbirth pains, and other maladies.[22] A forest root valued in China was ginseng, and the Desauniers sisters, who are better known for their illegal fur-trading, developed a process for curing this plant.[23] The forest also furnished dyewoods that were used by Agathe Saint-Père as a cheap way of tanning deerskins since no oil was required, helping make those garments (worn beneath a coarse *surtout*) common in Montreal at the beginning of the eighteenth century. Grasses, rushes, porcupine quills, and wood were used to fabricate all sorts of items, including the boxes and birchbark baskets that Indian women crafted, and the carved boxes and statues that convents produced for sale. Did women perhaps also manufacture the wooden utensils mentioned by Peter Kalm as being packed, along with wheat and peas, into holds of ships outbound from Quebec to the West Indies?[24]

Dwarfing all such smallwares were the enormous timbers felled and milled for the shipyards at Quebec, Rouen, and other ports. Prominent here was the family left in debt by the death of its patriarch, the Montreal Governor Claude de Ramezay. He left a mainly female clan behind to mourn. The widow Charlotte and later her daughter Louise stepped up to join the few entrepreneurs willing to ship masts and boards of oak and pine. It was initially a matter of trial and error for all concerned. The story of this family will unfold in our later chapters. Suffice it here to say that *Veuve* Ramezay led an operation filled with error, while her daughter fared better. Others ventured into the timber business too. Geneviève de Chavigny was given a Cap-Saint-Ignace fief by Intendant Jean Talon in recognition of services to the Jesuits by her husband, trader/guide Charles Amiot. She received permission to harvest the oaks there for house and boat construction.[25] Widow Baron de Lupien, mother of ten, entered the business for just a year, completing delivery on her husband's contract to cut and deliver Lake Champlain oak and other timbers to the Quebec shipyards after he died on the job. She received 34,000 *livres* for it,[26] probably mostly going to cover expenses. Others were in it for the long haul. Marie-Anne Hazeur, an orphan schooled by the Ursulines, at age twenty married the fifty-three-year-old physician Michel Sarrazin. The death of that well-regarded but ill-paid physician left his family struggling. During a long widowhood, Marie-Anne and her daughter sold spruce from their St Foy property for construction of Crown ships such as the *Castor* and the *Martre*.[27]

There were other players, large and small. In 1743, Madame Duberon pocketed 767 *livres* for furnishing wood for shipbuilding, and over the next few years drew several thousand more in connection with Quebec fortifications and other war-related expenses. Marguerite Saint-Ours Deschaillons, daughter of Agathe Saint-Père, besides looking after the business affairs of her husband posted in the west, had eastern interests too. She received 1800 *livres* from Crown accounts for construction and wood purchases, and supplied food rations for four different ships in 1747. Demoiselle Sabrevois and another lady were paid for wood made into rafts. Madame Desrusseaux was paid for wood taken from her land and made into rafts of timber specifically allocated for construction of the flute *Caribou*. Alongside bigger suppliers were petty ones, such as Dames Portneuf, Youville, and Marguerite Dupuy, and widow Françoise Lamoureux who sold wood in loads valued between fifty and seven hundred *livres*.[28]

An astonishing number of women appeared on Crown payrolls in connection with the shipyards established by Intendant Hocquart in the late 1730s. Some, such as Mademoiselle Bayeul in 1747, were compensated under the Construction and Wood Purchases account. But all manner of merchandise – wood, iron, nails, pots of water, cabbage, onions – was supplied, often by widows such as *Veuves* Lajus, Lagrois, Julienne Larche (whose husband had been a meat merchant), and by the Pommereaus (who further profited by renting out a room to a Crown employee). Among others providing housing for shipbuilders or for crews were Widow Lefebvre, Madame Girard, Madame Gouze, and Madame Duplessis, the last renting out two houses to the crew of *Le Martre* at fifty livres a month. Madam Langloiserie, Marie Charlotte Palin, Marie Paquet, and Marie Pement were other suppliers.[29]

Some of these women received bills of exchange, sometimes amounting to more than two thousand *livres*, for various (sometimes unspecified) services in connection with construction of ships such as renting here a room, there a stove to heat the construction office, or for supplying various ships' furnishings. Mesdames Berthier, Des Anges, and de la Richardière, and Mademoiselles de Sabrevois and Gouze were among their number. In the King's domain, entrepreneur Marie-Anne Barbel (whom we have met before) collected 2,000 *livres* for construction of vessels and provided the Crown with construction supplies and rental houses. Widows Cureux and Rampeau also received payment in connection with vessels at ports in 'King's Domaine, Acadia or Rochefort.' Also involved was Madame du Meloizes, a down-at-the-heels noblewoman from the Lotbinière family whose husband's roofing tile business had failed but whose daughter would soon revive the family fortunes by becoming mistress of Intendant Bigot. Marie Madeleine Duret, Marie Cluzeau, and Madame Jean Pierre were paid for '*façons d'ouvrages et blanchissage*' such as the twenty-one pairs of drapes and thirty coverlets laundered by the last-named for thirty-three *livres*. Marie La Garenne was a seamstress, perhaps of sails, coverlets, or workers' or mariners' clothing. Widow Raymond made several deliveries, including fourteen pieces of white rope or rigging for the *St Laurent*.[30] Marie Paquet, Marie Pement, and Julienne Larche nursed laid-up workers at the Hôtel-Dieu while Madame de Villeray watched over a field hospital set up for them in a private house.

Surprisingly, even nuns at the Hôtel-Dieu earned money from the naval yards. Year after year in the 1740s the convent appeared in the Crown accounts, for it supplied both food and medicine to workers there. The Hôtel-Dieu and Hôpital Général both were repaid for meals to ill or injured carpenters or seamen in their wards. But Hôtel-Dieu shipments of onions, shallots, garlic, lettuce, parsley, and other herbs for crews and shipyard workers seem to have been sold in lots, perhaps going either to workmen in their quarters or down into the holds of ships. Was there a similar destination for the thirteen different syrups and other remedies that were supplied by Madame de Ste Jean, apothecary of the Hôtel-Dieu, all in a single lot on 31 July 1745? While it was not unknown for sisters to go in person to field hospitals in wartime, it was probably convent servants who carried supplies to the men's quarters and to the ships.[31]

Provisioning the Crown

One of the leading industries of New France, as the historian W.J. Eccles pointed out, was war. For approximately a century of its century-and-a-half existence, the colony was embroiled in conflicts with the Iroquois, the Foxes, and other First Nations, as well as with the English. Certainly as the two great rival empires squared off in the eighteenth century, France began to pour massive amounts into military spending, escalating from the time of the 1744–8 War of the Austrian Succession until France's definitive North American defeat in 1759–60. Ten French ships annually plying the Atlantic to Quebec towards the beginning of the eighteenth century tripled towards the end of the regime.[32] Even in earlier times, wealthy Montrealers such as Widow Lemoine and Madame Perrot had contributed food and supplies for seventeenth-century Iroquois envoys; later, Madame You de Découvert and her husband had outfitted military detachments.[33] Suzanne Francoeur and Marie Compin (and likely many others) sewed and laundered for Crown storehouses well before the war began again in the 1740s.[34] When it did, the swelling Crown expenditures were allocated to a multitude of modest suppliers in a colony where there were few large companies. People who provisioned the fur trade in peacetime also looked to the Crown for alternatives when war paralysed trade.[35]

The officer class stood at the head of the line. Some noblewomen simply stepped into the shoes of husbands. As one leading merchant noted in 1744 at the outbreak of the War of the Austrian Succession, with the call-up of men to the front, many officers were transferring powers of attorney to their wives.[36] As in every ancien régime society, largesse flowed to the King's 'family,' the nobles. It became Crown policy to favour the widows and wives of military officers, both to boost morale and to compensate for military salaries (as we discuss in a later chapter) that failed to maintain officers' families in a manner considered fitting. One widow, Madame Philibert, who supplied bread at a steep price to colonial troops and seamen was being paid to keep quiet because a nobleman of the Repentigny clan had killed her spouse during a dispute about rent.[37]

Women of all ranks became cogs in a war machine that spread from the colony to its hinterland. Crown accounts of the 1740s listed them in connection with food and munitions supplied to the Quebec storehouse 'on the occasion of war' and supplies for the fortifications being built there. Others relate to goods or food delivered to Amerindian allies further afield. Dozens of women, many of them female relatives of officers, earned money in this way, amounts that ranged from a mere 124 *livres* up to 7,000. Recipients included Mademoiselles Beyeul, Manon Desauniers, Lestage, and de Ramezay; Mesdames Berthier, Cailleteau, De Cerry, De Lino, Des Plaines, Leuron, Lusignan, Nicolet, and Tapin; Widows Baby, Delaurier, Lafontaine, Petel, and Raymond. Alongside their flourishing trade in English contraband with the natives, the Desauniers sisters were food provisioners to French troops and to passing war parties around Montreal during the War of the Austrian Succession.[38] Several other suppliers of food were also on the payroll. In another line of work, 'she named Duval' and others pocketed some pay for washing the clothes of sick soldiers.

The war machine required uniforms, trade goods, tents. At Montreal, a seamstress Geneviève LaTerreur collected nearly 1,200 *livres* in the last four months of 1745, Marie Coupin a tenth of that. Marie Daneau sewed thirteen tents for 156 *livres*. Marianne Metivier made fifty-seven *capots* and twenty-five *capots galonnés* for 160 *livres*. Josette Metivier and Thérèse Dyon sewed culottes for troops and other items for Crown stores.[39] Dame Poulier sewed 139 trade shirts for 52 *livres*. Dame DeNoyelles earned 230 by furnishing the following:

Seven soldiers' short jackets
Seven breeches
Seven pairs of stockings
Seven hats
Fourteen neckties
Fourteen shirts
Thirteen pairs of shoes

We have seen that the Montreal Hôpital Général furnished military garb too. Clearly some proportion of the thousands of pieces of military and trade clothing in Crown storehouses came from the hands of *canadiennes*.

Traders also arranged deliveries to the *pays d'en haut*. Julienne Larche, for example, who was supplying the vessels *Rubis* and *Caribou* at Quebec in 1741–4, was by 1745 furnishing livestock, a canoe, and snowshoes to commanders at Fort St Joseph, a fort that was also provisioned by Marie-Madeleine de Colon de Villiers. Marie Louise Lefaivre gave service in the upper country 'on the occasion of movement of natives.'[40] Some, such as Madame Baby, are known to have provisioned the trade from Montreal. She, as well as Mariane Lafayette and Widow Magnon sent goods such as porcelain war collars, red copper kettles, and vermillion, as well as glass, and, for some reason, paper cornets. The several varieties of cloth (1,200 *livres'* worth) that Widow L'Espérance supplied perhaps also went to the western trade.[41]

A lingering question is the extent to which provisioning represented teamwork of wives and husbands. Intendant Hocquart wrote in 1737 that 'many wives of businessmen govern their husband's business affairs,' which he moralistically attributed to men of the business and officer classes being attracted by gaming and other amusements.[42] But as we have seen, wives were not the only females to labour for Crown cash. The accounts list convents providing miscellaneous supplies. In addition to those we have already mentioned, nuns prepared 820 meals for 'salt smugglers and other prisoners' in the last half of 1740 and fancy work such as a decorated chasuble for which Sister Sainte-Agnes received 117 *livres*. Wartime also meant a spike in payments to religious orders for the rations of hospitalized soldiers and aboriginal allies alike.[43] Single laywomen were involved too. It would seem what was true of female income-earners in London around 1700 was also true for the colony: 'There seems to have been no objection to women working – quite the contrary.'[44]

Living on the Land

Everywhere one saw wives, widows, and single women working that most plentiful of all natural resources, *la terre*. This basic commodity in an agrarian society was subject to the laws of inheritance, commonly part of the community of goods and dower that fell to widows, and the chief legacy to be divided up among children. It was normal for widows to make use of family assets. Josette Brun indicated that in the towns of Louisbourg and Quebec, widows frequently stepped into the shoes of the deceased in 'certain professional activities' including whaling rights, forging, tanning, and providing fuel or construction materials for forts and lighthouses, and we have now added other activities to the list.[45] In the country, where so many families eked out a very modest living, wives with husbands away and widows with underage children often had little choice but to keep the farm running, resulting in many female-headed farms.

In this society that drained many men away for war or trade, wives with absent husbands were numerous, the phenomenon being particularly prominent in the seventeenth century. An official dispatch of 1679 observed women and children farming and tending livestock, and attributed it to the absence of five to six hundred *coureurs de bois*. Within two years the figure shot up to 'eight hundred or more,' and it was noted at the time that this made it difficult to make an accurate census.[46] Early in the eighteenth century a Montreal governor claimed there were four hundred such men in the Ottawa country alone.[47] There was also a disproportionate number of single women, which was noted from the second decade of the eighteenth century onward. In 1717 the governor and intendant noted the shortage of nubile men, and the Marine Council discussed the problem of two to three thousand more girls than boys, due to 'boys who go to war, to the woods and the fisheries.'[48] Around the same time Bishop Saint-Vallier specified there were twice as many marriageable women as men in the colony, since many of the latter went to war, the forests, or the fisheries and did not return, leaving between two and three thousand surplus young women in the colony, three hundred of them concentrated at Montreal. Three decades later Peter Kalm reported, 'All agree here that the men are much less numerous in Canada than the women, for the men die on their voyages.'[49]

Although men who went away for a trading season or military campaign may have been counted in colonial censuses, that did not mean they were around. An influx of young single women from the country into town[50] may reflect this lack of rural marriage partners. With or without men at their side, women farmed. The upper ranks managed seigneuries and participated in buying, selling, and developing both rural and urban lands. *Habitant* women tilled the fields and raised, processed, or manufactured a variety of consumer goods that found their way to markets.[51]

Let us look first at examples of major landowners and developers. Just as in the English colonies, the precarious conditions and limited population of the seventeenth century often left wealthy widows in control of estates. In New France this reached a remarkable extent. On seigneuries belonging to individuals in New France, in 1663 there were sixty-two lay seigneurs. Eleven of those were women, and they held slightly more land than did the forty-one male seigneurs combined.[52] Included in their number was Barbe de Boullougne, widow of Governor Louis D'Ailleboust. Thwarted in her attempts to become an Ursuline nun, she spent seven years administering the seigneurie of Coulonge as well as *arrière-fiefs* at Beaupré and Lauzon, distributing land to *censitaires*. Generally conducting business herself rather than through an agent, she oversaw operations more actively than her husband had done.[53] Particularly among the officer class, as we shall see in our next chapter, it was common enough, being (as Peter Moogk wrote) 'a task some ... officers left to their wives.'[54]

When officers were away on summer campaigns, off to command a frontier fort, or killed in action, wives and widows had to be ready to do whatever needed doing. We will cite just a few examples that emerged in official correspondence: Madame de Gaspé and Demoiselle Legardeur ratified new concessions, Marie Couillard (Madame de la Rivière) sold a piece of land, while Madame D'Ailleboust D'Argenteuil petitioned to expand her holdings. Marie Angelique Chartier de Lotbinière (*Veuve* Renaud d'Avène Des Meloizes) asked support for her plan to open a village in Neuville seigneurie. Madame Pean was reported exporting flour from her seigneurie even as the hungry colony was collapsing in 1759–60.[55] Future scholarly investigation of women as landowners that makes a thorough examination of notarial records will certainly produce a long list of transactions.

Some active seigneuresses carried their interest in land development far beyond their own seigneurie. Entrepreneurial wives such as Agathe Saint-Père and Marie-Madeleine Roberge, for example, were involved in varied exchanges with a long list of individuals.[56] Preferring to focus her energies on shipping what the land produced, *Veuve* La Roche was among those paid by the intendant for transporting wheat, flour, and peas into Quebec City to feed troops and civilians in the 1740s.[57] Thérèse de Couagne, as wife and then young widow, supervised workers, inspected crops and farm animals at her Saint-Michel farm, and funnelled crops into the fur trade.

Systematic analysis of such women has been initiated by the historian Benoit Grenier. In a study that identified twenty-nine widowed seigneuresses in pre- and post-Conquest decades, he was able to find evidence of fifteen who handed business concerns over to a male, and nine who conducted estate business themselves. Most commonly these latter had underage children, but a few persisted after their sons came of age. Marie Catherine Peuvret Duchesnay, for example, granted many concessions at Beauport, hired workers, collected receivables, and conducted court battles to defend her interests.[58]

Everywhere, in a colony where 80 per cent lived on the land, one saw women working in the fields. As early as 1679–80 Intendant Duchesnay had complained that the hundreds of men who would be the most capable farmers were leaving it to their wives and children to cultivate the land and livestock while they headed into the woods. Certainly when the men were home, they turned their efforts to the heaviest work of clearing, plowing, and reaping. The women could then spend more time on their traditional charge of vegetable gardening, dairying, poultry, soap- and candle-making, butchering, manufacture of cloth and clothing, and baking in the outdoor oven. If the wheat crop failed, the family fell back for survival on milk from the wife's cow, her marketable pork, butter, and eggs. The peas from her garden brought in cash as one of the more reliable exports to Louisbourg. In a good year, any of these activities might produce a surplus for barter or sale.[59] Even as the eighteenth-century fur trade moved further from the settlements and become more the preserve of professional traders than *habitant* husbands, men did not start monopolizing the outdoor farmwork. It was towards the end of the regime that Kalm observed how women, inured to hard labour, were a regular fixture in the fields, meadows, and stables, not spurning any sort of work.

Even taking the veil in a cloistered religious order did not guarantee an indoor life. As we shall see in chapter 7, a mother superior might go in person to inspect her convent's seigneurial lands. Members of religious orders worked the fields, supplying convent needs and selling the citizenry comestibles such as baked goods and meals for prisoners and shipyard workers. Religious women had farmed right from the start. Montreal's first governor described giving Marguerite Bourgeoys 'various land concessions which she had cleared at her own expense and had a farm established and supplied the necessary cattle.' Her young colleague Sister Marie Barbier toiled away herding, dairying, and hauling grain to the miller. By 1681 the Congregation of Notre Dame had 150 cultivated *arpents* and nearly two dozen cattle, plus sheep and horses,[60] employing thirteen men to help them. Productive lands supplied various orders with wood, grain, produce, and meat. Every convent had holdings. When Intendant Champigny visited the Ursuline convent at Trois-Rivières in 1701, he described the farm under supervision of the seven choir sisters and one lay sister. Wooden fences enclosed sixty-five *arpents* around the convent, with a garden, stone bakery, and stables, and a wooden barn containing several hundred *minots* of wheat, peas, and oats. In the courtyard grazed a horse, nine cattle, fifteen sheep, and some pigs, and a lower courtyard teemed with poultry.

These operations produced revenues for decades. In lean years convents might secure the bishop's permission to leave cloister to do the fieldwork, since they could not afford to hire anyone; in better ones they employed farmhands.[61] The Congregation of Notre Dame eventually operated three farms in the Montreal area (at Verdun, Pointe Saint-Charles, and Saint-Martin), hiring fifteen labourers and producing 700–800 *minots* of grain a year. The Montreal Hôtel-Dieu annalist reported that the 'most vigorous of our nuns have many times been ... to gather hay ... and to thrash the grain during the harvests, in the blazing sun.'[62] Their seigneurie doubtless provided some or all of the 600 *minots* of wheat, 180 of oats, 12 of barley, and other staples stocking the Hôtel-Dieu granary in 1734.[63] After Mother de Youville and her followers took charge of Montreal's hospice in the 1740s, they generated income by renting out pasturage and selling apples and cider. In 1751 they could count twenty-four steers, twenty-four cows, four horses, forty-nine sheep, and nine pigs. They increased their revenue by stabling other peoples' livestock and lending out their own animals. This sizeable operation by 1758 had twenty-two men (often ex-patients) working at their farms at Chambly and Point Saint-Charles; they would add the seigneurie of Chateauguay to their holdings shortly after the Conquest.[64]

Further east around Quebec, the Hôpital Général oversaw three seigneuries and numerous farm animals, while the Hôtel-Dieu harvested enough hay to sell surpluses to the army in wartime.[65] When a growing populace created a housing squeeze, the authorities looked covetously at properties such as the Hôtel-Dieu's fourteen rental lots near the fortifications, fuming that 'the greater part of Quebec lots belong to religious orders' and that their walled gardens full of herbs and legumes were obstructing urban growth and circulation.[66]

Cloistered or lay, married or single, many women garnered revenues from the land at their feet. As in France, men, women, and children sometimes worked together in the fields at haying and harvest time, sometimes separated for more gender- or age-specific tasks. Everyone was expected to contribute, even children being conscripted to mind younger siblings as well as livestock. With men absent on travels for trade or war – phenomenon officials frequently noted – the pre-industrial reliance on the family may have been heightened in Canada, just as it was in certain districts of France such as Auvergne, where the men took to the road in search of work. Intendant Hocquart was impressed by the disposition Canadian women had for business, mentioning that in 'nearly all ranks' they showed wit, adding that men in the countryside concluded 'nothing of consequence' without consulting their wives.[67] Our examples of both elite and ordinary women show they found ways to insert themselves in the cycle of economic production and exchange, and that they did so to an extent that people arriving from Europe found noteworthy. Intendant Hocquart, by singling out this phenomenon and explicitly noting how it crossed the class spectrum, offered some support for the difficult-to-prove proposition that female bargainers may have been more prevalent than in France itself, where regional differences were endlessly complex. As we shall see in our next chapter, colonists had the benefit of the particular code of French law (Parisian) most likely to facilitate female access to family assets.

To perceive the situation accurately, one must move beyond anachronistic dichotomies of 'homemakers' and 'businesswomen.' There *were* some of the latter, especially among widows such as Mesdames Pascaud and Fornel, among single women such as Louise de Ramezay and the Desauniers sisters. In general though, in pre-industrial societies work patterns tended to be fragmented for both sexes, and particularly for women. Multi-tasking was common where home and workplace were one and the same, and households often contained children old enough to care for younger siblings, freeing mothers for remunerative activity. The fragmentation in early modern Europe was characterized quite categorically by historian Judith Bennett, who believed that 'no matter what the actual occupations of women, they tended to work in low skilled, low status, low paid jobs, and they also tended to be intermittent workers, jumping from job to job or juggling several tasks at once.' Historian Alice Clark cast this in the more positive light, suggesting, 'Owing to the greater complexity of a woman's life her productive capacity must be classified on different lines from those which are generally followed in dealing with the economic life of men.'[68]

The result? Our evidence suggests that much more commonly than one encounters the Pascauds and Desauniers, one finds petty or occasional traders, who were most often married with children. If only the occasional colonial wife headed west or ran a store, most produced something that found its way to market. They did their part to earn a little cash, selling a little wood that came to hand, delivering a cartload of clean regimental laundry, bringing onions or pots of drinking water to men at the shipyards, offering the peas in the garden to an itinerant merchant. Those were the rhythms of everyday life. Were we to carry the model forward in time, we could note that remunerated work characterizes mothers in contemporary post-industrial societies, just as it did in pre-industrial economies. It became *less* prevalent at times and places where an ideology of female sequestration combined with sufficient affluence to induce married women to withdraw from market activity, or at least to perform any such activity (as nineteenth-century Montreal pieceworkers did) within the hidden recesses of the home. In New France, they were more visible. They collected, grew, or manufactured goods, and they were at work on shorelines and farms, in artisanal shops, in convent gardens and workrooms too. They show up in records of travellers and notaries, and in the financial records of the Crown. Regularly, and quite visibly, women across the class spectrum produced and marketed goods. Women, like men, were breadwinners in early Canada.

Conclusion

In a colony where the vast majority lived in the countryside, men, women, and children spent much of their lives outdoors, absorbed in the endless routines of feeding livestock, sowing and reaping crops, travelling in open boats on rivers, and by cart, carriage, horseback, or foot across the land. All had to seek shelter, of course, against the ice and snow that set in as early as November and did not vanish until April, when the river would thaw at last. Those involved in trade might spend the winter months socializing around the fire with kin or trading partners, sewing trade goods, preparing bundles of cargo, or working over the ledger books, turning to rock the cradle if a whimper arose. Then, when spring arrived and the rivers and streams once again ran their sparkling courses, the colony came to life like an anthill. The populace began the outdoor work of gathering, processing, selling, and shipping the natural resources of fish, marine oils, timber, earthenware, fibres, and foodstuffs produced on farms or culled from waters and forests. All this did not involve just a few exceptional women, nor was it a slightly larger 'network' that clung together for mutual support. As in France, economic production and exchange was common to both religious and laywomen of all classes. In a later chapter, we turn to look more closely at noblewomen who were proud to be involved in such production, oblivious to the stigma that was beginning to attach to female commerce in more 'advanced' parts of the eighteenth-century world. Supporting the family was the ordinary business of men and of women too, still happily oblivious to Rousseau's bugle call to retreat into the bastion of nursery and kitchen.

PART THREE

Transatlantic Codes

Chapter Five

Comparing Laws of Property

To understand the economic agency of French-Canadian women that looms so large in this book, it is important to take a little time to comprehend one source of such agency: their position before the law. It is time to examine a few key issues that affected women who wanted to manufacture shirts for sale, send fur-trade goods westward, or ship timber across the Atlantic. Could only women without husbands legitimately do these things, since married women in so many legal jurisdictions had little legal authority? To what extent could *any* woman control property? If a creditor defaulted on a female merchant, could she go to court for redress? In discussing law, we must underscore the limitations of the subject as well as its importance. As Louise Dechene pointed out, the law lay rather lightly on members of the nobility. There was a curious vagueness in inventories of their property, as if officials wished not to pry too closely into their affairs.[1] At the other end of the spectrum, the popular classes had a tendency to conduct transactions informally, having no interest in depleting their meagre resources to pay a notary.[2] Casting the net still wider, we find that it was not only those at the top and the bottom of society upon whom the law could weigh lightly. Many persons of all ranks, male and female, operated outside the law in the colony's leading export activity, since fur-trade transactions 'under the table' may at times have surpassed duly recorded legal trade.[3] And yet, despite all the ways people scuttled out from under the letter of the law, its provisions regarding property remain a matter of considerable importance. In societies where family farms were the primary source of livelihood, inheritance systems affected the population more extensively than they do today, and were no small matter for the 70 to 90 per cent of French Canadians who lived in the countryside during the two centuries we discuss in this book.

Because Canada's laws can be appreciated only in context, this chapter begins by sketching the evolution of women's right to property under common law in Britain and America and under civil law in France. Thereafter it turns to legal customs in New France, which were to persist under British rule well into the nineteenth century. Transnational comparisons help us place the colony in perspective. All of the legal codes discussed here assigned more privileges to men than to women (discrimination that remained common until the second half of the twentieth century). Equality was simply not on the table. The significant variations lay in the *degree* of male privilege and female incapacity. Comparing legal systems will lay the groundwork for this book's closing discussion of the post-Conquest period, when Canada would manage to dodge, for a while, some of the gendered legal restrictions when their grip tightened in the other jurisdictions. After a brief *tour d'horizon* of transatlantic legal developments, our discussion will shift to Canadian legal practice.

Evolution of Female Property Rights in Other Jurisdictions: England and America

Customary property rights began shrinking for women in both England and America during the course of the seventeenth century. Scholarship by Susan Staves, Eileen Spring, and Amy Erickson presented a battery of evidence that English widows after 1600 became less apt to control substantial property (assuring that medieval widows who endowed five of the colleges of Oxford and Cambridge were a thing of the past). The goal, scholars believe, was not so much to impoverish widows as to curtail their independence. Many men used their growing discretionary powers to provide for their spouses quite fairly. However, as has often been observed, one must assess the quality of laws not by the behaviour of good men but of bad ones. During the seventeenth century, the latter got a freer hand. As the authors of a text on women in early modern England summed it up, 'Changes in legislation ... caused the widow's financial position to deteriorate to the advantage of the male heir.... By the later seventeenth century, there are many examples of fathers and sons acting in collusion to break settlements.' More generally, 'the legal situation of the majority of women underwent serious erosion in early modern England.'[4] Their contingent legal status, combined with value systems that made a husband's business the priority, deprived female-run ventures of capital.

The erosion occurred on many fronts. Widows' traditional right to one-third of their husbands' estates after creditors were paid was weakened by an act passed in 1670. In large landowning families the right of a widow to one-third was replaced by a provision determined before marriage, generally for less. Androcentric 'rationalization' of the legal system made the law more recondite and lawsuits more expensive, making it less likely women would understand and claim entitlements. Many different ways to bar dower were devised, too. Prescriptive literature of the day condemned or ignored ways that brides might keep control of assets. 'Widows and women abandoned by their husbands in England were among the least protected in the world,' Amy Erickson writes, 'let alone in Europe, where a restitution of dowry was legally required.'[5] Other traditional protections faltered as ecclesiastical and manorial courts, which once heard a large proportion of female litigants, declined in importance. The custom in London and some other towns of dividing up one-third of the estate among children of both sexes gradually fell by the wayside too. Wives became less apt to be executors of husbands' wills, which suggests less shared financial responsibility during marriages. Husbands' testamentary freedom also rose markedly in the latter half of the seventeenth century. What drove these trends? Some have pointed to a conservative backlash following restoration of the monarchy, others to 'the overt identification of the individual with the male individual in contemporary political and property theory.'[6] In any case, scholarship at the turn of the twenty-first century seemed to support Alice Clark's 1919 judgment that seventeenth-century changes 'deprived married women and children of the property rights which customs had hitherto secured to them.'

American trends followed those in England. Elaine Foreman Crane found evidence of growing legal constraints as the colonial period progressed. In the first decades of settlement in Massachusetts, some widows retained more than their one-third right to realty (indeed sometimes the whole property), and there was extralegal buying and selling of property by wives and widows. As time went on though, courts sought to regularize these sales, placing them after 1692 under control of male trustees. Increasingly they put creditors' demands ahead of widows' claims. Such developments stripped Massachusetts women of independence they had possessed in the settlement's early decades.[7]

Studies of inheritance patterns by Marylynn Salmon, Carole Shammas, and Michel Dahlin further documented such erosion. 'American primogeniture, the testamentary freedom to will property outside of the lineage, and married women's lack of property rights ... [were] among the biggest surprises encountered by immigrants from Europe,' they observed.[8] Inheritance rights among Englishwomen in America compared unfavourably to those of Dutch, German, and Spanish neighbours in the middle colonies and the southwest. Anglo-American widows typically received one-third of real estate and sometimes one-third of other possessions as well, but had no power to sell them. Probably a majority of property was transferred by wills, in which men tended to be more generous than dower stipulated, but often with provisos: a widow would lose her inheritance if she remarried, when a child reached majority, or some other circumstance decreed by the husband. Her legal status became more and more contingent. There was a growing tendency to exclude widows as executors and to lessen daughters' shares. Widows were a notoriously impoverished group in colonial society, and 'the main beneficiaries of the economies practiced on widows were male heirs.'[9] The scholarship seems to justify the conclusion that between 1600 and 1800 common law in England and America grew more restrictive towards women's rights to property.

France

French law was more effective than the common law of England and America in protecting female claims to property. Partible inheritance systems (which divide the property among the children rather than favouring one heir) and the general absence of primogeniture among commoners encouraged more equitable division of family assets among children of both sexes. Across much of France, various legal codes also created a marital 'community of property' and placed safeguards on wifely property and dower (including entitlement to a portion of a husband's premarital real estate) that were missing in English marital regimes. A common concern of customary codes was protecting lineage property for blood kin through rules of succession that greatly restricted testamentary freedom. A dearth of scholarship on the evolution of women's legal position under the ancien régime hinders generalizations about French law, which was nearly as diverse as the distinctive peasant costumes that varied from village to village.[10] Customary codes of the north contrasted with written, or statutory, Roman-based law used mainly in the south. Espousing 'simple equality' among heirs was the code used in Paris and Ile-de-France, as well as those in Brittany, Anjou, Poitou, and much of western France – regions that sent many immigrants to Canada.[11] Less protected were females in Normandy and in some Roman-law areas such as Languedoc, where 'women could be virtually servants.'[12]

None of the codes created equality between man and wife. French wives always suffered some degree of legal incapacity, just as English ones did.[13] In general the husband was legally entitled to manage the family finances, decide the place of residence, and determine how the children would be raised. The wife could not make contracts or appear in court without his permission, though she did have certain legal remedies against a husband's mismanagement, notably a separation of goods. Still, wifely legal incapacity, Barbara Diefendorf writes, was 'so thoroughly implanted in *ancien régime* France that the husband's permission for the alienation of his wife's property was almost always included in legal contracts, even in cases where it might not have been technically required.'[14]

Studies that try to bridge 'the considerable distance between the theory of law and the common practice' have shown wives exercising what Diefendorf calls 'a significantly greater measure of responsibility, autonomy and equality within the family than has generally been assumed.'[15] Ongoing research into local practices continues to address the mystery James Traer identified, that 'although the customary law of northern France permitted some kind of inequality of succession rights among non-noble children it is unclear whether significant numbers of parents sought to use the option to favour one child above others.'[16] Julie Hardwick's study of notarial families in Nantes found that 'imperatives of Breton customary law and practice in many ways countered the power of fathers and husbands over their children and wives, power that the royal decrees of 1530–1630 so increased … customary law, rather, fostered … kin consultation and strict partibility.'[17] Hardwick found that dowries and movables for daughters matched the costs of establishing sons, that the 'roughly equal treatment of children, boys and girls alike … is striking'[18] and contrasts with nineteenth-century practice there. A study of Dauphinée commoners' wills similarly did 'not suggest that daughters were in any way "sacrificed" in order to preserve the family's greatest wealth for its sons.'[19]

Survivor rights were very important, since at least a quarter of spouses in eighteenth-century France died less than fifteen years after the wedding day.[20] In statutory law regions the widow was entitled to return of her dowry, plus an additional *augment*.[21] The most egalitarian of the customary codes was that of Paris, the one that was applied in New France. It entitled the widow to a return of her lineage properties. She received lifetime use of half of the properties of the marital community (in contrast to one-third under some other codes). She also could claim lifetime usage of certain lineage properties of her husband. Customary dower rights continued after remarriage, though adultery or debauchery could jeopardize them.[22] The *préciput* entitled the widow to withdraw certain goods and capital before the estate was parcelled. These provisions combined to make widows in France considerably better protected under the Custom of Paris than they were even in the late twentieth century.[23]

Though we await further scholarship, the positive tenor of these assessments suggests that any deterioration of women's property rights was less dramatic than that seen in English law after 1600.[24] Diefendorf believes that change – positive *or* negative – was not the hallmark of the French system, that 'family practices did not change dramatically between the sixteenth century and the end of the *ancien régime* ... there is a rather remarkable continuity throughout the period.' Apparently the legal status of French women experienced no sharp decline between 1600 and 1789 comparable to that across the Channel.

After 1789, changes came with dizzying speed, and there were a few positive measures. Modifications in the law of succession did guarantee daughters equality of inheritance with sons and male relatives, and divorce became freer. On the other hand, Revolutionary tampering with widows' rights to family assets plunged a number of widows into distress.[25]

Just after 1800, the Code Napoleon of 1804 represented a backward step for women. James Traer concludes, 'Napoleon favoured subordination of wife and children to the authority of the head of the family ... and obtained this goal.'[26] Although the law continued to favour significant legacies for unmarried daughters, other opportunities, new and old, tended to shrivel. The code devised a double standard for divorce, permitting wifely action only if a man housed his mistress under the family roof. A husband's consent was required, even for an independent businesswoman or separated wife, to represent herself in court. Fathers re-acquired unchecked power over a child's person and property until age twenty-one. Widows' protections became discretionary entries in marriage contracts. Napoleonic principles would eventually be incorporated into the reformed Civil Code of 1866 in Lower Canada, bringing its retrograde traditions to the St Lawrence in an echo effect more than a half-century later.

More than one commentator has seen the changing legal order in Europe negatively. Wally Seccombe took a long view across the centuries and noted the way economic and legal change conspired to erode the status of widows: 'The situation of older working-class women was grim by comparison with their peasant predecessors. Peasant women rose in community stature upon their husband's decease, controlling children's fortunes as executors of family estates. Proletarian women sank into abject poverty ... (and) often ... had to appeal to their children for support.'[27]

To summarize our comparison of national differences, ancien régime French law was more gender-equitable than English law. In both systems, wives suffered legal incapacity, though both made provision for exceptionally entrepreneurial wives to act as *marchandes publiques* or *feme sole* traders. But for ordinary wives and daughters, French systems offered more protections. After 1650, Anglo-American jurisprudence in England and its American colonies saw many constrictions of women's position. However, in 1804 the Napoleonic Code curtailed the legal rights of French women too. Fortunately for *canadiennes,* well into the nineteenth century their colony was spared both the Napoleonic Code and the full force of common law. Let us turn now to examine the Custom of Paris in Canada.

The Custom of Paris in Canada

What was the situation in Canada? Canadian authorities consulted French legal treatises and precedents, and modelled their work on the Custom of Paris as implemented in the mother country.[28] They subscribed to the two great principles behind the *Coutume de Paris:* 'protection of family interests and equality among heirs.'[29] Both principles carried benefits for women that were missing from some of the other French codes as well as from British common law. Let us look at the rights of four groups in turn: inheriting daughters, single women, wives, and widows.

Inheritance Rights of Daughters and Single Women

Daughters were thought more appropriate heirs under the Custom of Paris than under common law. English and American jurisdictions tended to favour either primogeniture (the eldest son receiving the family land) or modified forms of it that divided land among the sons, while daughters might receive some share of the movable property. Still, all kinds of arrangements were possible, and paterfamilias typically made the decision. He, as we have seen, had extensive testamentary freedom under common law, allowing him to favour one child over another. The

Coutume, by contrast, left less power in the hands of pater (or widowed mater) and showed more solicitude for children's rights to inherit, guarding them from a step-parent who might not have their interests at heart.[30] In contrast to common law favouritism toward sons, there stood the principle of equal treatment of all heirs, male and female. If parental land was allocated to one child (usually a son or son-in-law) in order to keep it intact, he was expected to reimburse his brothers and sisters for their shares of the total value.

There were strong limitations on parents' ability to single out a favourite child. The early-eighteenth-century French legal authority La Ferrière saw it as a truism that 'Nature obliges parents to nurture those they have brought into being, and there is scarcely an animal that does not submit to that law.'[31] So that all *would be* nurtured, it was required that major gifts, dowries, and other advances made to children during the parents' lifetimes be taken into account later when inheritance was allocated.

Scholars have tried to discern how the principle of equality worked in practice. According to a study by Beatrice Craig, at first the plentiful landholdings in the St Lawrence settlement might be divided equally among all inheriting children. After a generation or two it would become more common for one child, usually male, to inherit the land and compensate his siblings. Such compensation did not always result in strict equality (for example, land scarcity would enhance the value of land in relation to movables). A study of the Ile Jesus in the eighteenth century by Sylvie Dépatie found deeds of gift in advance of the parents' deaths perpetuated a rough but not absolute equality. She, and also Louis Michel who studied Varennes and Verchères, noted some heirs used cash shares to buy new or partly developed land, complicating the picture. Total equality existed only in a minority of cases, but 104 of the 118 cases revealed the children received at least the minimal requirement of their *légitime*, one half of their entitlement. Inheritance studies to date have covered only limited regions and time periods, and we await further studies. Findings do seem to point to difficulty in preserving strict equality as land resources became scarcer, sometimes at the expense of daughters who seldom got their shares in land.[32] However, after the daughter married, her rights to revenues of her husband's lands would partially compensate.

Let us move on, to women in other stages of life. We can quickly deal with unmarried women who reached the age of majority (twenty-five). They could sign contracts and go to court on their own behalf. Such women did not suffer legal incapacity. Falling into this category of *filles majeures* were some of the major economic players discussed in this book, single women such as timber exporter Louise de Ramezay, and the Desauniers sisters who dealt in contraband fur.

Property Rights of Wives

What about the vast majority of women, those who became wives? The basic marital arrangement under the Custom of Paris was a community of goods. It was usually written into contracts. Where no contract was written, community was automatically created.[33] Frequently each partner would bring some wealth into a marriage. According to Nathalie Pilon, who studied 114 marriages on Montreal Island in the 1740s, men seem most often to have brought land or money. More typical of brides was Charlotte Guilbault's presentation to her husband of an armoire, hutch, table, kitchenware such as frying pan, yellow copper casserole pot (*poêlon*), big covered cooking pot (marmite), and pewter plates and platters, as well as items for the bedroom such as wool coverlet, drapes, mattress, feather bed, and bedding.[34] Each spouse retained, outside of the community of goods, management of such *propres* as these. A wife needed her husband's approval to sell hers. For his part, he could sell crops from a field she brought into the marriage as her *propre*, but he required her permission to sell the field itself.

Aside from those *propres*, the marriage created a community of goods that belonged to the two spouses together. Any earnings, purchases, or income from inheritance property during the marriage entered this community. As its overseer, the husband had the lion's share of managerial power. However, as Yves Zoltvany noted, the *Coutume* established an equilibrium between husband and wife. Although he administered the community, if he mismanaged, she was not obliged to submit to those consequences but was entitled to seek a separation of goods. If she arrived at widowhood, additional options would present themselves.

Property Rights of Widows

Widows were a very substantial and relatively youthful group that one historian compared to the pool of divorcées in our own day. A study of Montreal determined that widows were perennially twice as numerous as widowers, attributing this to the later marrying age for men, the dangers of male occupations, and the tendency of widowers to remarry

quickly.[35] The widow might survive for decades, and she was less likely to
remarry than her male counterpart was. A study of the town of Quebec
during the French regime determined that in 57 per cent of unions the
husband died first, largely due to the fact that he was typically about five
years older than his wife. The consequence was a society rich in widows.
In Quebec, they outnumbered widowers three to one.[36]

What happened when a woman lost her husband? In further compensation for yielding control of the community to the husband during
his lifetime, a widow had redress: if he died leaving a heavily indebted
community, she could renounce the community, after first collecting –
ahead of any creditors – her dower. The dower customarily gave her the
usufruct – crops or rents accruing to lands or buildings, for example – of
half the inherited land or real property the husband owned at the time
of marriage (his *propres*). Zoltvany notes, 'This right of the wife to her
dower was fundamental and the Custom contained numerous provisions
to assure its enjoyment. Thus it could not be used to pay debts of the
community and any act by the husband to dispose of those goods was
subject to annulment.'[37] (This contrasted with the English dower, which
was often meaningless, because many men left estates heavily encumbered in debt). In addition to her dower, the French-Canadian widow
was also entitled to ownership of half the community of goods – the
assets acquired during the marriage (movable ones such as rents, furniture, and tools, and immovable ones such as land and houses).[38] Over
this property she gained some powers of management, though they were
not complete. She could sell her own *propres* brought into the marriage,
but for the protection of the next generation of heirs, she was required
to secure consent of a family council or her children's' financial guardian (tutor) if she wished to dispose of the goods of the dissolved community.[39] If no action was taken upon the husband's death to dissolve
the community, it continued to function for the widow and the children
or other heirs.

In other ways too, a widow acquired resources and authority. She now
assumed marital authority or *puissance paternelle* to manage the community on behalf of the family. She acquired judicial authority, the right to
make contracts and go to court. Widows also sometimes took over the
family's trade, harking back to old French guild practices. As we have
seen in our earlier chapters, quite a number of widows were involved
in family businesses large and small. Owning property provided access
to credit for expanding the business or purchasing stock. Pilon's study
of Montreal widows concluded that these provisions meant widows were

generally left with the means to manage their own futures. The tendency for those who remarried to select men who were a few years younger than themselves[40] also hints at their new authority. Wealthier widows were less likely to remarry, eschewing (as Montreal gentlewoman Elisabeth Begon put it) 'a new master.'

Looking at the situation more broadly, law and custom worked together to create a society in which the average widow, coming from a family that held a little land, was not thrown to the mercy of others. The law did not entitle a husband to cut her off without a penny, or do so posthumously if she remarried. It was a common practice among the elderly, female and male alike, to set up a *pension viagère* when the time came to turn over the farm to the younger generation. A notarized contract would specify the living space and the amount of food, firewood, clothing, and so on that the retiree was to receive annually.[41]

A benefit of retaining property and a legal personality was the way it positioned a woman to contract with kin in exchange for services. The widow Louise Margane de Lavaltrie, for example, made a donation of her half of two properties to a granddaughter and her husband in exchange for their care in her final years.[42] Thirty-year-old Marie-Françoise Huppe, a blacksmith's widow, had a brother who helped her in some of her financial dealings; later her nephew Augustin was affectionate and 'for many years fed and cared for her without monetary award.' At age sixty-five she bestowed all her property on the nephew on condition that he provide her with housing, food, fuel, and maintenance for the rest of her life. Likewise a widowed labourer with six youngsters contracted to cover rent payments for his mother-in-law (whose husband was absent) and feed her on condition she 'take care of his family as she had already been doing.'[43] The language of such contracts does not suggest a lack of affection or the need to force people to meet their family obligations; it does bespeak a system that did not assume women should make it their particular speciality to act as sentimental, selfless creatures who could live on air, blithely entrusting their finances in the hands of a male relative – who might turn out to be an angel – or a cad. They held a card or two in their hands. For example, when the second husband of one seventeenth-century Montreal wife failed to provide for her needs, her grown son did so; from her own patrimony, she had the means to reward that behaviour with twenty acres of forested land. The contracts from New France indicate that both men and women were expected to display filial affection – *and* to have a contract stipulating where their food and firewood was coming from next winter!

Such options compare favourably with the widow's situation in English Canada described by Susanna Moodie, 'ironing the fine linen, or boiling over the cook-stove' while her daughter-in-law 'held her place in the drawing room,'[44] the property having passed to the son. Common law saddled wives with what Nellie McClung called the responsibilities of an adult partner and the legal status of a child. Still, one must refrain from too optimistic a view of French Canada's code. All the legal safeguards in the world meant little to a family with only rags and a hovel to divide, and widows of that class formed a sizeable proportion of the urban poor. A weak heart, a failing mind, a bullying relative of either sex could all make the law more a theory than a practice. But the automatic right to dower, the customary and contractual protections of women pointed in the right direction, acknowledging compensation for work within a marriage as a right, not a favour.[45] They offered the ordinary country widow the opportunity to live in dignity, even to call the tune, for she managed the family community and had control of property until the children came of age. When they did, she could still depend on her dower and her half of community goods and other entitlements, sometimes supplemented by a contracted pension as described above. A woman was not at the mercy of a husband, brother, or son to the same extent as under the common law.

Women's Participation in the Judicial System

Several scholars have examined court records at the Prévôté de Quebec, an active court located in the port city, to determine the extent of female participation in the judicial process. Knowing what causes brought them there helps define their civil status and their economic concerns. Did judicial incapacity of wives mean they seldom appeared in court cases? Scholars have come to disparate conclusions about what Prévôté records reveal. One study basically deemed the glass as half-full, while another deemed it half-empty. Let us look at the different perspectives in turn.

France Parent, in her thesis and in a subsequent article co-authored with Geneviève Postelec, focused on Prévôté records for the year 1686. One person in six involved in the cases was female. 'A strong proportion, forty per cent of them, presented themselves in person at hearings, compared to fifty-two per cent of men ... [which] reflects an image of women who were very active on the judicial scene in New France.'[46] They were not rich people: one-third of them were from the *habitant* class, 17.0 per cent artisanal, about 14.0 per cent mercantile, 8.5 per cent professional.[47] Parent and Postelec were struck by an involvement in the judicial process greater than the formal provisions of the law anticipated for married women.[48]

What brought these women to the courts in 1686? While the majority of cases were family matters, only a fifth of these women appeared in person to deal with those, since the husband administered the marital community. Nearly two-thirds of women who appeared came on matters of commerce or real estate, with city dwellers from the artisanal milieu being the most active. Parent hypothesized that they were delegated by husbands who were tied up at the shop or elsewhere, especially during spring and fall busy seasons. More than half the women present were acting as *procuratrices* or agents of their husbands, in an economizing measure that wealthier mercantile families perhaps did not need. Other women, such as laundresses and innkeepers, showed up to defend their own business interests. Parent concluded, 'Their numerous mentions in cases of an economic character ... gives the impression of constant implication of women in colonial business' and of more openness to female judicial participation than customary restrictions would suggest.[49]

Josette Brun, studying the same Quebec court's records for a later period, the first half of the eighteenth century, saw things quite differently. Brun was struck by the conservative nature of judicial operations in New France in regard to women: 'The analysis reveals that marital authority was not at all in peril in New France and that it assumed all its sense and its importance under the formal plan. Nevertheless the rights and the role of spouses under the plan of succession were generally respected.'[50]

Brun's study of 137 notarial cases indicated that men rarely delegated authority to their wives. Joint transactions were somewhat more frequent, reflecting the wife's rights and roles in the transmission of her own property, the cases where her consent was legally required. The male heads of family carried out 75 per cent of the notarized transactions; about 20 per cent were made jointly, and wives alone in only 4 per cent of cases. Brun notes that the active participation of some wives and widows indicates a variety of experiences, making certain widows, particularly those who were in their thirties and forties (who might have experience with the business and children old enough to assist them) better equipped than others to take over their husband's responsibilities after his death.[51] Among the small numbers of women who were active, she found mercantile wives more commonly involved in business-related proceedings (6 per cent of them) than artisanal wives (1 per cent). This contrasts with the heavier artisanal representation in Parent and Postelec's findings. Brun's study, covering a later, longer time span, sounded a caution that *puissance paternelle* was the prevailing pattern, and judicially active women were the minority.

This conservative assessment has been called into question by a new research project by Benoit Grenier and Catherine Ferland. The somewhat wider parameters of eighteenth-century procurations at Quebec allowed them to identify 265 procurations involving 221 different women, a much larger number than Brun uncovered. Half of the women were bourgeois and 80 per cent of them were married. Ninety per cent of these women were acting as the legal representative of a close family member (usually a husband). Thirty-three per cent of the absentee men had gone to France, 17 per cent to the *pays d'en haut*, and 10 per cent to French ports in Newfoundland or Acadia.[52] This unfolding research promises a more complete picture of the active judicial and commercial participation of the *canadienne*. We also await study of courts around Montreal, where male departures for fur trade and military expeditions may have led to even greater female involvement in commerce.

Conclusion

Having examined women's property rights in several countries as well as in Canada, we may now draw some conclusions. These rights were eroded in Britain and America during the seventeenth and eighteenth centuries. In France they deteriorated in the Revolutionary and Napoleonic periods. Did the situation in Canada diverge from these patterns? The major new research project by Grenier and Ferland tends to confirm early suggestions of considerable commercial activity in New France, though (as chapter 8 discusses) this would gradually recede after the British takeover in 1760. Brun cautioned that the economic activity she found among widows in midlife was 'a phenomenon whose existence has been observed for other societies and other chronological periods ... nothing in it would allow us to state that the colonial context of New France especially "favoured" women.'[53] The question of whether the Custom of Paris favoured women is of course a relative one, for it depends on the comparison group. If one is asking whether the Custom favoured women in comparison to men, of course it did not. In comparison to Iroquois women (who had jurisdiction over the fields and longhouses), there too *canadiennes* were in a weak position. In comparison to the property rights of women in pre-Revolutionary France who lived under the Custom of Paris, we lack comparative data, but one suspects there was no great difference; after all, a number of judicial officials came from France, and the same legal texts were consulted in colony and mother country.[54] Yet in comparison to women living under the common law in Britain and North America, *canadiennes* were certainly favoured. Because it would retain the Custom of Paris largely intact for four decades after it was jettisoned in post-Revolutionary France, French Canada would preserve, well into the nineteenth century, a degree of security of property for wives, widows, and daughters that was missing in common law and in the Code Napoléon – both of which gave men more freedom to sell or will away family property. The Custom would have a long life in Canada, surviving into the nineteenth century, and in that sense time was on the side of colonials. Daughters could look to the rule that they as well as their widowed mothers were entitled to a significant inheritance. When they married, as Brun's study showed, the courts tended to be assiduous in upholding the letter of the law as far as their relatively generous marital rights were concerned. As a number of historians have noted, it is too sweeping to make a blanket statement about women in New France as being 'favoured.' It is particularly ill-suited to the many who lived in quite rudimentary conditions as subsistence farmers or urban workers. However, in the sense that the Custom of Paris left generation after generation of women in enjoyment of property rights that were fading elsewhere, that was a favour indeed.

Chapter Six

Noble Codes, Colonial Translations

Much ink has been spilt over the question of whether New France was a 'backward' or underdeveloped colony. As we have noted, its legal codes offered women relatively secure property rights. Moreover, it bettered the mother country in reducing the hunger, desperation, and disease that plagued the poorest classes in France, and it avoided the extremes of opulence and penury seen there. Subsistence, however, should not be equated with dynamism. The colony lacked the vigorous commercial class that had such a profound impact on the economic and political evolution of the thirteen colonies lying to the south of Canada. It had the misfortune to develop in the shadow of a long French depression,[1] and what profits there were, often accrued to metropolitan merchants rather than colonial ones. Moreover, there was little to nourish an intelligentsia. Some colonial elites could barely write, the place had no printing office or bookstore, and scholars who appeared on the scene tended to be temporary visitors from France. One of the things this book explores is the irony that while Canada *was* a decidedly distant outpost of its brilliant metropolis, its very remoteness allowed elite *canadiennes* to retain certain powers even as they were receding in France as well as England and America.[2] Ladies in distant colonies, with their men away and no one to read the *Encyclopédie* to them, sometimes fell back on older, more robust assumptions about their duties and abilities.

The particular families we examine in this chapter were guided by codes of the ancien regime *noblesse*. Their activities were not so much innovative as part of a long European tradition in which gentlewomen had commonly engaged in public activity. As the eighteenth century progressed, such activities were increasingly decried in western Europe by philosophic, political, and scientific literature that posited men and women as creatures with separate natures. The new views resulted in the growing restrictions on female rights and activities we discussed in chapters 1 and 5. Here we attempt to understand the ancien régime mentality of the Canadian upper classes. The discussion reveals concern about their families' economic and social status as a key motivator of noblewomen's actions. It concentrates on the way noble codes of honour interacted with what (from an elite perspective) were relatively crude colonial conditions. Noble codes and colonial circumstances combined in a way that encouraged female public activity.

Although the outlook had many traditional aspects, it is true that New World and ancien régime influences cannot be tightly compartmentalized. Women of two of the noble families we are about to consider, Agathe Saint-Père and Louise de Ramezay, have already made an appearance in our discussion of trade in the natural resources found along the river. Their work ties in with the book's environmental theme, for they trafficked in North American products such as wood, fur, native fabrics and dyes, clay, bricks, and tiles. Not even elite families could afford to ignore the New World's bounty; however, their lives were not fundamentally shaped by it. On the whole, nobles marched to a drummer who was different from the commoners', dancing to tunes that emanated from Versailles, or from stone halls of medieval times. The cultural imperative to fulfil the duties and protect the privileges of caste were a fundamental concern. We will illustrate this by reconstructing the stories of three noble families whose women were particularly prominent.

It is perhaps unnecessary to alert the reader that the people we are about to discuss do not represent 'Everywoman.' They are leaders rather than representative figures. Previous chapters discussed some more ordinary women involved in trade, mentioning, for example, the labours of farmwomen, fort laundresses, smugglers, seamstresses, and canoemakers. It would be foolish, though, to avoid discussing leading figures because they are not 'ordinary' people. When we turn our eyes to elites we are, to borrow Laurel Ulrich's phrase, looking for 'what was permissible, not what was probable.' In eighteenth-century Canada a number of high-ranking women carried on public activities – mostly commercial, occasionally political – that were gradually becoming either legally difficult or socially unacceptable in more 'advanced' places where new gender doctrines were emerging.

Three Public Families

It may be helpful to approach elite women by accepting, for the moment, their own premise that they were quite different from others of their sex. A rigidly *gendered* social system in the Western world from the late eighteenth century through the mid-twentieth has tended to obscure the gender flexibilities of the more rigidly *hierarchical* social system before that time. One realizes, of course, that both patriarchy and hierarchy always co-existed and intertwined, both before and after the eighteenth century. Our initial chapter indicated, however, that pre-Revolutionary patriarchy was not infrequently trumped by other forms of privilege. *La Grande Mademoiselle* was able to lead troops during a crisis not just by force of personality but because she belonged to one of the highest-ranking families in France. Elites were Ladies and Gentlemen, and the others were not. (The new order turned all of us into Ladies or Gentlemen, as many a washroom door proclaims). As Merry Wiesner concluded in her study of European women, at some point a little before 1800, in many countries 'the perception of women as marginalized by gender became stronger than the perception of women as divided by class.' Prior to that time, privileges of caste were more widely accepted and had a better chance of outweighing favouritism towards the male sex.

Despite their privileges, noble lives (male *and* female) were driven by their own narrow and exacting set of constraints. Many ladies immersed themselves in 'public' service, not only to meet immediate family needs but also to carry out larger responsibilities to the Crown that the *noblesse* considered part of its mandate. They seem to have passed much of their time in the midst of a crowd of kin, servants, visitors, and members of their political clique, in some sort of 'Big House,' be it an urban dwelling, rural manor, or stately convent. Often there was no male head of household in attendance. Since the 'warrior class' in New France was indeed preoccupied with war, its females commonly directed affairs in those old-fashioned, communal settings. But rather than being forerunners of some future, more 'liberated,' feminine condition, the women discussed here were dilatory, slow in adopting new rigidities of gender that were beginning to supplant the rigidities of caste in Europe. They were in some ways throwbacks to an earlier age of medieval fortresses and walled towns. Such strongholds offered women their own forms of freedom, but it was the rather stiff freedom not of ambitious, free-wheeling individuals but of players in a pageant: dressed in costume, they were able to ad lib their script, to speak and act dynamically only to the extent that they remained within the codes of their aristocratic order. In their public enterprises they were not aiming to step *outside* established roles but to adapt the conventional duties of members of military nobility to colonial circumstances.

Here are their stories.

Agathe Saint-Père (Madame de Repentigny)[3] is considered the founder of French Canada's textile industry. She was well named, for the feast of Sainte-Agathe (5 February) was one on which women were supposed to take charge. Take charge she did: the death of her mother when Agathe was barely fifteen left her to raise ten step-siblings, including a newborn baby. At age twenty-eight she married Pierre Legardeur de Repentigny, a warrior from one of that frontier town's most distinguished families. The couple raised one son and seven daughters. In her middle age, with her husband still on active military duty, Agathe went into business. A 1705 shipwreck led to an absence of the imported cloth the colonists wore. Madame Saint-Père de Repentigny ransomed nine New England weavers who had been captured by the Indians and hired them to work for her. She had copies made of the town's one loom and arranged for Canadians to serve as apprentices to the skilled New Englanders. The strong, coarse cloth her St Joseph Street manufactory produced provided working-class Montrealers male and female with *chemises*, the shirts/shifts worn closest to the body. The two highest colonial officials, the governor and intendant, wrote to the French minister to request support for her venture, saying it was a real boon to colonists at a time when cloth was so scarce that colonists were reduced to recycling old woollen yarn, getting a little more wear by spinning it together with crude drugget. When the weavers opted two years later to return to Boston, the newly trained apprentices were able to continue the operation. Some remained at Saint-Père's workshop, while other men and women plied the looms she distributed to their homes. In 1706, Intendant Jacques Raudot said that without this enterprise half of 'the poor people in that poor country ... would be without shirts.' That year Saint-Père reported that twenty-eight people were weaving; by 1707 about seventy were at work.[4] It seems she had adapted her production to the climate, for an official dispatch of 1708 gave the news that the *habitants* were wearing *surtouts* (overcoats) of *droguet du pays* over their deerskin garments. For these contributions in the early years of the century, Agathe Saint-Père would receive emoluments of 200 *livres* per annum for forty years to come. Successive intendants were sufficiently impressed to continue the bonus, partly because so few government-approved manufactories ever developed in Canada. In addition to her cloth manufactory, Saint-Père also experimented with making cloth from local hemp, nettles, and cottonweed. After about ten years of operation, she sold the textile manufactory. She looked after the family's assets in other ways, making a number of land purchases. While

it is difficult to know the profitability of these ventures, there seem to
have been ample resources for dowries for her half-dozen daughters who
either married noblemen or entered convents.

Another prominent Montrealer was Louise de Ramezay, who would
develop timbering, tanning, and milling enterprises.[5] Raised in a sylvan
riverside chateau, Louise had a father who was town governor. Louise's
mother (Charlotte Denys de la Ronde) had married Montreal's future
governor, Claude de Ramezay. After his death in 1724, Madame de Ramezay took control of the family timber and sawmilling operation located in the Richelieu valley where they held seigneurial land. In 1726
she declared herself in a position to fill the hold of the King's ship with
planks of oak and pine. However, many vicissitudes befell her business,
just as they had when her husband had run it.[6] A flood carried away the
sawmill, a legal dispute with neighbouring landowners dragged on ruin-
ously, a careless ship captain let the timber rot in Quebec rather than
transporting it to France. Finally, her workers and equipment perished
in a shipwreck that also killed Madame de Ramezay's own son. All this
led the widow to conclude the timber venture was too risky to continue,
thus becoming another example of what Governor Beauharnois called
Canadian 'timidity' in such enterprises.

The daughter Louise succeeded where her mother had failed. Managing to settle the land question amicably, she restored and expanded the
business, securing additional timber reserves and supplying the Crown
in the 1730s. She entered a twenty-five-year partnership with another
seigneuress, Marie-Anne Legras (Madame J-B-F Hertel de Rouville). The
sawmills were on the Rivière des Hurons and the Ruisseau Notre-Dame
de Bonsecours. She was able to establish sixty-two colonists on the rivers
in the family's Ramezay and Bouchemin seigneuries. In 1749 she purchased a Montreal tannery complete with house, stables, oven, and wa-
termill, bringing a master tanner into partnership with her. Sometimes
managing her businesses herself and sometimes employing foremen,
Louise de Ramezay travelled frequently between Montreal, Chambly,
and Quebec to oversee operations. In acquiring additional properties
and making them profitable, she is credited with restoring the family's
flagging fortunes. Louise de Ramezay did not join her brother and other
friends and relatives who migrated to France at the time of the British
Conquest in 1760, but remained in business until her death in 1776.

Women of a third powerful family exercised control that was political as well as economic. Born in the Acadian backwoods, Elisabeth de
Joybert (Madame de Vaudreuil) provides an aristocratic variant of the

rags-to-riches story. Loss of her father when Elisabeth was five left the family strapped. A dissipated grandfather, who was a judicial official at Quebec,[7] purloined what was left of her mother's wealth. Young Elisabeth received government assistance to attend the Ursuline school in Quebec City, where her teachers described her as having solid virtue and superior wit and 'all the graces that charm elite circles.' Rare sagacity, the convent annalist observed, tempered her lively character. Her face was lovely, 'enhanced by the most naïve expression of modesty.'[8] She married a man who was eventually appointed governor general of New France.

Here we see an unusual case of a Canadian mother-daughter team who positioned themselves at the French court. Madame de Marson, Elisabeth's mother, managed to secure audiences with French officials, using this influence so effectively on behalf of her daughter's Canadian family that she was reported by the Quebec nuns to have been responsible for Vaudreuil's appointment as governor. In 1709, when political enemies were spreading rumours and seriously undermining the position of Governor Vaudreuil (a man once criticized by the intendant as being ignorant of all subjects except military ones), Elisabeth herself sailed to defend her husband's interests at Versailles. There, no doubt, her mother coached her in the ways of the court and introduced her to the right people.[9]

Elisabeth won the ear of the minister of marine, Jerome de Pontchartrain, to such an extent that he permitted her to read the complaints of her husband's enemies – which they naturally thought they were making in confidence. The bonds with the Crown grew even closer when Madame de Maintenon and several others highly placed at court recommended the charming colonial lady for the position of under-governess to the family of the Duc de Berry, who was a grandson of Louis XIV. Duly appointed, Elisabeth Joybert de Vaudreuil thus graced the French court in the closing years of the Sun King's reign, a period when (as we saw in chapter 1) women enjoyed unusual political influence.

Madame Vaudreuil's success lay, according to her biographer Yves Zoltvany, in getting Pontchartrain to take a personal interest in the family, helping assure support for the governor and appointments for their sons. She made 'clever use of her influence by recommending various Canadians for appointment and advancement ... [surrounding] herself and her husband with a network of clients.'[10] During the time Elisabeth was in France, cries of outrage emanated from her husband's enemies back in Quebec. 'She controls all the positions in Canada,' wrote Attorney General Ruette d'Auteuil. 'She writes magnificent letters from all sorts of places to the seaports about the power she can exert over him [Pontchartrain] ... she offers her protection, she threatens to use her influence.' He added, 'She causes great fear and imposes silence on most of those who could speak against her husband.'[11] That official claimed that Pontchartrain had inordinate control over Canada – and she had inordinate control over him.

Elisabeth Joybert de Vaudreuil was the most powerful of all the Canadian women we encounter in this book. In ministerial audiences and correspondence stretching over more than thirty years (and two successive ministers of marine), Madame de Vaudreuil defended her husband and made suggestions for government policy. She also lobbied for new procedures to place more colonial appointments and patronage in the hands the governor. While the French minister of marine did not always support her proposals, his comments on the margins of her letters, including a number of approvals, indicate they were taken seriously. Basking in the favours that frequently emanated from the minister, Madame Vaudreuil besieged him with requests for their friends and allies in Canada, commissions for officers, pensions for widows, financial aid for convents, permission for the governor to appoint a chaplain, a secretary, a surgeon. And there was the family: would Monseigneur please grant a naval officership for one of their sons, a benefice for another studying at the Jesuit seminary, and favours for brother Soulanges and cousin Lotbinière too?

Across the years many rewards flowed into the requested channels: 'Bon,' wrote the minister beside her 1711 request for an ensignship for her eldest son; 'Bon' again for the second son's lieutenancy; and the third son's ensignship was fine with him too. On one of her lists nominating appointees and requesting fuller appointing powers for her husband, the minister indicated approval for some and deferred decision on others.[12] Nothing was a foregone conclusion, it all took work and tact. In her glory years, at the height of her influence in 1712, Pontchartrain had to warn her to 'use moderation because his Majesty would not approve of too frequent requests.'[13] Moderated, they continued for years. As they did, Madame Vaudreuil's progeny continued to advance up the ladder. All the eligible sons received their military or naval commissions and two rose to top positions in the colonial government. One son received the governorship of Trois-Rivières and then a promotion to governor of Montreal. Another progressed from governor of Louisiana to win, after his mother's death, his father's old position of governor general of

New France. Among other rich proceeds the family received were the seigneuries of Vaudreuil and Soulanges, well placed just above Montreal to receive furs from traders before they reached town. More than two decades after Elisabeth de Vaudreuil's first trip to France, the King himself was still approving her requests. A pair of noble correspondents agreed in 1750, 'None could be happier than the Vaudreuil family ... on every side they succeed in all they undertake.'[14]

In an era when colonial appointments often depended on which faction reached the French court first, Madame de Vaudreuil's long presence there, her indefatigable lobbying, and her acceptance into the royal household must be placed alongside her menfolk's military talents and amiability in making the family's fortunes. The outcry from officials at Quebec, the deliberations on her proposals by the minister and Marine Council, and the fact that the court informed her first of some of the favours the family received suggest her influence; so does her long residence at the notoriously fickle French court. 'To her,' Zoltvany concluded, 'belongs a good deal of the credit for the successful careers of Vaudreuil and his sons.'[15]

Leading a colonial cabal was not for the faint of heart. In 1710 it was alleged that Elisabeth de Vaudreuil helped cover up the misdeeds of an ally who had slit an infant's throat. 'Witty but dangerous,' Lamothe de Cadillac declared her. As commander at Detroit, Cadillac, along with Colony Company agent Georges Regnard Duplessis complained that Madame and Monsieur Vaudreuil were conspiring to ruin them. Another Quebec official wrote, 'Everything is in a wretched state; a mere woman is in control, to the same extent when she is absent as when she is here.'[16] He added that Vaudreuil was entirely governed by his wife. Be that as it may, her 'somewhat phlegmatic'[17] husband enjoyed a longer term of office than any of his counterparts, and six of their seven sons received coveted commissions, including the colonial governorships. For two decades a range of highly placed colonials spoke of Madame Vaudreuil, '*La Gouvernante,*' as a formidable force.

In a sense the women of the Repentigny, Ramezay, and Vaudreuil families are only the most outstanding of the long list of publicly active women in New France, women of all sorts whom we have already observed trading across the vast hinterland from Bordeaux to the *pays d'en haut*. Yet, in another sense they were quite exceptional. Their families were members of a tiny ruling caste, never more than 3.5 per cent of the population, shrinking after 1735 to 2.0 per cent of a growing populace.[18] Their caste made these women 'personages' whose status allowed them to command people and resources. They belonged to the Second Estate, the nobility, theoretically so far above the common people as to have different blood (hence 'bluebloods') from the ordinary *vilains* or 'vile persons.' A few, such as Agathe Saint-Père de Repentigny, whose grandfather was a craftsman, had only recently risen to that status, but she lost no time in assuming the outlook of the nobility. Such crossovers were facilitated by royal exemptions, which permitted colonial nobles to engage in both retail and wholesale commerce.[19]

A Warrior Nobility

To understand colonial nobles, it is important to note the beleaguered situation of New France, and the low priority it usually held in the eyes of its mother country. The government of France, inefficient in finance, frequently at war in Europe, and rife with discontents was, we know in retrospect, destined to come crashing down in 1789. While New France was less burdened with palaces and courtiers, it was in its own way an even clearer case of a too-grand edifice built on shaky foundations. A look at the map tells the story. As early as 1701 France claimed territory stretching from Acadia on the Atlantic seaboard, westward past the Great Lakes, north to Hudson's Bay, and down the Mississippi valley to the Gulf of Mexico. When the Treaty of Utrecht in 1713 ended several decades of French–English war in North America and parcelled large portions of the territory to England, it ominously failed to determine precise boundaries. The disputed areas were rimmed with great stone fortifications and patrolled with the help of numerous native allies. The idea of a heavily fortified enclave surrounded by dangerous forest harked back to medieval times (nineteenth-century tourists wandering their ruins would call them 'French castles'). The alliances conjured up, to those who heard of the tomahawking of peaceful inhabitants of Schenectady and Deerfield in their beds at night, an even more antique image: Roman use of barbarian mercenaries in the empire's dying days.

Eighteenth-century New France was a pawn of imperial military strategy. The idea was to send just enough French troops, supplies, and trade goods to seal the native alliances that kept Anglo-American rivals terrorized and hemmed in along the seaboard. Less than 1 per cent of the French budget was allocated towards its Canadian outpost, yet should the issue come to total war, so many British troops would be needed to capture the far-flung fortifications of New France that they would be drained from more important combat zones in Europe, India, and the Caribbean.

Ursuline Convent at Quebec. In 1639 when Quebec was just a tiny clearing in the woods, three French Ursulines and three hospital nuns arrived. The Ursulines soon erected a three-story stone convent, the largest building there. The house of their patron Madame de la Peltrie is in the foreground, along with the tipis of Algonkian families who placed their daughters in the Ursuline school. Arriving before France established governing institutions and a military presence, female missionaries used funds from aristocratic donors to set up schools and hospitals at Quebec and Montreal. While not very successful in the goal of converting First Nations, they offered essential services to settlers. Detail from a painting by Joseph Legaré, Courtesy of Musée des Ursulines de Quebéc, Collection du Monastère des Ursulines de Quebéc.

Marie de l'Incarnation. This image of the first Quebec Ursuline superior was painted by one of the sisters in the mid-nineteenth century, a composite of earlier images. This rendition captures the iron character, learning, and heavenly preoccupations of the Founder. As early as the seventeenth century, each Ursuline nun possessed a 'Room of One's Own' a small cell with candelabra, books, and writing materials. Courtesy of Musée des Ursulines de Quebéc, Collection du Monastère des Ursulines de Quebéc.

Marguerite Bourgeoys and her pupils. In contrast to the austere Marie de l'Incarnation who founded a cloistered convent and boarding school, Marguerite Bourgeoys was a populist who resisted class distinctions. She dispatched a band of followers overland and by canoe to set up free schools for ordinary settlers across the St.Lawrence Valley and beyond. This has been characterized as Canada's first system of public education. Bourgeoys' Congregation of Notre Dame also worked among First Nations with the help of two Canadian aboriginal women who took the veil. From E-M Faillon, *Mémoires Particuliers pour Servir à l'Histoire de l'Eglise de l'Amerique du Nord.* Courtesy of Thomas Fisher Rare Book Library, University of Toronto.

Two centuries separated Montreal's first school in a stable (1658) set up by Marguerite Bourgeoys and the large, fashionable 1854 boarding school opened by her order, the Congregation of Notre Dame. By the mid-nineteenth century the Congregation was educating more than two thousand girls annually at its boarding and day schools in Lower Canada. Eventually the order spread across Canada and to Africa and South America. From the time of its founding the Congregation offered opportunities for female education that were often lacking elsewhere. From E-M Faillon, *Mémoires Particuliers pour Servir à l'Histoire de l'Eglise de l'Amerique du Nord.* Courtesy of Thomas Fisher Rare Book Library, University of Toronto.

Jeanne Mance, ranked by seventeenth century sources alongside Governor Maisonneuve as the co-founder of Ville-Marie (Montreal) in 1642. She attracted essential funding from aristocratic female donors for an outpost to convert peoples of the continental interior. Mance established a hospital where she tended First Nations and colonists. When Iroquois resistance placed the settlement in peril, Mance handed over her hospital's endowment funds to raise troops in France. This assured the survival of what has become in our own day the second largest primarily French-speaking city in the world. This nineteenth-century image by L. Dugardin is said to be an authentic copy of an original portrait. Courtesy of Hotel-Dieu Museum of Montréal.

The Sisters of St Joseph arrived from France in 1659 to help Mance run the Montreal Hotel-Dieu. Sister Judith Brésoles was a renowned pharmacist and healer. An incident in which an Iroquois patient in the ward attempted to crush her behind a door offers early testimony that not everyone saw missionary work in the same glowing light its chroniclers did. The Hotel-Dieu remains a busy downtown hospital to this day. I. Massard illustration in E.M. Faillon, *Mémoires Particuliers pour Servir à l'Histoire de L'Eglise de L'Amerique du Nord*. Courtesy of Thomas Fisher Rare Book Library, University of Toronto.

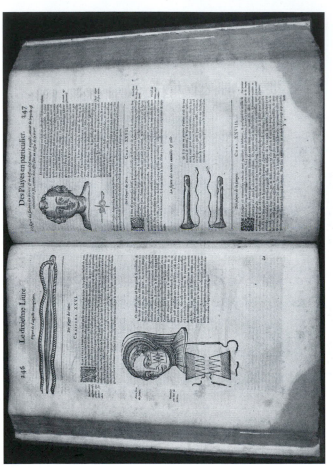

Pages of a text by sixteenth-century French surgeon Antoine Paré, who made medical knowledge more widely available by publishing in French rather than Latin. Though physicians, when available, directed treatment, several sisters at the Quebec and Montreal hospitals were said to rival them in knowledge and skill. Epidemics, invasions and physician shortages required sisters to step in as needed. Skilled needlework would have prepared them to perform sutures such as these pictured in the Hotel-Dieu's edition of Paré. Courtesy of Hotel-Dieu Museum, Montreal.

Madame Celles Duclos bringing weapons to unarmed Montrealers during an attack by the Iroquois in February 1661. In the belltower, Sisters from the Hotel-Dieu sound the alarm. Long after such dangers passed, Montreal remained a centre of female enterprise. In the eighteenth century some women ran mills, brickworks and tanneries, while others participated in the fur trade. Three un-married Desauniers sisters became notorious purveyors of smuggled furs, col-luding with Kahnawake residents who paddled beaver pelts to Albany to trade for English blankets and luxury goods. I. Massard illustration in E.M. Faillon, *Mémoires Particuliers pour Servir à l'Histoire de L'Eglise de L'Amerique du Nord*. Cour-tesy of Thomas Fisher Rare Books Library, University of Toronto.

Travel chest (*coffre de voyage*). The brides who came to Canada usually stored their worldly goods in plain wooden travel chests which became the first furniture in their cabins along St Lawrence. Some women even lined chests with serge and slept in them to ward off the cold. One surviving inventory of the contents of such a chest suggests poverty as well as preparation for winter. It contained a wool housedress, camisole, two tattered petticoats, headcoverings and handkerchiefs, two coats, one jacket, a muff, and sheepskin gloves. © Canadian Museum of Civilization, 91-38, photograph by Harry Foster, D2007-08502.

Ursulines at Trois-Rivières, watercolour by James Duncan 1853-4. This illustration pictures activities of a group of Ursulines, who from the 1690s supplied the little town with both school and hospital. By the mid-nineteenth century date of this painting, there were about two hundred students and a hundred patients. In the foreground are the grille through which the cloistered nuns communicated with visitors. A nun delivers a math lesson on the blackboard, an instrument stands ready for a music class, and a student carries some of the needlework for which the Ursulines were famous. In the background a cart delivers a patient to the hospital. The Ursulines also tilled their own fields in early decades when they could not afford labourers. Courtesy of Montreal City Archives.

Canoe building at Pepper's Island. This image gives some idea of the industry during the French Regime at Trois-Rivières, where a visitor recorded that women and girls built large military canoes under government contract. They perhaps toiled alone because the men were away for war or trade. Above, both sexes are working to build canoes in the Ottawa valley in 1838. In a pattern typical of woodland cultures, the men are building the frame while the women are making the birchbark covering. From W.H. Bartlett, *Canadian Scenery*, courtesy of Robarts Library, University of Toronto.

'View of Quebec' by Benjamin Beaufoy, detail, circa 1850. Two industrious French Canadian farmwomen are pictured along with the men, taking their produce to the Quebec market. One assumes a commanding stance while another paddles the craft. This contrasts with their more languorous 'betters' such as the seated gentlewoman in the rowboat to the right who might incur opprobrium if she toiled outdoors or served as a breadwinner. Courtesy McCord Museum M19891.

Apple-pickers near Montreal circa 1832. Although the city was expanding rapidly when this image was made, pre-industrial patterns lingered. Visitors commented on the frequent sight of women engaged in outdoor agricultural work,
a practice which was declining in Britain and America. Here they are harvesting
apples near Montreal. Detail from J. Bouchette, *The British Dominions*, courtesy of
Robarts Library, University of Toronto.

This crude drawing by an unknown German visitor to Canada ca. 1780 captures the main thrust of the story we present in *Along a River: The First French Canadian Women*. The habitant woman displays an adaptation to the New World environment that combines three key elements: aboriginal practice, French tradition, and market activity. As was common in French Canada, she wore moccasins, adding here native leggings too. Her bodice and skirt are in French style, shortened to facilitate rugged outdoor work on a bushy or snowy farm. She carries two marketable items (also inspired by native culture) that women sold to settlers and troops, baskets and snowshoes. Indeed, the *canadienne* commonly manufactured – or acquired by barter with woodland neighbours – all her items of apparel. Such economic activity persisted long after the British captured the French colony in 1760. Detail from *Genre Studies of Habitants and Indians*, courtesy of the Royal Ontario Museum.

As might be imagined, this prospect was not well designed to draw settlers from the richest, most populous country in Europe. The *filles du roi* and other seventeenth-century immigrants – largely soldiers[20] – slowly generated a French-Canadian population, and its ranks were slightly enlarged by handfuls of salt smugglers and other immigrants in the following century. Those who came found the omnipresence of war reflected in everyday parlance; what was called a village in France was often called a fort in Canada.[21] Forts were needed, for on the vast ground that France claimed, the number of French settlers remained pathetically small. There were fewer than 6,000 colonists in 1680, when the colony of New York alone had about 18,000. In 1700, compared to about 225,000 in the combined American colonies, there were just 14,000 in New France. A little later Governor Vaudreuil counted up the armed men and estimated Canada could muster 5,000, in comparison to 60,000 from the English colonies.[22] Given this disparity, it was no small accomplishment to ward off conquest until 1760, at which time the American colonies had 1,500,000; Canada, 70,000. This underpopulated colony could sustain itself only with swords drawn and cannons roaring. To fire the cannons and muskets, all men aged sixteen to sixty were organized into active militia units, and the colonial elite was groomed to lead them into battle.

Military nobles were unusually numerous in the colony. In the mother country, rich bourgeoisie and educated administrators of the *noblesse de la robe* intermarried with the warrior *noblesse d'épée*, and a centralizing monarchy groomed many nobles for a courtly role. In Canada, the more warlike variant continued to predominate. Well over three-quarters of the Canadian nobility sprang from military families,[23] and the few non-military colonizers and merchants who were ennobled hastened to enrol their sons in the one career befitting a Canadian gentleman. Colonial officials informed the court in 1727, 'This succession from father to children in the occupation of warfare is the source of the nobility ... and creates for the King men on which he can count.'[24] Their education, Intendant Hocquart admitted in 1737, was defective: they did not know the first elements of history or geography, and many could scarcely read or write. The local officers possessed few books or paintings and risked embarrassing themselves with their awkward, phonetically spelled letters. It was those who came from France who were more cultured, Governor Frontenac who arranged witty theatricals, Governor La Galissonnière who discussed scientific classifications, Mother Sainte-Hélène Duplessis who wrote graceful letters and annals. Home-grown colonial salons, enlivened by home-grown wits, were slow to emerge.[25]

The administrative elite, and most of the sovereign councillors, who
came out from France, sought out members of their own set for dinner
parties and marriages. Most colonials had little in common with these li-
terati. With economic opportunities scarce, wilderness omnipresent, and
war perennial, shabby colonial nobles often continued to resemble the
old *campagnard* or minor country nobility in the French provinces: down
at the heels, somewhat rustic, but full of bravado – a bravado so often put
to the test that it tended to signify genuine valour. The Canadian gentlemen did like a fight. They were reported by one French visitor to 'love
war more than any other thing.'[26] Another visitor observed that most
of the military officers were nobles, that indeed New France possessed
more of the ancient (that is, military) nobility than any other French
colony, perhaps more than all the others put together.[27] In return for
their efforts, they did not expect to live like mere soldiers; wanting to live
nobly on an officer's meagre pay, they got into trouble for pressing foot
soldiers to serve as their personal valets.

The Ramezay, Repentigny, and Vaudreuil families that engage us here
all belonged to the colonial military elite. Generation after generation
of males posed for their portraits with the coveted red and gold Croix
de Saint-Louis, awarded for long and valorous service, proudly displayed
on their breast. The portrait all too often took the place of the man. For
the women of this elite, a central fact of life was the loss of fathers, husbands, brothers, sons: their departure for overseas service, their absence
on summer campaigns in the interior, their arrival home with wounds
– or failure to return at all. Agathe Saint-Père's life was certainly shaped
by war, since her father, grandfather, uncle, and son were all killed by
Indians. But one of the deaths allowed her mother, a craftsman's daughter, to remarry advantageously, into the LeMoyne family (merchants who
gained titles of nobility): Agathe then sealed the family's ascent by marrying a warrior from one of the colony's leading families. Her husband's
Norman clan of Legardeur de Repentignys and Legardeur de Tillys
would eventually boast nineteen '*chevaliers de St Louis*' who served their
government not only at Saratoga, Michilimackinac, and Labrador, but
under the exotic skies of Martinique, and Pondicherry in India. The line
would continue to serve into the Napoleonic period. Pierre Legardeur
de Repentigny, Agathe's husband, received his Croix de Saint-Louis after
four decades of campaigning against the Iroquois, the Fox Indians, and
the New Englanders. The years, the wounds, and many nights in the field
weakened his body but not his spirit; at age sixty-five he was described by
the governor as still 'a very good officer, although more fitted to serve in

a fort than to march on a campaign.'[28] Their son, already serving at age twelve, was fourteen when his mother asked the minister to make him an officer.

In the same vein, Louise de Ramezay's father campaigned against the Iroquois and defended Quebec City from a fleet sent up from Boston in 1690. As for Louise's four brothers, the eldest, Claude, died at age nineteen fighting with the French navy at Rio de Janeiro. Louis died at age twenty-one, leading thirty Frenchmen into battle against the Cherokees. Charles-Hector perished at age thirty-six in a shipwreck. The sole surviving one, Jean-Baptiste-Nicolas Roch, an ensign in the colonial troops from age eleven, was awarded at age seventeen his dead brother's lieutenancy. A highly esteemed officer, Roch de Ramezay fought Fox Indians in Illinois, the Ojibway in Wisconsin, the English on Hudson's Bay and in Acadia, where he led his own sons into battle. He was appointed the high position of King's lieutenant in Quebec City just in time to see James Wolfe's fleet sail up the St Lawrence for the final encounters of 1759–60.[29] His sisters Geneviève and Elisabeth married officers and produced another generation of candidates for the Croix de Saint-Louis.

Elisabeth de Joybert's destiny also revolved around war. Her father came to Canada in 1665 in the Carignan-Salières regiment. Captured by the English, he lived only a short time after his ransom. Elisabeth's husband, Philippe Rigaud de Vaudreuil, came from a military family that could trace its Langeudoc ancestry back fifteen generations. Preoccupied in the first years of their marriage with a campaign against the Onondaga, he won encomiums ('We have grown accustomed to his valiant deeds, and he has the King's service so much at heart, that those who know him will not wonder at his latest exploits,' an official reported). Two years later he received the coveted Croix. Appointed governor of New France in 1703, he ordered the bloody raid on Deerfield, Massachusetts. The Vaudreuil sons too received commissions, several fighting with French forces in Europe.

The predictable life course of these men sprang from their membership in a tightly knit ruling class in New France, which historian William Eccles aptly described as a military caste system,[30] 'characterized by hereditary status, endogamy, and social barriers rigidly sanctioned by custom, law, or religion.'[31] More rigid than class systems, caste systems prevent flow between strata by defining and maintaining the boundaries. It was not that the bourgeoisie never rose into the nobility; but once they did, they adopted a new set of rules. In any case, the issue seldom arose. There were only eleven ennoblements in comparison to 170 founding nobles whose status was inherited, passing down from fathers to sons. This group of 181 noble families intermarried to the extent that within a few generations they were nearly all related to one another.[32] Death and outmigration reduced the male pool, encouraging many a noble daughter to enter a convent rather than lose noble status by marrying a commoner. Nobles had a distinctive demographic profile that included slightly longer life, much higher celibacy rates, and larger families. While commoners typically conceived in spring, nobles conceived in the autumn when summer campaigns were over.[33] Noble families occupied their own separate pews at the front of the church. They laid claim to the highest ecclesiastical offices and administrative positions in convents.[34] They were, in many ways, a breed apart.

There were other caste signifiers, too. Manual labour was forbidden. The noble's duty was to spill his blood if necessary in the King's service, in contrast to commoners whose task was to toil on the land, fabricate goods, engaging in tasks that dirtied their hands actually or symbolically. Though prohibitions on wholesale commerce by nobles had been modified by decree in the mother country, trade was an adjunct to military or administrative service and was not to interfere with 'living nobly,' entertaining, and keeping up a certain style. Indeed, one pious early governor was criticized for an ascetic lifestyle – living like a servant, eating pork and peas like a craftsman or a yokel – that was seen as disgracing his station. Living nobly, serving the Crown, and having documentary proof of pedigree have been identified as the three criteria of nobility in New France.[35]

Pedigree brought its privileges. Because they had a separate status before the law, nobles were punished more lightly for crimes than common folk, and they could not be hanged. (In parody of the noble's right to be beheaded by sword was the wholesale decapitation by guillotine in Revolutionary France.) Nobles used their position to take liberties with servant maids and plunge into tavern brawls, as did Pierre Lagardeur de Repentigny; to slap and kick in anger, as did Governor Vaudreuil; or even murder a too-pressing landlord, as did one Repentigny nephew. Pierre de Saint-Ours, whose sons married de Ramezay and de Repentigny daughters, was placed in a Montreal jail after raping a sixteen-year-old but was soon released because 'imprisonment was unbefitting his station.' (He was allowed to indemnify her with a thousand *livres* instead.) The father of Elisabeth de Joybert, a brash and querulous officer of fourteenth-century pedigree, was similarly let off a rape charge. The Repentigny murderer, exiled from the colony for a time, ended up with a governorship in another French colony.[36] How completely the King forgave his own!

The last thing nobles wanted to do was blend in with the crowd. The Canadian ladies, Intendant Hocquart wrote in 1737, loved pomp. The ladies and the gentlemen both dressed to display their rank. The warrior had his armour and sword. Both sexes had powdered wigs, floral brocades, satin and velvet garments, trimmings of braid and ribbons, silk stockings and silver buckled shoes, which it was their prerogative to wear, and they did so as they entertained or attended functions of church or state. Another trademark, more difficult to usurp, was a physical grace developed from childhood. Little French nobles learned how to bow precisely the appropriate degree to persons of varying rank, to ride, to fence – and to dance, which was a particular Canadian passion. A noble dancing body itself was invested with social significance and was supposed to be kept straight from the chest to the eyes, bending neither the waist nor the inside of the knees.[37] These graceful, well-dressed bodies were meant for show. So were the words that came out of their mouth, for skilful and witty language was considered another mark of superiority. Positioning oneself in this pageant was a matter of great import. Top officials quarrelled over the right to occupy the most prominent place at church, to have archers and guards to swell their retinue, to have a tambour sound their proclamations.[38]

In return for such privileges, loyal service was expected. When Intendant Jean Talon asked the King to create new nobles in the 1660s, the purpose was 'to better uphold the authority of the King, to form a little corps that will attach itself more strongly to his Majesty's interests.'[39] The height of serving his Majesty was not to save one's life but to lose it. Valorous deeds served the lineage too, redounding horizontally to the glory of the whole extended family, and vertically through the centuries to all the members of the line. The noble was a link in a long chain, which must not be broken by failure, cowardice, or discourtesy to other nobles. For Crown purposes, the system worked. Visitors to the colony noted the Canadian officers' valour, hardihood, and willingness to campaign, their patience in waiting long years for promotions.[40]

The Public Household

In 1705, when Montreal was still a small town of about two hundred houses, mostly wooden, there began to take shape on Notre Dame Street near the waterfront an imposing stone mansion with four chimneys and walls about three feet thick. The proud owner, Claude de Ramezay, described it as 'unquestionably the most beautiful in Canada.'[41] The chateau was in chaste Norman style. From the windows could be seen gardens, orchards, and fields stretching down towards the St Lawrence. Not long after the foundations were laid, Claude began imploring the Crown for subsidies, since the governorship required so 'much expense to sustain ... with honour.'[42] Honour meant providing for the couple's ten children (the girls must go to the classy Ursuline school at Quebec, not the humbler Congregation of Notre Dame one at home). It meant hosting visits from Madame de Ramezay's kin and allies, the governor's military cronies, and an array of official visitors to Montreal. A French aristocrat's style was to be constantly on show, 'forever courting the public opinion of his "equals" so that they may pronounce him worthy.'[43] Fortune first smiled when, as governor of Trois-Rivières, Claude had built a fine stone house for visiting dignitaries and won Governor Frontenac's accolade as 'a real gentleman.'[44]

Opening the stately door of the Ramezays' Chateau in Montreal or the Vaudreuils' in Quebec, one could expect to see the coats of arms that signified noble rank on stained-glass windows, furniture, and knick-knacks around the room. Walls would typically be hung with tapestries, portraits of the royal family and of ancestors. The usual trappings would be gold-framed mirrors, armoires, chess and other board games, and copper-trimmed bellows to assure a blazing fire. Coats of arms might be emblazoned on stained-glass windows to call up the family's status as defenders of the Crown over the centuries. There was also the rare sight – in that colony where most were illiterate and no newspaper ever saw publication – of a few books and a writing desk. At mealtime one sat down to fine china and silver tableware.[45]

If anything was missing, it was privacy. The interconnected rooms were thoroughfares, with beds of assorted size scattered about, even in kitchens and vestibules. These were the days when French servants – sometimes of a different sex – still slept close by their masters or mistresses, when royal weddings included public nightgowning and newlyweds holding court from their beds. Colonial bedrooms were not private places really; in the 1750s a lady of the Vaudreuil family entertained distinguished visitors from her sickbed, and a visiting military engineer shared a bedroom with a married couple.[46] Agathe Saint-Père and her husband shared their Montreal home with the textile factory, retaining the right to use the courtyard door to reach the upstairs apartments of their own large family. A little convent of Ursulines lived with the Ramezays in their stone house in Trois-Rivières before the family was transferred to Montreal. The Chateau St Louis, Quebec home of the Vaudreuils and successive governors general, was full of all sorts of live-in guests – adopted Indian children, New England captives, and envoys who stayed so long suspicions arose they were spies; children's boarding-school friends and others from France; and servants such as the cook, wine steward, carpenters, and scriveners. An entourage of sixteen such domestics sailed with Governor Vaudreuil when he returned home in 1716 from a visit to France.[47] All such hands were kept busy in the 1720s when some forty people occupied the chateau during the busy autumn and winter season, most of them sitting down to breakfast and dinner every day.[48]

One person not necessarily at home was the mother. She might depart, without her husband, as part of the entourage of an intendant travelling around the colony, as did Mesdames Daine, Péan, Lotbinière, and Marin in the 1750s.[49] A noble materfamilias might cross the Atlantic to present the family's seigneurial or trade claims to the court. Governor de Ramezay wrote to the minister in 1704 that Madame de la Forest, an active member of his fur-trading faction, would explain to the court any gaps in his letter regarding fur-trade abuses; two years later she was there again, voicing her own grievances against the intendant.[50] Another wife and mother, Madame de Frontenac, never set foot in the colony but remained in France; while her husband went out to serve in the colonies, she represented his interests at court. Nor was Elisabeth Joybert de Vaudreuil the only colonial summoned to serve in the royal household; her protégé Madame Beaujeu would sail from Quebec in 1728 to serve as a *remueuse* for younger members of the royal family. In Governor Vaudreuil's 1723 transatlantic entourage were two fur-trading ladies, Mesdames d'Argenteuil and Lusignan.[51]

The most spectacular of the court-bound wives was, of course, Madame Vaudreuil. She set sail to look after family legal affairs in 1696–7 when her husband was too involved with military concerns to go himself. She left again in the autumn of 1709, turning over to a nursemaid the baby Marie-Elisabeth, who was about two months old. She did not return home until 1721, but the governor did come to France for a long visit and the daughters at some point joined her. Her 1721 return to Quebec lasted just two years and then she sailed off to France again because she wanted to curry favour with the new minister of marine. Coming back to Quebec only briefly in 1724, she departed shortly after her husband died in 1725; at that time she left the now teenaged Marie-Elisabeth and her sister behind for another six months before bringing them to France. Every spring

the governor, with or without his wife, would decamp from the chateau
to spend the summer in Montreal. The chateau's furnishings suggested
the family's peripatetic existence: clothes were stored in portable chests
rather than dressers, and the governor kept his old camp bed.[52]

Nobles experienced very little of what would today be considered private family life. This is well symbolized by the elaborate curtained beds
of the period, which basically served as bedrooms. Even when the bed-
curtains were drawn, the intimacy of the conjugal couple may have been
rather limited by modern standards. How much empathy was there between forty-seven-year-old veteran officer Philippe de Vaudreuil and his
seventeen-year-old bride Elisabeth Joybert? Agathe Saint-Père and Charlotte de la Ronde were more typical in being just a decade younger than
their mates.[53] But how much meeting of the minds was there between
seasoned officers and fresh graduates of convent schools? They did their
duty by spending enough time together in that curtained bed to produce heirs. By the 1720s, though, wealthy families such as the Vaudreuils
were beginning to build their chateaux with separate apartments for
Monsieur and Madame, reflecting their essentially separate lives, especially given the long periods of widowhood – sixteen years for Elisabeth
Joybert, but a half-century for her mother. It was just a decade for Agathe
Saint-Père, but eighteen years for Charlotte de la Ronde and thirty-three
for her daughter Geneviève. Agathe's daughter and namesake was thirty-
seven years a widow.

Historians of early modern families have long debated another
question – their degree of attachment to their young. French observers on a number of occasions criticized Canadians for being too indulgent towards their children. But members of the nobility, in Canada as
elsewhere, relied heavily on domestics and probably had a somewhat
formal relationship with their children. In the towns, noble infants a few
months after birth were typically ejected from their home, sent out to
nursemaids in the countryside until the age of two. Thus there were few
cooing and crawling infants in the manors. These and other childrearing practices were so unhealthy that infant mortality rates among the
eighteenth-century colonial *noblesse* climbed to a shocking 50 per cent
around 1750 – double the rate of the rest of the population.[54] Those who
managed to survive came home for a few years before going off, again,
perhaps down the river to board at the elite Ursuline convent in Quebec,
where future entrepreneur Louise de Ramezay was packed off with her
elder sisters at the age of five;[55] or heading off for regimental training,
sometimes (another de Ramezay choice) to the military academies in

France. They might also pass time in another household to begin the lifelong cultivation of relationships with other 'people of quality.' Even when they were in the parental home, the French custom was to modulate displays of affection lest they interfere with public signs of deference owed to parents and superiors, and thereby undermine social order.

The evidence is not that mothers tried to keep children at home, but quite the contrary. Lest there be an interval between schooling and career, Madame Vaudreuil and other mothers besieged the Crown with letters begging that their sons be admitted into the army at younger ages. When the King reduced the age to fifteen in the 1720s, they implored that their fourteen-year-olds at least be placed at the top of the waiting list.[56] So hot was this lethal quest that Madame de Ramezay, who lost her three eldest sons to war, responded to the shipwreck death of the fourth with a letter to France, praying for an army commission for the sole surviving son. Madame de Verchères did the same after losing a husband and three sons. Maintenance of caste seemed to take precedence over mere physical survival, or even what might be thought of today as prudent financial planning by sending some sons to a safer career. When the son of Joseph de Hertel de Saint-François was killed at age fifteen, he was making his sixth raid against the American colonies. Children of these families played with little toy cannons, and perhaps nine-year-old ensign François-Pierre de Vaudreuil was still enjoying the models when he began to move among the deadly originals.

The careers and marriages of such children were as much matters of parental strategy as of youthful taste. It was accepted that love should be part of marriage, and stories of the lovelorn – such as a Repentigny daughter who entered a convent in grief after her suitor died in battle – survive from the period. But there was considerable parental pressure to make an astute choice. Historian John Bosher pointed to the necessity for parental consent (normally until age twenty-five) and the signatures on marriage contracts by diverse cousins, aunts, and uncles as indicators that a good marriage was a step up for the whole family.[57] Foreign military service, which often resulted in settlement abroad and dangerous careers, meant there were not enough noble grooms to go around. The number of noblewomen who took the veil while still nubile may have indicated piety, but it also reflected parental pressures to avoid marriage to a commoner. The childrearing, career, and marriage practices of these people suggest that their lives, like their houses, served public purposes. Private interiors – of both houses and people – were not much in evidence.

Sex

One wonders whether colonial noble couples, who were often apart, often different in age, were faithful to each another. Did the lovely Madame de Vaudreuil, for example, sleep her way to success at Versailles? Her beauty was an attribute her mother mentioned in recommending her to the court, but others noted other valuable assets: wit and (in her youth) modesty. The minister in telling the governor why she was chosen to serve the royal family cited her discrete conduct. The court had not yet reached its late-eighteenth-century height of libertinism,[58] but the memoirs of the Duke of Saint-Simon make it clear that affairs were common enough. One would think Madame Vaudreuil's enemies would have aired scandal about her if they knew any, and their written complaints related instead to undue influence, vindictiveness, and greed, not adultery. In any case, she was in her late thirties when she first began to influence ministerial decisions, and she continued to do so into her late fifties.

Certainly by the eighteenth century the colony, which had once attracted mystics, no longer exuded the pure air of a mission. Elites tended to roll their eyes if clergy thundered against dancing and décolletage. The letters of Madame Elisabeth Begon, widow of a Crown official, described a constant round of parties and balls.[59] She was amused when her friend the Baron de Longueuil lavished praise on one young thunderer for his splendid sermon, while at that very hour the baron's daughters were dancing at one of the all-night parties being condemned. Madame Begon and others thought Mademoiselle de la Ronde very witty when an earnest curé attempted to catechize her on her upcoming nuptials, enquiring whether she knew the meaning of the sacrament of marriage. She sweetly informed him she did not, but if he was curious, she would give him the news in four days. If that was the spirit, what was the practice? Did nobles who mocked priests also mock church laws?

Seemingly so. Being a colony under arms required some men to postpone marriage, with predictable consequences. The bishop charged Governor Vaudreuil with forcing some military men to wait eight to ten years to marry, turning them into libertines and 'giving the colony an infinity of illegitimate children.' The situation induced both officers and men to resort to do-it-yourself marriages *'à la gaumine'* in which the couple stood up during the most solemn moment of the Catholic Mass, with friends as witnesses, and declared themselves man and wife. Others didn't bother. Both sons of Attorney General Ruette D'Auteuil were accused of scandalous liaisons with women.[60] A woman impregnated by the Sieur de la Durantaye initially gave her baby to Indians at Lorette, leading to pressure on the Crown to provide for abandoned bastards; and a council order against giving French children to natives suggests that this was no isolated case. Marie-Aimée Cliche's study of unwed mothers noted that elite fathers were overrepresented in cases of pregnancy out of wedlock. Fathers could be called upon to provide for, even take into their households, illegitimate offspring, and a man who compromised a woman of rank would pay particularly high damages. A Montreal magistrate made a revealing comment to Pierre Saint-Ours after he impregnated another officer's daughter: Why had he set his sights on her when there were 'plenty of girls of lower birth at his beck and call with little risk involved'?[61] Discretion regarding elite misconduct frustrates any attempt at quantitative analysis. But the evidence points in the direction of nobles being out of step with the general population, which had lower illegitimacy rates than those in France.[62]

Another question is also of interest: Did the usual, gendered, double standard apply to nobles? Some historical studies of plebeian insults in Europe and its colonies have contended that the most highly prized virtues were chastity in a woman and honesty in a man, though some take issue with this view.[63] As historian James McMillan observed, that code clearly did not extend to nobles in pre-revolutionary France, where 'in practice, if not in theory, the double standard of morality no longer applied to many women of the French upper classes.'[64] Did the colonial male *and* female nobility emulate the infidelities for which French elites were famous? We know that the bishop was sufficiently concerned about officers having liaisons with married women to issue a *mandement* against it in 1694, and in the following decade the intendant instructed Montreal men to stop housing their mistresses in town. Yet these were probably typically women of a lower class, as Cliche's study suggests.

Other evidence, too, suggests that noblewomen in Canada were more restrained than their male counterparts. Discouraging libertinism was the fact that birth control techniques do not seem to have been employed; while French noble birth rates dropped from 6.5 in the seventeenth century to 2.0 in the eighteenth, the colonial rates remained high. The 6.2 per cent rate of *pre*-nuptial conceptions among colonial noble couples was about the same as that of the general population.[65] In the early eighteenth century, the strong action taken against one particularly black sheep seems to suggest that open libertinism was far from the norm. Notorious among single women was the twenty-five-year-old daughter of Pierre André de Leigne, a Prévôté de Quebec official. She 'had long lived a life contrary to good morals and good order' the authorities wrote, and her father tried to ship her back to France to a house of correction. When two young noblemen helped her escape in men's clothing before the ship departed, her father refused to have her back under his roof. The Saint-Vincent family seem to have been part of this wild crowd, the son helping Demoiselle André de Leigne jump ship, the daughter becoming pregnant out of wedlock.[66] Several other noble daughters too were impregnated out of wedlock, though the degree of consent is unknown.

Morals apparently grew looser with the passage of time. During the Seven Years' War when French forces flooded the colony, mores followed those of France; illegitimacy rates climbed among the populace, and there were scandalous liaisons at the social summit. Angelique Renaud d'Avène des Méloizes, witty twenty-five-year-old wife of Chevalier de Pean, became the mistress of the middle-aged Intendant Bigot, sharing in his gambling parties, a situation accepted by her husband as a path to his advancement. There is some evidence that Louise-Geneviève des Champs de Boishebert de Ramezay, granddaughter of the former Montreal governor, had had an extramarital liaison with General de Montcalm and possibly had a child by him. Even Louise-Geneviève's grandmother, the governor's wife, was suspected of having an affair with a Montreal official.[67]

Overall, cases of noblewomen consorting with men who were not their husbands do not seem plentiful. It is possible, of course, that elite families were good at guarding their secrets, and that incriminating documents or lore were suppressed as French Canada moved into its long ultra-Catholic period after 1840. The most suggestive comment I have been able find about elite libertinism is an observation by the often-reliable John Lambert at the beginning of the nineteenth century that 'the number of unfaithful wives, kept mistresses and girls of easy virtue exceed in proportion those of the old country ... However, husbands generally wink at the infidelities of their wives.'[68]

Among the noble families that are our main focus, the most shocking case (all the more so because it seems the perpetrator went free) concerns Pierre Legardeur de Repentigny, husband of Agathe Saint-Père. A great frequenter of taverns, de Repentigny was notoriously libertine. His assaults upon an employee reveal the vulnerability of a servant, Marie Lugré, left alone with a brutal superior. According to the servant's testimony,

The sieur Darpentigny forced her to remain in his service for a third and final year. He made every effort to corrupt her and to have his carnal pleasure. Seeing that the complainant did not want to give what he wanted from her, he took her honour by force. When she resisted his passions and brutality, and defended herself from his approaches, he had recourse to threats and even to his sword. On four different occasions he seemed to want to gorge her, and to pierce her chest. He cut the hooks of her skirts. He put all his forces to action during the absence of his wife and children, whom he sent away on purpose in order to have more ease in satiating his brutality, to violate the honour of the complainant, who found herself persecuted and threatened with being shot to death if she didn't consent to his base desires and violence and shameless touching. In the end, her forces and means of resisting him being exhausted, and not being able to leave his house, she found herself giving in.[69]

This incident occurred within a year of Repentigny's 1685 marriage to Agathe Saint-Père, when they were both aged twenty-eight. De Repentigny repeatedly demanded sex of the servant when his wife was away until he at last impregnated her; then he threatened to kill her if she revealed him as the father. The assaults occurred, the servant said, when Agathe Saint-Père was at Mass, or visiting Lavaltrie (where she had relatives) and when younger members of the household were asleep. The portrait of the ruthless officer and the servant brutalized and sexually exploited helps us understand why Canadians were reluctant to enter service. The wife who was frequently away, and the infidelity within a year of the wedding day, suggest a rather lose marital bond. It is true, however, that Repentigny was one of the most notorious officers in this regard. It is also true that scandalous affairs could disqualify a man for office. Lieutenant General Raimbault's efforts to curb Montreal illegal trading alienated many parties and was said to have spurred particularly vicious gossip about his liaison with a widow. The attacks on his character were so forceful as to interfere with his advancement.[70]

Was Female Enterprise Unusual?

Among colonial elites, the father of the family was often, through no fault of his own, an undependable breadwinner. From the 1670s requests began to multiply for government assistance for Canadian nobles unable to support their large families. La Potherie wrote that Canada was a poor country, heavily dependent on Crown gratifications. The lack of commercial agriculture prevented seigneuries from approaching levels of prosperity often attained by noble landowners in France. In 1686 the intendant reported that Pierre Saint-Ours's daughters had even been reduced to tilling the fields. More commonly, officers relied on fur-trading to supplement their income. But it often remained true that 'the officers who are married have only their appointments to sustain their families; their wives are in distress when they die.'[71] Intendant Hocquart felt he should allow poor officers and their widows the petty commerce involved in provisioning the posts with foodstuffs in 'this country which has so much need of aid.'

Dispatch after dispatch from the governor and intendant solicited pensions, fur-trading licences, and the King's 'graces' or gratifications for impecunious wives, widows, and their children.[72] When Elisabeth de Vaudreuil's father died, the intendant wrote in 1685 to supplicate the Crown on behalf of his widow and two children, who were 'so reduced in fortune as to be without bread'[73] – a formulaic phrase probably indicating not actual hunger but lack of any secure source of income. Mesdames Vaudreuil and Ramezay remained rivals for favours long after both husbands had died. A number joined Madame de Ramezay in trying to stretch Crown largesse by having their pensions passed down to daughters or even granddaughters. It is hard to know the extent of hyperbole in petitions, but it seems noble 'poverty' did sometimes cut close to the bone. Possibly it did so with the officers at Fort Fréderic in 1742 who were reported to be so poor their wives turned to the intendant for rations.[74] Governor Frontenac in 1679 beseeched the Crown for some means of subsistence for Messieurs d'Ailleboust, Denys de la Ronde, and Repentigny, and it seems likely that such insecurity helped spur the entry of women of all three of those families into trade.

The de Ramezays struggled for a long time after the governor's death in 1724. Governor General Vaudreuil commented that the Montreal governor had served 'with honour ... and lived very comfortably, having always spent more than his salary, which is the reason he has left only a very small estate to his widow and children.'[75] Fortunately Madame de Ramezay was already familiar with handling estate business, as were the wives of many other seigneur-officers who were much away. Sitting down at the writing desk to pen supplications, the widow secured a pension for herself, a captaincy for her son, and small gratifications for her single daughters. Favours flowed from the highest officials for years after her husband's death. Even so, she remained saddled with debts that would today be seen as the responsibility of government, such as the governor's purchase of artillery.[76]

One served the family line. Even an unmarried daughter such as Louise de Ramezay was likely motivated by the dynastic interests that loomed so large for the nobility. Louise developed the family properties on behalf of her sisters and her last surviving brother, who was preoccupied with his illustrious military career. The King instructed him to build a mill on the family properties so the *habitants* could grind their wheat, but the records suggest it was Louise who eventually constructed one. When he yielded Quebec City up to General Wolfe's army in the winter of 1759–60 and followed the defeated army to France, Louise remained in the colony, looking after family interests by selling a good part of the now-productive property to her widowed sister, whose children would continue the line in Canada.[77]

The de Ramezay clan indicates how 'normal' female enterprise could be, even in a leading family in which it was probably not a matter of strict necessity.[78] The family tree reveals sisters, mothers, and daughters all carrying on commercial ventures, ranging from fur-trading and transatlantic shipping to brick and timber operations. We know that Louise's aunt, Marie-Louise Denys de la Ronde (Madame D'Argenteuil), exploited family lands well placed for the fur trade at the west end of Montreal island, and exported furs and hides across the Atlantic. We saw how Louise's widowed mother, Charlotte Denys de la Ronde de Ramezay, assumed control of the family timber and sawmilling operation located in the Richelieu valley, and actively pursued seigneurial interests.[79] Louise's sister Geneviève de Boishébert, whose husband was crippled in war, was yet another family member who involved herself in trade, a receiver of large shipments of imported goods. We might add Louise's sister Charlotte, a nun who variously served as the financial officer and the superior of her Quebec Hôpital Général, overseeing its seigneurial lands and its commercial windmill in town. On the maternal side of the family, Madame Des Muceaux was another relative involved in the fur trade. Her daughter (Louise's first cousin) married into the trading Pierre Margane Lavaltrie family and played a part in the family business. Another maternal aunt of Louise's, Françoise Denys, also engaged in money lending and land sales. A seventeenth-century relative of theirs, Marguerite Denys de Lanougière, had directed the family seigneurie both as a young bride and for decades after becoming a widow at age twenty-one. Likewise, Louise's aunt Madame D'Argenteuil[80] made most of her money during her thirty-seven years of widowhood. Here again, we have a picture of successive generations of sisters, mothers, and daughters involved in enterprises in which female public activity was part of the ordinary course of things.

What about the Vaudreuils, occupying the lofty mansion of the governor general? They and their kinswomen worked their government connections. We know the widowed mother of the governor's wife had been involved in fur-trading in Acadia. She reaped richer rewards when she managed to ingratiate herself at Versailles. Her daughter Elisabeth's own profitable years at Versailles followed. Back in Quebec, Angelique Chartier de Lotbinière, aristocratic wife of the Crown attorney (and relative of Madame Vaudreuil), ran a drapery shop, following the footsteps of other titled ladies in trade. Other government wives did the same. In the late seventeenth century at the governor's mansion, Madame de Denonville ran a boutique.[81] The wife of a Treasury commissioner and several officials' wives also had things for sale. Elisabeth's kinswoman and goddaughter Louise Chartier de Lotbinière (Madame Denys de la Ronde) was by a 1734 procuration empowered to administer her husband's business affairs while he was pursuing his unsuccessful copper-mining venture near Lake Superior, and she persuaded the French court to let the family retain the post after his death.[82] Madame Vaudreuil's daughter-in-law, Jeanne-Charlotte de Fleury Deschambault, made a move not uncommon for ancien régime widows when she married a younger man (Vaudreuil was fifteen years her junior). Evidently she was enterprising, for she involved herself in commerce in Louisiana when her husband was governor there. She also perpetuated family tradition by making appeals to the minister of marine for his advancement.[83]

Hands-on business also characterized the family of Agathe Saint-Père de Repentigny. Female relatives followed her into trade. In 1717 one 'Mademoiselle de Repentigny' was recorded as exchanging furs with a government-approved company. We know that Agathe's daughter Marguerite, who married officer J-B de Saint-Ours Deschaillons, took charge of his business affairs in the colony when he went west for a number of years; she also at various points shipped timber and managed seigneurial affairs.[84] Another daughter, Agathe's namesake, married merchant François-Marie Bouat, who died in 1726. 'Madame Bouat' was listed on Crown bills of exchange for shipments to Ile Royale in 1731, fourteen years later for tonnage on a ship carrying iron, tar, and fish oil to Rochefort.[85] Agathe Saint-Père's sister-in-law was Labrador trader Marie-Charlotte Charest, who in turn was maternal aunt of the smuggling Desauniers sisters. Madame Lusignan was part of that clan too. Casting the net a little wider, we find another relation of Agathe's, Marie Anne Legardeur de Saint-Pierre de Repentigny, marrying into another family with a fur-trading mother (to whom we shall return): Marie-Anne La Marque, wife of the Detroit commander Tonty.

Were these entrepreneurial gentlewomen seen as mavericks? Comments by contemporaries indicate that female trade was not uncommon. Intendant Hocquart noted that wives made the governors' and intendants' mansions their places of assembly, flocking there to solicit favours for their husbands, children, and friends; that Canadian women had a 'disposition for business.'[86] As we have noted earlier, the intendant also concluded that women of almost all classes in the colony were more astute than the men, though he said he did not understand how this had come to be. Colonial officers were so regularly posted away from home that it was not uncommon for them to delegate powers-of-attorney to their wives or female relatives, as in the case of both Agathe Saint-Père and her daughter when their male relatives headed west. Merchant Pierre Guy reported widespread transfer of business powers to wives when war broke out in 1744.[87] Numerous women, noble and otherwise, provisioned the Crown during that war, as we saw in chapter 4. More than a few benefited from a Crown policy that gave the widows and families of officers preference in that regard.

In many noble families, both sexes made active efforts to secure Crown favours, good marriages, and whatever revenues would allow them to 'live nobly' – or at least keep the wolf from the door. In all these – and many other – families, female economic activity throughout the period of French rule was not an aberrant calling but a perfectly normal one. Was famous frontier fighter Hertel de Rouville marching off to war? Then his wife Marie-Anne Legras would stay on the seigneurie and form a long-term sawmilling partnership with Louise de Ramezay. Was there an untimely death? A widow in a mercantile family such as Marie-Madeleine Roberge (*veuve* Charles Perthuis) would continue the enterprise, trade to Louisbourg, and, across the Atlantic, buy up flour produced by the Quebec Seminary, supply religious orders with French goods, and venture into Quebec real estate.[88] Many of the interrelated elite families had multiple women, spanning generations, involved in trade. Indeed, given the close kin ties in the ruling class, one suspects every Canadian noble could name a female relative who conducted some business affairs. Some could easily rattle off half a dozen.

Proud Entrepreneurs

Agathe Saint-Père did not go into business because she did not value her noble status. Indeed, she initiated legal proceedings to prevent her half-brother from marrying a commoner and assiduously specified that habitants on her lands must pay homage by planting a maypole in front

of her manor.[89] The lady valued her hard-earned blue blood. In light of
changing standards on the other side of the Atlantic about what befitted
a lady, it is noteworthy that she was proud, not ashamed, of her economic
activity. She wrote to the colonial minister in 1705 with news of her textile enterprise and proposals for developing Canadian buffalo wool, cot-
tonwood clothing, and maple sweets (with samples enclosed). She had
ideas about using lake rushes for bed ticking and a rot-resistant fibre
for ship's rigging.[90] She said nothing about being a 'mere woman' and
made no mention of her husband's military service. Hers was good old
self-aggrandizement in the style of the *gentilhomme campagnard*: 'I repeat
to your lordship that the woolens here are incomparably better than
those of France. I would never finish, Monseigneur, were I to indulge myself in revealing all the knowledge I have of the advantages to be found
in Canada ... only my courage has prevented my ceding to difficulties
and expenses that I had to make in these beginnings.... The country ...
would receive endless fruits from the use of these resources which until
now have been enveloped in obscurity from which I have raised them.
My imagination, Monsieur, has procured me the honour to enter into a
little part of your intentions.'[91]

Knowledge, courage, and imagination – what unladylike virtues! But
incipient forms of ladyhood would take a long time to reach the gentry
living out on the colonial fringe. The idea of feminine modesty had not
yet supplanted the noble mandate to show off, to brag about answer-
ing the King's' call for public-spirited enterprise to relieve shortages. In
a similar vein, Chambly's Madame de Thiersant immodestly informed
the colonial minister in 1731 that it was she who had given the state the
means to eject the illegal trade of the English from Canada, a signal contribution to the colony's commerce. Hence, she informed the Crown,
the paltry emolument the Indies Company gave her should be converted
into a more fitting reward.[92] Her neighbour, timber and tanning merchant Louise de Ramezay, who was of higher rank than Thiersant or
Saint-Père, did not suffer any loss of face from her activities either, receiving honours and patronage from both church and state.[93] In Canada it
was still a fine thing for a lady to involve herself in the Crown's economic
objectives – and she expected compensation for it, too.

The ideal of the 'separate sphere,' that ethereal planet devoid of female breadwinners, is perceived as rising in the skies of France and England sometime during the eighteenth century. It was incontestably in
view by 1750, with the upper classes being the first to feel its gravitational
pull. But the 'sphere' rose too late and too far away to have much impact

on New France. The noblewomen there did not consider their activity in any way déclassé or degrading. 'I have worked all my life,' wrote Marie-Anne La Marque to the colonial minister in 1729, shortly after the death of her husband, Detroit commander Alphonse de Tonty. Her mother had been baptized at the French court, her godmother being Madame de Guercheville who had financed missionaries to New France – facts that La Marque proudly noted in her petition. Even for a lady of such high pedigree, admitting to working all her life was not shameful. That distinguishes these gentlewomen from those of subsequent generations, epitomized by the nineteenth-century lady said to 'but touch any article, now matter how delicate, in the way of trade, she loses caste, and ceases to be a lady.'[94]

Ladies in the Napoleonic and Victorian eras would clearly be the inheritors of the ancient noble prohibition on dirtying the hands with soil or lucre, as that (always elusive) ideal was transferred from nobles of both sexes to gentle*women* in particular. Isolation and necessity would perpetuate the working 'lady' in the colonies long after eighteenth-century philosophers and conduct writers began to stigmatize her in France and England. Governors' wives and daughters earned their bread by lobbying officials or working on their seigneurial accounts. Officers' wives continued to dirty their hands with ledger books and packets of beaver at Canadian towns and posts.

All in all, there were a number of ways noble families lacked the rigid gender specialization that would be expected of their nineteenth-century granddaughters in Victorian Canada. The mothers seem questionable nurturers, sanguine about losing half their babies to nursemaids, about losing sons to war. The fathers seem equally inept as breadwinners. Oblivious of the gender codes that a later age would impose so dogmatically, gentlewomen presumed that they, like their men, must cobble together the family's fortunes. We have seen in earlier chapters that female involvement in various kinds of economic activity was a normal part of life for ordinary women in town and country. Ladies at the top of the social scale, too, applied themselves to meeting family economic needs, and they were also conscious of another responsibility, one sometimes called noblesse oblige. Often enough, when they signed their names they signalled awareness that they represented both their noble family of birth and the second one into which they had married. Far from being the nameless 'Mrs' of some man, they represented two great families; listing no first name, they simply signed 'Denys Ramezay' or 'Joybert Vaudreuil.' Some of those at the apex might serve not just as economic actors but as public servants too. To that more rarefied calling we now turn.

Noble Public Service

Nobles took seriously the call to serve the Crown. The Ramezay family, for example, presents a picture of starry-eyed, though somewhat star-crossed, idealism. Growing up in the public eye, Louise de Ramezay and her siblings present a picture not so much of self-indulgent luxury as of stressful royal service. Their mother, herself raised in an aristocratic family, knew the requirements of 'living nobly.' They included hosting lavish banquets and all-night balls, being present at military and civil ceremonies, and in her particular case, smoothing over the quarrels of her irascible husband, who had an unfortunate habit of attacking superiors.

It is no wonder ladies were reported to mix water with their wine. At table and in the hall they were on duty, steering the conversation the right way, whether it involved carefully calculated matchmaking or dunning officials for a favour. The officials had to guard their backs, for 'wicked talk' could be sufficiently poisonous to threaten their careers, as Montreal Lieutenant General Raimbault discovered. Matchmaking was serious business too; a *mésalliance* that offended the governor could result in exile. Governor Beauharnois complained in 1727 that gossiping and backbiting reigned in the colony, fostered by long idle winters with little news of the outside world. Malicious though it might be, this was an opening for 'woman's speech,' which historians have identified as a source of power, though it was a power already on the decline in parts of Europe after 1650.[95] Indeed, French Minister Pontchartrain warned Governor Vaudreuil not to listen to 'women's talk.' But Canadians were all ears. Intendant Jacques Raudot complained that Madame Vaudreuil's salon was a regular forum for slanderers. The women hosted the salons, and both sexes dropped in to indulge in the sport. Governor de Ramezay told the minister he was intimidated by slander associating him with the brandy trade. He then lobbed accusations of his own at Madame Vaudreuil, intimating that she had purloined military supplies to build a road to her new house on the outskirts of Montreal.[96]

Amidst all the stresses relating to gossip, factional feuds, and fur-trade rivalries, Madame Charlotte Denys de la Ronde de Ramezay sitting in state at her banquet table may have stolen a glance at the pattern on her china, which pictured sheep grazing on a quiet meadow. A family story recounts her rather mournful sense of duty, with the younger generation recoiling from life at the head of a pageant. Colonial balls were known to last until three in the morning. Two of her daughters expressed surprise at seeing their mother up again a few hours after hosting such a party. This interchange is reported:

> 'It's as it should be, my children,' responded Madame de Ramezay, 'your father has to go before nine to the Champ-de-Mars to review the new regiment, whose principal officers we had here last evening.'
>
> 'But you are pale ..., Mother, doesn't this noisy and dissipated life vex you? ... '
>
> 'I must admit we'd have more happiness and peace if we could live retired on our seigneurie; but what would people think of us, if we refused to associate with his Majesty's officers, with high-ranking citizens? ... '
>
> Catherine cried out: 'You have more cares than pleasures! ... permit your daughters to embrace a state which never offers such vexations.'[97]

They were the Crown's public servants. Entertaining officers and reviewing troops was the duty of noble men, women – and even children, who were reported to have accompanied their parents that morning to the ceremony.

There are other indications of a strain of idealism in the De Ramezay family. Young graduates of the Quebec Ursuline school, Louise and her sisters were described as 'living a life worthy of the first Christians.' Emulating parental public service, and perhaps their brothers' battlefield sacrifices too, Louise and two of her sisters offered to take the place of nuns who had died caring for the sick during an epidemic.[98] In return they requested only to be buried in the nuns' chapel should they perish. Such altruistic behaviour might suggest that Louise's motive in developing the family seigneuries was not her own wealth and comfort but to keep the estate intact while her sole remaining brother was fighting for the colony's survival; transferring it to her widowed sister and her children further suggest goals that went beyond personal acquisitiveness. In a letter written after 1760 to her brother-in-law, Louise spoke very warmly of his young children before going on to give detailed information about deeds and titles to family properties. It seems they all heard a call to serve.

The two girls in the family story about the late-night ball later assumed administrative positions in convents, and another sister spent her life as a lay volunteer caring for the ill at the Hôtel-Dieu. Perhaps it was in reaction to her stately upbringing that Catherine de Ramezay later made a name for herself by exhorting her students at the Ursuline school to shun one impressive earthly vanity of the day, the voluminous *panier* skirt. Her sister Marie-Charlotte, as Mother Saint-Claude of the Quebec Hôpital Général, would render Crown service to the end, it seems, by spreading rumours of French victory in hopes of demoralizing British troops in the hospital at the time of the Conquest, as our next chapter will discuss.

Elisabeth Joybert de Vaudreuil's many years abroad perhaps also qualify as heroism in service of the Crown, though the circumstances were scarcely edifying. Troubles began when she first rushed over to France, during time of war, in hopes of allaying growing criticism of her husband. When her ship was captured, she, like her father before her, became a prisoner of the English. When at last she arrived at Versailles, she was, as we have seen, successful in ingratiating herself both with the royal family and the minister of marine. However, it may have been her discretion, and the fact that she would one day return to a distant colony, that qualified her for service to the King's grandson, the Duke of Berry. It was a disordered and scandal-ridden household. The duke, so poorly educated that his courtiers had to script even the shortest of his speeches, disgraced himself at the time of the Treaty of Utrecht by becoming too tongue-tied to say a word to those gathered in state to hear him. His wife was an imperious creature who became so drunk at table that she passed out; who grew so bold in infidelity that she tried to persuade one of her courtiers to elope with her. Although having personal duties in the royal household was an honour, this particular assignment must have had a tortuous side. Those in attendance needed to avoid taint from the scandals and to be discreet in managing and concealing their employers' follies.[99] The Duchess of St Simon, who also served there, wrote that the position was beneath Madame Vaudreuil, a woman of considerable talent, who had accepted it in order to advance the interests of her large family – as indeed it did.

Madame de Vaudreuil's court service and influence gave her a stature surpassing that of some top Canadian administrators – who were generally respected in the colony but sometimes considered nonentities at Versailles.[100] When she finally sailed back to Quebec in 1721 after her twelve-year absence, ensconced in the captain's quarters and surrounded by servants, the former charity case from Acadia held her head high. Landing in Canada, the Ursulines' once 'modest' student was reported to have acquired the air of a great and proud noblewoman. She instigated a grand rebuilding of the chateau. She got her own kinsman appointed head of the Quebec Recollets. Now the gubernatorial couple, according to a somewhat intimidated Bishop Saint-Vallier, was in a position to sweep around Quebec speaking 'very forcefully' about their schemes and their enmities. Madame Vaudreuil left the bishop sputtering about this overbearing conduct, complaining of Madame's cavalier disregard of cloister as she dropped into convents with her entourage of ladies and girls.[101]

Madame Vaudreuil, like Agathe Saint-Père, considered business of state to be *her* business. She was not the first woman to represent a governor's political interests at court; we have seen that Madame de Frontenac had performed that role in the 1680s, and Madame de La Forest later represented Governor de Ramezay. But Madame de Vaudreuil spoke loud and long. While not all her advice was taken, she clearly enjoyed a number of successes, both before and after the death of her husband. Historian Guy Fregault noted that she involved herself in 'le grand politique' – in military and political planning. For example, an urgent letter she penned at court to the minister of marine outlined intelligence she had just received from an English ship of a planned attack on New France's east coast. She implored the minister to ship arms to the colony. Since the news had reached her suddenly, she had no time for consultation with her husband, and the expertise appears to be her own:

Versailles, 15 February 1710

Monseigneur

I learned yesterday evening from an English vessel captured and brought into St Malo that the English are putting into execution the project they formulated last year to go attack Canada by sea and by land, that vessels from London will embark at once to join the Boston fleet. This news, Monseigneur, has every appearance of being true. I beseech you to instantly give your order to send powder and muskets to Canada where they have scarcely any; since the ships of Granville and Bayonne are leaving this month for Plaisance, they could carry the powder Monsieur de Costebello is sending by these ships to Quebec, for there are many muskets at Plaisance from the capture of Saint John. I implore you also, Monseigneur, to order that some be sent to Quebec and if the two hundred troops destined for Canada could also carry them that would be greatly beneficial. I have the honour to be with profound respect, your very humble and very obedient servant.[102]

After Acadia fell to the English, Madame Vaudreuil suggested strategies for its recapture, specifying the different kinds of equipment needed according to whether the campaign took place in winter or summer.

There was both knowledge and power here. In 1711 she proposed reinstalling military garrisons in Canada's three towns. In another letter she made a detailed list of the various supplies needed to secure Indian alliances. Another discussed the merits of building a fort at a point near Montreal to forestall enemy attacks. For two decades successive ministers reiterated Madame de Vaudreuil's 1710 advice to the court to reduce the number of horses so Canadians would retain the snowshoeing skills needed on winter raids. The Marine Council accepted her as a player in Canadian policy, for it deliberated on her suggestions and her nominees for colonial positions just as it deliberated on those sent by the governor and the intendant. With the help of Intendant Jacques Raudot, the Vaudreuils prevailed over their opponent Attorney General Ruette d'Autueil, who was ignominiously dismissed from office. Later it was the turn of the intendant himself to fall prey to the Vaudreuils' enmity and superior connections, his ears burning with satirical verses Madame Vaudreuil composed about him that were sung in the streets. When Raudot denounced this malice to Versailles, it was not taken very seriously – woman's speech again. In the colony, though, it hit its mark.[103] Governor de Ramezay was afraid of her too.[104]

In the Vaudreuil family, and a number of others we have discussed, the roles passed down through the generations. We have seen that both Madame de Marson and her daughter Elisabeth de Vaudreuil were heard at court; Elisabeth's daughter-in-law in her turn would appeal to the court on behalf of her own husband, Governor Pierre Rigaud de Vaudreuil. Like her mother-in-law and her husband's grandmother, she felt qualified to offer advice on matters of state. The *Marquise de Vaudreuil*, sixteen-gun warship built on Lake Ontario in 1756, attested to the prestige of the Vaudreuil wives. On the eve of the Conquest, though, this wife of the second Governor de Vaudreuil would earn a scolding from General Montcalm, who informed her that ladies must not discuss war. He added that if Madame de Montcalm were present she would certainly provide a model of silence.[105] But how could they keep silent? Even in convents, nuns drawn from these same Canadian noble families knew about the battles their menfolk were fighting, discussed military strategy, and looked for ways to subvert the enemy. Backward as usual, the colonials were slow to conform to the shrinking sphere being designed for the eighteenth-century European lady. At Versailles, as we saw in chapter 1, after the reign of Louis XIV there had been a gradual decline in the ability of royal wives and mistresses to influence policy and political appointments.[106] Women's ability to be taken seriously during the Sun King's reign permeates the story of Elisabeth de Vaudreuil. But forty years later, in Canada's last years as a colony of France, the boorish colonials had not yet absorbed the new, more gendered forms of discretion, the more ornamental feminine role established at the court of Louis XV and his successor. It took the *campagnard* ladies a while to realize that affairs of state were no longer their business.

Times would change soon enough. Within a decade or two of the British Conquest, the Versailles-trained Lady Carleton and her entourage would be teaching Canadian ladies how to fly into 'hysterics' (eliciting Madame Baby's acerbic comment that were a Canadian girl to try it, her mother would box her ears).[107] Loyalist petitioners arriving in Canada in the 1780s from America would glorify their husbands' wartime courage and heroism while remaining silent about their own, as the work of Janice McKinnon has shown. Ladies would by then try to cover up any evidence of female entrepreneurs in the family tree. Both Lady Carleton and the Loyalists would have been shocked by Agathe Saint-Père's unladylike boasting about her grubby manufacturing business.[108]

Conclusion

It is perhaps now clear that the enterprising noblewomen we have examined here, if more dynamic or successful than others of their caste, were not so much stepping outside an established role as fulfilling one. Their place was not in the bosom of a small private family of modern conception. The non-existence of such families is suggested by the outsiders living within the manors, by the sending away of infants and children, by absences of not only fathers but also of mothers.

The fate of Madame de Ramezay, burning the candle at both ends with her public duties, losing four sons, left widowed and in debt, shows that this demanding role did not necessarily reward its practitioners with either happiness or security. Her own attempts to restore the family fortunes were not very successful. Her single daughter, Louise, however, became a long-term entrepreneur with a considerable range of operations. She may have had both a taste and a talent for business; the duty to safeguard an indebted family property while her male kin were busy defending the colony also propelled her into action, just as it had propelled her mother before her. Agathe Saint-Père, who raised ten of her mother's children and then eight of her own, probably seldom called an hour her own. Overseeing food and clothing for all those youngsters, developing colonial resources, or employing New England weavers do not fall neatly into public and private categories but were all part of her duties towards her 'own,' a circle that included her immediate kin, the nobility as a whole, and as her confident letter of 1705 suggests, the colonial minister and the King. Elisabeth Joybert de Vaudreuil and her mother both carried service to *their* own all the way to the glittering halls of Versailles. Elisabeth, and later her daughter-in-law too, thought it quite fitting to mix military advice with appeals they might be making on behalf of family and protégés. It is indicative of the 'normal' nature of such activities that in all three of these leading families we have discussed, it was not just some outstanding individual but an array of mothers, sisters, and daughters who embraced public activities, just as their men followed one another into glorious but underpaid military careers.

Despite a certain arrogance, these people probably had little sense of themselves as unique individuals. That awaited the later romantic awareness of self and valorisation of private emotions. Death struck too often and too early for them to delude themselves that they were singular or irreplaceable. They were aware of themselves as links in noble chains, upholders of the family line. Although their business journeys, their willingness to delegate childcare to others, and their economic and political initiative resemble those of latter-day career women, we find scant evidence that they wanted to be remembered for the money they made. They were not ashamed of it, but it was not the wellspring of their pride; their bloodlines were. The requests they made for Crown favours and subsidies, the military commissions they coveted for brothers and sons, their entrance into convents so they would not lose caste by marrying commoners suggest they were preoccupied with family 'honour' and livelihood more than with their own individual ambitions. Indeed much of their public activity was evidently an ordeal rather than a pleasure.

These figures operated so much within the rules of caste that it seems accurate to place them within an entrenched, highly ritualized order of Old World origin. The most successful noblewoman we have met here, Elisabeth Joybert de Vaudreuil, was more than ready to exchange the dubious charms of the Canadian wilderness for a foothold in France. Shortly after her husband's death she rejected the crude profits of beaver skins, offering to swap valuable family land astride trade routes to Montreal for the more refined pleasures of a heather-filled forest in Languedoc.[109] Ultimately she set up house with her daughters, mother, and mother-in-law in Paris, never to see the rugged cliff of Quebec again.

Madame de Vaudreuil and the other noblewomen we have met in this chapter were enterprising, but they were not innovative. These were not 'new women' on the frontier, for they gloried in the conventions of their caste. The parvenu or rustic ones strutted, boasted, and started factories; the more refined ones developed a haughty demeanour and French connections. All were keenly aware of their rank with its privileges and duties. As in board games, they could move only along well-established lines; but by moving deftly within the rules of the game they could out-manoeuvre opponents and outrun adversity.

The situation is well captured in a game of theirs that has come down to modern times. The rules of chess reflect a similar concern with maintaining family, caste, and religion in service of the Crown. All strive to protect their King and defeat his opponents. The knights can make short, devastating charges. The rooks or castles – those of landed wealth such as Louise de Ramezay – can use it to move energetically across the board and prevent disaster. The bishops have their own considerable, if oblique, power: representatives of a hierarchical church that placed high-born sons and daughters well. As for the Queen – even though this was an age in which monarchs desperately desired male heirs – for some reason the Queen is the most powerful piece on the board. The King – who must not be taken – is of course the most important, but is too stately for manoeuvre. The Queen's might lies in the fact that she can strike suddenly from across the board and win the game. Who knows why these long-ago people gave her such clout? Certainly it was not often the case in real life. But, as Madame Vaudreuil might tell you, the rules of the game did open up the possibility.

Chapter Seven

Decoding the Eighteenth-Century Convent

Just as the traditional outlook of French elites pervaded noble homes, it also pervaded convents. There too privileges, duties, and connections shaped the way a group of women dealt with the challenge of life along the St Lawrence. Convents followed French models to develop a system that was in many ways more hierarchical than communal. Well-developed systems developed over the centuries in Europe regulated their lives of prayer, the way they nursed and educated growing numbers of colonists, tended their own fields and gardens, and turned natural products into sources of revenue. When the time came, their institutional strength and aristocratic connections allowed them to face an invading army that came down the river and demanded entry. This chapter is a study of the social and economic capital of convents, and the importance of noble clientage systems in assuring their well-being and survival.

Our investigation reaffirms viewpoints expressed by various scholars about the importance of colonial convents in making 'a vital contribution to colonial development.'[1] We observed in chapter 2 the vital activities of Marie de l'Incarnation and other members of religious orders in colonizing early Quebec and Montreal and setting up the first publicly available systems of schooling and medical care. When we take a closer look here at the modus operandi of convents, it supports another scholarly assertion, that they were able at times to withstand the 'intransigent wills' of bishops bent on altering their rules or their mandate.[2] What was the source of authority in these single women, who were nominally subservient to a male hierarchy (and certainly lacked any husband to protect them)? Tallying up their various kinds of economic and social capital can help us understand how, even in a patriarchal society, convents at times shocked officials with what was deemed 'open resistance' and 'rebelliousness.'[3] Pondering why they were not controlled by male administrators to the extent that convents in France were, the governor and intendant mused that it might date to the fact that nuns had arrived in the colony before it possessed a bishop or an intendant. They retained some of their founders' rights even as pioneer missions evolved into more conventional establishments on eighteenth-century streets.

We select, as our prime example in this discussion, the most aristocratic of the convents, the Hôpital Général or General Hospice of Quebec. Its workings did, however, have parallels in all convents, and this chapter will visit them all. They include two Hôtel-Dieu hospitals, one in Quebec and one in Montreal. There were also two Ursuline establishments, consisting of a school at Quebec and the combined school and hospital at Trois-Rivières. The large, and relatively populist, Congregation of Notre Dame at one time or another conducted fifteen schools across the colony. Along with Quebec's General Hospice there was also one in Montreal, which in the regime's closing decades was removed from the hands of a male order and placed in the hands of lay sisters, the *soeurs grises*.

Having discussed religious motivations in chapter 2, here we note only tangentially the spiritual dimensions of the sisters' work. Those, of course, persisted; but with the death of the last of the sisters who had known Marie de l'Incarnation, Jeanne Mance, and Marguerite Bourgeoys, the legendary mission days became more a revered memory than an everyday reality.[4] However, it is important to recognize, even as we focus on secular sources of power, that the religious and the secular were thoroughly intertwined. Even the most combative or imperious nun was probably convinced that success would permit her to better serve the Lord and his people. If she solicited the Crown for help against a local opponent, she was not appealing to a 'secular' ruler but one viewed in Christian doctrine as upholding a divine covenant with the ruled.

Waiting in the wings to guide us on this tour of the eighteenth-century convent is Marie-Charlotte de Ramezay. Like most nobles, she was proud of her lineage and proved it when she took the vow and assumed the name of her father (Montreal Governor Claude de Ramezay), becoming Mother Saint-Claude de la Croix. Observers singled her out for her stately air and commanding stature (nobles ate better than the common people, and she evidently had the height to prove it). It is instructive to compare the two phases of Mother Saint-Claude's life. As a child she lived in the Norman-style Chateau de Ramezay with its four chimneys and massive stone walls, the estate from which her father governed the town between 1704 and 1724. The second phase began when at age nineteen she entered the novitiate of the Quebec General Hospice, the most prestigious convent in the colony. Her new surroundings in many ways replicated those of the chateau in which, as we have seen, a lady in New France could be economically and politically active without loss of caste.[5] The same was true of the convent.

In both cases, authority sprang not from gender but from noble privileges of command over people and resources. Writers on ancien régime clienteles point to spousal connections and discuss the occasional woman as an active agent. Even nuns, who receive little mention in the literature on clientage, would seem to be candidates for inclusion, for the convent cases that began to come before French Parlements in the eighteenth century required powerful protectors in addition to legal counsel. Inspecting the Hôpital Général de Québec will make it clear that the system of clienteles pervaded even sacred spaces, penetrating the walls of cloisters.[6] The story of Mother Saint-Claude speaks for many other nuns who also had an elite background.[7] They possessed a sophisticated skillset that allowed their orders to flourish in peacetime and avert disaster when Protestant invaders came up the river.

To include a cloister in the political process is consistent with recent writing about Renaissance and ancien régime government. It acknowledges that the formal, abstract state based on an ideal of impersonal public service did not exist in the early modern period. Unofficial groups, noble and clerical factions, and family connections have sometimes been viewed as private, illegitimate interferences with proper government, but historians have come to perceive them as the very essence of the pre-modern state.[8] Since major offices in France ennobled their holder, sooner or later those at the centre of clienteles generally belonged to that estate. New France historian Peter Moogk observed that in New France real power lay with 'high appointees from France who each built up a following from members of different families,' to the extent that one official exclaimed, 'Be a relative or a friend of one of the members of high society and your fortune is made!'[9] Still, clientage systems also connected 'high society' to the general populace. As historian S.J.R. Noel observed of a later period, colonial clientage constituted a broad strand of government 'woven into the total fabric of the community,' with an effectiveness 'all the greater because it was not exclusively political.'[10] Even in the Continental absolutist state, clientage systems offered a flexibility that created areas of 'choice and voluntarism in French political life.'[11] One example of such flexibility was the bargaining power that convents possessed, regardless of their lack of direct representation in the councils of state.

Caste and Clientage among the Nobility

To be a noble, according to Lorraine Gadoury's study of the 181 noble families of New France, one had to meet certain requirements. First of all, there must be documentary proof, such as registered letters of nobility, marriage certificates, or other documents identifying ancestors by noble titles such as *écuyer* (esquire) or *chevalier* (knight). Documents proved Mother Saint-Claude's family was noble as far back as 1532; they had a coat of arms and passed muster with the intendant of Paris that they 'issued from noble race.'[12] Particularly before 1760, the term *race* was frequently used in connection with the ancien régime nobility. Guy Chaussinand-Nogaret identified the belief in eighteenth-century France that nobility conferred 'supériorité séminale ... l'affirmation d'une excellence biologiquement transmise.'[13] In contrast to bourgeois honour, which accrued to the individual, noble honour attached to the lineage. As noted in chapter 6, nobles were seen as a race apart, with separate rules, laws, and customs that made them almost a caste. They had to 'live nobly,' avoiding manual labour and keeping any commercial activity secondary to serving the Crown through military, ecclesiastical, administrative, or ceremonial duties.

The family life of Mother Saint-Claude illustrates what noble performance entailed. Born in 1697, she was baptized Marie-Charlotte de Ramezay. We are already familiar with the Chateau de Ramezay's handsome furniture, mirrors, tapestries, and picturesque grounds that her father boasted made his estate 'unquestionably the most beautiful in Canada.'[14] We know that those who assembled there decked themselves in powdered wigs, floral brocades, velvet, and other markers of noble status, moving gracefully and cultivating witty speech. On the day she replaced her ornate gowns with the plain black-and-white habit of an Augustinian nun, Marie-Charlotte de Ramezay did not shed the noble demeanour, the inbred signs of superiority.[15]

Noble fortunes were advanced through clientage systems. They were usually based on face-to-face contact and reciprocal exchanges over a period of time. Often they involved material benefits such as land or employment in return for loyalty. Typically these were voluntary, vertical alliances between people of unequal status. Both the language of master–servant and of affectionate friendship were employed in these relationships. The bonds were often strengthened by kin or marriage ties.[16]

Sometimes patron–client relations were not face-to-face, but were mediated by brokers. In France, intendants served as brokers for the Crown, using patronage to win the loyalty of provincial nobles and institutions in the peripheral provinces.[17] Many intendants sprang from great families, giving them another attribute of brokers – an independent power base.[18] So important were those connections that in New France all but one of its fifteen intendants were relatives or protégés of two French ministerial families, the Colberts and the Phélypeaux de Pontchartrain (the family with whom Elisabeth Joybert de Vaudreuil ingratiated herself). When Jérome Phélypeaux's relative François de Beauharnois arrived as intendant in 1702, a priest at the Quebec Seminary observed to a colleague, 'He is related to the minister ... and no one dares say anything.'[19] His brother Charles would later serve as governor, becoming a familiar visitor and patron of the General Hospice. Since colonial weather and distance severed communications seven months of the year, the intendant and two other Crown agents, the governor general and bishop, often had to make their own decisions while awaiting court instructions, which made them powerful brokers indeed.

Convents needed political brokers. Bishops (their formal superiors and protectors) were often absent from the colony. Moreover, in the colony the Crown exerted more control than it did in France over basic aspects of colonial convent life such as dowries, number of recruits, and decisions about expansion.[20] Convents thus needed to find powerful friends who would represent them in court circles. Though the present chapter focuses on activities within the colony, the hospice was clearly part of a chain that extended upward, for it had a procurer at Versailles. It also had a friend in Madame Vaudreuil, who was known to ask at court for help with dowries for noble postulants. For their part, convents offered the reciprocal loyalty and service at the heart of the patron–client relationship. They were agents of state social control. They were the institutional destination for potentially unruly beggars, prostitutes, and the insane as well as the elderly and disabled. During epidemics they served as a quarantine station for soldiers and sailors from the King's ships. They performed various other services for their patrons, including accepting as postulants or boarders women who were protégées of the governor, intendant, and the minister of marine. It was clearly a reciprocal arrangement, with nuns providing loyal service in exchange for the protection of the mighty at Quebec and Versailles. The Crown compensated the nuns for these services. Like other faithful clients of the Crown, they continued to serve even when compensation failed to arrive.

Such practices came naturally to the *noblesse*. Certainly in the household in which Mother Saint-Claude was born, building clienteles had always been part of everyday family life. In order 'to display the wealth that promised generosity to his clients ... a great noble needed to maintain a large household.'[21] Her parents had hosted many a travelling dignitary in their chateau as they pursued that strategy. When an extravagant lifestyle left the family in debt upon the governor's death,[22] his survivors could turn to a supportive network. Attending the elite Ursuline convent school in Quebec City, to which Marie-Charlotte and her sisters had been packed off as little girls, they made connections with other noble girls and their families. After the governor died, officials who had likely savoured de Ramezay banquets and balls, helped the widow to procure pensions, timber contracts, and a captaincy for her son Nicolas-Roch.

Despite their privileges, the nobility did not exist merely to decorate the earth. They served the Crown, often at the cost of their lives. Marie-Charlotte's brothers, father, brothers-in-law, cousins, and nephews were all military officers. We know three of her male siblings died in action, leaving only Roch, who served creditably for four decades. Wives, mothers, even nuns of warrior families discussed military strategy and, as we saw in the last chapter, served the Crown in various ways, a few even acting as spokespersons for Canadian governors at the French court.[23] Contemporary terminology recognized the familial responsibility, terming official wives 'La Gouvernante' and 'L'Intendante.' Wives, and children too, stood at attention for troop reviews and other functions. A further aspect of noblesse oblige was the volunteering by de Ramezay daughters to nurse victims of smallpox.

The Convent Enterprise

Said to have been fatigued with the family's public life, Mademoiselle Charlotte de Ramezay took the veil at the General Hospice, an institution founded by the aristocratic Bishop Saint-Vallier, former chaplain at Louis XIV's court. The bishop actively recruited noblewomen to his order. He helped pay their dowries and encouraged them to assume convent administration. Hospice historian Micheline D'Allaire calculated 37 to 46 per cent of its nuns were noble. By Lorraine Gadoury's stricter definition, some 22 per cent were noble.[24] Either proportion is high, for only about 3 per cent of the eighteenth-century colonial population held noble status. Because the elite nuns occupied the more visible positions, it seemed to visitors that nobles were in the majority. Charlevoix (1720) wrote that 'most are daughters of rank,' Kalm (1749) that 'most of them are noble.' Pascau du Plessis (1756) identified them as 'all girls of rank.'[25]

Despite its purpose to serve the poor, the *hôpital* must have conjured up memories of home for Mother St Claude. Visiting the colony in 1720, the French historian Charlevoix pronounced the Hôpital Général 'the most beautiful house in Canada,'[26] which was precisely the distinction her governor-father had claimed for *his* mansion. The nuns' estate overlooked meadows, woods, and a meandering river. As with the Chateau de Ramezay, private space was meagre, public space expansive. The nuns slept in small unheated cells, struggling to keep warm in their blue-curtained beds. The communal rooms, though, were handsome and well heated. The church in particular was magnificently adorned, just as Marie-Charlotte's home had been. There were gold and silver fixtures, oak wainscoting, grand portraits and landscapes, and handsome tapestries. Like the de Ramezays, the nuns put on a fine show. When Swedish botanist Pehr Kalm visited, a large flock of nuns showed him around. They presented a banquet with dishes 'as numerous and various as on the tables of great men.' It was he who described Mother Saint-Claude as 'the daughter of a Governor ... [and having] a very grand air.'[27]

The nuns also duplicated another aspect of the chatelaine's lifestyle: they commanded a multitude of underlings. Noble nuns usually held the highest administrative offices. Between 1700 and the end of French rule in 1760, the mother superiors at the hospice were noble more than two-thirds of the time.[28] As administrators, they supervised the wards, the novices, and the finances.[29] When Marie-Charlotte de Ramezay became Mother Saint-Claude, she was predestined for such a role. She was the convent's depositary (financial director) for twenty-six years, and superior for six.[30]

Inside the convent, Marie-Charlotte encountered the same sharply drawn hierarchy she had known at the Chateau. Choir nuns and converse (or lay) sisters inhabited the same building but different worlds. *Converses* addressed even adolescent choir nuns as 'Mother.' Choir nuns, drawn from the higher classes, passed much of their day in prayer, meditation, and song, though they spent some time in the wards and teaching the poor.[31] The *converses*, on the other hand, were typically illiterate daughters of the working class. Their dowries were much lower. While choir nuns wore shoes, they wore clogs. Their bed linen was coarser. Required to be healthy, robust, and docile, *converses* took care of the barnyard and did the heavy work in garden, laundry, and stable. These 'Cinderellas of the convents' could not sing in the choir or vote in convent elections. They came to community meetings only to confess their faults.[32]

Choir nuns directed not only the lay sisters but all the numerous inhabitants of the institution and its three seigneuries. There were as many as thirteen domestic servants. Hundreds of *habitant* farmers paid dues and homage to their convent seigneuresses. Choir nuns, including Mother Saint-Claude, personally crossed the river to inspect their Saint-Vallier seigneurie. This was not, as we shall see later, the only relaxation of cloister, which theoretically required nuns to remain in the convent behind locked high walls, barred windows, and double-locked gates, segregated in their churches and parlours from the public by grills.[33] While the Quebec nuns ignored these strictures to act as seigneuresses, they performed another task typical of that station, becoming godparents to new babies, who were then named after them. They also employed carpenters and builders, harvest crews, and male nurses. Though the nuns may have felt deference towards some residents such as the bishop and an occasional military officer in their wards who might outrank them, most who entered their gates were in a subordinate position, outranked by the religious and dependent upon them.[34]

Like the wealth of the military *noblesse* in general, the nuns' wealth was based on varied sources of income and a good deal of womanly enterprise. Besides Crown and seigneurial revenues, they had two kinds of paying pensioners. Aging women and men often lodged there. Some paid through service. One pensioner took it upon herself each spring to cross the river to the Saint-Vallier seigneurie to collect rents for the convent.[35] A widow whose husband had been nursed at the hospice offered to serve as *soeur tourière* (gatekeeper) for life. When it opened a school in 1725, the convent acquired a second set of pensioners – young ones. Aware of a lack of milling for local *habitants*, the nuns erected a huge windmill that became a major source of revenue.[36] Sisters, inmates, or servants busied themselves with farming, dairy and poultry, churning, preserving, baking and hunting to supply the table, as well as weaving, sewing, and shoemaking. The nuns ran a pharmacy and performed such ladylike arts as filigree embroidery and artificial flower-making. Other income came from donors who admired the sisters' work, from court fines levied on petty offenders, and from legacies of people without heirs. Alms of all kinds arrived in such quantity that they rivalled seigneurial earnings as the largest source of revenue.[37]

The other convents, too, had lands, seigneuries, manufactories, and grants. Indeed religious orders held so many lots in the town of Quebec that they were blamed for the housing shortage there in the 1740s and forbidden to acquire more land.[38] Not only farm produce but prepared food, baked goods, woodcrafts and religious objects, embroidered garments for ecclesiastics, even shirts their pensioners sewed for the fur trade, combined to glean revenue for convents, with Canadian hospital sisters relying more on such productions than their French counterparts did.[39] There was also annual Crown compensation for care of ailing soldiers, sailors, shipyard workers, and native allies. Apart from helping with special expenses and emergencies (such as epidemics or fire damage), the Crown also made annual grants to each community; for example, a 1715 account allocated 6,500 *livres* to the Jesuits for all their missions and 400 for their regent, 1,200 to Quebec Recollets, 1,500 to Quebec Ursulines, and 6,500 to be shared by the two Quebec hospital communities. At Montreal, the Hôtel-Dieu received 2,000, the Congregation of Notre Dame 3,000.[40]

The assets described above were impressive, especially when one considers the straitened situation and unappetizing employment prospects of single women in eighteenth-century Europe, particularly in Protestant countries.[41] Security and solidarity were possible for those who banded together in religious orders. Wealthy women could escape the scorn that dogged even elite spinsters in Britain. Middle-class women could avoid the grating dependence of living in other households as governesses or maiden aunts. Poor women could escape penury, find a home and hopefully a calling too, as *converses*. Unlike many a domestic servant, they could count on food and shelter in their old age.

Another aspect of these institutions was self-government. Nuns would meet to elect their chief officers, rotating some offices yearly. The Rule of the Quebec Augustinians (who conducted the hospice and the Hôtel-Dieu) stipulated that those who had been choir sisters for at least six years were to select the major officers (about a dozen) by secret ballot. A mother superior could not be elected for more than two successive three-year terms, which helped prevent the position from becoming the fiefdom of a powerful individual; an elected council to advise her helped democratize decision-making.[42] The legal documents personally signed by many nuns imbue them with the dignity of adults with decisions to make and assets to distribute.[43] Convents were no utopias; there were no doubt difficult personalities and grating duties. Still, the degree of material and political self-determination contrasts with the pictures often painted of patriarchal states and patriarchal families of the day.

Nonetheless, it would be misleading to regard even convents that ruled over two or three seigneuries as affluent. It took a good deal of juggling of the various sources of revenue to make ends meet. The bishop observed in 1738 that the Quebec seminary and all the female religious communities were in debt, that he could not name ten families in the colony in a position to pay the 5,000 *livre* dowry without subsidy. Help was needed even for those wanting merely to educate their daughters at convent schools. Gone were the days, the bishop noted, when a well-connected predecessor, Bishop Saint-Vallier, had been able to secure hefty donations for colonial institutions in France from clergy and laity, reaching up to Madame de Maintenon herself.[44] Part of the lull was temporary, since the Crown expenditures that lubricated the colonial economy would soar upward in the two closing decades of French rule. All in all, convents offered women unusual financial security, a legal existence, and possibilities for a purposeful, companionable life.

Making use of these assets, institutions such as the General Hospice carried out the noble mandate to serve the Crown. The institution was founded, as were a number of Hôpitaux Généraux in France in the seventeenth century, to take charge of a growing number of beggars, prostitutes, petty criminals, and vagabonds, the great *renfermement des pauvres* that has been variously analysed by historians as calculated social control or helpful social service.[45] It had aspects of both. The Quebec hospice housed about forty inmates in 1730, double that number by 1748.[46] A year of smallpox or famine could send the numbers temporarily much higher. A *hôpital* was not a hospital but an institution that combined the functions of correction in the manner of a workhouse with custodial care of disabled, orphaned, and other needy or homeless people. Nonetheless, in times when the regular hospital (the Hôtel-Dieu) was full or incapacitated, the General Hospice would also serve the sick. This it did in wartime, and during epidemics of 1756–7 when ten nuns lost their lives caring for stricken soldiers and sailors.[47] The intendant reported general praise for the sisters, and he added that the meals they served did even more than their medicines to restore health.[48]

Convents served people of all conditions. In 1717 the bishop wrote that besides looking after cripples and handicapped, the Quebec hospice had a manufactory that instructed children of both sexes in 'works of all sorts.' Besides its boarding school for elite daughters and rooms for elite widows, it functioned as a hostel for female travellers and wartime refugees.[49] Its windmill ground grain for the government and for farmers for miles around. The sisters' varied activities were termed 'indispensable service' by the Crown brokers above them, and were much used by the local inhabitants. Indeed, overwork often sent sisters them-

selves to the infirmaries. It took a particularly heavy toll of Congregation
of Notre Dame sisters who travelled long distances and lived in primitive
conditions as they set up country schools.

For their part, the Hôtels-Dieu were more exclusively dedicated to the
sick. The authorities noted in 1731 that the Quebec Hôtel-Dieu patients
included soldiers and *habitants* 'who are nearly all without distinction
transported to the hospitals when they are ill.'[50] Soldiers were covered by
their pay and Crown subsidies, a few indigents were treated free, and the
others paid between ten and fifty *sols* and one *écu* per day, which covered
food, dressings, and medicine, making separate arrangements if attended by the doctor. When the Quebec Hôtel-Dieu cared for the sick who
embarked from the ship *Rubis*, two nuns died and many others fell ill.[51]
Medical wisdom of the day left much to be desired, of course, and sisters' skills would have varied. One hopes the better ones were conversant
with the medical texts in convent libraries, and were more skilled than
the barber surgeons or the incompetent physician who caused alarm at
Trois-Rivières in the 1730s. There were signs of popular sympathy when
the Montreal Hôtel-Dieu burned down in the winter of 1734. Officials
reported forty patients were commonly treated there, mostly for free.
Having 'a special affection for that community,' the populace came forward to help. Country dwellers sent wood and wheat, Montreal workers
donated labour, and donors quickly contributed three thousand *livres*
towards rebuilding.[52]

The Convent and Clientage

It took some time for convents to master the art of securing protectors.
Bishop Saint-Vallier's initial decision to found Quebec's General Hospice
and staff it with Augustinian nuns from the Hôtel-Dieu was done much
against the will of the Augustinian Order (which, as we have seen, first
established itself in Quebec as a missionary group in 1639). The sisters
did not wish to see their forces spread too thin, but the bishop overpow-
ered them. He employed the emotionalism that characterized some patron–client relations; he visited the Hôtel-Dieu and wept to soften their
hearts. They cried too, but did not budge. He proceeded to the French
court, and there he won his cause. Once the hospice was established, the
bishop became its powerful protector. Convents also had friends in the
secular arm of government. Madame Vaudreuil left Bishop Saint-Vallier
sputtering about the overbearing politicking of the gubernatorial couple, about the cavalier way they broke cloister by dropping into convents

with their entourages of officers or of ladies and girls.[53] However, having friends at the Chateau Saint-Louis gave the sisters a place to turn against overbearing ecclesiastics.

The nuns' powers were put to the test when Saint-Vallier died in 1727. Infighting among clerical and lay leaders brought one faction to the doors of the hospice where his body lay. Fearful that his request to be buried at his beloved institution would be countermanded by the other faction who preferred the cathedral, Mother Superior Geneviève Duchesnay, a noblewoman, permitted them to conduct an impromptu midnight service. The poor held the candles, the Mass was sung, and the bishop duly buried. When the rival ecclesiastical faction discovered this, they denied the hospice chaplain the right to administer sacraments to the nuns and proceeded to replace Mother Duchesnay as superior.[54] The majority of the sisters rebelled against this and continued to obey her.

This was the first of a series of brushes with ecclesiastics who seem to have detested the nuns. The Quebec sisters were making decisions ordinarily made by men, for *hôpitaux* in France were at this time administered by laymen. The clerics seem to have been repelled by the independence of the sisters. In 1730 Bishop Dosquet would accuse them of 'bad conduct' and an abusive 'spirit of independence and liberty,' claiming that half of them had no vocation and that none of them had the least regard for their rules. He asked the minister to reduce their numbers.[55]

The nuns responded to the coup against Mother Duchesnay by soliciting patrons. In the face of ecclesiastical hostility they could turn to secular rulers, because colonial bishops faced more state control than French ones did.[56] The nuns wrote directly to the minister of marine with their versions of events. Mother Duchesnay, in the master–servant language of patronage, 'took the liberty to write to your Lordship to supplicate very respectfully the honour of your protection,' hoping he would apply his 'penetrating mind' to their problem. She noted, in the affectionate language of patronage, how (the minister's kinsman) Governor Charles de Beauharnois, like 'a good father full of charity,' had come and restored peace to the convent.[57] Yet she also enclosed, and endorsed as 'simple and truthful,' the memoir of Sister Agnes.

Sister Agnes, in her office of convent secretary, signed her note 'on behalf of the whole community.' She claimed that Governor Beauharnois had himself divided their community, forcing some of the younger or more timid nuns to bow to authority on false pretences.[58] The governor was evidently a frequent visitor, convincing some of the more impressionable sisters only 'after a thousand entreaties.' But on behalf of the convent in general Sister Agnes reiterated firmly, twice, that sentiments were ever the same, for retention of their chaplain and their rights.[59] The letter shows that in seeking help from the authorities, the nuns were not altogether beholden to them. Particular care was needed, since the governor initially sided with the faction hostile to the mother superior. Still, Governor Beauharnois proved to be a friend. He protested against the arbitrary condemnation of Mother Duchesnay and used his authority to have the interdiction lifted.

A second imbroglio occurred when Mother Duchesnay died in 1730. The bishop's representative was determined to break the rule of the proud noblewomen at the head of the hospice,[60] to humble nine of the eighteen nuns who were daughters of officers and gentlemen. He arbitrarily appointed a non-noble nun as superior. This violated the order's constitution that called for election by secret ballot. Mother Saint-Claude and seven others of the noble faction retired to their cells during this illegal procedure, taking care first to disable the convent bell.[61]

After inspecting the convent's constitution, Governor Beauharnois (related to the Phélypeaux clan) and Intendant Hocquart (related to the Colbert clan) both agreed with the nuns and asked the minister to call for a new election. They added that vexations (*tracasseries*) were common in convents, and they insisted that the nuns generally conducted themselves appropriately. By charitably attending invalids and the insane, they provided an 'indispensable service' to the colony. The Crown did not go so far as to remove the appointee, but Mother Duchesnay's younger sister was elected superior in 1732, and for the rest of the time until the Conquest, the superior was always a noblewoman. Nor was there further complaint of ecclesiastics interfering in elections.[62] Historian Micheline D'Allaire described the nuns as being adroit 'in the way they assured themselves of protection of the powerful.'[63] However, in their rather extravagant claim to the dead bishop's palace on the grounds that they were his universal legatees, the nuns lost their case. Mother Duchesnay wrote to condemn the efforts of the absentee Bishop Mornay to saddle them with the costs of renovating the palace. Her words exude the confidence of the daughter and sister of warriors: 'Isn't it burdensome enough for the … nuns to have paid … reparations without taking any benefit from a donation made with such generosity and good faith by M. de Saint-Vallier! And could not His Majesty, by way of compensation, make M. de Mornay desist from his exorbitant pretensions.'[64]

The governor and intendant backed her up, informing the minister that the nuns certainly should not be required to meet the bishop's 'exorbitant' demands.[65] They wrote in glowing terms of the convent's work and supported the sisters' desire to have dowry fees made less prohibitive. From 1732 onward, according to D'Allaire, the Crown looked with favour on the convent. By 1737, with friendly advocates in the government, the number of choir nuns would grow to thirty-four, with six *converses*, soaring to fifty-five in all two decades later. Indeed Intendant Hocquart revealed the new policy when he wrote to the minister in 1744, 'I presume your intention is that I treat that Hôpital better than the others.' The nuns also succeeded in fending off Crown efforts to saddle them with lay administrators.[66] By 1750 the General Hospice, far from being threatened with extinction, was setting terms on which it would absorb other institutions and was receiving a Crown gratification more than twice as large as that of the other convents.[67]

Other cloisters showed signs of independence too. Furious dispatches from Intendant Dupuy accused the Quebec Hôtel-Dieu of being entirely out of line with French practice in insisting on administering hospital funds independently, without oversight by lay administrators. In a dispatch of 20 November 1727, Dupuy accused them of having a 'genius for avarice,' avowing 'that he had never known such a rebellious religious order,' one that even refused to hand over the accounts when he asked. They were hucksters who would sell anything, avariciously exacting money, even from poor people and domestics. They also had taken it upon themselves many times, he fumed, to harbour fugitives from justice, requiring Governor Vaudreuil at one point to send sentinels to keep miscreant soldiers from eluding justice that way. Unlike the other Quebec communities, the Hôtel-Dieu refused to sell land needed for housing and defence, even building a wall that obstructed access to the fortifications. Intendant Dupuy retaliated by ordering them to cease construction on their property, threatening to shut them down altogether. One of the superior councillors made the further charge that avarice alone made the Hôtel-Dieu extract fees from certain patients. The nuns averred that all this hostility originated in a theft charge against a servant of Madame Dupuy. The girl (who had formerly been a patient in the hospital) after her flight from the intendant's palace was taken in by one of the young nuns. This resulted in a furious interrogation and a search by guards that extended even to the nuns' beds. Government sentries whom the nuns sometimes encountered in their wards at night were another bone of contention. The problems were symptomatic, Dupuy concluded, of the sisters' 'open resistance to order and justice in a country in which one inhaled Independence.'[68] A few years later the calmer voices of Gover-

nor Beauharnois and Intendant Hocquart confirmed that 'the nuns of
the Hôtel-Dieu of this town among others maintain they are not held to
render any account, not even to the Bishop, which will not do at all. It
would be to the good order ... of this community if they had lay administrators.'[69] Two decades later Intendant Bigot was well aware of their
independence, which included their refusal to divert convent funds to
build a new wing the government wanted. Bigot advised that 'if the King
doesn't take measures to force them, they will simply do nothing.'[70]

At Montreal, nursing sisters had apparently inhaled such air too,
for some defied their physician by ignoring his prescribed treatments
in favour of their own. The Montreal sisters had been granted 'full administration' of their goods by the Sulpicians in 1677, although their
constitution required the bishop's approval for land sales. They built an
independent income on land revenues and investments locally and in
France, as well as the produce they grew. They also had income derived
from *congés* (fur-trading licences they could sell to others) and from baking, sewing, preparing pharmaceuticals, weaving fabric, making rope,
even cutting windowpanes for Montrealers, all supplementing the alms
and Crown subsidies that came their way. In fact, 82 per cent of their
revenues came from their own assets and labours.[71]

The General Hospice at Quebec, with its unusually high proportion
of noble nuns, provides the clearest example of how convents could
use connections to preserve their treasured independence. Patron–client linkages were generally face-to-face, so it is hard for historians to
trace them. We do know, however, that there was an unusual amount of
visiting at the hospice by governors and their wives, successive bishops
fulminating against not only Madame Vaudreuil dropping in but her
husband doing the same thing, sallying into the building with his retinue
of officers and friends. That broke cloister to the extent that both Saint-
Vallier and his successor, Bishop Dosquet, appealed to the court to stop
the outrage.[72] The nuns even went to dinner parties at the chateaux of
the governor and the intendant, and it was alleged some townspeople
saw the convent as a place for 'promenades and amusement.'[73] During
the decade in which the colony fell, both the appalled Bishop Briand
and the delighted novelist Frances Brooke agreed that the nuns were
very worldly. Brooke characterized their conversation as so polite and
animated that one forgot the nun and saw only the lady of distinction.
The austere Briand fumed, 'What is one to think of the introduction of
the abuse of having one's own money at her disposition [this applying to
Mother Saint-Claude] ... buying her own food ... liquors ... clothes?'[74]

He went on to accuse the nuns of talking indiscreetly about sexual scandals, of rising late, of neglecting prayers and rules of silence, and of being libertine in recreation time. These ladies were not letting the veil interfere with the art of cultivating friends in high places, or with dining and conversing in the style to which they were born.

What the bishop saw as sin others saw as accomplishment. Mother-Saint-Claude's service as a depositary during some of the war years was lauded in the convent annals. While her vocation made her 'humble, modest and devoted,' she was 'obliged by her employment to have daily dealings with people of all ranks, [and] she showed herself, by the nobility of her manners and the delicacy of her behaviour, always worthy of her high birth.'[75] She also staunchly defended the convent's seigneurial claims. And, like her father before her, she distinguished her reign by constructing a bigger, more palatial establishment.

Along with links to the polite world of colonial government, nuns in Quebec, Montreal, and Trois-Rivières also had the reliable network of kin to reinforce their position. Unlike priests, nuns were typically Canadian born. With many relatives in the town's shops and warehouses, Council seats and government posts, reciprocal patron–client relationships blossomed. Hospice supplies were purchased, and donations arrived, from families such as the Soumandes, Hazeurs, Hichés, and de la Chesnayes, who were related to the superiors.[76] Loans were extended or forgiven, lands were swapped for services. Officials contributed to dowries for needy noble postulants, which meant women aspiring to the clerical state did not face the problem that thwarted male vocations, that few colonial families could pay for priestly training.[77] Nuns educated officials' daughters and cared for their widows. They taught their own nieces (many of whom also took the veil) and boarded their elderly relatives, such as Agathe Saint-Père, who passed her last days at the Quebec hospice, where her daughter was a nun, and left a legacy to the order. Amidst so many kin, graduates, and friends, convents were well fixed to weather what storms might come.

The Fall of Quebec

The storm that arose in 1759 was one of the most devastating imaginable. Having endured four years of battle between French and British imperial forces, the underpopulated and poorly supplied colony was hungry and exhausted. That year British-American forces were massing along invasion routes converging on the St Lawrence. In midsummer

General James Wolfe's army, well supported by the British Navy, sailed up the wide river, ensconced itself on the shore opposite Quebec City, and began shelling. One young noble, Mother Sainte-Elizabeth Adhémar de Lantagnac, set up a field hospital right at the scene of skirmish, where a brief encounter with an enemy soldier who held a sword to her throat 'seemed to inspire her with fresh zeal.'[78] Wolfe studied ways to lay siege to the well-fortified city on its looming cliff. Meanwhile his forces ravaged nearby settlements and continued to shell the town until most of its buildings were in ruins.

During the siege, the General Hospice's suburban location was a godsend. Kin and townspeople came pouring into the building with their belongings. Both the Ursuline and Hôtel-Dieu nuns also fled their crumbling convents and came streaming over the fields, carrying their bedding. Soon every attic, hall, barn, and outbuilding was crammed with refugees, patients, inmates, and nuns. Buildings designed for 120 people braced to receive 800.[79]

On the fateful night of 12 September 1759, Wolfe's troops slipped past French sentries and crept up a path leading to the Plains of Abraham. The sisters, who customarily rose at four, were among the first to learn of the landing. Taken by surprise, Montcalm rushed out to meet the invader, without even waiting for nearby reinforcements. One of history's most famous battles was over in less than half an hour, as French forces broke ranks and ran back into the walled town. The nuns watched in horror from their windows. After the battle, hundreds of French wounded were carried to the hospice.[80]

That night, the nuns carrying soup to patients were frightened by the loud knock of a British officer at the door. But he entered to declare himself their protector, for the nuns had already woven the victors into their network. From the time Wolfe sailed up the river, they had accepted British wounded captured in various skirmishes.[81] Mother Saint-Claude herself had nursed British officer David Ochterloney. In gratitude for services rendered, General Wolfe declared that should fortune of arms favour the British side, he would extend his protection to her and to the hospice.[82]

Captain John Knox was a British officer dispatched to guard the big hospice outside the town walls and ensure that it gave no help to French forces still lurking in the neighbourhood. Fortunately he kept a journal that allows glimpses of convent life at the time. The captain was ambivalent when he first came into contact with the nun who had served as superior for several years, Mother Saint-Claude de la Croix (whom the reader will by now know well as a governor's daughter who emanated 'a very grand air.') On one hand, Captain Knox admired Mother Saint-Claude's hospice, which provided identical care to both French and English wounded. His eye did not fail to note a number of lovely young nuns (said to have joined for safety concerns during the war). The wards were nice too, clean and airy, with a curtained bed for each patient. Knox observed that 'when our poor fellows were ill, and [transferred here] ... from their own odious regimental hospitals ... they were ... rendered inexpressibly happy.'[83] However, wounded French-Canadian officers at that desperate hour were not uniformly able to maintain the courtesy expected towards British officers housed in the same wing of the institution. Better schooled in noblesse oblige, Mother Saint-Claude had personally cared for the young British officer, weeping when he died. Even as Quebeckers reeled from the disaster on the Plains, she invited Captain Knox to join her in a private room for English tea and polite conversation.[84]

Even as he accepted her hospitality, Knox believed the stately old dame was at work demoralizing the British officers under her care. 'Madame de Saint-Claude,' he confided to his journal, 'is reputed the industrious inventress of ... many ... groundless rumours' about the defeat of Amherst's invading army and other British losses. Knox said he was credibly informed that the British Commander General James Murray had written her a letter of reproach, chiding her that 'it is his opinion a woman who had shut herself up in a convent and retired from the world, has no right to intermeddle with what passes in it.'[85] Knox said Murray taunted Mother Saint-Claude that 'if she is tired of living out of the world, and will change her habit for that of a man, she being of a proper stature, his Excellency will inroll [sic] her as a grenadier.'[86]

When the regrouped French forces returned to fight a second battle at nearby St Foy in April 1760, the boom of cannons shook the hospice. The nuns saw brothers, fathers, uncles, and nephews fall and be carried in, nearly five hundred men in all. The convent annalist described the scene: 'It requires another pen than mine to paint the horrors ... the cries of the dying and the sorrows of the watchers. Those moments required a force above nature to bear it without dying ... We had in our infirmaries seventy-two officers; thirty-three died. One saw nothing but severed arms and legs.'[87]

It was a time for rising above feelings – at least rising above them in the wards. All through the bitter war years, the sisters nursed French and British soldiers alike. Still, it is impossible to read the annals of any of the town's three convents without recognizing their passionate attachment to the French cause. The nuns chronicled battle after battle, the Ursulines even including dispatches sent to them by General Montcalm from the front. The *hôpital*, where a full 40 per cent of the choir sisters were daughters of Saint-Louis Cross–holders,[88] was no less patriotic. The nuns vigorously protested thefts by the British guard, but accepted it with equanimity when French forces purloined the cattle and grain they needed to feed their own patients. They maintained secret communications with the French General Lévis and they helped spirit recovered soldiers back to the French lines.[89] If Mother Saint-Claude spread false rumours of French victories, it was in keeping with the obvious patriotism of the nuns.

Mother Saint-Claude never ceased plying paths she had practised since childhood. Scarcely a week after her brother, town commander Nicholas-Roch de Ramezay, yielded the starving place to the British, Mother Saint-Claude sent the British officer Monckton some preserves the nuns had made. They were, she wrote, 'eager to present their respects' to his Excellency, to express their deep appreciation for his protection, wishing him health.[90] Writing to a nun in France, she expressed fear that 'all the world' would shun them. Mother Saint-Claude's concern to maintain connections and supporters had been developed from earliest days in the chateau, and it served her well. The French regime came to a close with the capitulation of Montreal in September 1760. Fortunately for the nuns, the colony fell into the hands of gentlemanly British officers with similar concepts of honour and of clientage.[91]

With new connections made, the order weathered the change of empires. For a while, its survival hung in the balance, for it was the hardest hit of any of the colony's seven convents, experiencing deep losses when French bills of exchange were redeemed at only a fraction of their face value. The sisters were also stunned when the French court refused to repay the expenses they had incurred as a military hospital in the final years of the war. To meet debts, they were forced to sell their most valuable seigneurie, Saint-Vallier. The new governor of Quebec, James Murray, wrote that the hospice nuns belonged to the best families in Canada, whose families were their principal source of subsistence, but that now the nobility in general was plunged into distress.[92]

At this juncture the friendship of the English rulers was crucial. Clearly forgiving any white lies the nuns may have told, Governor Murray donated flour and lard to the *hôpital* and paid the expenses of the British patients. After the war, he lobbied both the French and English governments to aid the indebted hospice. The British government stepped into the role formerly occupied by France, providing annual grants in return for care of the infirm and insane, in a practice that continued into the nineteenth century.[93]

Outside the aging walls, a new gender order was emerging in the Western world. Segregation by sex would gradually become as caste-like as the old segregation by rank that preceded it. In France, the revolutionary decades that began in the 1780s were hard on chatelaines, court favourites, and powerful women in general. Even as colonial women outside the convents began to face increasing constraints, the General Hospice and the other convents would continue to provide a range of occupations and administrative positions for talented and strong-minded individuals (whom their annals identify as *femmes fortes*) in centuries to come. When the elderly Mother Saint-Claude died in 1767 after a lingering illness, she could rest secure. Even the restrictive gender notions of the Victorians would not stifle her order of nuns, who to this day work and worship in the ancient convent.

The other religious orders survived by similar expedients. The Quebec Hôtel-Dieu, for example, relied on rents, sales of building lots, seigneurial development, boarders' fees, laundry services, and skill in decorative arts to finance the new convent-hospital built after the fire of 1755. Although their wards were taken over for a quarter century to serve as a British military hospital, the sisters maintained cordial relations with Governor Murray and the new rulers under Superior Marie-Louise Curot (Mother de Saint-Martin), daughter of a Fort Frontenac trading family.[94] In Montreal, the Hôtel-Dieu sisters resisted an offer of transfer back to France and continued to combine agriculture and artisanal production with other revenues. Their care of British troops led General Amherst to channel support from the new Crown in their direction. In the late eighteenth century they were taking in pensioners, marketing their own candles, medicines, boxes, sewing, gilt work, even soap made from cast-off army butter. From their bakery they sold Montrealers about two hundred six-pound loaves of bread every day.[95] The ever-resourceful Congregation of Notre Dame would continue to open Canadian schools, venturing eventually not only to Marguerite Bourgeoys's native Troyes but to Latin America, Africa, and Japan as well. Likewise the Ursulines at both Quebec and Trois-Rivières offered useful service to English newcomers as well as French Canadians, while retaining as much as they could of their long-time holdings and fabricating goods for local markets.

Having forged their ties to the populace and the new rulers, Mother Claude and the other nuns of the military *noblesse* certainly fared better than many of their brothers. Many of the Canadian officers went to France when the defeated French army was evacuated.[96] With weaker connections than the French officers, the Canadians faced a nasty scape-goating. Governor Pierre Rigaud de Vaudreuil was thrown into the Bastille for a time. Roch de Ramezay faced recriminations for surrendering Quebec. Denied permission to publish documents proving he had done so on the advice of his superiors, he was ignored by a court obsessed with the health of Madame de Pompadour. He was reduced to the relative poverty of an eight hundred *livre* pension, which, true to aristocratic form, he applied towards purchasing silk hose and stylish wig to keep up his station.[97]

The officers who remained in Canada fared badly too. There was an influx of Anglo-American merchants who mocked down-at-the-heels nobles, taunting them as *'l'épées'* (the swords). Philippe Aubert de Gaspé, scion of one of those military families, noted the common strategy to bury the family history in order to prosper under the new regime. Though his uncle had fought at St Foy, 'Strange to say, he never mentioned the glorious part he played there at sixteen.... But the truth is that at the time, these things were only spoken of in whispers, for fear of appearing "French and bad subjects," as the English put it.'[98] By contrast the sisters did not have to bury their talents and their past.

Conclusion

When the Seven Years' War broke out in 1754, the sisters at the Hôpital Général de Québec, like their brothers on the battlefields, gave their all to the cause, many dying in the line of duty. Nobles that they were, they conducted themselves in ways that answered both the call of honour and the imperatives of a clientage system. Their mastery of that system is suggested by the triple role that history has assigned to Mother Saint-Claude: tearful nurse to dying British officers, lady of high breeding serving them tea, and secret agent working on behalf of the French. Here was 'woman's speech' again, words of power that were capable of attracting the authorities' attention – and, gentlewomen increasingly found, their condemnation. Officers from both France and England were known to chastise French-Canadian ladies for political meddling.[99] Whether Mother Saint-Claude's rumoured role as French agent is accurate or apocryphal, the story bespeaks a distrust of powerful women. And it is undeniable that Mother Saint-Claude and her sisters supported their own brothers who fought beneath their convent windows. They took it upon themselves to house hundreds of French refugees and calmly let French forces pillage their supplies. All the while – obeying both noble codes and religious vows – they cultivated the esteem of the British commanders who would soon rule Quebec. When their brothers faced ridicule and exile, the nuns stayed in a colony that continued to appreciate them.

Privileges and connections bolstered the ability of convents to survive the change of empires. Travellers to New France, and then the gentlemanly army officers who ruled after the Conquest, repeatedly expressed their admiration for the gentility and generosity of the nuns. Even relatively weak or unskilled convent administrators could rely on a well-developed system, one honed during imbroglios with ecclesiastics during the French regime. Though none of the other convents had as many nobles as did the General Hospice, the five large, long-established ones in Montreal and Quebec all had at least 14 per cent.[100] They too could benefit from whatever networks such nuns could command, and they adjusted successfully during the post-Conquest period when both male officers and male clergy faced plummeting numbers and morale.[101]

Our study of the eighteenth-century convent supports scholarly views of clientage as a pervasive form of power lying outside regular political channels. We see that an appreciation of noble networks can be particularly helpful in explaining the control certain women exerted in New France and other ancien regime societies. Not only influential wives such as Elisabeth de Vaudreuil, but also convents with noble daughters within their gates, represent 'interests and societal forces joining clienteles to achieve a degree of flexibility and independence within the absolutist state.' An ingrained code of honour made even cloistered nobles want to serve the Crown – and Crown administrators want to serve them. Authority flowed through Crown brokers to convents such as the Hôpital Général de Québec. The convent in turn had hundreds of ties to the local populace, and it had aristocrats at the top who parlayed with governors and ministers.

In the centuries that pre-dated our modern, binary notions of public and private, sacred and secular, Mother Saint-Claude and other brides of Christ did not shed the persona of proud and well-connected elites when they knelt to take their vows. They knew how to joust with fuming officials and domineering bishops. Greater peril arose when a Protestant invader sailed up the river and took the town. More than ever, Mother Saint-Claude and her sisters needed the self-confidence of the blueblood, and skill in the noble art of making connections. This form of politics was certainly elitist, but it did incorporate *some* women at commanding levels, while most nineteenth-century 'democracies' incorporated none. Well-connected, the convents along the St Lawrence lived to see another day even as French government crumbled and French armies sailed for home.

PART FOUR

River of Memory

Chapter Eight

Continuities in British Quebec

In 1763 a cloud of uncertainty blanketed the St Lawrence. That year the Treaty of Paris decreed the captured heartland of New France had become the British colony of Quebec. From the time French forces had capitulated three years earlier, unease had inevitably pervaded the hundreds of households along the river. Would French Canadians be dispossessed, perhaps even deported as the Acadians had been? Most officers of the administration and the army had already sailed to France. Would the entrepreneurial class, with its ties to Bordeaux, be the next to disappear? Would the common law, which privileged eldest sons, supplant the more egalitarian Custom of Paris? What would happen to the numerous women who, following the customs of France and northern Europe,[1] involved themselves in trade? Would the religious orders be disbanded, their lands confiscated? Right away, some fundamental adjustments touched elite women of the *noblesse* and the urban bourgeoisie, and our attention will turn to them first. However, our sketch in this chapter of French-Canadian women under British rule during three-quarters of a century following the Conquest is not, primarily, a discussion of change.

In one of the few works to assess effects of the Conquest on gender roles, the authors of *Quebec Women: A History* concluded that the change of regimes made little difference. They presented the eighteenth and early nineteenth centuries as a single, continuous, pre-industrial period; most families continued to work on farms, assuring that 'from 1701 to 1832, the life of most women in the St Lawrence Valley changed very little.'[2] That interpretation is essentially correct. For that vast majority of *canadiennes* who lived in rural areas, traditional forms of economic and social organization did indeed persist into the 1830s, that is, for more than seventy years after the British Conquest. A French ambassador doubtless exaggerated when he judged them 'a population that is today absolutely as it was a hundred years ago, with the same feudal regime, customary law, lack of education, simplicity of manners and … faith of the past century,'[3] but many other observers echoed the theme. Most changes that *did* occur affected the small proportion of French Canadians who lived in or around Quebec and Montreal, rather than the enormous rural majority. In the country, there is evidence that women remained true partners within marriages, vital economic teammates, spouses characteristically respected and consulted by their husbands. They remained partners in the legal sense too: the colony retained, for more than three-quarters of a century, customary legal protections for wives, widows, and daughters, even as such protections became increasingly obsolete in Britain, France, and America. Sidestepping the path of change had its compensations.

This is not to suggest that Quebec was some northern Arcadia, frozen forever in time. Seven decades that saw a tenfold growth in population could not pass without transformations, especially at a time when momentous industrial and political revolutions were shaking Britain, France, and America. In British Quebec (renamed Lower Canada in 1791), changes in consumption were everywhere to be seen. British patterns showed up on coverlets and cheap India cotton nightdresses; by the early nineteenth century, tea-drinking – a curiosity in 1760 – had reached even the small farms, where they boiled water in a skillet while they saved up for a kettle.[4] *Habitant* farmhouses by the early nineteenth century did reflect increasing economic differentiation, some having four rooms, some just one. Yet even as sharp-eyed an observer as English traveller John Lambert could not help admiring the egalitarian spirit of the inhabitants: 'Their behaviour to strangers is never influenced by the cut of a coat, or a fine periwig. It is civil and respectful to all, without distinction of persons. They treat their superiors with that polite deference which neither debases the one nor exalts the other. They are never rude to their inferiors because they are poor, for if they do not relieve poverty they will not insult it.'[5]

Certainly one does not quarrel with scholars who point to material differences that affected rural areas, such as the opening of new markets and new villages, and gradually emerging economic gradations.[6] The question is not whether such things occurred, but how deeply they affected the lives of most farm families. The stark fact remains that French Canadians turned their backs on towns and became progressively more rural in the decades after the Conquest. They underwent an astonishing demographic reversal from being 75 per cent rural at the end of the French period to 95 per cent rural in 1800.

Rural isolation, which helped buffer them from English language and mores,[7] could even be strengthened by locally controlled commercial development. Even as the ranges further back from the river were cleared and settled, most were still oriented towards the 'one continuous village' stretching along both banks of the St Lawrence for four hundred miles. The small wooden dwellings, offset by the occasional church or manor, now boasted a sawmill, smithy, or some other modest commercial enterprise employing two or three workers. On the fields, pastures, and meadows looming above the steep banks of the river, families continued to grow traditional crops of wheat and peas, exporting some but consuming most themselves. When the nineteenth century began, there were scarcely more ships carrying outbound cargoes than there had been a half century before. While some new opportunities emerged, other ones shrank, as land gradually became more scarce in the early nineteenth century and wheat crops faltered more frequently. New niceties of gender that city folk could study in conduct books had little to do with them, for few of them could read and fewer still aspired to be ladies or gentlemen. For any *habitant* families that were clearing back acres or trying out new crops, and for the many scraping by on old tracts of land, the same arduous physical work they had known ever since the first days of New France required both male and female hands. Thus our major theme in this chapter, which assesses the gender order in French Canada under British rule from the 1760s to the 1830s, is the persistence of old ways. Though the upper ranks of society did begin to see significant changes, the rural majority continued to experience work, social organization, property rights, and conjugal conduct that in many ways approximated those seen under French rule.

Property Rights

Rather surprisingly, the first British governors of Quebec looked favourably on the old ways. Governors James Murray and Guy Carleton appreciated the martial values of French Canadians, while Lady Carleton, who had spent part of her youth at Versailles, re-enforced ancien regime manners at the Chateau St Louis. They shared a resentment of the querulous Anglo-American merchants who stepped ashore with a keen sense of entitlement to the spoils of a conquered colony. Their remarkable judgments echo down through Canadian history. Governor Murray declared the conquered *habitants* 'perhaps the bravest and the best race upon the Globe,' and Governor Carleton asserted that 'barring Catastrophe shocking to think of, this Country must, to the end of Time be peopled by the [French-]Canadian Race, who already have taken such firm Root.'[8] The threat of revolution in the American colonies led Carleton in particular to court the French Canadians, who numbered over eighty thousand in comparison to fewer than one thousand English-speaking settlers in the colony. In 1774 he lobbied for the Quebec Act, which ended a period of legal uncertainly by officially re-installing the Custom of Paris, the old civil law of the French regime.[9] Confirming that priests could still collect tithes and seigneurs could still collect dues, the Act also validated most of the customary practices regarding marriage and inheritance.[10]

Thus the Quebec Act enshrined timeworn legal principles. While husbands were entitled to manage property during marriage, other members of the family were treated more respectfully than in many other jurisdictions. All male and female children (except for seigneurs' sons) were supposed to inherit equal shares. Between spouses, there existed a community of goods rather than husbandly ownership of them. Similarly, widows had dower rights to the revenue or use of half of the husband's inherited real property. This customary dower remained quite secure, taking precedence over all other creditors. The relatively generous female property rights under the Custom of Paris were to remain largely in place for eight decades after the Conquest, while any such provisions became ever more obsolete in eighteenth-century common law, as well as in post-Revolutionary France.

Remarks about women's 'superiority' in French Canada have intrigued historians for years. A whole series of travellers, officials, and new settlers from the 1740s through the 1820s made such comments, along four common themes: that women enjoyed substantial property rights, spoke up, conducted business with acuity, and had unusual degree of influence within marriage. One allows that some travellers were more knowledgeable than others, but what makes the body of remarks persuasive is that they came from both French and English sources, that they persisted over a seventy-year span, and that there was such a consensus. It is difficult to uncover any remarks about the abject or servile state of Canadian women. Quite the opposite.

The Chevalier de Lapause, an officer in Montcalm's forces, reported in the last decade of the French regime that among all social orders the 'women are ... in general, wittier than the men.'[11] This was an affirmation of Intendant Hocquart's assertion a decade earlier that the women's wit 'gives them a superiority over men of nearly all ranks' and that men in the countryside concluded 'nothing of consequence' without consulting their wives.[12] At the beginning of the nineteenth century John Lambert, one of the best-informed British observers, reported the women were in close touch with the priests and 'better instructed or at least better informed ... Hence they generally acquire an influence over their husbands.'[13] Frenchmen the Duc de La Rochefoucault Liancourt in the 1790s and D. Dainville (pseud.) in 1820 both reported the women better instructed than the men; the latter observed that 'the Canadian always consults his wife on business of any importance and seldom does he fail to follow this advice.'[14] Another of their countrymen, Isidore Lebrun, attributed the happiness of families to the women and asked how many husbands in Europe would act more wisely 'if they followed the Canadian example and concluded no transaction without consulting their wives.'[15] Country wives who held property – and opinions that mattered – struck a whole series of visitors from France and the British Isles as a sufficiently unusual order of things to be worthy of remark. Articulate women who said what they thought, and a conception of marriage as a socio-economic partnership, were alive and well in Lower Canada.

Sojourning English merchant Hugh Gray explicitly linked the unusual influence of women in the French tradition to their property rights (though the Napoleonic Code was at that very time eroding them in France). His oft-quoted remark seems to go to the root of unions in which consultation, not 'marital authority,' was the basis for decisions: 'The law ... [makes] marriage a partnership in common ... the wife being invested with a right to half a husband's property; and being rendered independent of him, is perhaps the remote cause that the fair sex have such influence in France; and in Canada, it is well known, that a great deal of consequence, and even an air of superiority to the husband, is assumed by them.'[16]

Besides the travellers, another group was also struck by the relatively strong position of French-Canadian women – and they did not like it. Two thousand Loyalists settled in the Laurentian area in the wake of the American Revolution. Then, after the Napoleonic wars ended in 1815, a larger surge of British immigrants disembarked each year at the port of Quebec. They arrived with more androcentric traditions of the common law in which, in Blackstone's dictum, 'husband and wife are one person ... the very being or legal existence of the woman is suspended during the marriage.' As they grew in numbers and in confidence, the newcomers raised a chorus of disapproval against the family-oriented, 'feudal' nature of the laws that had been given a second lease on life by the Quebec Act. 'They ranted,' Bettina Bradbury wrote, 'against community of property and widows' dower rights, for giving wives and relatives too great a claim on a man's property.'[17] Partly this reflected the fact that English-speaking immigrants were concentrated in the towns, giving Quebec in the 1830s and Montreal in the 1840s English-speaking majorities. Montreal was the vanguard of the new order, surging from a population of about nine thousand in 1800 to forty-four thousand in the early 1840s, with rapid turnover of properties and businesses. Newcomers unfamiliar with the French system found it hard to keep track of dower claims that were unrecorded or obscurely filed away at a notary's office.[18]

English-speaking officials in Lower Canada were not content to accept the situation as a quaint anomaly. Several of them, as Bradbury's work has shown, launched a concerted campaign against customary dower, insisting that no claim should take precedence over other creditors unless formally registered. They argued that dower claims led to fraud and business losses and discouraged investors. Hardly ever discussed in the debate, even by those who defended dower, was one of the purposes of the customary or unwritten dower: to assure an automatic, inalienable legacy for widows and children – as J-F Perrault put it in 1810, 'an entitlement of the widow to the property of her husband to provide her with an honest living according to the condition of her husband.'[19] Such a guarantee made it more likely that the widow of a mercantile or seigneurial family would have resources to continue the operation if she wished. It contrasted with the common law tradition in which, as Susan Staves has noted, increasing restrictions were designed not to impoverish widows but to curb their independence. By contrast, the two colonial legal treatises that appeared before 1840, that of F-J Cugnet in 1775 and Henri Desrivières Beaubien in 1832, acknowledged women as legal personalities with a key set of rights. Cugnet noted that the widow's ability to renounce an indebted community was only fitting as a compensation for giving up management during marriage. He insisted that dower was a wifely right, not a 'liberality' granted by the husband; he took pains to point out how it differed from the weaker English dower. Beaubien's 1832 treatise devoted a full fifty pages to dower rights, revealing that sometimes even nuns and adulteresses might collect them.[20]

Into the 1830s, prominent French-Canadian jurists and politicians continued to defend their more humane legacy. Along with concern for dower, there was also some awareness of the dilemma of dutiful daughters, who were supposed to be treated equally with sons but could encounter fathers who ignored traditional principles and embraced English notions of unrestricted male ownership, freely disposing of property that they were supposed to have held in trust for all their children. One 1827 case featured Marie Amable Fortier, one of five young girls whose mother died early. Their father, as he aged, 'took up the habit, common enough, to dispose of goods of which he had only the guardianship, including a good part of the community of goods and *propres* of his wife. The children and relatives preferred to suffer than to embitter his old age in calling him to account ... and they let him finish his career in peace, having let him enjoy their property for more than thirty years.'[21]

In the early nineteenth century a small but growing proportion of propertied Montrealers, initially drawn from the English community, exercised the option to draw up marriage contracts that renounced community of property and dower. These sometimes substituted other provisions to support a widow, but those did not enjoy the traditional priority over creditors' claims. At that point the vast majority of urban French Canadians, like their rural brethren, still adhered to traditional conceptions of marriage as an economic partnership.[22]

Urban Transformations

Business practices also began to change. Newcomers with new customs arrived in the Lower Canadian ports year after year. We have seen earlier in this book that a number of historians of France, England, and America have identified growing constraints on female autonomy and public activity between 1600 and 1800. At worst there could be an apartheid-like exaggeration of the difference between men and women, conceptualizing them as practically two different species. In outlying regions, it should be noted, aboriginal and Metis women did continue their essential role in the fur trade as cultural intermediaries and producers of food and clothing. However, the end of the French monopoly regime seems to have removed the rationale for illicit trade through Albany, which had once recruited numerous colonial and aboriginal women in the St Lawrence and Hudson valleys.

Post-Conquest elites were imbued with a sharper sense of segregation, and contractions accordingly began at the top. At Crown posts, military officers from the British Isles supplanted the French officers' families once involved in commerce at the posts.[23] The financial and supply centre shifted from Bordeaux, with its transatlantic trading families, to London, where transatlantic trading took place through incorporated companies composed of males. French-Canadian entrepreneurs in general suffered displacements; subjected to narrow British-American concepts of what a 'lady' could undertake, entrepreneurial women faced double discrimination. With the added influx of English-speaking fur-traders after the American Revolution, there opened a period of particularly violent rivalries between Montreal-based companies and the Hudson's Bay Company, and the brawling culture developing at the posts was certainly no place for gentlewomen. When the North-West Company arranged for transatlantic shipping in its own vessels, that also put a squeeze on independent players.

We have as yet uncovered little evidence that female participants persisted in the upper ranks of suppliers to the fur and timber trades. French-Canadian women of a few families stayed active; we know, for example, that Madame Benoit's shirt-making operation still functioned in Montreal in the 1760s.[24] From the Conquest onward, though, female entrepreneurs become harder to find, and among the transatlantic traders they seem to vanish altogether.[25] Mesdames Courtemanche, D'Argenteuil, and Fornel were no longer seen supervising the loading of ships. Within twenty years of the Conquest, major female staples dealers had become a thing of the past. When timber, milling, and tannery entrepreneur Louise de Ramezay died in 1776, it marked the end of an era.

One does not know the precise mechanisms of these displacements. Ambition alone probably would have militated against female entrepreneurship now considered déclassé and likely to lower the family currency on the cross-cultural marriage market. It would hardly do for women from good families to come with hands dirtied by trade, even if their mothers and grandmothers had sensed no degradation there. The highest ranks of society were moving towards the more rigid gender segregation of tasks that was becoming de rigueur for ladies in more affluent and cosmopolitan cities of the Western world: not only Paris, London, New York, and Boston, but also, by the late eighteenth century, the provincial English towns studied by Leonore Davidoff and Catherine Hall, and the towns of woodsy Upper Canada.[26] In England Mary Wollenstonecraft complained in 1791 that even a laudable attempt to earn a living sank women 'almost to the level of prostitution. For are not milliners and mantua-makers reckoned the next class?'

On the other hand, *Lady* now became a much more inclusive term than it had been under the ancien régime. It had once denoted those in the highest ranks of society, those with noble lineage and landed estates. Now middle-class women too could claim the position, if they embraced practices once identified with nobles of both sexes: elaborate and cumbersome dress, downplaying of business interests, a focus on gracious living and hospitality, and an ideal of service. Now, however, private service to family tended to displace older notions of serving the Crown, which had a public dimension and had led certain noblewomen into actions that were politically significant, as when Madeleine de Verchéres defended her family's fort, or Madame de Vaudreuil advised the Court on colonial policy.

At lower levels of urban commerce, the wide range of pre-industrial occupations shrank more gradually. Still keeping a foot in the door, for example, were thirteen female 'traders,' twelve grocers or dry-goods dealers, seven tavern-keepers, and one auctioneer among about fifteen hundred occupations in the 1819 Montreal directory, which recorded the more sizeable operations and tended to name husbands without mentioning active wives.[27] We know that some women shipped goods across distances, as did Vénérande Robichaux, member of a Quebec-Acadian trading family, who marketed maritime fish, furs, sugar, and Micmac boxes to Quebec buyers. Another pre-industrial survivor who 'moved goods' of a different sort was the female funeral director. Omnipresent at markets were female vendors, who were captured on the sketchpads of early-nineteenth-century military officers as they stood hawking things to eat, homemade straw hats, and bolts of cloth. Not for them the niceties of certain English farmwives who had by then come to consider vending their wares at public markets degrading.[28]

At Quebec in 1807 John Lambert described the way ladies, members of Parliament, servants, and military men jostled as they vied for supplies that *habitant* wives and daughters stood selling from five in the morning until noon, even in the snowy months of winter, while their men repaired to nearby taverns. A very young salesgirl purveying sweets at a church door surprised American tourist Joseph Sansom in 1820 by running after him to return a coin when she thought he had overpaid. Women, perhaps single or widowed, leased in their own names four of thirty-one stalls in Montreal's Ste Anne market in 1834. Fifteen years later, Henry David Thoreau found urban women still selling merchandise on tables near the river. They appear to have been active too in the Quebec-area neighbourhoods where 'almost every house had a grocery at one end of it.'[29]

There was also artisanry. A female tinplate manufacturer and tallow chandler listed in Montreal's 1819 directory echoed the earlier, wider, pre-industrial range of family production. Probably there were quite a few other wifely artisans and producers who did not make it into such directories. Hinting at that wider range are the female blacksmiths, coachmakers, mercers, gardeners, and farmers identified in Jacques Viger's 1825 Montreal census.[30] Since there were as yet few ready-made garments for sale, women sewing at home still made most of the clothing worn by ordinary people in Montreal.[31] Convents also persisted as centres of small industry. For example, the Grey Nuns who ran the Montreal Hôpital Général, assisted by the elderly women living there, supplied fur-trade ventures with shirts in the same way French-Canadian women had done for generations. Besides making clothes and ornaments for the North-West Company, the sisters and those in their care printed and bound books and worked in the fields of their seigneurie. Outside the convent, wives' continuing common practice of using their own last names rather than that of their husbands also bespoke a certain independence,[32] which went hand-in-hand with the still-considerable female economic production.

Lower Canada was only slowly making the leap to the new gender order. In 1820 Quebec and Montreal were modest towns, and old ways changed slowly. Menservants were still in fashion; not until later in the century did cook and household servant become overwhelmingly female occupations. An elite family might still turn to a traditional female healer rather than call the physician and have to submit to his favourite cure-all: bleeding the patient.[33] Nor had femininity become narrowly identified with nurturing. When the nineteenth century began, it was still common to send upper-class babies to nursemaids. Other infants stayed with siblings or grandparents when mothers were busy in the family workshop, yard, or store. Mothering remained an avocation rather than a destiny.

Still, changes did gradually begin to touch the middling classes in the towns, especially in the commercial hub of Montreal. The longstanding female activity of dressmaking initially expanded as ever more textiles arrived in British cargoes. Five of the six largest dressmaking operations in Montreal in the 1820s and 1830s were run by female entrepreneurs who employed substantial capital and labour, as the research of Mary-Anne Poutanen has shown. Dressmaker Eliza Graham, for example, recorded some two thousand pounds worth of inventory in 1829; in the following decade, her colleague Margaret Major was employing thirty apprentices, more than any competitor.[34] The leading names in this field were not, however, French Canadian, and the newcomers initiated a shift away from pre-industrial practices. The new masters and mistresses resisted the custom of housing and caring for apprentices. They turned to shorter apprenticeships and were known to exact twelve-hour days without compensation, simply in return for instruction in the trade.

While these big dealers were tightening up their operations, marginal traders began to be labelled a nuisance. Hawkers and pedlars, a feature of urban streetscapes around the world since biblical times, were seen as a stain on newer, wider streets. Did they not undercut the enterprising merchants who invested in handsome display windows to entice customers inside? It was a sign of the times when one illiterate female fixture in the Montreal market in 1820 hired a male intermediary because she needed him to handle paperwork with the newly established Bank of Montreal. As research by Brian Young indicated, special venom was directed towards hawkers who went door-to-door, tempting the servant who opened it 'to waste time and money.'[35] As English-speakers became a majority in Quebec and Montreal in the 1830s and 1840s, the old ways increasingly fell out of favour. However, one could still take a short ride out from the towns and find people who were impervious to any gender innovations in the towns.

The Rural Majority

In the countryside, where 95 per cent of French Canadians lived when the nineteenth century began, women remained secure in their traditional position for a much longer time after the Conquest. They had not yet experienced a 'consumer revolution,' which typically entailed more time indoors for women in order to raise standards of household organization, cleanliness, and comfort. British traveller Basil Hall could detect no such standards when he travelled through Montmorency County in 1816, finding 'dirt much in evidence' among the homespun-clad habitants, but he conceded that they seemed sociable, self-sufficient, and content. Another traveller complained that they would never name a price for goods or services, saying, 'Pay what you please, sir,' with nary a grumble about whatever he gave. This was not a well-developed consumer society. Even seigneurial manors were deemed no better than the dwellings of ordinary New England farmers, beginning with grounds that announced 'little attention to trees for shade or ornament.' At Kamouraska the Couillard stone manor was 'furnished in the plainest manner, much perhaps as were those of our country gentlemen a century ago; that is, much wainscoting, no papering, little or no mahogany, plain delft ware, a rustic establishment with two or three little girls to wait, instead of a footman, and as many large dogs for porters.'[36] Most country dwellings had so few treasures to safeguard that they remained innocent of locks.

One hallmark of traditional peasant agriculture is the female field-worker. We know that in the 1740s the traveller Peter Kalm observed that women in parts of England and America had withdrawn from fieldwork, an innovation signifying 'separate spheres' ideology across western Europe and North America over the course of the eighteenth and nineteenth centuries. When he came to Canada though, Kalm found the women still toiling in the fields. He applauded this unstinting and versatile female labour, which he had seen in his native Sweden. After Canada came under British rule, *canadiennes* continued to don their straw hats and work under the sky, being observed there throughout the first half of the nineteenth century. Such female fieldwork, though it remained common for slaves in the American south and some itinerant workers in Britain, increasingly became an anomaly that elicited unfavourable comment from travellers. 'Many of the women,' George Heriot recorded in 1804, 'are handsome when young, but as they partake of the labours of the field, and expose themselves upon all occasions to the influence of the weather, they soon become of a sallow hue, and of a masculine form.'[37] About the same time John Lambert wrote that 'the girls from manual labour become strong, bony and masculine.'[38] French visitors reported that looks and dress of French-Canadian women recalled Norman peasants, that in contrast to American farmwomen who were no longer taxed with heavy labours, the *canadiennes* 'lose their beauty ... attributable to a life too laborious and occupations too masculine.'[39] Fifteen years later, Henry David Thoreau saw 'women and girls at work in the fields, digging potatoes alone, or bundling up the grain which the men cut ... with a great deal of colour in their cheeks ... broad-brimmed hats and flowing dresses. We afterwards saw them doing other kinds of work; indeed I thought we saw more women at work out of doors than men.'[40]

Thoreau's report indicates that the transition from wheat to newer crops such as potatoes was not accompanied by a gender change in the outdoor workforce. Even the sisters of the Congregation of Notre Dame often worked in the fields. On Canadian farms in general, growing vegetables and fruit characteristically fell to a female gardener and arborist. Dairy and poultry work as well as manufacture of soap and candles also kept the farmwife at her accustomed post as a producer of goods. Many stepped outside for domestic baking, commonly done in outdoor stone ovens. The bracing routine carried over into leisure, startling a French visitor who spotted farmers and merchants' wives dashing in sleighs across fifty miles of snowy terrain for social visits.[41]

On offer in the Quebec market early in the nineteenth century was an array of products that were either wholly or partly produced by women. From their garden plots and orchards they harvested the carrots, turnips, peas, beans, beets, celery, asparagus, potatoes, herbs, berries, melons, pears, and apples for sale there. The cheese, butter, and eggs, the chickens, turkeys, and geese in the market typically came from women's poultry and dairy operations. Men and women, boys and girls probably worked together to raise and butcher the livestock that was sold in the market in the form of beef, mutton, pork, and veal. The partridges, pigeons, and hares were most likely products of hunting by the men, who likely also supplied most of the firewood, flour, and fish. Both sexes might have a hand in producing the moccasins, maple syrup, tobacco, and fur products that were for sale, while the women likely manufactured the lard, tallow, hats of knitted wool and plaited straw, and the bolts of homespun cloth.[42] This was family production through and through.

Canadiennes certainly fabricated most of the cloth and clothing that country people wore. It was not a pretty sight. On weekdays both men and women wore basic homespun outfits, with socks, 'beef' shoes or moccasins, toques or straw hats – all homemade, often patched or recycled.[43] 'The dress of the women is old-fashioned,' John Lambert observed in 1808. 'There are numbers who wear only cloth of their own manufacture, the same as worn by men,' although some of the young were starting to discard long waists and big caps for the styles servant girls wore in towns.[44] On Sundays, people would show off their store-bought things, sometimes in gaudy colour combinations. But the same short jacket and calf-length skirt remained standard feminine attire over the course of two centuries. Some observers linked it to the skirt worn by aboriginal women. In both cases, the wearers worked in fields and trudged through snow to do their chores, and sensibly stitched a hemline that would not hobble them.

Home manufacture, in fact, expanded in Lower Canada. Though spinning and weaving seem to have occurred on a relatively modest scale in New France, by the 1790s nearly a third of farm families in the regions around Quebec City owned looms; by the 1820s, nearly half of them did, and about a third of families around Montreal did too. Seventy per cent in both regions possessed spinning wheels, enabling women to make yarn to knit at home and take to a weaving neighbour if they did not own a loom themselves. A 'trend in self-sufficiency in domestic textile production began in the latter part of the eighteenth century and continued to gain strength in the early nineteenth century,' according to historian David-Thiery Ruddel.[45] For this purpose, families began keeping larger herds of sheep. While both sexes had woven in New France, the nineteenth-century weaver was typically female. The colony in 1833 numbered thirteen thousand weavers, who were 'nearly all women.'[46] Lower Canadian textile production peaked in the late 1820s (with 8.3 yards per family) but persisted throughout much of the nineteenth century while the art died out elsewhere in North America. The 1851 census recorded production of just 15,000 yards of linen in (more populous) Upper Canada in contrast to 900,000 yards in Lower Canada.[47]

Linen production was a particularly complex activity involving work teams composed of both sexes. It required growing flax, cutting and spreading it in the sun to remove resins, then drying it over a fire. The dry fibres were pounded in a flax brake to loosen woody wastes, then beaten with a scutching sword to separate them. After a hackle was used to untangle the fibres, they were at last ready to be spun and woven. Producing linen was so embedded in popular culture that a number of songs and rituals grew up around it, such as 'Recule toi de la,' 'Quiprocquo,' 'Madame demande sa toilette,' 'On vend du plomb,' and 'On loge les gens du roi.' The mixed party of workers passed around a glowing firebrand to play the game 'The little gentleman still lives.' Collecting wages was called 'gathering cherries from red cheeks,' and who knows what went on when couples played the game 'One takes leave of the convent.'[48]

Apart from producing comestibles and clothing, countrywomen perpetuated a wide range of pre-industrial occupations. Licence lists reveal some who worked as pedlars and operated ferries.[49] In L'Assomption parish in the 1830s, women added another item to their traditional production of trade clothing when the Hudson's Bay Company commissioned them to make *ceintures fléchées* (colourful woven sashes). In Saint-Antoine-de-la-Rivière-de-Loup, over sixty women (10 per cent of the village population) were at work embroidering birchbark. In Trois-Rivières they made baskets, purses, and toys. In Saint-Eustache, as Serge Courville has shown, there were in 1831 one or more female innkeepers, embroiderers, carders, singers, traders and merchants, shoemakers, bakers, couturières, cooks, cultivators, school principals and teachers, domestic servants, *engagées*, and day labourers. There were also female spinners, caregivers, governesses, laundresses, masons, joiners, mercers, stylists, musicians, plasterers, nuns, purveyors or new and second-hand merchandise, midwives, secretaries, tailors, tanners, and weavers. The majority of those women were working in some form of production. Twenty years later, in 1851, a smaller proportion were employed and fewer than a third of them were involved in production. By then, domestic service had become the leading female occupation. Transatlantic trends that saw women withdraw from cottage industries eventually did reach French Canada, but they were a long time coming.[50]

On the whole, families could muster, as they had during the French regime, a small surplus that permitted an occasional cash purchase, while continuing to produce most of their own food, clothing, tools, vehicles, and shelter (the last three being male specialties). If few people went hungry, most were far from affluent. There were repeated observations about female producers at their wheels and looms, as well as in the fields. It is indicative of the changes taking place elsewhere in the Western world that, by the early nineteenth century, visitors now deemed women who did heavy outdoor work disagreeably 'masculine.'

Women as Citizens

Ancien régime societies often privileged rank over gender, making it acceptable for some women, as the result of birth, wealth, or achieved status, to exercise authority over lower-ranked men. Such authority could extend well beyond directing menservants within the confines of a mansion. My own research and that of others has found management of sizeable estates by both lay and religious women who supervised workmen. We know that certain well-connected mother superiors, as a result of their own prestige or their connections with ruling factions, sometimes won the day in disputes with bishops. We know the remarkable power Madame Vaudreuil had to influence colonial policy after she gained favour at the French court, a power Madame Frontenac exercised to some degree as well. The point is not, of course, that women ruled New France. It goes without saying that women did not hold formal military or political office, such as generals, judges, or councillors. Women did, however, 'work for the government,' being on Crown pay lists as suppliers of oils, ropes, and timber, as provisioners of food and lodging for officials, soldiers, and Crown employees, as laundresses, seamstresses, and hospital administrators. Some also worked to implement Crown directives, as did Agathe Saint-Père with her subsidized textile factory, as did nuns who addressed needs of settlers, soldiers, and First Nations allies for shelter, food, and health care. Even in matters of public policy it was within the realm of possibility for female opinions to prevail over male ones; certainly in the case of Madame Vaudreuil, her view determined some appointments and shaped some ministerial directives. We know this because the attorney general and other officials complained loudly about it, and because the minister of marine signalled his acceptance or rejection beside her recommendations in the colonial correspondence. If one looks ahead to British rule in 1820, or Canadian rule in 1920, one cannot imagine a woman shaping policy in that way. The ancien régime, for all its inequities, awarded, to a special few, an agency that would become unthinkable in more 'democratic' times that lay ahead.

Female political leadership also appeared in lower ranks of society. Historians have found that women were active participants in pre-industrial crowds on both sides of the Atlantic, in situations as diverse as the English Civil War, the French Revolution, and land disputes on Prince Edward Island. They gathered for public protests against bread shortages, merchants who hoarded grain during famines, and overly exacting landlords. Although this form of popular politics had its drawbacks, it was more inclusive on the gender front than the all-male franchise of a later date. In New France, several instances of female rioters were recorded. Women in a crowd that protested relocation of a parish church threatened to kill the offending bailiff and toss him into the marsh. During the Seven Years' War, groups of women in Quebec City took to the streets to protest against horsemeat rations. They made allusion to the proverbial *habitant* love of horses, telling the authorities they were disgusted because 'the horse is friend of mankind' and also because 'our religion forbids it.'[51]

After the Conquest, there were some active female fomenters among the numerous *habitants* who welcomed the American Revolutionary army when it invaded Quebec in 1775. Three officers of the Crown who went from parish to parish to recruit *habitant* militia to fight the Americans made a record of seditious actions. At Pointe-aux-Trembles 'the wives of Joseph and Jean Goulet have gone from door to door to defame [*noirceur*] those who recruited youths last autumn to march with Mr McLean, saying that they were being led into carnage.' At least two female agents were sufficiently well-known to earn the nickname *la reine d'Hongrie*, an allusion to Queen Marie Thérèse of Austria, Hungary, and Bohemia (1717–80). At Saint-Pierre on the Ile d'Orléans the officers discovered that 'the wife of Augustin Chabot whom the habitants have ironically named the *reine d'Hongrie* has perverted nearly all the habitants by visiting the houses from one end to the other. It seems this woman has a powerful tongue [*beaucoup de langue*] and according to a number of *habitants* has made a great impression on many minds.'[52]

There was another of these queens at Saint-Valier: 'The widow Gabourie, nicknamed *la reine d'Hongrie,* has done more harm in this parish than anyone else. She often held at her house assemblies where she presided, tending to turn spirits against the government and animate them in favour of the rebels.' Officials added, 'To better achieve her detestable aim she plies them with hard liquors.' Twenty years later, 'the menaces of five hundred Women' greeted authorities attempting to arrest Quebec-area men who were protesting a corvée to repair roads.[53]

Around the beginning of the nineteenth century, women were still construed as creatures with civil rights. The *Quebec Magazine* (edited by reformer John Neilson) devoted three separate issues to lengthy excerpts from Mary Wollenstonecraft's *Vindication of the Rights of Woman* beginning in the spring of 1794. Mary would have rejoiced to know that women already *did* vote in Lower Canada. When Canadians with modest property holdings were enfranchised under the Constitution of 1791, women were not explicitly excluded, and they proceeded to exercise the right. A study of surviving Lower Canadian poll books by Nathalie Picard yielded the names of 857 women who voted between 1792 until 1834. At that point the vote was withdrawn temporarily, followed by a definitive withdrawal in 1849.[54] Feminine voting was especially strong during the tense pre-Rebellion years 1827–34, with the heaviest turnout in 1832. Such voters were particularly active in Montreal and William Henry village, and in Leinster and Huntingdon counties. Around that time a number of women voted in Trois-Rivières too, though not in Quebec City. Overall, female names constituted 2–3 per cent of the voters recorded in surviving poll books. In certain hotly contested elections it rose higher, notably to 14 per cent in Montreal West in 1832, where one study raised the possibility that nearly all widows who headed households and met the property qualifications may have voted, while at a minimum one-third of them did.[55] The fact that women voted at all is noteworthy, since they did not do so in England, France, and most American states during this period.[56]

What kind of women came to the polls? In 1832 Montreal, most were widows (638), but there were also a number of single women (*filles majeures*). There were some wives who lived under the regime of separation of goods from their husbands, therefore able to manage their own property. This configuration reflects an extension of the basic principle of the Custom of Paris, that those not under marital authority of a husband possessed authority of their own. Voting came under the ancien régime rubric that it was one's status, not one's gender per se, that conferred rights.[57]

Trouble in Arcadia: The French-Canadian Professionals

However purposeful women may have been about exercising the franchise that the 1791 Constitution allowed, after 1830 very chilly blasts of air wafted towards the *citoyennes* of Lower Canada. In the 1830s leading Canadian professionals began publicly to question the wisdom of traditional gender-inclusive practices. Gradually, anglicized legal practices and occupational segregation narrowed a woman's ability to function as a citizen, as a person with authority in the public sphere.

Certainly there was a fresh spirit of male entitlement that some must have found hard to resist. Early in the nineteenth century, as Fernand Ouellet and other historians have shown, a new group of college-trained French-Canadian professionals were upwardly mobile, searching for a future in the new parliamentary regime. Alive to currents of European liberalism and Jeffersonian and Jacksonian democracy, they became the first spokesmen of a nascent French-Canadian nationalism. These lawyers, notaries, doctors, and merchants jostled for place in a colonial regime that tended to favour English-speaking aspirants. Often rising from the farming class, the *canadien* professionals took particular pains to distinguish themselves from humbler folk. Despite incomes that were sometimes precarious, they spent more than merchants did on clothing – some 20 per cent of their wealth. Lawyers were the first French-Canadian group to cast off colourful ancien régime breeches, silk stockings, floral vests, and frilled shirts and replace them (as their Parisian cousins also did) with the dark, clean-cut, modern English-style suit with black top hat and Wellington boots, set off by an immaculate white shirt.[58] Scraping the soil from their heels, they rallied round a new system that seemed more modern and efficient. They would not have been immune to the gender privileges that English law offered, along with its commercial efficiencies. Still, it is unsettling to observe the very men who led the quest for popular rights – culminating in an armed uprising of some eight thousand men – spearheading *removal* of women's rights.

Much can be laid at the door of eighteenth-century French philosopher Jean-Jacques Rousseau. Women who ventured into the political arena were disparaged in his influential writings – which made their way into the English canon too. His romantic invocation of what was 'natural' and his resentment of libertine noblewomen culminated in a prescription that females of all ranks had best stay home, out of the limelight, and cultivate virtue in the bosom of the family. Admittedly, his espousal of maternal breastfeeding was good advice. Sending infants to wet nurses so often led to their deaths that when Lower Canadian governor's wife Lady Milnes encountered the practice among Quebec elites, she underwrote publication of a Rousseau-inspired tract calling for change.[59] Unfortunately Rousseau's prescription of a stint in the nursery somehow ballooned into a lifetime of banishment from civic affairs, since, the philosopher claimed, there was 'no good conduct for women outside of a withdrawn domestic life … the dignity of their sex consists in modesty.'[60] Even in Rousseau's day it was commented that this concern for female modesty was somewhat disingenuous in a philosopher who together with a friend purchased a girl to be their shared sexual slave, and who deposited five children he conceived with an illiterate servant-mistress in a foundling home. Nonetheless, Rousseau's domestic angel, sketched in honeyed and idealistic terms, reached cult status among educated people of both sexes across the Western world. By the 1820s even Lower Canada's English-language press was informing readers that a woman could not appear in the pulpit or 'at the polls … without disparagement of her sexual character.'[61] The romantic maunderings about the lack of female virtue outside the private sphere ensured that any who bucked the trend would pay dearly for it, opening themselves to sexual innuendo. Since occupational opportunities were shrinking too, women were more dependent than ever on a good reputation to contract an opportune marriage.

Louis-Joseph Papineau was Saint Jean-Jacques's most prominent French-Canadian acolyte. Elected Speaker of the House of Assembly in 1815, Papineau emerged as the charismatic leader of the nationalist movement. He echoed Rousseau's injunctions about childrearing and the unsuitability of women expressing political views in his letters to his wife.[62] In 1834, on the day he urged fellow legislators to exclude them from voting in Lower Canadian parliamentary elections, he proclaimed, 'As to the practice of having women vote, it is right to destroy it. It is ridiculous, it is odious to see wives dragged to the hustings by their husbands, daughters by their fathers, often against their wishes. The public interest, the decency, the modesty of the female sex demands that these scandals not be repeated. A simple resolution of the House, excluding those persons from the right to vote, would prevent such improprieties.'[63]

There is nothing factual about this statement. The poll books suggest some 70 per cent of the voters were widows – unable to be dragged by husbands and unlikely to be dragged by fathers. Papineau's house was in downtown Montreal, and record numbers of women, including friends of his family, voted in the constituency he held for two decades. As Bradbury has shown, they generally came without men, arriving throughout the days of open polling, not as last-minute recruits to sway a close contest. Papineau personally greeted voting women at the polls, and his own cousin D-B Viger reported the preponderance of widows in Montreal elections to a legislative committee. It is unlikely Papineau was unaware of the reality.[64] Nonetheless the offending bill passed in 1834, with no substantive objections and little discussion. Although it was revoked in 1836 by the Legislative Council, for reasons unrelated to female franchise, few women appeared at the polls after the 1834 ban. An Act of the Parliament of the United Canadas in 1849 later eliminated women's vote until the early twentieth century.[65] An encyclopedic reader of French, English, and American literature of all kinds, Papineau was a harbinger of new gender dogma from abroad.

Some of Papineau's followers, too, may have seen female political activity as disgraceful. Political passions ran high in the 1830s, and it is hard to distinguish new ideas about women in public from run-of-the-mill sexual slurs, which were as old as the hills. By the 1830s Montreal newspapers of both languages tended to discuss female voters negatively, deriding political opponents for resorting to such questionable supporters.[66] Allan Greer has argued that Rousseau's ideas had reached even rural Patriots by the 1830s. Such ideas had, after all, made their way into radical ideologies during revolutions that served as models for the Patriot uprising. Though female citizenship briefly became a rallying cry during the French Revolution, it had been repudiated with the banning of female revolutionary clubs in 1793 and exclusion of women from the franchise and from public or armed service.[67] Pornographic portrayals of Marie-Antoinette reinforced salacious views of commanding females. In the wake of the French and American Revolutions, the articulation of 'the rights of Man' and the 'rise of the common man' held out the prospect of civic entitlement to men of all classes, but conceiving citizenship as a *human* right was too radical for the radicals. The most suggestive echo of this exclusionary philosophy in rural French Canada was the cry of a Patriot merchant in Contrecoeur who responded to a prayer of thanksgiving for the coronation of Queen Victoria by leading dissidents out of the church with the insult, 'It is painful to have to sing the Te

Deum for the damn Queen, damned whore with her legs in the air.'[68] Papineau himself belittled the English monarch more politely, drawing laughter from a political rally in 1837 with his remark that the young queen was thinking more about getting a husband than about politics. Thomas Jefferson was invoked in the 4 July 1837 Patriot press, pontificating that women 'to prevent depravation of morals, and ambiguity of issue, could not mix promiscuously in the public meetings of men.'[69]

Despite such discouragements, women did participate in the rebellions of 1837–8. They wove the homespun that replaced boycotted British cloth, made banners, and organized patriotic banquets. One woman used that age-old female political weapon, the tongue, to compose satirical songs against the local curé who supported the government. Several formed a Patriot group. When the uprising began, some made bullets. Some allowed rebels to use their homes as battlements, and others hid fugitives from the authorities. Several religious women offered aid and comfort to the Patriot side: Emilie Tavernier-Gamelin served as a go-between for imprisoned rebels and their families, and the sisters of Montreal's Hôpital Général sheltered families of rebels at their Chateauguay manor.[70] On the government side, Papineau's own cousin Rosalie Cherrier not only wrote newspaper commentary but resisted a menacing crowd that beset her house for two nights; either she or someone else inside there fired wounding shots. Hortense Globensky was another bold partisan, who donned her husband's clothes and arms to confront Patriots.[71]

Nonetheless, it was not an impressive showing. It seems there was no parallel to the *reines d'Hongrie*, the female leaders who in 1775 were identified by the authorities as 'making a great impression on many minds' or 'doing more harm in this parish than anyone else.' In those days they had nicknamed female political leaders after Queens; sixty years later, they scorned female leaders and they called the real Queen a whore. Allan Greer pointed out that among some thirteen hundred names on official lists of political prisoners during and after the uprising, not one can be identified as female, and that 'thousands of depositions and other narrative sources convey a similar impression that nowhere did women play ... a very active role.'[72] As Greer observed, the Patriot movement 'clearly stood for a masculine – indeed a masculinizing – politics in which women were not welcome.'[73] Nor did the defeat of the Patriots lead to a restoration of citizenship rights for women. One-time *Patriots* such as L-H Lafontaine and G-E Cartier would return to the fore of French-Canadian parliamentary politics in ensuing decades, bringing with them the same

exclusionary outlook. Nor, for decades to come, would any party anywhere on the political spectrum challenge those 'masculinizing politics
in which women were not welcome.'

Restrictions on Property

Some of the same Patriots who voted to remove women's electoral rights
also decided in the 1830s that traditional property rights under the
Custom of Paris were in need of reform. Some participants in Patriot
rallies of 1837 proposed resolutions against customary dower, and they
appeared again in Robert Nelson's 1838 Declaration of Independence.
Some nationalists, including post-Rebellion Reform leader L-H Lafontaine, believed such encumbrances must be removed; as attorney general and prime minister in the next decade, he would advance that goal.[74]

The Special Council set up to govern Canadians after the rebellions,
which was composed predominantly of members of the anglophone
economic elite, rushed to pass the Registry Act, which a number of its
members had long sought. It required registry of dower in order for it to
retain precedence over demands of creditors. Married women could now
release their customary dower on any property their husbands wished to
sell during marriage, and dower rights were narrowed to land that the
husband owned at the time of his death. As Bradbury observed of the
1841 Registry Act, it 'jettisoned the inviolability of dower under French
law' and 'changed the nature of the marriage bargain in the province,
since freedom of contract for men overrode society's prescription of the
proper proportion of wealth that should be made available to a widow
... [boosting] individual male rights to decide whether to be benevolent
or not.'[75] Over the next four decades, judicial rulings and further legislation – most notably the recodification of 1866 – further restricted dower
claims. Although it is true that dower rights were less important to urban
groups than to families living on the land, Quebec remained a predominantly rural society until the 1920s. The Registry Act of 1841 narrowed
what had been a residual property right. Ironically, this occurred only a
few years before concerted campaigns arose in common law jurisdictions
to remedy the inadequate property rights of women there. With the Act
of 1841, Lower Canada began moving in the opposite direction. Ironically too, Canadian women definitively lost the vote in 1849, just one year
after American activists at Seneca Falls began to demand it.

What was the impact of the combined reduction of women's occupational range, their rights to dower, their rights to franchise? The fact that

women no longer voted gave legislators and administrators less cause to take their needs and interests into account. As for marital property, no doubt there were, as in Upper Canada, chivalrous judges who were interested in mitigating some of the harsher effects of the law, at least in cases that aroused their sympathies.[76] Such is hardly a substitute, though, for automatic legal entitlement to revenues or use of one-half of a husband's inherited real property, and the economic options that that allows. Declining dower rights cut widows off from one source of the security and autonomy they had always enjoyed in French Canada.

Although we have been examining dark trends, there was one area of public life in which urban women continued to shine: social assistance, or as it was called at the time, the work of benevolence. In that field, they retained considerable authority, controlled substantial assets, and made a key civic contribution. Here too, some critics brandished Rousseau's charge of public action as a stain on female honour. For example, in 1818 a correspondent to *Le Canadien* wondered how the nuns 'could decently prepare to treat certain shameful maladies. How could they assist with childbirth ... Impossible!' A decade later Papineau took another tack, assailing convents' abilities to manage their own finances, despite their two hundred year colonial history of doing so. He was exercised about 'their removal from the world rendering them incapable to administer the revenues of such an institutions ... It is up to us [the Assemblymen] to remedy this, to direct and control their finances.'[77] This time, however, the attempted withdrawal of female powers was forestalled. In closing, we turn to inspect this last bastion of feminine leadership outside the home.

Lingering Benevolence

Urban women led in shaping social welfare throughout the period covered in this book – the two centuries between the 1630s and the 1830s. Design and development of social assistance in Lower Canada remained primarily a feminine enterprise. To a large extent, so was the financing of those systems in that period of minimal state intervention. It remained a vital area for feminine public activity at a time when both citizenship and many of the more remunerative occupations were becoming masculinized. We direct our discussion to the rapidly growing town of Montreal, to show that even there, at the centre of growth and change, benevolent women maintained a vigorous presence in the public domain. Convents continued to house the needy, now joined by laywomen who founded new organizations to assist unprecedented numbers of destitute immigrants. Nuns and laywomen were still initiating major projects in 1832, when cholera created an emergency in the town. Women drawn from both major language groups provided for those unable to supply their own food, clothing, fuel, housing, childcare, schooling, or health care.

Convents carried the major burden of social welfare in Lower Canada after the British Conquest of 1760. From the seventeenth century, Congregational nuns had provided free schooling to working-class children; they added two new Montreal locations to their Notre Dame motherhouse in the early 1830s.[78] Other groups of nuns cared for the orphaned, indigent, aged, and ill. Having begun in the seventeenth century as a dedicated group of missionaries funded by private donors and their own lands and labours, the nuns had provided services that in some ways compared favourably with hospital care and female education in France itself.[79] After the Conquest, despite financial difficulties, their role expanded. Having cared for British as well as French cases during and after the Seven Years' War (their own blend of charity and *politique*), the nuns were permitted to recruit in Canada at a time when the Jesuit and Récollet orders were forbidden to do so, and vocations to the parish priesthood were languishing. In 1825 nuns outnumbered clergymen in Montreal by four to one. Moreover, the colonial government, which balked at financing male orders, regularly funded sisterly work in Lower Canada's three urban centres. The sum of £17,103 was awarded to nunneries in Montreal alone between 1800 and 1823 to help sponsor their care of the sick and homeless in the expanding town.[80]

Receiving financing from the colonial government during an era of rather weak ecclesiastical control, the nuns continued to enjoy considerable autonomy. Just as this had irked officials during the French period, it had caused the nationalist party leader Papineau to turn a covetous gaze towards their government-funded institution, while others questioned their medical activities. However, the sisters rode out the criticism and no fundamental change was made before 1840.

One of the operations aided by government funds was the Hôtel-Dieu, located on the bustling business street of Saint-Paul. This thirty-bed hospital consisted of two wards until a late-1820s expansion provided more space, allowing the sisters to treat some thirteen hundred patients a year. One of its administrators, Sister Lacroix, was noted as being 'gifted with much talent and ability for temporal affairs.' She served as both architect and overseer of construction for the hospital and its street-level shops that proffered the sisters' farm produce, baking, preserved goods, and

artisanal work. Though the Hôtel-Dieu benefited from pro bono ward visits by Dr William Selby, physicians were in scarce supply. Thirty-five nuns
carried on day-to-day duties, including those of apothecaries, ward supervisors, and hospital administrators. A visitor in the 1830s noted, 'The
apothecary ... is extensive and arranged in a manner that would gladden
the sight of the New York college of Pharmacy. The jars and gallipots ...
of dark-blue and white china ... [and] shelves perfectly uniform. Two of
the nuns are in constant attendance on the establishment manufacturing and preparing medicine. They also cup and bleed. The physician in
attendance merely prescribes, and they execute his orders.'[81]

Combining women's pre-industrial role as healers with the work of
nursing, the more skilled among them can be characterized as nurse-
practitioners.[82]

Montreal's Hôpital Général, run by Madame Youville's Grey Nuns
since the 1740s, was a larger establishment with about eighty beds and
a range of social services. Unlike the Hôtel-Dieu (which turned away
children, maternity cases, communicable diseases, and several other categories), the hospice had an open door. It nursed a number of indigent
invalids and mental patients. It looked after orphans of both sexes as
well as women in various kinds of trouble. It also housed paying pensioners who used it as a retirement home. It was, according to Micheline
D'Allaire, the first Canadian organization to make daily home visits to
the poor. Sheltering a number of Irish orphans and other victims of a
typhus outbreak in 1822–3, the *hôpital* received legislative commenda-
tion for fostering the town's 'uncommon degree of health at that time.'
In the latter year it treated 485 Protestants and 367 Catholics, consisting
of residents and drop-ins in roughly equal numbers. Of these, it was reported, only 41 died.[83] Lower Canadian hospices, even during epidemics, were not among the proverbial places where the poor went to die. By
1840 the *hôpital* counted 160 residents and employed a sizeable pay list
of servants and other attendants.

Like the Hôtel-Dieu, this large establishment owed its prosperous
condition to enterprising directors. One was bursar Marie-Marguerite
Lemaire, who warded off interlopers attempting to farm or timber on
the *hôpital's* two seigneuries. She personally drew up land rolls and supervised improvements at the sisters' Chateauguay seigneurie, pulled up
squatters' crops, even rescued travellers trapped on ice floes. Equally
resourceful was Thérèse-Geneviève Coutlée, *hôpital* director from 1792
to 1821.[84] The daughter of a day labourer, Coutlée had entered the convent in 1762 and was singled out early for her intelligence and judgment.

When appointed superior, she wept at the responsibility. However, she soon displayed the business acumen that we have seen in so many ancien régime women. When the *hôpital* faced financial difficulty due to the French government's failure to pay certain annuities, Sister Coutlée did her best to restore a sound footing. She rented out part of the land, and she developed workshops where the nuns made candles and vestments, embroidered cloth, and bound books, exercising a traditional range of craft skills. Sister Coutlée was also an innovator who went to some lengths to import a spinning machine for the *hôpital*.[85] The premature death of several fieldworking nuns apparently persuaded her that the order's overtaxed energies were better used indoors. Doctors, legislative councillors, and all parties involved in the 1824 'Enquiry into Establishments for the Insane, Foundlings and the Sick and Infirm Poor' spoke with respect of the dedication of the Grey Nuns and their 'great and unremitting exertion' to feed, clothe, and care for all those in their charge.

The Hôpital Général's Foundling Street location bespoke its other major function, to receive abandoned infants. Madame Youville had initiated this practice at the outset of the Seven Years' War, as the number of foundlings soared in a colony full of troops.[86] The nuns sent them out to wet nurses, paid them, provided them with baby clothes, and visited to check up on their tiny charges. When they turned two, the babies were brought back to the *hôpital*, and later sent out for adoption or contractual placement with 'respectable families.' This infant care, which might have been one of the Grey Nuns' more cheerful tasks, was in fact a grim business, for the majority of infants died. As Montreal developed into a sizeable port, military base, and reception point for immigrants, increasing numbers of children were abandoned. The nuns received seventeen infants in 1760, thirty-nine in 1800, and eighty-six in 1823, many barely clinging to life when they arrived.[87]

The Hôpital Général, Hôtel-Dieu, and sister institutions successfully made the transition to a new regime by diplomacy with their British rulers and by the continuing tradition of dedicated care, now broadened to include non-Catholics. Above all, they survived and expanded because they filled a vital need, to which the considerable government grants stand testimony. In Montreal there were no other hospitals available until 1816 and no sizeable Protestant institution until 1822, despite a preponderance of Protestant patients.

Perhaps influenced by the sisters' activity, Protestant laywomen in Lower Canada entered the arena. Evidently they were unimpressed by the Assembly's 1816 plan to deal with surging pauperism by fining beg-

gars and those who gave to them. The historian of the Female Benevolent Society, which was established that year, recorded that a house on
Craig Street, where the society began to care for the sick poor, was the
embryo for the first Protestant general hospital.[88] Doige's *Montreal Directory* of 1819 corroborates the claim: 'The bright example of superior
benevolence evinced by the female sex in this institution has at length
aroused the energies of the gentlemen, who have lately caused a public
dispensary to be established, which, with the increase of the population
and the difficulties of the times ... has made necessary.'

While female paying occupations became *less* respectable, it appears
that benevolent activity became *more* respectable over time. The 'Females'
(whose first leader came from a family of tailors) recast themselves as
'Ladies' in 1832 to reflect changing sensibilities and an influx of genteel members. Such ladies perhaps felt safer with the society's increasing
focus on helping women and children.[89] Several committee members
worked to establish a national school while others formed a committee
of the Society for Promoting Education and Industry.[90] From 1822 the
society had run a Protestant orphan asylum with twelve members serving
as managers. None of this prevented them from going door to door to
help those afflicted with cholera in 1832.

The impoverished immigration of the 1820s and 1830s also stirred
other lay efforts. An heiress of the aristocratic Longueuil family founded
the Catholic Dames de Charité in 1827 to provide housing, education,
and employment to needy women and children. The group opened an
orphanage a few years later. A close ally was Emilie Tavernier-Gamelin,
who soon attracted followers and began setting up hostels that would
grow into the extensive work of the Sisters of Providence. Leaders such
as the Baronne de Longueuil, who married David Alexander Grant, and
Marguerite Baby, who married Dr Selby, fostered an ecumenical spirit,
and Catholic and Protestant laywomen collaborated in bazaars where
their manufactures fetched impressive sums.[91]

So even in Montreal's time of sharp transition after 1815, a notable
aspect of welfare was the centrality of the work of women. A couple of
visitors from abroad thought the Lower Canadian activism in benevolent
work and education outdid that of women in England and France.[92] The
Canadians did not operate peripherally, as auxiliaries to men's groups;
they initiated the response to many of the most pressing public needs.
The Ladies Benevolent Society records indicate that 'this Society was the
pioneer philanthropy of British Montreal, and that its work led directly
to the founding of the Montreal General Hospital and the Protestant

Orphan Asylum and to an organised assistance for that vast throng of immigrants continually progressing towards Upper Canada.'[93] As late as 1820 other groups were still so ephemeral that the Ladies' Benevolent Society was the only Protestant charity mentioned in the *Montreal Directory* that year. A workhouse opened in 1819 but operated only sporadically during the next decade.[94] Beyond that, there appears to have been little besides stonecutting for unemployed men and the bread line at the Récollet Church. Until the opening of the commodious Montreal General Hospital in 1822, the Catholic and Protestant institutions for the ill in Montreal were all founded and administered by women.

Thus did this last bastion of female civic leadership persist in the British colony of Lower Canada. It is significant that several of those who headed their ranks also appeared at the polls to vote, until that right was taken away.[95] It has been observed that the indifference of the state and the relatively weak Catholic Church of the post-Conquest decades left women a certain leeway to develop social welfare institutions according to their own lights. Some of the leading beneficiaries of such work were girls, who constituted 58 per cent of Montreal's free pupils by the mid-1830s.[96]

The hope expressed in Doige's 1819 *Directory* that men would soon follow women's lead in the benevolent field had become a reality by the time the 1839 directory appeared. By then, men led a plethora of societies devoted to relief, reform, and immigrant aid,[97] and had taken over leadership of the new Montreal General Hospital and of the new Montreal Lunatic Asylum. Though women were no longer alone in the field, one sign of their continuing importance was a special exemption from tightening gender restrictions, a legal provision granting laywomen who administered benevolent work the right to make contracts without spousal permission.[98]

There is a French term for these administrators in skirts: *femmes fortes*. Although religious orders would continue to supply outstanding figures throughout the nineteenth century, *femmes fortes* among the laity would become rarer after the 1830s. Independent public enterprise by bourgeois women would begin to seem out of place. As we have seen, older family-oriented property systems were increasingly replaced by more individualistic (which in this era meant androcentric) British law and custom. When that happened, a woman had less to bring to the public domain. She was less apt to have independent property or the kind of business acumen her grandmother may have acquired through managing the family business or estate. Even among the nuns, work would be more closely supervised by the male hierarchy, particularly by Montreal's overbearing Bishop Ignace Bourget, who began his long reign in 1840. After the early nineteenth-century decades under review here, projects would increasingly be initiated by male clergy, philanthropic business-men, or civic officials. While continuing to supply much of the labour, women were less apt to supply the direction.[99] That, however, is another story.

Conclusion

Our account in this book has tracked women in the public sphere in early French Canada. It has sought out instances of female agency and found them in great profusion. Surprisingly, many of these opportu-nities endured for a full seven decades after the British took over the colony in 1760. For more than seventy years after the Conquest, most of the French Canadians (who comprised 84 per cent of the Lower Cana-dian population in 1827) continued to operate within a pre-industrial economy and a pre-Conquest, pre-Revolutionary legal framework. Sur-veying the post-Conquest period, we have seen women maintaining a public profile in economic production, and leadership in educational and benevolent organizations, claiming their place in public squares to sell their goods, even casting votes for members of the Legislative As-sembly. They had managed to keep their foothold in the public sphere even as Lower Canada began its transition away from the ancien régime into the world of steamboats, elected Assemblies, massive British immi-gration, and urban growth. In the countryside, they continued to be economic producers on the farm and to increase their output at the spinning wheel and the loom. Most people in Lower Canada remained firmly tied to an economy based on farming and natural resources. The majority of women were country dwellers who engaged in some form of economic production and exchange, just as their great-grandmothers had done.

Changes that were emanating from the capitals of the Western world could not be warded off indefinitely. Among the landmarks were disap-pearance of female transatlantic traders, the 1834 disenfranchisement, and the reduction of property rights in 1841 when dower began to be hedged with restrictions. By then the changes on those and other fronts seemed inevitable, for French-Canadian liberals had begun to embrace both economic change and a newer set of ideas about gender. That tran-sition warrants a book of its own.

Our story has been a different one. From the seventeenth century into the early nineteenth, women were actively involved at all levels of economic life, in very visible ways. We have met managerial gentlewomen and nuns whose patterns of behaviour were greatly influenced by metropolitan codes and traditions, as was typical of the nobility. Trading women of lesser rank were often responding directly to the resources of the North American environment that lay at their feet. All groups built, in one way or another, on modes of life and trade that had been developed centuries earlier by First Nations. They built too on the fledgling society shaped by two distinct groups of seventeenth-century immigrants, the *dévotes* and the *filles du roi* who had sailed up the St Lawrence River to begin a new life. The missionaries had been drawn to the forested environment of the new colony, specifically to the forest peoples they hoped to Christianize. Going beyond the economic, we have discussed diverse female initiatives in the two centuries that followed the arrival of Marie de l'Incarnation in 1639. Of political importance were the deeds of redoubtable figures such as Jeanne Mance, who co-founded Montreal and provided the funds to prevent its abandonment, and Elisabeth de Vaudreuil, who influenced colonial policy, speaking into the ear of the minister at Versailles.

We have turned our attention, too, to the ranks of very 'ordinary' women. First among them were the brides who managed to cross the ocean at a time when one in ten passengers could expect to die en route, who faced the unknown, settled along the river, and became the founding mothers of a new, northern people. The French Canadians are in our own day a force that is seven million strong in Canada, with others scattered across the continent. The immigrant brides of the seventeenth century, standing at the very beginning of that line, were physically transformed by the healthful conditions of the colony, with its clean air and water, fish, game, and fertile soil far outweighing any dangers its native peoples and wintry climate might pose to them. They enjoyed exceptionally long life and high fertility, giving birth to vigorous sons and vigorous daughters. Like Jeanne Mance, they too made an essential contribution to the colony at a time when its survival was precarious. As agriculturalists in days when all capable hands worked outdoors, they were essential economic producers. Economically productive too were petty dealers, the *métisse* crafter of snowshoes, the whole lot of small vendors, seamstresses, fort laundresses, convent artisans, and canoe-makers. Innumerable are those who contributed something, large or small, to the operations of army, fur trade, fisheries, timber, and shipbuilding.

Looking out over the forested hinterland that stretched away from the St Lawrence River, there occasionally loomed up a clearing containing an isolated fishing station, a convent farm, a native village, a wooden trading post, or an imposing stone fort. Along the vast chain that stretched from pristine interior waterways, down along the big river past the populated centres of Montreal and Quebec, out to the Gulf of St Lawrence, and then over salt waters to Bordeaux, thousands of people were at work. Year after year they gathered, grew, processed, traded, packaged, and shipped the products that made their way to New World settlements and Old World markets. When we search along the shores for Canadians involved in this vast pattern of exchange of goods, many a *canadienne* steps into the light.

Notes

Introduction

1 As Micheline Dumont pointed out at the turn of the millennium, there remained a disappointingly small body of writing about French-Canadian women in subsequent decades too, though things are beginning to change. See Micheline Dumont, 'Un champ bien clos: L'histoire des femmes au Québec,' *Atlantis* 25, no. 1 (2000): 102–18. A breakthrough was the conference 'Femmes, culture et pouvoir' held at the Université de Sherbrooke in May 2009, with a sampling of its scholarly presentations on women in New France and later eras subsequently published in both the Conference Proceedings and in a special issue of *Revue d'histoire de l'Amérique française* 63, nos. 2–3 (2010).

2 Lynn Hunt, *The Family Romance of the French Revolution* (Berkeley: University of California Press, 1992); Joan Landes, *Women in the Public Sphere in the Age of the French Revolution* (Ithaca: Cornell University Press, 1988); James F. Mc-Millan, *France and Women, 1789–1914: Gender, Society and Politics* (London: Routledge, 2000).

3 The nagging is described in W.J. Eccles, *The Canadian Frontier 1534–1760* (Toronto: Holt Rinehart Winston, 1969), 92; the charms in Richard Colebrook Harris, *The Seigneurial System in Early Canada* (Montreal and Kingston: McGill-Queen's University Press, 1966), 164.

4 Louis Franquet, *Voyages et mémoires sur le Canada* (Montreal: Éditions Élysée, 1974), 193.

5 Carol Devens, *Countering Colonization: Native American Women and Great Lakes Missions, 1630–1900* (Berkeley: University of California Press, 1992); Susan Sleeper-Smith, *Indian Women and French Men: Rethinking Cultural Encounter in the Western Great Lakes* (Amherst: University of Massachusetts Press, 2001);

Sylvia Van Kirk, *Many Tender Ties: Women in Fur Trade Society, 1670–1870* (Winnipeg: Watson and Dwyer, 1980).

6 One might perhaps say instead that the frontier thesis has shifted to more westerly parts of New France. There are certainly vestiges of the idea of new societies shaped by environment in the study of the country north of the Great Lakes, by Richard White, *The Middle Ground: Indians, Empires, and Republics in the Great Lakes Region, 1650–1815* (Cambridge: Cambridge University Press, 1991), which discusses the hybrid cultural forms that developed. Related themes regarding mixed marriages in the Great Lakes region are advanced in Sleeper-Smith's *Indian Women*. For a survey of earlier work, see Michael S. Cross, ed., *The Frontier Thesis and the Canadas: A Debate on the Impact of the Canadian Environment* (Toronto: Copp Clark, 1977).

7 Among the numerous influential scholars of New France who owe much to the *Annales* tradition are Catherine Debarats, Louise Dechene, Lorraine Gadoury, Allan Greer, and Louise Lavallée. For discussion and examples of such work, see Sylvie Dépatie, Catherine Desbarats, Danielle Gauvreau, Mario Lalancette, and Thomas Wein, *Vingt ans après Habitants et marchands: Lectures de l'histoire des XVIIe et XVIIIe siècles canadiens* (Montreal and Kingston: McGill-Queen's University Press, 1998).

8 William Eccles, 'The Social, Economic and Political Influence of the Military Establishment in New France,' *Canadian Historical Review* 52 (1971): 1–22; Dale Miquelon, *New France 1701–1744: 'A Supplement to Europe'* (Toronto: McClelland and Stewart, 1987).

9 Thomas Wien, in Dépatie et al., *Vingt ans*, 12, 160.

10 *Oxford Canadian Dictionary*, s.v. 'environment' (Toronto: Oxford University Press, 1998). Useful definitions of environmental history, including classic essays by William Cronon and Donald Worster, are found in Carolyn Merchant, ed., *Major Problems in American Environmental History* (Toronto: D.C. Heath, 1993). See also Alan MacEachern and William J. Turkel, *Method and Meaning in Canadian Environmental History* (Toronto: Nelson, 2009).

11 Peter Moogk, *La Nouvelle France: The Making of French Canada – A Cultural History* (East Lansing: Michigan State University Press, 2000), 188, 268.

12 Ibid., 161, 188, 207, refers to wives as dependents.

13 Ibid., 229, notes the compromise in practice; for the suggestion of continuity, see 268.

14 Young's work is discussed in chapter 3 of this book. As for single women in convents for whom the closest male authority figure was the bishop, Marguerite Jean showed long ago (and our chapters 2 and 7 shows again) that they were happy to disagree with His Lordship, and it was not unknown for them to get their way.

15 One can note, too, that Allan Greer's influential interpretation of the political discontent, *The Patriots and the People* (Toronto: University of Toronto Press, 1993), suggests that Patriot agitators employed traditional folkways such as the charivari.

16 Gerald Craig, ed., *Lord Durham's Report* (Toronto: McClelland and Stewart, 1963), 28.

1. Transatlantic Trends 1600–1800

1 Louise Dechene's 1974 book appeared in translation as *Habitants and Merchants in Seventeenth-Century Montreal* (Montreal and Kingston: McGill-Queen's University Press, 1992), 281.

2 Attesting to this was Canadian Attorney General Ruette d'Auteuil, who attributed it to the abundance of firewood, grain, and fruit, and the readily available products of fishing and hunting. At around the same time another colonial official, Gédéon de Catalogne, asserted that Canada was the best place in the world for the labourer because there was not one who did not eat good wheat bread, and one encountered few beggars. Library and Archives Canada (LAC), MG1, C11A series (hereafter C11A), 1712, vol. 33, fols 210–36; 1715, vol. 34, fols 176–92; and vol. 40, fols 241–51.

3 Dechene, *Habitants*, 124–5, 285.

4 A. Clark, *Working Life of Women in the Seventeenth Century*, ed. A.L. Erickson (London: Routledge, 1992); Pamela Sharpe, 'Continuity and Change: Women's History and Economic History in Britain,' in *Women's Work: The English Experience, 1650–1914*, ed. Sharpe (London: Arnold, 1998), 26. For a discussion of how subsequent studies have challenged the idea of continuity in women's work prior to the seventeenth century, see Barbara Hanawalt, 'Women and Household Economy in the Preindustrial Period: An Assessment of *Women, Work and Family*,' *Journal of Women's History* 11, no. 3 (1999), 10–16.

5 Alice Clark, *Working Life of Women in the Seventeenth Century* (1919; repr., London: Cass, 1968), 292–3.

6 Ibid., 145.

7 Ibid.

8 Ibid., 304.

9 Ibid., 196. She was sometimes imprudently categorical too, stating, for example, that apart from 'exceptional cases of illness or incompetence, the share which the wife took in her husband's business was determined ... by ... whether he carried it on at home or abroad' (294).

10 Ibid., 304. Historians now situate the major industrial transformations in the eighteenth century rather than the seventeenth.

11 Ibid., 13.

12 Ongoing interest led to two further editions of *Working Life of Women in the Seventeenth Century* in 1982 and 1993.

13 *New Oxford Dictionary of English*, s.v. 'patriarchy.'

14 Bridget Hill, *Women, Work, and Sexual Politics in Eighteenth Century England* (Oxford: Basil Blackwell, 1989), 50. In her classic study of women workers, Clark's contemporary Ivy Pinchbeck, *Women Workers and the Industrial Revolution, 1750–1850* (London: Routledge, 1930), noted that female control of dairying, as well as female fieldwork, waned at quite an uneven rate, persisting in certain pockets of England well into the nineteenth century. See part 1, 'The Employment of Women in Agriculture.'

15 Hill, *Women, Work*, 50–67, 259–63.

16 See, for example, Jane Humphries, 'Enclosures, Common Rights and Women: The Proletarianization of Families in the Late Eighteenth and Early Nineteenth Centuries,' *Journal of Economic History* 50 (1990): 17–42; and Keith Snell, 'Agricultural Seasonal Unemployment, the Standard of Living, and Women's Work, 1690–1860,' in Sharpe, *Women's Work*, 73.

17 Sharpe, 'Continuity and Change,' 28, citing Robert Allen. See also Deborah Valenze, *The First Industrial Revolution* (Oxford: Oxford University Press, 1995). Scholars continue to probe this subject, noting the need for local, regional and sector studies. See Nigel Goose, ed, *Women's Work in Industrial England: Regional and Local Perspectives* (Herefordshire: Local Population Studies, 2007).

18 Cited in Leonore Davidoff and Catherine Hall, *Family Fortunes: Men and Women of the English Middle Class, 1780–1850* (Chicago: University of Chicago Press, 1987), 315. However, Davidoff and Hall were not quite correct in saying, 'Mrs Ellis expressed this view with chilling finality.' In fact, she went on to advise ladies to 'employ themselves in the business of their fathers and husbands, rather than to remain idle,' even though they would have to brave the abovementioned 'vulgar prejudices prevailing in society' against women in trade. My thanks to research assistant Erin Strazhnik for this find in Mrs Ellis's *The Women of England, Their Social Duties and Domestic Habits* (London: Fisher and Son, 1839), 345.

19 An investigation of wills and trust in industrial Birmingham and Sheffield, for example, found more nineteenth-century female control of property than *Family Fortunes* suggested would be the case. See Maxine Berg, 'Women's Property and the Industrial Revolution,' *Journal of Interdisciplinary History* 24, no. 2 (Autumn 1993): 233–50.

20 Judith Bennett claims perennial low status for women's work in 'Medieval Women, Modern Women: Across the Great Divide,' in *Culture and History 1350–1600: Essays on English Communities, Identities and Writing*, ed. D. Aers

(Detroit: Wayne State University Press, 1992), 158. Margaret R. Hunt, *The Middling Sort: Commerce, Gender and the Family in England 1680–1780* (Berkeley: University of California Press, 1996), chap. 5, points out that women's presence was hidden because legal and insurance documents were often placed under a male name, and the same applied to urban directories (which also tended to omit smaller concerns). She notes that rising consumer demand and breakdown in guild controls did benefit some eighteenth-century women in trade (145).

21 Bennett, 'Medieval Women,' 159.

22 Ibid., 157.

23 The phrase comes from Deborah Simonton, *A History of European Women's Work, 1700 to the Present* (London: Routledge, 1992), 2.

24 Amanda Vickery, 'Golden Age to Separate Spheres? A Review of the Categories and Chronology of Women's History,' *Historical Journal* 36, no. 2 (1993): 411–12. See also 402–4.

25 Ibid., 413.

26 Ibid., 409; and Amanda Vickery, *The Gentleman's Daughter: Women's Lives in Georgian England* (New Haven: Yale University Press, 1998), 166.

27 Vickery, *Gentleman's Daughter*, 11; and Vickery, 'Golden Age,' 392.

28 Vickery, 'Golden Age,' 404.

29 Peter Earle, 'The Female Labour Market in London in the Seventeenth and Early Eighteenth Centuries,' in Sharpe, *Women's Work*, 121–47, reprinted from *Economic History Review*, 2nd ser., 42 (1989): 328–53. See also Earle's *The Making of the English Middle Class: Business, Society and Family Life in London, 1660–1730* (Berkeley: University of California Press, 1989).

30 Earle refuted Clarke's contention that couples commonly worked together, finding only 10 per cent of his sample of employed women worked with their husbands. For discussion of Earle's research design, see B. Hill, 'Women's History: A Study in Change, Continuity, or Standing Still,' in Sharpe, *Women's Work*, 95–6.

31 Earle, 'Female Labour Market,' 138.

32 Robert Shoemaker, *Gender in English Society, 1650–1850: The Emergence of Separate Spheres?* (London: Longman, 1998), 116–22ff.

33 Cited in ibid., 174; for the other changes, see 153–4, 183–4.

34 Laurel Thatcher Ulrich, *Good Wives: Image and Reality in the Lives of Women in Northern New England, 1650–1750* (New York: Vintage, 1991), 240–1.

35 Ibid., 36.

36 Ibid., 97.

37 Ibid., 37–43. Allan Greer employs this concept in his chapter on women in *The People of New France* (Toronto: University of Toronto Press, 1997).

38 Ulrich, *Good Wives*, 249n. Coton Mather's *Ornaments for the Daughters of Zion*

(1692), which includes some favourable discussion of independent action by (religiously motivated) women, is mentioned as also relevant, but I can find no reference to a deputy husband on the page cited or adjacent pages.

39 Even Ulrich's own annotated diary of a late-eighteenth-century Maine midwife, *A Midwife's Tale: The Life of Martha Ballard, Based on Her Diary 1785–1812* (New York: Vintage, 1991), suggests a more independent wife than the hypothetical 'deputy husband' types appearing in *Good Wives*. Martha Ballard earned professional income, attended autopsies, competed with local physicians to provide healing and obstetric services, leaving home for days at a time to attend her patients. She also farmed, attended church council, and gave deposition in a criminal case. Before, during, and after her husband's eighteen-month imprisonment for debt, the diary makes little mention of any direction from him about her activities. The contrast in the two major works by Ulrich shows how different the results can be: her midwife who speaks in her own words seems quite autonomous and forceful, while the collective 'good wives,' drawn largely from masculine idealizations, are much less so.

40 Gloria Main, 'Gender, Work and Wages in Colonial New England,' *William and Mary Quarterly*, 3rd ser., 51, no. 1 (1994): 65.

41 Carol Berkin, *First Generations: Women in Colonial America* (New York: Hill and Wang, 1996), 87.

42 Deborah Rosen, *Courts and Commerce: Gender, Law and the Market Economy in Colonial New York* (Columbus: Ohio State University Press, 1997), chaps 5 and 6; and Rosen, 'Women and Property across Colonial America: A Comparison of Legal Systems in New Mexico and New York,' *William and Mary Quarterly*, 3rd ser., 60, no. 2 (2003): 377. See also Elaine Forman Crane, *Ebb Tide in New England: Women, Seaports and Social Change, 1630–1800* (Boston: Northeastern University Press, 1998). See also the nuanced discussion of this issue in Serena Zabin, *Dangerous Economies: Status and Commerce in Imperial New York* (Philadelphia: University of Pennsylvania Press, 2009).

43 Main, 'Gender, Work and Wages,' 54.

44 Olwen Hufton, *The Prospect before Her: A History of Women in Western Europe*, ed. Natalie Z. Davis and Arlette Farge, vol. 1, *1500–1800* (London: Fontana, 1997), 152–3.

45 Ibid., 70, 146–9. Just as in England, young women from the humbler rural groups commonly worked on neighbouring farms; even quite modest operations hired servants. Alternatively they might work in town to amass the capital and household goods critical to establishment on the land, expecting their suitors to provide the rented farm and field implements. To my knowledge, historians have not uncovered either of these patterns in early Canada.

46 Wally Seccombe, *A Millennium of Family Change* (London: Verso, 1992), 251–4.

47 Our chapter 8 notes the nineteenth-century comment of Henry David Thoreau about seeing more women than men working the Lower Canadian fields. Henry David Thoreau, *A Yankee in Canada* (Montreal: Harvest House, 1961), 48–9.

48 Massimo Livi Bacchi, *The Population of Europe: A History* (Oxford: Blackwell, 2000), 110–14. This was despite the fuller training that midwives received in France, making French midwives renowned in England. In Paris they served apprenticeships, observed dissections and anatomies at the Hôtel-Dieu, and sat for exams. There were over two hundred midwives in Paris in 1800. Numbers and training were less impressive outside the capital.

49 Olwen Hufton, 'Women, Work and Family,' in *A History of Women in the West*, ed. Natalie Z. Davis and Arlette Farge, vol. 3, *Renaissance and Enlightenment* (Cambridge: Harvard University Press, 1993), 27.

50 Hufton, *Prospect*, presents vast numbers of French peasants locked in an economy of scarcity. For a discussion of the way poor social distribution undermined the benefits of very substantial agricultural improvement, see Paul Butel, *L'Economie française au XVIIIe siècle* (Paris: Sedes, 1993), chap. 5. On inferiority to English living standards but superiority to the European average, see Françoise Bayard and Philippe Guignet, *L'Economie française au XVIe, XVIIe et XVIIIe siècles* (Paris: Ophrys, 1991), 180. The French situation elicits the same debates as in England about whether proto-industrial spinning and other piecework helped keep families intact, forestalling itinerancy and outmigration.

51 Seccombe, *Millennium*, 253.

52 Julie Hardwick, *The Practice of Patriarchy* (University Park, PA: Pennsylvania State University Press, 1998), 157–8.

53 For a rich discussion, see Martine Sonnet, 'A Daughter to Educate,' in Davis and Farge, *History of Women*, 3:101–31; also Hufton, *Prospect*, 112; and John McManners, *Church and Society in Eighteenth Century France* (Oxford: Clarendon, 1998), 550. Unlike most teaching orders, the Ursulines valued classical culture. They instructed students in Latin as well as writing – subjects too often neglected in female schooling focused on domestic arts and the reading of Catholic manuals as well as folk tales. Elizabeth Rapley, who has written extensively about the Ursulines, has concluded that they did more than anybody else to introduce seventeenth-century Frenchmen to the concept of feminine schooling. On the numbers and impact of cloistered teaching orders, see Elizabeth Rapley and Robert Rapley, 'An Image of Religious Women in the *Ancien Régime*: The *États des religieuses* of 1790–91,' *French His-*

tory 11 (Fall 1997): 387–410; and Elizabeth Rapley, 'Fénelon Revisited: A Review of Girls' Education in Seventeenth-Century France,' *Histoire Sociale / Social History* 20 (1987): 299–318. See also E. Rapley, *A Social History of the Cloister* (Montreal and Kingston: McGill-Queen's University Press, 2001).

54 McManners, *Church and Society*, 560, 568. See Marie-Claude Dinet-Lecomte, *Les soeurs hospitalières en France aux XVIIe and XVIIIe siècles: La charité en action* (Paris: Honoré Champion, 2007), for a rich and authoritative discussion of the sisters' work that, among other things, shows initiatives too numerous, localized, and diverse to sustain any theory of centralized social control. Among the battles McManners discussed were sisters resisting physicians' attempts to take corpses away for dissection, considering it too demoralizing to the local populace. A sister might also hold her own in Montreal. Sister Marie Morin recorded in the Hôtel-Dieu *Annales* that in regard to the remedies of her contemporary Sister Judith Bresoles 'the richest and most fastidious people had more confidence than in those of … [Montreal's] skilled surgeon.' In another contest of the sexes, Montreal's Hôtel-Dieu mother superior was sent surgical instruments by the Crown with instructions that the military surgeon could not borrow them without express permission from Versailles.

55 Jacques Dupaquier, *La Population française aux XVIIe et XVIIIe siècles* (Paris: Presses Universitaires de France, 1979), 267–79; Olwen Hufton, *Women and the Limits of Citizenship in the French Revolution* (Toronto: University of Toronto Press, 1992), 58; and Hufton, 'Women without Men,' *Journal of French History* (1984): 371. See also Colin Jones, *The Charitable Imperative: Hospitals and Nursing in Ancien Régime and Revolutionary France* (London: Routledge, 1989), 80, 113, 167–8, 194–7. Jones observes that the sisters performed some surgical functions and offered their patients a 'diluted medical culture' in place of folk remedies or the dubious ministrations of the physicians of the era. Dine-Lecompte elaborates on the role of the sisters in promoting medicalization and their fortunes during the Revolution in *Soeurs hospitalières*, chap. 7 and 'Conclusion.'

56 Wiesner, *Women and Gender in Early Modern Europe* (Cambridge: Cambridge University Press, 2000), 76. The figure tended to be about 10 per cent among the peasantry and urban poor, as high as 25 per cent among elites. Sara Grieco, 'The Body, Appearance and Sexuality' in Davis and Farge, *History of Women*, 3:70. Regarding England, Pamela Sharp writes, 'Up to 25 per cent of the people of marriageable age were celibate at the end of the seventeenth century' ('Continuity and Change,' 7). In assessing the French sisters' overall impact, we should note that despite all the nuns who ran

schools for girls, female ability to sign was higher in England. Admittedly the meaning of this is somewhat unclear, since French girls were taught to read but seldom to write.

57 Lynn Abrams, *The Making of Modern Women* (London: Pearson, 2002), 35. *Filles séculaires* constituted only about one-sixth of female religious, according to Claude Langlois, *Le catholicisme au féminin* (Paris: Éditions du Cerf, 1984), 78. There is discussion of both cloistered nuns and *filles séculaires* in Canada in our chapters 2 and 7.

58 In a similar vein, Deborah Simonton writes, 'After the Revolution, the overwhelming influence of the doctrine of dual spheres is striking ... A clearly articulated and formulated ideology of womankind emerged which was relevant to European women of all classes. What was new was 'the unprecedented scale on which it was propagated and diffused' (*History of European Women's Work*, 69). Olwen Hufton, 'Women in History: Early Modern Europe,' *Past and Present* 101 (1983): 126.

59 See Wiesner, *Women and Gender*, 7, 134, 311.

60 Elinor Accampo, 'Integrating Women and Gender into the Teaching of French History, 1789 to the Present,' *French Historical Studies* 27 (2004): 268, discusses the tendency towards female activism in periods of crisis.

61 Sara Mendelson and Patricia Crawford, *Women in Early Modern England, 1550–1720* (Oxford: Oxford University Press, 1998), 394, 406. On female Levellers' assertion of political rights, see also Stevie Davis, *Women of the English Revolution: 1640–1660* (London: Women's Press, 1998).

62 Mary Beth Norton, '"The Ablest Midwife That Wee Know in the Land": Alice Tilly and the Women of Boston and Dorchester, 1649–1650,' *William and Mary Quarterly*, 3rd ser., 55 (1998): 105–34, esp. 128.

63 Mary Beth Norton, *Founding Mothers and Fathers* (New York: Knopf, 1996), 403.

64 Ibid., 286.

65 Kathryn Norberg, 'Incorporating Women/Gender into French History Courses, 1429–1789: Did Women of the Old Regime Have a Political History?,' *French Historical Studies* 27 (2004): 244–5, cites the work of Diefendorf, Goodman, Hanley, and Neuschel (all cited elsewhere in this book) to support these findings. Nonetheless, Norberg detects a pattern of gradually waning autonomy of queens, regents, and favourites from the fifteenth through the eighteenth centuries, though the situation continued to provide 'arenas of public speech and performance by women' that compared favourably to that following the Revolution. Among numerous works on Rousseau and women are Mary Seidman Trouille, *Sexual Politics in the Enlightenment: Women Writers Read Rousseau* (Albany: SUNY Press, 1997); and

Lynda Lange, ed., *Feminist Interpretations of Jean-Jacques Rousseau* (University Park, PA: Pennsylvania State University Press, 2002).

66 For seventeenth- and eighteenth-century comments on learned females, see Elise Goodman, *The Portraits of Madame de Pompadour: Celebrating the Femme Savante* (Berkeley: University of California Press, 2000), 4, 34, 100. Foremost among the learned was Emelie de Châtelet, a physicist who translated Newton's *Principia Mathematica* and published works explaining Newton and Leibnitz to a French audience. Famed beyond the borders of France, de Châtelet conversed with the leading mathematicians and scientists of her day, and conducted experiments with pipes, rods, and wooden balls in the chateau she shared with Voltaire.

67 This account is drawn from Hubert Carrier, 'L'action politique et militaire des femmes dans la Fronde,' in *Encyclopédie politique et historique des femmes: Europe, Amérique du nord*, ed. Christine Fauré (Paris: Presses universitaires de France, 1997), 97–137.

68 Anka Muhlstein, *La femme soleil: les femmes et le pouvoir: une relecture de Saint-Simon* (Paris: Denoel/Gonthier, 1976), 97–8; see also 32–9.

69 Goodman, *Portraits of Madame de Pompadour*, 11; see also C. Pevitt Algrant, *Madame de Pompadour: Mistress of France* (New York: Grove, 2002), 194, 203, 212–15, 248, 284; and Thomas Kaiser, 'Madame de Pompadour and the Theatres of Power,' *French Historical Studies* 19, no. 4 (Fall 1996): 1025–44.

70 Marie-Antoinette studies have reached the status of an industry. For a sampling, see Dena Goodman, *Marie Antoinette: Writings on the Body of a Queen* (New York: Routledge, 2003).

71 Mendelson and Crawford, *Women in Early Modern England*, 4.

72 Ibid., 58.

73 See Thomas Laqueur, *Making Sex: Body and Gender from the Greeks to Freud* (Cambridge, MA: Harvard University Press, 1990).

74 Clark described the decline of older, more family-oriented English government in these terms: 'Thus it came to pass that every womanly function was considered as the private interest of husbands and fathers, bearing no relation to the life of the state, and therefore demanding from the community as a whole no special care or provision ... [creating] a state which regards the purposes of life solely from the male standpoint ... and [she concluded wistfully] robbed us of so large a part of the joy of creation.' Clark, *Working Life of Women in the Seventeenth Century* (London: Cass, 1968), 307–8.

75 John Smail, *The Origins of Middle-Class Culture: Halifax, Yorkshire 1660–1780* (Ithaca: Cornell University Press, 1994). This political exclusion was, however, incomplete, since well after 1800, in many parts of England, ordinary women 'continued to demonstrate and to protest over food prices, infringe-

ments of common rights, industrial and trade issues, and a wide range of religio-political concerns' (Mendelson and Crawford, *Women in Early Modern England*, 429). None of this is meant to discount the feminism of women who worked to maintain autonomy through separate marriage settlements, support for female-oriented philanthropy, and legacies designed to promote female heirs' independence. See Hunt, *Middling Sort*, chaps. 5 and 6. As government became more androcentric, traditional powers of female speech to affect public policy also declined. Susan Amussen argued that diminishing domestic production, together with a concern to restore order after England's civil war, tended to discredit families as key units of local government. Now taken less seriously, disorder in families was less often referred to courts, and insults uttered by women began to be ignored. Susan Amussen, *An Ordered Society: Gender and Class in Early Modern England* (New York: Blackwell, 1988), 180–7.

76 New England historians Elaine Foreman Crane, Jane Kamensky, Carol Karlsen, and Ruth Wallis Herndon together create a portrait of the late seventeenth century into the eighteenth as a time of tightening masculine controls over commerce, civic and property rights, and church governance – findings echoed in Karin Wulf's studies of colonial Philadelphia. These eighteenth-century colonies moved to consolidate what Mary Beth Norton deemed 'pervasive pubic/private distinctions, and … a world in which all women were categorically excluded from the public' (Norton, *Founding Mothers*, 10). Norton further builds the case in *Separated by Their Sex: Women in Public and Private in the Colonial Atlantic World* (Ithaca: Cornell University Press, 2011). See also Elaine Foreman Crane, *Ebb Tide in New England: Women, Seaports and Social Change, 1630–1800* (Boston: Northeastern University Press, 1998); Jane Kamensky, *Governing the Tongue: The Politics of Speech in Early New England* (Oxford: Oxford University Press, 1997); Carol Karlsen, *The Devil in the Shape of a Woman: Witchcraft in Colonial New England* (New York: Norton, 1987); Ruth Wallis Herndon, *Unwelcome Americans: Living on the Margin in Early New England* (Philadelphia: University of Pennsylvania Press, 2001); and Karin Wulf, *Not All Wives: Women of Colonial Philadelphia* (Philadelphia: University of Pennsylvania Press, 2005).

77 While women produced fewer than 0.5 per cent of all published works in England between 1600 and 1640, this figure doubled to 1 per cent during the Civil War and Interregnum. By 1750–69 women accounted for at least 7 per cent of all novels published (likely higher, since the sex of one-third of novelists is unknown). Between 1780 and 1830, ten of the twelve most popular English novelists were female (Shoemaker, *Gender in English Society*, 284–5). On women in the public sphere, see also Linda Colley, *Britons: Forging the Nation, 1707–1837* (New Haven: Yale University Press, 1992); Ellen Donkin,

Getting into the Act: Women Playwrights in London, 1776–1829 (London: Routledge, 1995); Brean Hammond, *Professional Imaginative Writing in England 1670–1740: 'Hackney for bread'* (Oxford: Oxford University Press, 1997); and Paula McDowell, *The Women of Grub Street: Press, Politics and Gender in the London Literary Marketplace, 1678–1730* (Oxford: Clarendon, 1998).

78 Claude Dulong, 'From Conversation to Creation,' in Davis and Farge, *History of Women*, 3:396.

79 McMillan, *France and Women*, 9. Among the proliferating discussions of seventeenth- or eighteenth-century learned women, see Susan Dalton, *Engendering the Republic of Letters* (Montreal and Kingston: McGill-Queen's University Press, 2003); Dena Goodman, *The Republic of Letters: A Cultural History of the French Enlightenment* (Ithaca: Cornell University Press, 1994); and D. Haase-Dubosc and E. Viennot, eds., *Femmes et Pouvoirs sous l'ancien régime* (Paris: Rivages, 1991).

80 Bonnie Anderson and Judith Zinsser, *A History of Their Own* (New York: Harper and Row, 1989), 2:109.

81 Ibid., 2:105–6. David Parker, *Class and State in Ancien Régime France: The Road to Modernity* (New York: Routledge, 1996), 148, concurs.

82 Anderson and Zinsser, *History*, 2:113.

83 Merry Wiesner, *Women and Gender in Early Modern Europe*, 2nd ed. (Cambridge: Cambridge University Press, 2000), 202. For the view that French women, too, exerted considerable influence on the public sphere, replacing the oral culture exemplified by salonnières and fishwives with 'dramatic expansion of their presence in print culture after 1789,' see Carla Hesse, *The Other Enlightenment: How French Women Became Modern* (Princeton: Princeton University Press, 2001). Like Vickery's argument for England, this tends to beg the question of exclusion from professions and decision-making of church and state. There is a less optimistic assessment of late-eighteenth-century developments in Fauré, *Encyclopédie politique*: see 'Des droits de l'homme aux droits des femmes: une conversion intellectuelle difficile,' 220. Of interest, too, is Catherine Larrère, 'Le Sexe out le rang? La condition des femmes selon la philosophe des Lumières,' 169–201, in the same volume.

84 For de Gouges's view, see Dorinda Outram, 'Le langue male de la vertu: Women and the Discourse of the French Revolution,' in *The Social History of Language*, ed. Peter Burke and Roy Porter (Cambridge: Cambridge University Press, 1987), 126. On Vigée-Lebrun, see Anderson and Zinsser, *History*, 2:120.

85 For a discussion of Abigail Adams and her inability to reach a larger circle, see Elaine Forman Crane, 'Political Dialogue and the Springtime of Abigail's Discontent,' *William and Mary Quarterly*, 3rd ser., 56, no. 4 (Oct. 1999): 744–60.

86 John Cashmere, 'Sisters Together: Women without Men in Seventeenth Century French Village Culture,' *Journal of Family History* 2 (Jan. 1996): 44–62. Jacques Guilhamou and Christine Lapied, 'L'action politique des femmes pendant la Revolution française,' in Fauré, *Encyclopédie politique*, 159, note the preponderance of women around the guillotine.

87 For a rich summary, see Guilhamou and Lapied, 'L'action politique,' in Fauré, *Encyclopédie politique*, 139–65.

88 Ibid., 147–51. Hufton, *Women and the Limits of Citizenship*, 472–89, discusses provincial counter-revolutionaries.

89 Guilhamou and Lapied, 'L'action politique,' 143. James McMillan qualifies that verdict somewhat, concluding that bringing the king to Paris was an action 'initiated by women, but completed by men' (*France and Women*, 22).

90 Guilhamou and Lapied, 'L'action politique,' 155 (my translation). For a full account, see Dominique Godineau, *Citoyennes Tricoteuses: Les femmes du peuple, à Paris pendant la Révolution français* (Aix-en-Province: Alinea, 1988). See also McMillan, *France and Women*, 23–5.

91 Cited in Guilhamou and Lapied, 'L'action politique,' 149.

92 Ibid., 160. See also Dalton, *Engendering the Republic*, especially chap. 3 on Mme Roland; and Felicia Gordon and P.N. Furbank, *Marie Madeleine Jodin 1741–1790* (Aldershot: Ashgate, 2001). Women were also quite active among the counter-revolutionaries protecting banned clergy as well as church property, whereby 'they increasingly carved out religious expression as their own arena within church and community.' Suzanne Desan, 'The Family as Cultural Battleground: Religion vs Republic under the Terror,' in *The Terror*, ed. Keith Michael Baker (New York: Pergamon, 1994), 188.

93 McMillan, *France and Women*, 25. In 1792 the Republic introduced 'universal' suffrage, given to all independent males (male domestic servants were excluded) over the age of twenty-one.

94 Elinor Accampo, 'Class and Gender,' in *Revolutionary France 1788–1890*, ed. Malcolm Crook (Oxford: Oxford University Press, 2002), 101. See also Lange, *Feminist Interpretations*.

95 McMillan, *France and Women*, xiv. In the end, the Revolutionaries granted citizenship to Protestants, Jews, and free Blacks, but not to women.

2. River of Promise

1 From 'The Relation of 1654,' in *Marie of the Incarnation: Selected Writings*, ed. Irene Mahoney (New York, Paulist Press, 1989), 108–10; see also *Dictionary of Canadian Biography* (hereafter *DCB*), s.v. 'Marie de l'Incarnation.'

2 Described in Reuben Gold Thwaites, ed., *The Jesuit Relations and Other Docu-*

ments (hereafter *JR*) (Cleveland: Burrows, 1896–1901), 1636, 9:173; 1647, 30:255–73.

3 Thwaites, *JR*, 1634, 6:261. The Relation of 1635 followed up on this appeal by addressing philanthropists, noting the blessings that would flow if the extravagant expenditures of certain ladies in France were redirected to this holy work.

4 See Marie-Florine Bruneau, *Women Mystics Confront the Modern World* (New York: SUNY Press, 1998), 23–5, 95–6. Elizabeth Rapley, *The Dévotes: Women and Church in Seventeenth-Century France* (Montreal and Kingston: McGill-Queen's University Press, 1990), 119, writes that it was not until the late seventeenth century that women in France 'became catechists, and their involvement in this sacred occupation ceased to shock.' Rapley describes the 'feminized Catholicism of seventeenth-century western Europe,' epitomized by Mary Ward, founder of dynamic (and later proscribed) English 'Jesuitesses.' Ward proclaimed, 'I would to God that all men understood this truth, that women, if they will be perfect, and if they would not make us believe that we can do nothing – that we are but women, might do great matters…. I must and will ever stand for this truth, that women may be perfect, and that fervour must not necessarily delay because we are women' (Rapley, *Dévotes*, 33). As for the enthusiasm, 'They wrote with such fire and in such numbers from so many diverse places that … one could form a city of nuns with ten teachers for every student,' the Jesuits recorded. The year before the female missionaries set sail, their patron, the Duchess of Aiguillon, was already catechising a young Iroquois in France, two Montagnais girls were being baptised at the Parisian Carmelite convent with the Princess of Condé as godmother, and Dieppe Hospitallers were teaching another to make lace. Some of these new Christians were already in precarious health. Thwaites, *JR*, 1638, 11:93–7. See also L. Choquette, 'Ces Amazones du Grand Dieu: Women and Missions in Seventeenth Century Canada,' *French Historical Studies* 17 (1992): 627–55.

5 Bruneau, *Women Mystics*, insightfully compares the two.

6 See Dominique Deslandres, *Croire et faire croire: Les missions françaises au XVIIe siècle* (Paris: Fayard, 2002), 384–9. A few individual women had migrated earlier, most notably Madame Hebert, who with her husband established the first French farm at Quebec.

7 Besides producing scholarship on specific figures and their writings, Dom Oury has helped place this period in context. He observed the exceptional nature of the clergy who worked in New France, compared to their French counterparts, pointing out that early Canada accounts on its own for a good quarter of the saints and the beatified of the seventeenth-century church of

France, if not more. In Canada, he observed, missionaries stamped a special mark, giving the country's beginnings a specific character quite unusual in modern history. Dom Guy-Marie Oury, *La Croix et le Nouveau Monde* (Montreal: CMD, 1987), 13, 23, 27. On the secretive Compagnie de Saint-Sacrement, see E.R. Adair, 'France and the Beginnings of New France,' *Canadian Historical Review* 25 (1944): 246–78; Raoul Allier, *La Cabale des Dévots* (Paris: Colin, 1902); and Claire Daveluy, *Jeanne Mance 1606–1673* (Montreal: Fides, 1962), 97–9. One of the company's major accomplishments was the foundation of the Parisian Hôpital Général, source of so many of the *filles du roi* who are discussed in this chapter. A sampling of scholarship on the question of sainthood in connection with race, gender, and empire is found in Allan Greer and Jodi Bilinkoff, eds., *Colonial Saints: Discovering the Holy in the Americas* (New York: Routledge, 2003).

8 See Bruneau, *Women Mystics*, 25, 106–15, for a revealing comparison of texts; also Natalie Davis, *Women on the Margins: Three Seventeenth Century Lives* (Cambridge, MA: Harvard University Press, 1995), 112–22.

9 For an example of changing portrayals of secular heroines over time, see Colin Coates and Cecilia Morgan, *Heroines and History: Representations of Madeleine de Verchères and Laura Secord* (Toronto: University of Toronto Press, 2002). For discussion of evolving perceptions of Bourgeoys, Mance, and other founders of Montreal, see Fernande Roy, 'Une Mise en Scène de l'Histoire: La Fondation de Montréal à travers les Siècles,' *Revue d'histoire de l'Amérique français* 46, no. 1 (1992): 7–36.

10 'The Relation of 1654,' in Mahoney, *Marie of the Incarnation*, 133.

11 The incident is discussed by Dom Oury in *Marie de l'Incarnation* (Quebec: Presses de l'Université Laval, 1973), 2:324–6. See, too, Marie's own account in Mahoney, *Marie of the Incarnation*, 133–4. See also Davis, *Women on the Margins*.

12 See the letter of Father Paul LeJeune, *JR*, 1639, 16:19–20.

13 Marie de l'Incarnation, from 'The Relation of 1654,' 138, and from her letter to the Ursuline superior at Mons, 1 Oct. 1669, 273, both in Mahoney, *Marie of the Incarnation*. Credulity about visions was found among the Jesuits, too, as in their account of a heavenly lady in white who clothed and fed a settler's child so she could head off to her parish devotions. Thwaites, *JR*, 1666, 50:51–3.

14 More details of this first hospital are found in Thwaites, *JR*, 1641, 19:9, 23, 25–7; 1642, 20:249–57; 1643, 22:173; 1647, 31:161–4. For the perspective of an expert on hospitalières in France on the mission to Canada, see Marie-Claude Dinet-Lecompte, 'Les hospitalières françaises en Amérique aux XVIIe et XVIIIe siècles,' *Revue d'Histoire de l'Eglise de France* 84 (1998):

261–82. The hospital work in Canada became firmly associated with suffering (Hôtel-Dieu Mother St Augustin informed a relative in the Bayeux motherhouse that she was 'attached to the Cross by three nails': God's will, salvation of souls, and her vocation to live and die in Canada), and French hospitalières of St Joseph (the order sent to Montreal) characterized a Canadian posting as 'l'éloignement de toutes satisfactions des sens, la mort continuelle de tout l'humain.' Cited in Dinet-Lecomte, *Les soeurs hospitalières*, 420–1. See also Deslandres, *Croire*, 374–5. The classic case of a zealous convert of the French missionaries, Catherine Tekakwitha, has been the subject of a full-length study by Allan Greer, *Mohawk Saint: Catherine Tekakwitha and the Jesuits* (Toronto: Oxford University Press, 2005), which makes admirable use of feminist perspectives, ethnohistory, and the latest scholarship on early modern Catholicism to delve into a subject that tends to perplex readers impatient with 'things unseen.'

15 From 'The Relation of 1654,' in Mahoney, *Marie of the Incarnation*, 138–9.

16 The Ursulines had taught eighteen Indian girls by autumn 1640, at least forty-eight a year later. In the four decades after their arrival, they taught more Huron and Iroquois than other nations. They went beyond French practice when they instructed both males and females in their parlour. Marcel Trudel, *Les écolières des Ursulines de Québec 1639–1686* (Montreal: Hurtubise, 1999), 49–62. See also Dom Guy Oury, *Les Ursulines de Québec, 1639–1953* (Sillery: Septentrion, 1999); and Nadia Fahmy-Eid, 'L'éducation des filles chez les Ursulines de Québec sous le Régime français,' in *Maîtresses de maison, maîtresses d'école*, ed. N. Fahmy-Eid and M. Dumont (Montreal: Boreal, 1983), 49–76. The clothing is described in Thwaites, *JR*, 1641, 18:159; 1673, 56:247–63, contains the testimony of Marie de l'Incarnation.

17 Joyce Marshall, *Word from New France: The Selected Letters of Marie de l'Incarnation* (Toronto: Oxford, 1967), 216–17, 222–3. The Jesuits also occasionally recounted stories of female leaders such as a 'sorceress' at Trois-Rivières who went from village to village imparting fear of an Iroquois attack and threatened with a knife a missionary who tried to stop her (Thwaites, *JR*, 1636, 9:113–17). Father Lafitau's famous tribute to the authority of Iroquoian women will be discussed in chapter 3 of this book. On Marie de l'Incarnation as a 'femme forte,' see Deslandres, *Croire*, 303. Chapters 23 and 24 of Deslandres's book contain rich coverage of 'La Mission des Femmes' in early Quebec and Montreal.

18 Marshall, *Word*, 233. The ability of the Ursulines to affect diplomacy is also suggested in a comment by Father Lalement (Thwaites, *JR*, 1646, 28:297) in which the governor negotiated the return of a Huron student Thérèse Khionreha, who had been captured by the Iroquois, for whom 'the Ursuline

Mothers have spared no pains, and have moved Heaven and Earth to procure her liberty, causing the Governor to cooperate in the matter with all
his power.'

19 Mahoney, *Marie of the Incarnation*, 6.

20 The seventeenth-century French edition of her writings, edited by her son
    Claude Martin, noted it 'may well cause surprise as women do not ordinarily
    write many letters.' Cited in *Marie of the Incarnation [1599–1672] Correspon-
    dence*, trans. Sister St Dominic Kelly (Sligo: Irish Ursulines Union, 2000),
    vi. Intendant Talon and the Princess of Conti were among those who spon-
    sored Quebec Ursuline pupils. Thwaites, *JR*, 1672, 54:275–7.

21 See the early statement of purpose cited in Dom Guy-Marie Oury, *L'Homme
    qui a conçu Montréal: Jérôme Le Royer, Sieur de la Dauversière* (Montreal: Édi-
    tions du Méridien, 1991), 133.

22 These were found in her inventory after death. For early documentation,
    see Soeur Maria Mondoux, *L'Hôtel-Dieu, premier hospital de Montréal, après
    les annales manuscrites, les documents originaux … et autres sources 1642–1763*
    (Montreal: n.p., 1942); and Marie Morin, *Histoire simple et véritable: annales de
    l'Hôtel-Dieu de Montréal*, ed. G. Legendre (Montreal: Université de Montréal,
    1979).

23 Françoise Deroy-Pineau discusses Mance's medical methods in saving
    tomahawk victims in *Jeanne Mance: de Langres à Montréal, la passion de soigner*
    (Montreal: Bellarmin, 1995), 95–6.

24 Daveluy, *Jeanne Mance*, 96n. See also Daveluy's *La Société de Notre-Dame de
    Montréal* (Montreal: Fides, 1965). Hôtel-Dieu annalist Marie Morin noted
    Mance's eloquence.

25 Another new donor was Princess Charlotte-Marguerite de Montmorency,
    mother of the duchess of Longueville, a famous Fronde warrior.

26 For a reproduction of the whole text of *Véritables Motifs*, see Daveluy, *La So-
    ciété de Notre-Dame*. The justification of female proselytizing appears on page
    7 in the original document.

27 The papal missive to the founders of Montreal appears in Daveluy, *Jeanne
    Mance*, 113.

28 François Dollier de Casson, *Histoire de Montréal* (Montreal: Hurtubise, 1992),
    recounts this episode. See also Daveluy, *Jeanne Mance*, 123–44, as well as 113
    for the papal letter. Another contribution occurred later, when the French
    company that had founded Montreal was dissolved, and Jeanne Mance
    sailed to France to negotiate transfer to the order of Sulpician priests that
    would henceforth run the seigneurie of Montreal. Micheline Dumont,
    Michele Jean, Marie Lavigne, and Jennifer Stoddart, *L'Histoire des femmes au
    Québec depuis Quatre Siècles* (Montreal: Quinze, 1982), 41, write that 'les histo-

riens s'accordent a dire que le rôle de Jeanne Mance a été plus déterminant dans ce projet que celui de Maisonneuve.' Nineteenth-century church historian Étienne-Michel Faillon, twentieth-century historian Gustave Lanctot, and the biographical entry on Mance in *DCB* tend to support this interpretation, while Marcel Trudel in his annotated version of Dollier de Casson's *Histoire de Montréal* considers that saying Mance 'saved Canada' overstates the case. Daveluy in *Jeanne Mance*, 130n, says most historians place casualties at seventy of the first Montreal inhabitants of the period 1642–57. The toll of dead and wounded has elsewhere been estimated as about half of the population in the initial decades. John Dickinson, 'La guerre iroquoise et la mortalité en Nouvelle-France, 1608–1666,' *Revue d'histoire d'Amérique français* 36, no. 1 (1982): 31–54, makes a careful count.

29 Cited in Daveluy, *Jeanne Mance*, 143–4.

30 Her parents were both from artisan families; her father, however, was also ranked as a merchant and town official. Patricia Simpson, *Marguerite Bourgeoys and Montreal, 1640–1665* (Montreal and Kingston: McGill-Queen's University Press, 1997), 19–20. Simpson has covered the life of Bourgeoys there and in a second volume, *Marguerite Bourgeoys and the Congregation of Notre Dame, 1665–1700* (Montreal and Kingston: McGill-Queen's University Press, 2005).

31 From the writings of Bourgeoys, cited in Simone Poissant, *Marguerite Bourgeoys, 1620–1700* (Montreal: Bellarmin, 1982), 24. See also *The Writings of Marguerite Bourgeoys* (hereafter *WMB*), trans. M.V. Cotter (Montreal: Congregation of Notre Dame, 1976). Regarding Bourgeoys's role in caring for Maisonneuve's linen, her biographer Patricia Simpson notes that she did not regard any kind of service as demeaning; she points out Maisonneuve's respectful treatment and also the fact that service to a governor was a more exalted position than would be implied by the term *servant* today. Simpson, *Marguerite Bourgeoys and Montreal*, 102–7.

32 Poissant, *Marguerite Bourgeoys*, 25. Details of the harrowing journey through countryside ravaged by the *Fronde* appear in Simpson, *Bourgeoys and Montreal*, 57–61.

33 *WMB*, 178. Dollier de Casson recorded that Bourgeoys also upset her colleagues by refusing an offer of much-needed patronage. For leadership issues, see Simpson, *Bourgeoys and the Congregation of Notre Dame*, 19–23, 77, 105, 153, 237; Simpson does point out that in certain ways the leader's business acumen compared favourably to that of other members of the order.

34 C11A, 1731, vol. 106, fol. 67. This source indicates that the country schools were free.

35 Soeur de Sainte-Henriette, *Histoire de la Congrégation de Notre-Dame* (Montre-

al: Congrégation de Notre-Dame, 1910–41), 1:270. The activities with New England captives and servants are described in William Foster, *The Captors' Narrative* (Ithaca: Cornell University Press, 2003), 41, 166; and in Simpson, *Bourgeoys of Montreal.* For more detail on the native sisters and on dress of the order, see Simpson, *Bourgeoys and the Congregation of Notre Dame*, 63–8.

36 Elaine Breslaw, *Witches of the Atlantic World* (New York: NYU Press, 2000), 261, discusses mental states of mystics. We also draw on the work of Bruneau, *Women Mystics*, esp. 19–25, 224–5.

37 Deslandres, *Croire*, 386–7; see also 361, 378, 384. See also Bruneau, *Women Mystics*, 204–5. For cases of resistance to empowerment of lowly mystics, see Douglas L. Winiarski, 'Souls Filled with Ravishing Transport: Heavenly Visions and the Radical Awakening in New England,' *William and Mary Quarterly*, 3rd ser. 61, no. 1 (2004): 3–46; for other instructive comparisons, Susan Juster, 'Demagogues or Mystagogues? Gender and the Language of Prophecy in the Age of the Democratic Revolutions,' *American Historical Review* 104 (1999): 1560–81. Visions that were a threatening embarrassment to Protestant divines were evidently less so to seventeenth-century Catholic missionaries, and both Marie de l'Incarnation and the Jesuits freely acknowledged the Christian Algonquin woman who was the first to hear a heavenly voice prophesying the earthquake of 1663, described in Marshall, *Word from New France*, 287–8; and Thwaites, *JR*, 1663, 48:53–7.

38 The incident appears in Marshall, *Word from New France*, 24, and in more detail in Oury, *Marie de l'Incarnation*, vol. 2.

39 Thwaites, *JR*, 1642, 20:229. Father Vimont's comment is in *JR*, 1643, 22:171–2.

40 The most detailed analysis of an array of conflicts is provided in Marguerite Jean, *Évolution des communautés religieuses de femmes au Canada de 1639 a nos jours* (Montreal: Fides, 1977). Simpson's two volumes on Marguerite Bourgeoys add further details. See also Mahoney, *Marie of the Incarnation*, 28–9. Laval waited until after Marie's death to change the Ursulines' constitution in ways she had opposed. While the 40,000 *livres* provided by the Duchesse d'Aiguillon and the 76,000 from the Duchesse de Buillon for the Hôtels-Dieu in Quebec and in Montreal were the most spectacular, there were many donations from townspeople, including the governor's widow, Barbe de Boulonge, who lived her last days as a pensioner and was a large benefactor. The family of the second superior of Montreal's hospital, Catherine Mace, moved in court circles and were able to secure her hospital's endowment.

41 These and other imbroglios are discussed in chapter 7 of our book. Some of the richest documentation on this is found in the outburst of Intendant

Dupuy on 20 Nov. 1727 (C11A, 1727, vol. 49, fols 124–55); see also 1730, vol. 52, fols 156–7. One official dispatch of 1665 suggested that at that point the bishop reviewed their accounts yearly (vol. 7, fol. 63) but the colony subsequently experienced quite a few years of absentee bishops.

42 Cited in Eleanor Leacock, 'Montagnais Women and the Jesuit Plan for Colonization,' in *Women and Colonization: Anthropological Perspectives*, ed. Mona Etienne and Eleanor Leacock (New York: Praeger, 1980), 25–42.

43 Greer, *Mohawk Saint*, 23. See also Nancy Shoemaker, 'Kateri Tekakwitha's Tortuous Path to Sainthood,' which stresses the strongly syncretic nature of native sainthood, in *Rethinking Canada: The Promise of Women's History*, 4th ed., ed. V. Strong-Boag, Mona Gleason, and Adele Perry, 17–31 (Toronto: Oxford University Press, 2002).

44 There are many anecdotes of the Ursulines and their pupils in P-G Roy, *A Travers l'Histoire des Ursulines de Québec* (Lévis: n.p., 1939). For an assessment of the methods and the impact of Ursuline instruction on Aboriginal pupils, see Claire Gourdeau, *'Les délices de nos coeurs': Marie de l'Incarnation et ses pensionnaires amérindiens, 1639–1672* (Sillery: Septentrion, 1994). Huron Geneviève Agnes de tous les Saints, who became a Hospital sister, died young in 1657.

45 Deslandres, *Croire*, 383 (my translation).

46 Letter of 1 Sept. 1668, reprinted in Dom Guy-Marie Oury, *Les Ursulines de Quebec 1639–1953* (Montreal: Septentrion, 1999), 64–6.

47 André Lachance and Sylvie Savoie, 'Les Amérindiens sous le Régime français,' in *Les marginaux, les esclus, et l'autre au Canada aux 17e et 18e siècles*, ed. André Lachance (Montreal: Fides, 1996), 190–3. For Ursuline acceptance of the change in their mission in the second decade of the eighteenth century, see C11A, 1719, vol. 40, fols 270–300. Deslandres estimates the Ursulines had some hundred live-in seminarians during the first thirty years of their mission, and vastly larger numbers of temporary or day students (*Croire*, 364–5). By the end of the seventeenth century, war and epidemics had made native students rare.

48 C11A, 1687, vol. 9, fol. 4. In 1659 Mance ceded the work of Montreal's Hôtel-Dieu to the Religieuses Hospitalières de Saint-Joseph. At that time, the annalist recorded, the sisters slept together in cells so cramped they could scarcely turn over.

49 One result of serving sailors and soldiers (a source of Crown revenue) was that they served primarily male patients. The Quebec Hôtel-Dieu in 1750 had twenty-four beds for men and ten for women; in 1744, two-thirds of the 657 patients admitted were male. Renald Lessard, 'Pratique et praticiens en contexte colonial: le corps médical canadien aux XVIIème et XVIIIème

siècles' (PhD diss., Université Laval, 1994), 281–2, 330. The Hôtel-Dieu was praised for refusing no one, be they rich, poor, or from the countryside (C11A, 1685, vol. 7, fol. 63). Hospital nuns were said to give preference to *habitants* over soldiers as patients.

50 Simpson, *Bourgeoys and the Congregation*, 111.

51 *WMB*, 136–7; Amédée Gosselin, *L'Instruction au Canada sous le régime français (1635–1760)* (Quebec: Laflamme et Proulx, 1911), 191–2, 244. Eventually the idealistic position on dowries was eroded.

52 Quoted in Simpson, *Bourgeoys and the Congregation of Notre Dame*, 120–1, who also describes her harrowing adventures on the Ile d'Orléans.

53 Bourgeoys specified that 'if one had to use punishment, which should happen only rarely, it should always be ... with extreme moderation, remembering one is in the presence of God.' She also cautioned her followers to make no distinction between poor and rich, relatives and strangers, the pretty and the ugly, the gentle and the grumbling, for 'to act otherwise was to ... serve nature and not God.'

54 Roger Magnuson, *Education in New France* (Montreal and Kingston: McGill-Queen's University Press, 1992), chap. 7, gives a useful overview of CND work in New France. In the early eighteenth century, six sisters were teaching over one hundred students at Quebec. For additional information on various schools see, Gosselin, *L'Instruction au Canada*, 175, 192, 244, 466, 477. Ten schools are listed in C11A, 1707, vol. 27, fol. 142. And C11A, 1701, vols 105–6, fol. 53v mentions that the Quebec Seminary was paying 225 livres rent to the Sisters of the Congregation, who conducted little schools in a house built for them on Beaupré seigneurie. Gedeon de Catalogne discussed their establishment and also their Indian mission in C11A, 1712, vol. 33, fols 210–36. For a time Marie Raisin taught at a *mission ambulante* at Trois-Rivières, according to the 1666 census. In addition to the fifteen schools listed here, there was evidently a short-lived one in the 1680s at Kahnawake (Simpson, *Bourgeoys and the Congregation*, 19, 106). Excluded from our calculations here are schools opened by the Congregation in Louisbourg and New Orleans.

55 Gosselin, *L'Instruction au Canada*, 178–9. Governor de Ramezay called them indispensable to the life of the colony (C11A, 1707, vol. 27, fols 3–16; see also C11A, 1708, vol. 28, fols 242–9 for Raudot's comments. Male counterparts in Montreal did not have their own school until 1686, when Sulpician superior de Queylus founded one; there were others in surrounding areas by 1700, which prepared boys for communion. See M. D'Allaire, *Les Communautés religieuses de Montréal*, vol. 2, *Les communautés religieuses et l'éducation a Montréal 1657–1900* (Montreal: Méridien, 2002). Securing enough school-

masters for boys was an ongoing struggle, although in 1721 the Marine Council did agree to subsidize eight school masters: two for the Montreal Hôpital-Général, and six for parishes and countryside, with a mandate to teach boys to read and write. C11A, 1705, vol. 22, fol. 33; and 1721, vol. 43, fol. 410. Canadian religious knowledge, said at the beginning of the eighteenth century to compare favourably with that in any province in France, was credited partly to the way the Congrégation reached even remote habitants (vol. 122, fol. 33). Simpson, *Bourgeoys and the Congregation of Notre Dame*, 127, discusses fees, which seem to have varied. Along with vows of poverty, chastity, and obedience, to provide free instruction was the order's fourth vow; but they were accorded permission to request twenty *sols* and a modest amount of firewood from their students. Gosselin, *L'Instuction au Canada*, 173ff.

56 Magnuson, *Education*, 135. The story of Soeur Marie Barbier in the snowstorm is from Soeur Henriette, *Histoire de la Congrégation*, 2:23. Praying for rain is mentioned in C11A, 1717, vol. 38, fols 220–5.

57 Historians of literacy now recognize that this makes the traditional literacy criterion – ability to sign one's name – problematic, since women were often taught to read but not to write. Dumont et al., *Histoire des femmes*, 87, estimated that since so many travellers commented on the superior education of women, it is likely that there were more women who could read, while there were more men who could write. However, Magnuson found considerable evidence that the Congregation of Notre Dame taught even country children writing as well as reading. For a detailed inventory and description of both French and native pupils of the Ursulines, what they were taught, and their living conditions, see Trudel, *Les écolières*. By 1657 the Ursulines had twenty-seven French day students, and the number seldom fell below this level in the ensuing three decades. Of French students of the Ursulines up through 1686, 73 were noble, 216 bourgeoise, and 194 commoners (Trudel, *Les écolières*, 70, 75).

58 C11A, 1729, vol. 51, fols 3–4. On habitant patients, 1740, vol. 74, fols 223–4.

59 Magnuson, *Education*, 90–100, 141.

60 Franquet, *Voyages et mémoires*, 31–2.

61 Soeur Henriette, *Histoire de la Congrégation*, 1:173; Poissant, *Marguerite Bourgeoys*, 86; Simpson, *Bourgeoys and the Congregation*, 101–2.

62 Gosselin, *L'Instruction au Canada*, 240–2.

63 Robert Lahaise provides a valuable discussion of 'L'Hôtel-Dieu de Vieux Montréal, 1642–1861,' in *L'Hôtel-Dieu de Montreal, 1642–1973*, ed. Michel Allard, 11–56 (Montreal: Hurtubise, 1973). It should be noted that even skilled sisters were not expected to circumvent male expertise, and patients

entering the hospital had to present a certificate indicating they had been examined by a physician or a surgeon (174). See also d'Allaire, *Les Communautés religieuses de Montréal*, vol. 1, *Les communautés religieuses et l'assistance sociale a Montréal 1659–1900* (Montreal: Méridien, 1997), 45–7, on the dubious practices of the colony's relatively unskilled surgeons. The figure on colonial physicians appears in Terrence Murphy and Roberto Perin, *A Concise History of Christianity in Canada* (Toronto: Oxford University Press, 1996), 44.

64 An official count of 1754 named choir sisters and CND teaching members but did not include converses / lay sisters, which increased the numbers significantly. For example, we know that about this time (1757) the Hôpital-Général had fifty-five sisters in total, including both choir and converse sisters, but the government tally of thirty would have omitted the latter. Micheline D'Allaire noted that converses or lay sisters brought the Montréal Hôtel-Dieu tally to forty, and there would have been similar increments to the other cloistered orders. D'Allaire, *Les communautés religieuses*, 1:65. Unknown too is the extent to which the CND figure included Montreal-based teachers then stationed in outlying parishes. The figures tallied in the 1754 colonial report were,

Quebec	
Ursulines	45 sisters
Hôtel-Dieu	40 sisters
Hôpital-Général	30 sisters
Congrégation Notre Dame	5 sisters
Trois-Rivières	
Ursulines	20 sisters
Montreal	
Hôtel-Dieu	25 sisters
Congrégation Notre Dame	50 sisters
Soeurs Gris	10 sisters

(Source: C11A, 1754, vol. 99, fols 226–7, 529–32)

65 Rapley, *Les Dévotes*, 141.

66 In addition to the many published sources on Wheelwright, archival material includes C11A, 1711–12, vol. 32, fols 94–6, 156–8; and vol. 33, fols 15–35.

67 Guy Frégault, *Le XVIIe Siècle canadien* (Montreal: Éditions HMH, 1970), 141–4, discusses Crown subsidies and landholding of various religious orders. The percentage calculations are mine. On the church in this period, see also Murphy and Perin, *Concise History of Christianity*.

68 There is detailed discussion of Hôtel-Dieu finances in Allard, *L'Hôtel-Dieu de Montréal*.

69 Dechêne, *Habitants and Merchants*, 151.
70 C11A, 1663, vol. 125, fols 213–19. Though there were, by Marcel Trudel's count, 1908 known male colonists and 1127 known female colonists in June 1663, so few of the latter were of nubile age and condition that marriageable men outnumbered them by six to one. See Robert Larin, *Brève Histoire du peuplement Européen en Nouvelle-France* (Sillery: Septentrion, 2000), 145.
71 This definition and count of the *filles du roi* is drawn from Yves Landry, *Les Filles du roi au XVIIe siècle: Orphelines en France, Pionnières au Canada* (Montreal: Leméac Éditeur, 1992), 21–5, and 44. (Landry citations refer to this 1992 volume unless otherwise indicated). Landry includes a summary of other definitions and counts by earlier historians. C11A, 1669, vol. 3, fols 33–5 also mentions payments for lodging upon arrival and gives additional information about dowries, which were sometimes spread over three years. For the demographic information in this section and the basic observation about how the environment transformed the *filles'* lives, I am heavily indebted to Landry's work. Also of considerable use is Gustave Lanctot's study, *Filles de joie ou filles du roi. Étude sur l'Émigration féminine en Nouvelle-France* (Montreal: Chantecler, 1952). Though he rides his 'the *filles* were pure' hobbyhorse too hard, the book is rich in archival material from Canada and France. See also Silvio Dumas, *Les Filles du Roi en Nouvelle France* (Quebec: La Société historique de Quebec, 1972). Colonial correspondence relating to the *filles* is assembled in *Rapport de l'archiviste de la province de Québec* (*RAPQ*), 1930–1; see also the 1926–7 volume.
72 There are regular references in the colonial accounts between the 1680s and 1718. In the latter year, Governor Vaudreuil and Intendant Begon advised the Crown to continue them, specifying it as 'les 3000 livres pour le distribution de 60 filles,' which would have amounted to the same fifty livres gratification given to most *filles du roi*. In some years this dowry was specified as being for 'filles françaises et indiennes.' The 1718 account, somewhat unusually, stipulates that a bonus was also paid to grooms aged sixteen to twenty (C11A, 1718, vol. 122, fol. 42), though it was common enough to subsidize soldiers who wished to marry. The suggestion was made in 1682 to reallocate dowries intended to prepare Ursuline Aboriginal pupils for marriage to Frenchmen (an unsuccessful project) to needy French-Canadian brides. For references to these dowries, see, for example, C11A, 1698, vol. 113, fols 36, 274–6; and 1711, vol. 32, fols 195–204.
73 Mario Boleda, 'Trente mille Français à la conquête du Saint-Laurent,' *Histoire sociale / Social History* 23, no. 45 (May 1990): 171, estimates that 450 women had stepped ashore by the end of 1659, though not all had stayed.
74 Yves Landry, 'Gender Imbalance, Les Filles du roi, and Choice of Spouse in New France,' in Bettina Bradbury, ed., *Canadian Family History: Selected Read-*

ings (Toronto: Irwin, 2000), 16, notes the imbalance, which became especially pronounced in 1665–8 when the Carignan regiment was stationed in the colony, reaching a ratio of 14:1.

75 Although love had begun to be deemed by French jurists as an important aspect of marriage, parental strategizing still tended to play a large role in marriages of elites.

76 In part, Lanctot was seeking to counteract the salacious view perpetuated of Louis Armand, baron de Lahontan, *Nouveaux Voyages de M. de Baron de Lahontan dans l'Amérique Septentrionale* (Las Haye: Frères L'Honoré, 1703), 1:11–12.

77 Landry, *Les Filles du roi*, 24, 90.

78 Leslie Choquette estimates that 75 per cent of all female immigrants who came to Canada during the French period were from towns and cities. Like the *filles*, the overall group tended to be young, 80 per cent of them under age thirty and unmarried. Leslie Choquette, *Frenchmen into Peasants: Modernity and Tradition in the Peopling of French Canada* (Cambridge, MA: Harvard University Press, 1997), 52, 156, 177.

79 C11A, 1670, vol. 3, fols 77–93 (Talon to Colbert, 10 Nov. 1670).

80 C11A, 1673, vol. 4, fols 32–43.

81 The passage is reprinted in Jacques Mathieu, *La Nouvelle France* (Quebec: Presses de l'Université Laval, 2001), 78.

82 Cited in Landry, *Les Filles du roi*, 101, a 1688 document from the Archives Nationales de France.

83 Ibid., 102.

84 Cited in Lanctot, *Filles de Joie*, 135–6.

85 Three other *filles* also fell victim to the Iroquois, at Lachine in 1689.

86 Landry, *Les Filles du roi*, 135, 260.

87 C11A, 1667, vol. 2, fols 306–20; on the rapidity of marriages, see also Landry, *Les Filles du roi*, 129, 142. Marie de l'Incarnation's letters are another source of information on the *filles'* initial days in Canada. A regulation levied fines on fathers with unmarried sons over twenty and daughters over sixteen, which seems to have evolved into grants to those who married young. The policy was reiterated in 1712 (vol. 33, fols 15–35), and marriage funds, which had apparently fallen into desuetude, were reinstated. There was a case of the intendant enforcing this regulation (on behalf of a twenty-three-year-old daughter whose father opposed her choice) in 1736. See C11A, 1718, vol. 122, fol. 42; and 1736, vol. 66, fols 17–18.

88 Lanctot, *Filles de Joie*, 82; and Landry, *Les Filles du roi*, 135, describe some of these marriage practices.

89 Dumas, *Filles*, 113, citing Marie de l'Incarnation.

90 C11A, 1671, vol. 3, fols 159–71.

91 C11A, 1671, vol. 3, fols 159–75; 1685, vol. 7, fols 115–116v.
92 Landry, *Les Filles du roi*, 207. The figure was higher for those who lived out their childbearing years.
93 Ibid., 207, 247–8. Danielle Gauvreau, 'La population pendant le Régime français,' in Dépatie et al., *Vingt ans*, 36.
94 Landry, *Les Filles du roi*, 237–8.
95 C11A, 1683, vol. 6, fols 177–80.
96 See the two December 1715 memoirs of Ruette d'Auteuil on this subject, CIIA, vol. 34, fols 176–92; and vol. 40, fols 241–51. In 1712 Gédéon de Cata-logne asserted that Canada was the best place in the world for the labourer because there was not one who did not eat good wheat bread, and one en-countered few beggars. C11A, 1712, vol. 33, fols 210–36.
97 C11A, 1747, vol. 87, fols 264–7, report of La Galissonière.
98 Landry, *Les Filles du roi*, 143–4.

3. Women and the St Lawrence Fur Trade

1 Graham Taylor and Peter Baskerville discuss the lack of systematic study of businesswomen in *A Concise History of Business in Canada* (Toronto: Oxford University Press, 1994), 66–7. On the more general dearth of research on French-Canadian women, see Micheline Dumont, 'Un champ bien clos: L'histoire des femmes au Québec,' *Atlantis* 25, no. 1 (2000): 102–18. On the importance of subsistence farming and the modest level of market involve-ment, see Allan Greer, *Peasant, Lord and Merchant: Rural Society in Three Que-bec Parishes 1740–1840* (Toronto: University of Toronto Press, 1985). James Pritchard, *In Search of Empire: The French in the Americas, 1670–1730* (Cam-bridge: Cambridge University Press, 2004), 228, makes the assessment that, in line with trends in Acadia, Cayenne, and Louisiana, 'in Canada ... com-merce does not appear to have been central to people's lives. There, fewer and fewer people participated in export trades or even produced for such trades. Local markets emerged slowly and remained quite small. Few colo-nists initiated commercial activities since they possessed virtually no capital.' In line with these interpretations, our discussion deals primarily with small, local, and occasional participants in the market, for whom the term *business-woman* is inaccurate and anachronistic. Readers who may prefer to read in French will find an abbreviated version of chapters 3 and 4 in 'N'étre plus la deleguee de personne: Une réévaluation du rôle des femmes dans le com-merce en Nouvelle-France,' *Revue d'histoire de l'Amerique francaise* 63, no. 2–3, (2010).
2 For example, *The Historical Atlas of Canada* (Toronto: University of Toronto Press, 1987), vol. 1, plate 48 shows the value of exports to France in 1736

consisting of Beaver, 43 per cent; Other Furs, 32 per cent; Hides, 19 per cent; Fish and Other, 6 per cent. (The compilers note that the Beaver were undervalued, bills of exchange not being included in the calculations).

A chart covering 1718 to the end of the French regime shows the upward trend of animal exports in the regime's last decades, a phenomenon also observed by Dale Miquelon. The amounts of Beaver, Other Furs, and Hides varied in different years, Hides or Other Furs frequently outperforming Beaver after 1735. A small proportion of exports consisted of exports of victuals, fish, and timber to the Gulf of St Lawrence (chiefly Louisbourg) and the West Indies, amounting to about 10 per cent of total exports in 1736. Plate 41 indicates in most years there were four to five hundred men recorded (apart from the illegals) in the trade by the 1730s and 1740s, soaring to almost seven hundred men employed seasonally in 1754. Whether these figures include some women, or whether the women should be added to the numbers, is difficult to say.

3 Mathieu, *Nouvelle France*, 195–8, basing the 3-*livre* figure on the intendant's observation in 1739.

4 The nagging is described in W.J. Eccles, *The Canadian Frontier 1534–1760* (Toronto: Holt Rinehart Winston, 1969), 92; the charms in Richard Colebrook Harris, *The Seigneurial System in Early Canada* (Montreal and Kingston: McGill-Queen's University Press, 1966), 164.

5 Carol Devens, *Countering Civilization: Native American Women and Great Lakes Missions* (Berkeley: University of California Press, 1992); Sleeper-Smith, *Indian Women*; and Van Kirk, *'Many Tender Ties.'*

6 On De La Salle's debts to Roybon d'Allone (claimed at one point to exceed two thousand *livres*), see C11A, 1706, vol. 25, fol. 280, and 1708, vol. 29, fol. 262.

7 Madeleine de Roybon d'Allone is also discussed in C11A, 1700, vol. 18, fols 220–7; 1701, vol. 19, fols 156–61; 1717, vol. 37, fols 140–3, and vol. 38, fols 119–20; 1718, vol. 40, fols 50–67v records her death. See also *DCB*, s.v. 'Roybon d'Allone, Madeleine de'; Lucie Lacomte, 'Madeleine de Roybon d'Allonne: intrépide commerçante … et célibataire,' *Cahiers d'Histoire* 23, no. 2 (2004): 65–79; and Kathryn Young, '… "sauf les périls et fortunes de la mer": Merchant Women in New France and the French Transatlantic Trade, 1713–1746,' in Strong-Boag, Gleason, and Perry, *Rethinking Canada*, 39–40.

8 C11A, 1707, vol. 26, fols 176–219; 1717, vol. 38, fols 101–16; 1729, vol. 120, fols 243–6; 1731, vol. 54, fols 282–5; 1753, vol. 99, fols 25–90. *DCB*, s.v. 'Tonty, Alphonse de.' There are numerous references to Madame La Pipardière in C11A, 1715–17, vols 35–8, 123; while 1717, vol. 38, fols 109–16 alludes to her journey to join Tonty after his marriage proposal was approved. On

Tonty's marriage, see 1717, vol. 37, fol. 297; 1721, vol. 43, fols 32–4, 320–1. For charges of wifely fur-trading, see 1707, vol. 26, fols 176–219; 1708, vol. 29, fols 140–3; 1717, vol. 37, fols 140–3, and vol. 38, fols 119–20. See also *DCB*, 2:584–5.

Contrats de mariage: Archives Nationales de Québec a Montréal (hereafter ANQ-M), Raimbault, P., 18 fév. 1712, and Lepailleur, M., 17 avril 1717. Lepailleur, M. 26 août 1724, procuration Alphonse de Tonty a M-A Lamarque; Adhémar, J-B, 16 juillet 1729, inventaire après décès, mentions her travel to Detroit. Marie-Anne La Marque, a rare only child in that colony of big families, ended up burying three husbands. Apparently alive to her interests, she arranged financial reserves for herself in her successive marriage contracts.

9 Young, '… sauf les périls,' 39–40.

10 Her mother was textile manufacturer Agathe Saint-Père, to be discussed in chapter 6. On Marguerite Legardeur de Repentigny, see ANQ-M, Lepailleur, M, 14 sept. 1717, *procuration*; Adhémar, J-B, 13 juin 1725, *obligation*, and 29 avril 1729 *société*; Danré de Blanzy, L-C, 12 juin 1740, vente d'une terre. See also *DCB*, s.v. 'St Ours Deschaillons, J-B.'

11 C11A, 1746, vol. 117, fols 91–3; 1747, vol. 118, fol. 104; ANQ-M, Danré de Blanzy, 22 juin 1753 procuration et obligation, 24 juin 1754 arrête de compte, 5 juin 1755, obligation; ANQ-M Simonnet, F, 12 juin 1762 decl par Marie Anne Magnan à Chappoton négotiant du Detroit.

12 ANQ-M Pinguet de Vaucour, JN, 5 oct. 1746 inventaire, 17 oct. 1746 renonciation.

13 ANQ-M Pinguet de Vaucour, J-N, 29 avril et 4 mai, procurations; 21 oct. 1734, obligation; C11A, 1747, vol. 87, fols 171–2v; 1748, vol. 91, fols 24–5v; 1751, vol. 97, fol. 201v.

14 Marie Louise Denys de la Ronde's activities are discussed in Lorraine Gadoury, 'Une famille noble en Nouvelle France: les D'Ailleboust' (MA thesis, Université de Montréal, 1982), see esp. 74–5, 107–15; and Louise Tremblay, 'La politique missionnaire des Sulpiciens au XVIIe et début du XVIIe siècle' (MA thesis, Université de Montréal, 1981), esp. 144–8; C11A, 1717, vol. 39, fols 217–18; 1731, vol. 56, fols 97–9; ANQ-M, Adhémar, J-B, 7 mai 1717, engagement; 21 sept 1723, convention et société. A very large marriage settlement for her daughter in 1732 suggests the enterprises were going well, as does the accounting in Gadoury's thesis. See also *DCB*, s.v. 'Ailleboust D'Argenteuil, Pierre d.'

15 The widow is described in Miquelon, *New France*, 132–3, 153.

16 *DCB*, s.v. 'Pascaud, Antoine.'

17 Kathryn Young, *Kin, Commerce, Community: Merchants in the Port of Quebec, 1717–1745* (New York, P. Lang, 1995), 41, citing Pritchard.

18 C11A, 1747, vol. 89, fols 84–103; 1748, vol. 92, fols 256–71.

19 C11A, 1722, vol. 37, fols 357–64; 1740, vol. 114, fol. 280.

20 *DCB*, s.v. 'Ramezay, Louise de.' For Saint-Père's persuasion of Montrealers, which does not appear in most accounts of her, see C11A, 1707, vol. 27, fols 142–3. Some of the trainees long continued at Saint-Père's workshop; other men and women plied looms, which she distributed to their homes. In 1707, when about seventy weavers were at work, 120 *aunes* a day were being produced. For forty years to come, successive intendants were sufficiently impressed to continue the bonus, partly because in 1748 they still found scarcely any formal manufactories in this country. Another important letter is in C11A, 1706, vol. 24, fols 331–52. The strong, coarse cloth her St Joseph Street manufactory produced provided working-class Montrealers with warm, heavy shirts or shifts (chemises). In 1706, when she informed the Court that twenty-eight people were weaving, Intendant Raudot Sr said that without this enterprise half of 'the poor people in that poor country ... would be without *chemises*.'

21 *DCB*, s.v. 'Grandmaison, Éléonore de.'

22 Notarial documents relating her to the fur trade include ANQ-M Adhémar, A, 11 août 1700, procuration; 9 août 1700 contre-lettre, 27 juillet 1703, société; ANQ-M Chamalon, 9 nov. 1702, and 6 déc. 1703, obligation. She appears frequently in the C11A correspondence in the first three decades of the eighteenth century. There are biographies of both Charlotte Françoise Juschereau de St Denys and of her brother Charles Juchereau de St Denys in *DCB*. See also *DCB*, s.v. 'Dauphin de la Forest, François.' On the wife of Simon Reaume (Therèse Catin), see C11A, 1720, vol. 41, fols 126–40v; 1722, vol. 44, fols 349–51, 356–63; 1723, vol. 49, fols 500–500v (also consult C-2387, 1722, oct. 20 for the 'cruel enemy' charge). See also Guy Frégault, *Le XVIIIe siècle canadien* (Montreal: Editions HMH, 1970), 179, 216–21.

23 *DCB*, s.v. 'Juchereau de Saint Denys, Charles de.' C11A, 1702, vol. 36, fols 411ff. Thérèse made some accusations of her own.

24 C11A, 1750, vol. 96, fols 104–8 gives the widow's own account of her pelt and marine oil operations. On her activities, see also 1717, vol. 37, fols 78–81; 1719, vol. 40, fols 63–7; 1721, vol. 43, fols 149–61v. Lilianne Plamondon's dissertation findings were published in article form in 'Une Femme d'Affaires en Nouvelle-France: Marie-Anne Barbel, Veuve Fornel,' *Revue d'histoire de l'amérique française* (hereafter *RHAF*) 31 (1977): 165–85. On the Labrador trade see also W.G. Gosling, *Labrador, Its Discovery, Exploration and Development* (Toronto: Musson, 1910), 131–53; and P-G Roy, 'La Famille Legardeur de Repentigny,' *Bulletin de Recherches Historiques* (1947): 195ff.

25 J.F. Bosher, *The Canada Merchants, 1713–1763* (New York: Oxford University Press, 1987), 23.

26 Young, *Kin, Commerce, Community*, 22.

27 Ibid., 40. Also among those with significant cargos (1000–6000 *livres*) shipped through the agents Havy and Lefevre, Young found Mesdames Boishebert, Chartier, Couagne, D'Auteuil, Duplessis, Fornel, Jeremie, Monfort, Ramezay, Reamur, and Texier.

28 Miquelon, *New France*, 81, 127. Notarial records show a series of transactions, including procurations empowering Pascaud's wife to act in a legal sense without his presence as early as 1697. ANQ-M, Adhémar, A, 03 oct. 1697, procuration. On Mme Pascaud, see also C11A, 1715, vol. 36, fols 321–4; 1723, vol. 45, fols 88, 121–3v; 1724, vol. 46, fols 253–61; 1734, vol. 61, fol. 13v; and John Bosher, *Men and Ships in the Canada Trade, 1660–1760: A Biographical Dictionary* (Ottawa: Ministry of Supply and Services, 1992), 101–3. That the Pascauds benefited from being in the good graces of the Vaudreuils and Intendant Raudot *fils* is apparent in reading the C11A, 1716–17 correspondence.

29 Peter Kalm caught one glimpse of that involvement on a road near Niagara, where he 'met with a great number of Indians of both sexes, who were engaged in carrying their skins and other goods to Quebec.' A. Benson, *Peter Kalm's Travels in North America* (New York: Dover, 1937), 696. Another glimpse is Governor Beauharnois's description of Ottawa chiefs who had promised him they would not go to Chouaguen, but their wives went in their place. C11A, 1742, vol. 76, fols 225–30v.

30 Father de Ricardie and Pierre Potier, extracts from *Journal des Jésuites* (1710–55) in Thwaites, *JR*, 69:261–75, 70:23–7, 91–9, cited in Katherine Lawn and Claudio Salvucci, *Women in New France: Extracts from the Jesuit Relations* (Bristol, PA: Evolution Publishing, 2005), 288–90.

31 Senneville in 1755, vol. 119, fols 278–84; and Mme Barrois in 1749, vol. 118, fols 378–9, appear in a fascinating record that gives a sense of what a hub Detroit was for a number of different tribes named in the document and is also instructive on the types and costs of trade garments. At another post, Marie Louise Lefaivre supplied commander Douville with flour for the Miamis. 1747, vol. 118, fol. 143.

32 C11A, 1747, vol. 117, fol. 443.

33 C11A, 1747, vol. 117, fols 144–6, 363, 383–4; and 1746, vol. 118, fols 30–1 (Laplante Bourassa); 1747, vol. 117, fols 364, 383, 459–62; 1748, vol. 118, fols 103, 178–85 (Manon Lavoine); 1749–50, vol. 119, fols 184, 284 (Blondeau). For a discussion of four native women traders in the western Great Lakes who were married to Frenchmen, see Susan Sleeper-Smith, 'Women, Kin and Catholicism: New Perspectives on the Fur Trade,' in *In the Days of Our Grandmothers: A Reader in Aboriginal Women's History in Canada*,

ed. Mary-Ellen Kelm and Lorna Townsend (Toronto: University of Toronto Press, 2006), 26–55.

34 Launay and some others are mentioned in C11A, 1742, vol. 114, fols 261–306v, see especially 289v; Veuve Laprairie 1720, vol. 42, fols 156–8.

35 Jay Gitlin, *Bourgeois Frontier: French Towns, French Traders, and American Expansion* (New Haven: Yale University Press, 2010), 16. Gitlin discusses native–French kin links, as does Sleeper-Smith, *Indian Women*. See also Carl Ekberg, *François Vallé and His World: Upper Louisiana before Louis and Clark* (Columbia: University of Missouri Press, 2002).

36 Franquet, *Voyages et Mémoires*, 17.

37 Cited in J.N. Fauteaux, *Essai sur l'industrie au Canada sous le Régime Français* (Quebec: L-A Proulx, 1927), 459.

38 Hilda Neatby, *Quebec: The Revolutionary Age* (Toronto: McClelland and Stewart, 1966), 72–3, refers to this activity shortly after the Conquest; Franquet encounted Madame Benoist in 1752–3 (*Voyages et mémoires*, 150). On women making clothes for trade, see also Louise Dechene, *Habitants et marchands de Montréal au XVIIe siècle* (Paris: Plon, 1974), 151–3, 187, 391. Some weaving was begun also at the Montreal Hôpital Général at the start of the eighteenth century, though what connection if any it had to Saint-Père's ransoming of the English weavers is unknown. See C11A, 1706, vol. 25, fols 261–4.

39 'Memoir of Father Claude Godefroi Coquart on the Posts of the King's Domain,' (April 1750) in Thwaites, *JR*, 69:91–3, cited in Lawn and Salvucci, *Women in New France*, 290.

40 C11A, 1740, vol. 114, fol. 274v; 1741, vols 74–5, fols 274, 295v, 325. Bread was so vital a commodity that Peter Kalm was forced to postpone his departure from Fort St Fréderic for a day until fresh bread was baked, because Englishmen stopping over for the night had taken away with them the previous supply (Benson, *Peter Kalm's Travels*, 580). On Crown efforts to reduce the numbers of women at the posts, see C11A, 1741, vol. 75, fols 324–8; 1742, vol. 77, fols 344–51v. The Texiers are mentioned in 1740, vol. 114, fol. 296v; 1745, vol. 115, fol. 218; 1746, vol. 85, fol. 329ff., and fols 392–4; 1747, vol. 88, fol. 246. The Fort St Fréderic cleaning lady received the same pay as the barber (sixty *livres* a year). Does this indicate the high status of women – or the poor quality of military haircuts! Indicative of multitasking, Marianne Texier was also paid as a couturière. 1742, vol. 77, fol. 393v.

41 While it is obviously impossible to know the extent of the illegal trade out of New France, it was estimated by historian Jean Lunn to be as high as half or even two-thirds of total Canadian beaver production in the early eighteenth century. Jean Lunn, 'The Illegal Fur Trade out of New France, 1713–60,' *Canadian Historical Association Historical Papers* (1939): 65. Intendant Begon

noted in 1715 that since establishment of the monopoly company, 'il n'est pas passé en France le tiers du castor qu'on envoyait tous les ans,' since they sold blankets too dear and paid too little for beaver brought to their offices. C11A, 1715, vol. 35, fols 332–4.

42 In English New York, Dutch customs lingered for more than a generation after the English conquest of 1664, just as French ones lingered long after the British conquest of Canada. It seems more than coincidental that the majority of non-native women known to have been involved in trade with the Iroquois came from Dutch and French cultures. Among both those groups of colonists, daughters as well as sons were expected to inherit equal or significant shares of the family property. Within marriages, there was a 'community of goods' regarded as the joint property of two lineages rather than the personal wealth of a husband. The wife's ongoing legal existence was reflected in Dutch and French wives' continuing use of their maiden names, in part or in full. Dower rights were also more generous than in the English tradition, allowing widows control of half of the communal property rather than the use of one-third that was typical under English law. Though the husband had considerable powers of management, the wife had protections against his mismanagement. Dutch women needed only verbal permission of husbands to engage in business, while the French sought written permission. Particularly important was the widow's ability to renounce an indebted community without losing her dower. Scholars of Dutch New York continue to view Dutch traditions as relatively egalitarian. See, for example, Linda Biemer, 'Criminal Law and Women in New Amsterdam and Early New York,' in *A Beautiful and Fruitful Place: Selected Rensselaerswijck Seminar Papers*, ed. N. Zeller and C. Gehring (Albany: New Netherlands Publishing, 1991), 73–6; David Narrett, *Inheritance and Family Life in Colonial New York* (Ithaca: Cornell University Press, 1992), esp. 48, 103, 207. On Continental Dutch practices, see Danielle van den Heuvel, *Women and Entrepreneurship: Female Traders in the Northern Netherlands c. 1580–1815* (Amsterdam: Askant, 2007); and for legal context, see Jan Bosch, 'Le Statut de la Femme dans les Anciens Pays-Bas Sepentrionaux,' *Recueils de la Société Jean Bodin: La Femme*, pt 2 (Brussels: Librairie Encyclopédique, 1962), 323–50. For information about verbal permissions entitling Dutch wives to trade, I am indebted to Kim Todt's presentation 'Maria van Rensselaer and the Trading Women of New Netherlands,' Université de Sherbrooke Colloque Femmes, Culture et Pouvoir, Sherbrooke, QC, May 2009. Biemer, 'Criminal Law,' 76, notes that the forty-six female traders seen in Albany during the last decade of Dutch rule declined in number under English rule, there being only six by 1685–94. The increasing eighteenth-century exclusion of female English New

Yorkers from commercial life has been documented by Deborah Rosen, *Courts and Commerce: Gender, Law and the Market Economy in Colonial New York* (Columbus: Ohio State University Press, 1997). We know there were some female English female traders who operated even without benefit of the more liberal laws of the other two cultures. For an instructive cross-cultural overview, see Carole Shammas, 'Anglo-American Household Government in Comparative Perspective,' *William and Mary Quarterly*, 3rd ser., 52, no. 1 (1995): 104–44.

43 Their forbearance was 'owing to their numbers (in 1700 they outnumbered French Montrealers), their proximity to French settlements and the precarious political situation.' Jan Grabowski, 'French Criminal Justice and Indians in Montreal, 1670–1760,' *Ethnohistory* 43, no. 3 (1996): 405–29.

44 J-F. Lafitau, *Moeurs des sauvages Amériquains comparées aux moeurs des premières temps* (Paris: Saugrain, 1724), 1:66–7. For Lafitau's comments on liquor at the mission, see C11A, vol. 39, fols 242–6. The mission initially consisted of as many as two-thirds Algonkian and Huron residents. However, many of them were prisoners of the Iroquois, whose customs likely prevailed.

45 Cited in Université de Montréal anthropologist Roland Viau's *Femmes de Personne: Sexes, genres et pouvoirs en Iroquoisie ancienne* (Montreal: Boreal, 2000), 93.

46 Viau examines a large array of primary sources. He supplements missionary accounts with those of several mid-eighteenth-century French commanders and agents who reiterated the importance of Iroquois women at councils. Viau identifies eleven terms used by a range of seventeenth and eighteenth-century European observers to indicate female leaders – terms such as *femme considérable, matrone, captainesse, dame du conseil,* and *femme de qualité.* These were the matrons who had power to select and depose peace chiefs and grant stays of execution to captives. They had a deliberative voice in councils and treaties, and they selected clan civil and spiritual leaders. At the ideological level, the primacy of Sky Woman in the Iroquois creation myth, religious celebration of the Three Sisters (beans, corn, and squash that women grew), and the preference for female infants all attest to esteem for women. The matrilineal and matrilocal practices, the autonomy with which women controlled their work, their sexuality, and their children, as well as the frequency of older brides / younger grooms and the existence of polyandry among one Iroquoian nation (the Seneca) all indicate that Iroquoian societies were strongly feminine. Viau believes this adds up to a rough equality of the sexes, in which relationships were not founded simply on exploitation or dependence, and neither sex commanded the other. But since it was *elders* of both sexes who ruled, Viau believes the society is most

accurately seen as a gerontocracy. Still, he singles out eighteenth-century Iroquoia as 'the human society which, from an anthropological point of view, appears to have come the closest to the definition of a matriarchy' (la société humaine qui, du point de vue de l'anthropologie, paraitra avoir été la plus proche de la définat du matriarcat) (108). Viau believes the powers of women increased during the contact period as the men were increasingly away from the villages for war or trade. Even stronger claims, based not only on written sources but on Haudenosaunee 'tellings' are made by Aboriginal scholar Barbara Alice Mann, *Iroquoian Women: The Gantowisas* (New York: P. Lang, 2000). In this extensively researched and sharply revisionist book that examines over nearly four centuries of sources on the subject of Haudenosaunee women, Mann contends that while 'the more dedicated racist skews' in writing about natives have been identified, the sexist ones have enjoyed a longer life.' Mann's use of Iroquoian 'tellings,' often 'women's tellings,' many of them based on nineteenth- and twentieth-century writings from elders and native ethnographers, sets the stage. Just as one cannot understand European culture without reference to biblical traditions (usually seen as symbolically, not literally, true), one gathers necessary understanding from Iroquoian foundational myths and their oral and written historical accounts, which introduce each of Mann's chapters. The author asserts that non-native observers and scholars have had trouble conceiving of certain women dominating councils and making decisions about going to war; that notwithstanding the numerous primary sources attesting to it, 'academic discussions of the League as a political entity almost exclusively concentrate on the men's Grand Council. The contrapuntal Clan Mothers' councils are studiously ignored, not because they were unimportant to the League ... but because western scholars are following the prescriptions of male dominance so central to European political history' (117). She gives the example of Governor Denonville's humiliating defeat in 1689. Although French-Canadian sources speak of this as a defeat at the hands of 'the Iroquois,' Mann cites Iroquois sources that commemorate this as a French defeat by a great female chief, the *Jigonsaseh*. Other European witnesses spoke of women being present at trade and political delegations but staying in the background, or kept there by their jealous husbands. Mann sees this as failure to understand that Iroquois 'etiquette' required a woman's council to delegate a male speaker to address men, just as men's councils would delegate a female speaker to address women.

47 C11A, 1745, vol. 35, fols 183–9.

48 Representatives of the Compagnie des Indes made this complaint about Intendant Begon and the Superior Council in 1715. Protests by the Desau-

niers and other fur-trading families about the ruinous effects of the French company's high prices for merchandise and low prices for beaver often went unheeded in France, but some colonial officials sympathized. C11A, 1715, vol. 35, fols 193–3v; 1721, vol. 44, fols 190–3.

49 Lunn, 'Illegal Fur Trade,' 61–76.

50 The information in this paragraph is drawn from Kees-Jan Waterman, ed. and trans., *'To Do Justice to Him and Myself': Evert Wendell's Fur Trade with Indians in Albany, New York, 1695–1726* (Philadelphia: American Philosophical Society, 2008). The editor notes that another, unknown hand in the books may have been that of their mother, Ariaantze.

51 Ibid., 164–5, 180, and attendant notes. The editor believes the priest who sent greetings was from the Montreal area. One of the Jesuits working there was later sent back to France by officials for purported involvement in illicit fur trading. For the proportion of female traders, see 48.

52 Ibid., 133, and attendant notes.

53 Sanders, whose French was sketchy, used the feminine article *la* to precede *porteur* for Conaquasse as well as for Agnesse and Marie-Magdeleine, using *le porteur* for Joseph and the other men. Still, one wonders if this person, whose name was spelled variously, might have been Canaqueese, a Metis man who travelled on diplomatic missions between Albany and New France. On Canaqueese, see Thomas Burke, *Mohawk Frontier: The Dutch County of Schenectady New York 1661–1710* (Ithaca: Cornell University Press, 1991), 89–90. See also Waterman, *'To Do Justice,'* 203, 206, for male identification of two phonetically similar names, Conossaasse and Cannasquaskje.

54 LAC, photocopy of Robert Sanders Letterbook, Sanders to Monièr, 19 8ber [*sic*] 1752, and 5 July 1753.

55 Ibid., 11 7ber [*sic*], 1753.

56 Dennis Sullivan, *The Punishment of Crime in Colonial New York: The Dutch Experience in Albany during the Seventeenth Century* (New York: Lang, 1997), 161. See also 72, 98–9. The screamer was named Temperance Loverage, suggesting some Englishwomen may also have been involved.

57 Ibid., 167–8.

58 Suspicions of the Desauniers and descriptions of smuggling at Fort St Fréderic are in C11A, 1744, vol. 81, fols 34, 167–9. Early activity was attested when a bill of exchange between Lachine trader Sieur Quesnel and Marie Anne Desauniers for exchange of eight hundred *livres* of beaver was confiscated. 1731, vol. 55, fol. 302. Did they make any use of the ship owned by Pierre Trottier Desauniers, their merchant brother in Quebec (1739, vol. 71, fol. 182)? More detail is contained in 1740, vol. 73; and 1742, vol. 77, fol. 19, including the initial command to close the store.

59 C11A, 1741, vol. 76, fol. 141v.
60 Female intermediaries in the western trade have been noted in work such as that of Devens, *Countering Colonization*; Sleeper-Smith, *Indian Women and French Men*; Van Kirk, *'Many Tender Ties'*; and Bruce White, 'The Woman Who Married a Beaver: Trade Patterns and Gender Roles in the Ojibwa Fur Trade,' *Ethnohistory* 46, no. 1 (1999): 109–47.
61 Another report, however, made them out to be sharp traders who bought the natives' corn and squash cheap in the fall and sold it back dear in the spring. C11A, 1741, vol. 76, fol. 142.
62 C11A, 1751, vol. 97, fol. 388.
63 C11A, 1750, vol. 95, fols. 174–5. The two Sault Saint Louis war chiefs Tega-nag8asen and Beauvais gave particulars (three canoe-loads of English goods shipped west in the past five days under the command of Agouirache).
64 C11A, 1751, vol. 97, fols 173–8 (see La Jonquière to the Minister, 1 Nov.1751). One cannot completely dismiss the possibility that the Desau-niers were unjustly accused – a position taken by Trois-Rivières Governor Vaudreuil (1741, vol. 76, fols 143–5), who asserted that (at least up to that point) numerous attempts to catch them red-handed had all failed. Evi-dence mounted when the two chiefs gave details of canoes they had five days earlier outfitted with English merchandise for prearranged transfer to voyageurs at Long Sault to take west to trade. Montreal Judge Lafontaine managed to entrap the Desauniers into selling English contraband to a na-tive agent. However, Lafontaine was an enemy of the Desauniers' brother. A native informant also had his own reason for wanting to please the authori-ties, hoping for return of a confiscated medal. Things never seem to be straightforward in this case. In his eviction order, Governor La Jonquière spoke of the sisters' 'greed,' and perhaps moral indignation made him too credulous of the Iroquois testimony. The bill of exchange found in the 1730s with Marie-Anne's name on it may be the firmest piece of incriminat-ing evidence (1731, vol. 55, fol. 302). The reluctance of a long series of of-ficials to act and their ongoing search for evidence suggests they were not minded to act on mere hearsay. The Mousseaux/Merceau mention in the merchant letterbook gives additional evidence of trade between Kahnawake and Albany. See 1741, vol. 76, fols 143–5; 1742, vol. 77, fols 353–4; 1750, vol. 95, fols 165–89, 262–3, as well as the discussion of Mousseaux later in this chapter. For the Desauniers' rejoinder, and testimonials on their behalf (some probably being private correspondence that they redirected to this purpose), see 1751, vol. 97, fols 378ff.; for their kinship with Montreal mer-chants, 1750, vol. 95, fol. 262.
65 1735 Lettre du Père Nau au Père Bonin, *RAPQ,* 1926–7, 284. The Desauni-ers developed a special process for processing the ginseng the Indians grew

for the China trade, and they would later claim that envy of this process of theirs was the root of all the accusations against them. C11A, 1751, vol. 97, fols 378–81.

66 C11A, 1751, vol. 97, fols 173–8.

67 Is it possible one or more of them gained a voice of authority in any way resembling that of clan mothers or women councillors? Adopted Europeans occasionally did so. Long-time New York trader Sarah McGinnis, for example, worked as a Tory agent during the American Revolution, just as Molly Brant did. Based within the Mohawk encampment, McGinnis used her position to prevent a wampum belt bearing demoralizing news of a British defeat from going further than her village, as noted in Barbara Graymount, *The Iroquois in the American Revolution* (Syracuse: Cornell University Press, 1972), 13. For discussion of McGinnis, the Desaulniers, and their ties with the Haudenosaunee, see David Preston, *The Texture of Contact: European and Indian Settler Communities on the Frontiers of Iroquoia, 1667–1783.* (Lincoln: University of Nebraska Press, 2009), chs. 1 and 2. McGinnis appeared in Robert Sanders's Albany trade book in the 1750s as a trader of porcelain beads or wampum. At Sault Saint Louis, it may have helped that outsider–insider distinctions were blurred in a village that included a number of different First Nations, people of mixed blood, European adoptees, and friends.

68 Sanders Letterbook, 11 7ber [*sic*] 1753. Madame de Merceau/Mousseaux was a kinswoman of Madame d'Ailleboust, who had also been accused of illegal trading. Both families were implicated as early as 1715 by Veuve La Pipardière. C11A, 1715–16, vol. 35, fols 64–9v, 81–6v, 170–1; vol. 123, fols 173–6. 'Madame Des Muceaux' brought furs to the company office in 1717 (vol. 37, fols 363–4). Suspicions that the family was involved in illegal trade date to the early eighteenth century, including a letter implicating 'Madame de Des Muceaux' and the younger Sieur de Coulonge, 1715, vol. 35, fols 170–1; see also 1719, vol. 124, fols 374–8v.

69 Her role as procuratrice for the couple and later for her son is documented in ANQ-M, Barbel, 20 mai 1735, Saillant de Collégian, 29 sept. 1764 , 1 oct. 1764. See also Franquet, *Voyages,* 56, 67–8, 200; and *DCB,* s.v. 'Lusignan, Paul-Louis Dazemard de.' Lusignan was considered a wise man by Intendant Hocquart, C11A, 1736, vol. 66, fol. 18. For the widow's post-Conquest petition, see 1766, vol. 89, fols 181–2.

70 C11A, 1700, vol. 18, fol. 333.

71 Other people got involved as counter-agents: Madame Thiersant in the Richelieu valley and Dame Gaillard at Bas de Fleuve sent the authorities reports about smuggling; the latter complained all the way to Versailles about a Recollet priest who recruited natives to smuggle furs. Madame de La Chauvignerie, who spoke native languages, was not only paid for hospitality

to Haudenosaunee and Algonquins but courted as an informant on smuggling. C11A, 1715, vol. 35, fols 192–3v; 1716, vol. 123, fols 306–7; 1730, vol. 52, fols 33–6v; 1731, vol. 55, fols 71–2. M. Chauvignerie, who was perhaps Madame's son, served as a French–Iroquois interpreter. C11A, 1750, vol. 95, fol. 165; see also volumes 18 (fols 152–3, 220–3, 329–32) and 25 (fols 192– 3v) and 1731, vol. 55, fols 71–2. Madame La Forest's dealings are extensively reported in the colonial correspondence, the smuggling appearing in 1703, vol. 21, fols 180–4. Gaillard appears in 1715–16, vol. 123, fol. 310. On Madame Couagne, see William Eccles, *Canadian Society during the French Regime* (Montreal: Harvest House, 1968), 61.

72 C11A, 1726, vol. 48, fols 79–88.

73 C11A, 1735, vol. 64, fols 13–14.

74 Even Thomas Norton, who examined the Wendell accounts, misled by the failure to name the women traders, undercounted them as 20 per cent of traders. Waterman, 'To Do Justice,' 18, 40–3, 212; see also Thomas E. Norton, *The Fur Trade in Colonial New York, 1686–1776* (Madison, WI: University of Wisconsin Press, 1974), 28n. On the certain participation of sister Hester Wendell and the possible participation of mother Ariaantje Wendell, see Waterman, 'To Do Justice,' 1, 10.

75 Waterman, 'To Do Justice,' 43.

76 Greer, *People of New France*, 68; Moogk, *La Nouvelle France*, 161, 207; Young, '"… sauf les périls,"' 405; see also the version in Strong-Boag, Gleason, and Perry, *Rethinking Canada*, 44n60, which mentions female 'networks.' Jan Noel, 'New France: Les Femmes Favorisées,' in *Rethinking Canada: The Promise of Women's History*, ed. V. Strong-Boag and Anita Clair Fellman, 33–56 (Toronto: Oxford, 1997), 51.

77 This phenomenon is analysed in my 'Women of the New France Noblesse,' in *Women and Freedom in Colonial North America*, ed. Larry Eldridge, 26–43 (New York: New York University Press, 1997), which discusses the economic contributions elite women made to their families. On the unenviable financial position of the upper echelons in New France, one of many examples is Intendant Raudot's 1706 remark that 'dans ce pays il n'y a personne de riche,' adding that without the King's help the people could not survive. It is true Kalm mentioned that in Quebec unmarried 'young ladies, especially those of a higher rank, get up at seven, and dress until nine,' then placed themselves at the window looking for suitors. But that in itself might be sound economic strategy in a port town where eligible gentlemen arrived and frequently married the locals. By contrast, Kalm mentioned that their mothers were occupied with 'all the business of the house.' At Montreal he found young ladies (one assumes he is discussing the higher classes) more industrious, rising early and always at their needlework.

78 Hufton, *Prospect before Her*, 1:70, 146–53. See also Daryl Hafter, *Women at Work in Preindustrial France* (University Park, PA: Pennsylvania State University Press, 2007); and Nancy Locklin, *Women's Work and Identity in Eighteenth-Century Brittany* (Aldershot: Ashgate, 2007).

79 Hill, *Women, Work*, 50–67, 259–63.

80 Peter Earle, 'The Female Labour Market in London in the Late Seventeenth and Early Eighteenth Centuries,' *Economic History Review*, 2nd ser., 42, no. 3 (1989): 346. Earle's turn-of-the-eighteenth-century sample suggested that at least in London, couples did not typically work together, and widows did not typically take over their husbands' trades, but tended instead to pursue their own forms of revenue generation, 'much of it of a casual nature.' See too Hunt, *The Middling Sort*, 128–9, on the further but frequently unrecorded participation of seventeenth-century women in family businesses, keeping boarders, doing laundry, and vending. Hunt also notes other work of Earle's in which an even higher percentage of women reported *some* paid income: 81 per cent of spinsters, 60 per cent of wives, 85 per cent of widows.

81 *Kalm's Account of His Visit to England on His Way to London* (London: Macmillan, 1892), 327–8. See also 80–95. The remarks of Kalm on Canadian women are found in Benson, *Peter Kalm's Travels*, 403, 417, 479, 525–6. An official dispatch of 1679 also observed women and children farming and tending livestock, and attributed it to the absence of five to six hundred *coureurs de bois*. C11A, 1679, vol. 5, fols 32–70. There are references to markets in the *côtes* where farm people satisfied what Intendant Hocquart deemed their love of luxury, and to *habitants* of both sexes coming to town, in C11A, 1741, vol. 75, fols 8–9; and 1742, vol. 77, fols 135–6. One of the many was a newly arrived French priest in 1737 who remarked that girls who tended cows during the week dressed up in lace and hoop skirts on Sundays. Eccles, *Canadian Society*, 74.

82 Cited in Shoemaker, *Gender in English Society*, 174.

83 Benson, *Peter Kalm's Travels*, 402–3, 525–6. Does the immersion of single women in economic activity help account for the tendency of courts in French Canada to place illegitimate children in the father's custody rather than the mother's? See Marie-Aimée Cliché, 'Unwed Mothers, Families and Society during the French Regime,' in Bradbury, *Canadian Family History*, 52–6.

4. Water, Woods, Earth: Making a Living

1 C11A, vol. 1 (*Procès-verbal*, 4 juillet 1651 and 10 juillet 1653).

2 *DCB*, s.v. 'Fornel, Louis.'

3 C11A, 1750, vol. 96, fols 101–7. On Fornel, see C11A, 1750, vol. 96, fols 101–8, which gives the widow Fornel's own account of her pelt and marine oil operations. For a summary of her activities, see Lilianne Plamondon, 'Une Femme d'Affaires en Nouvelle-France: Marie-Anne Barbel, Veuve Fornel,' *Revue d'histoire de l'Amérique française* 31 (1977): 165–85. See also C11A, 1748, vol. 91, fols 75–7, as well as 1721, vol. 109, fols 2–8.

4 *DCB*, s.v. 'Acoutsina.'

5 C11A, 1720, vol. 109, fols 75–91 contains Martel de Brouague's account of Acoutsina, the Inuit, and the perils to the fort as well as of his mother's heroism during the fire; see also *DCB*, s.v. 'Acoutsina.' The epidemic is described in 1722, vol. 109, fols 214–17. Other C11A correspondence with details on Charest are 1717, vol. 37, fols 78–82v; 1717, vol. 104 (or 109), fols 29–35; 1720, vol. 42, fols 164–75v; 1721, vol. 75, fols 70–2; 1722, vol. 109, fols 14–15v, 70–91, 110, 214–17; 1722, vol. 124, fols 52–3, 207, 555–9v. The family's continuing interest in Labrador trade is evinced in the career of Martel de Brouague, which lasted 'til the end of the regime; also in petitions and/or concessions to Marie Legardeur de Courtemanche (Mme Foucher) and Mlle Legardeur around 1740. See 1738, vol. 70, fols 209–10v; and 1741, vol. 75, fols 70–2. See reel C-2386, vol. 42, pp. 142–4 for Madame's alleged desire to keep the entire coast to herself. (My thanks to Molly Richter for this reference, and also for her research of the notarial records at the Quebec Archives at Montreal for this and many other sections of these chapters). There is further information in the *DCB* biographies of Augustin Legardeur de Courtemanche and his partner Raymond Martel, including Charest's 1703 suit for separation of goods from those of her debt-ridden husband. There are profiles of her son François Martel de Brouague in *RAPQ*, 1922–3, 356–8, and *DCB*.

6 *DCB*, s.v. 'Pommereau, J-B.'

7 Portneuf and Duchesné, C11A, 1747, vol. 89, fol. 73; Pommereau, 1742, vol. 78, fols 137–41; 1743, vol. 80, fols 217–18v, 303; 1744, vol. 82, fols 261–4; 1745, vol. 115, fols 165–85; 1747, vol. 115, fol. 171v. 1741, vol. 75, fol. 75 indicates that Madame de Boishébert was also planning to open a fishery of *loup marin* on the Labrador coast. While we do not know the nature of her involvement, a 1715 agreement of the Sulpician Order, seigneurs of Montreal, allocated to a widow (Anne Lemire, veuve Rupalley) the rights to all the places for sturgeon and other fish around Montreal Island, on condition the priests would get a third of their choicest catch (Fauteaux, *Essai sur l'industrie*, 522).

8 Mathieu, *Nouvelle France*, 180 (my translation). In addition to the weaknesses discussed above, 40 per cent Canadian apprenticeships were unpaid. There

were sometimes difficulties in finding work, and many people never worked in the field in which they apprenticed.

9 Isadore Lebrun, *Tableau statistique et politique des Deux Canadas* (Paris: Treutel et Wurtz, 1833), 389–90. Scholarship on manufacture of cloth and clothing in New France includes Bernard Audet, *Le costume paysan dans la région de Québec au XVIIe siècle: l'Ile d'Orléans* (Montreal: Leméac, 1980); Dorothy Burnham, *L'art des Etoffes: le filage et le tissage traditionnels au Canada* (Ottawa: Galerie nationale du Canada, 1981); Suzanne Gousse, *Les couturières en Nouvelle-France. Leur contribution socio-économique dans une société coloniale d'Ancien Régime* (MA thesis, Université de Montréal, 2009); Suzanne Gousse, 'Marie Catherine Demers Dessermon (1698–1785), cofondatrice oubliée. Interrogations sur le pouvoir d'effacement d'une religieuse montréalaise,' *Revue d'Histoire de l'Amérique française* 63, nos 2–3 (2010): 243–74; David-Thierry Ruddel, 'Domestic Textile Production in Colonial Québec, 1608–1840,' *Material History Bulletin* 31 (1990): 39–49. On post-Conquest manufacture of cloth and clothing, see our chapter 8.

10 Young, *Kin, Commerce, Community*, 25. Talon's manufactory produced *étoffes* and *linge*.

11 Cited in Fauteaux, *Essai sur l'industrie*, 459. On the Ursulines, see Davis, *Women Mystics*, 93. Denonville commented on the subject in 1685–6. Intendant Champigny in the 1680s urged *habitantes* to stop being *fainéantes* and *demoiselles*. He called for the raising and working of hemp, and the raising of *bestiaux*, though he conceded sheep were hard to keep over the long winters (C11A, 1687, vol. 9, fol. 18).

12 C11A, 1701, vols 105–6, fol. 53 mentions that the Quebec Seminary was paying 225 *livres* rent to the Sisters of the Congregation, who conducted little schools in a house built for them on Beaupré seigneurie.

13 Various war-related sewing by women, including uniforms, is mentioned in C11A, 1744, vol. 82, fols 254–5; 1745, vol. 84, fols 200–5, and vol. 115, fols 162, 192; 1746, vol. 117, fols 49–74; 1747, vol. 88, fols 248–54, and vol. 89, fols 77–9, 103v–7, and vol. 117, fols 68–74, 95–116; 1748, vol. 92, fols 236–55, 256–71.

14 C11A, 1748, vol. 91, fols 40–50 (when affordable); vol. 115, fols 183v, 194ff.; 1736, vol. 66, fols 15–21v (uniforms); 1737, vol. 67, fol. 95 (Hocquart).

15 See C11A, 1710–11, vol. 113, fols 261–2 for accounts of Madame Duplessis signed by Jaques Barbel; also see 1731, vol. 55, fols 217–22; 1734, vol. 61, fols 131ff.; and 1735, vol. 63, fols 173–83. See also *DCB*, s.v. 'Couagne, Thérèse de' and 'Marie-Joseph-Angélique'; Afua Cooper, *The Hanging of Angélique* (Toronto: Harper Collins, 2006).

16 Greer discusses the stoves in *Peasant, Lord and Merchant*; see *DCB* for biog-

raphies of 'Thérèse de Couagne' and also of 'Gastineau-Duplessis, J-B,' 'Olivier de Vezin, Pierre-François.' The C11A series references various female participants in the Forges operation, including 1715, vol. 61, fols 349–50; 1735, vol. 63, fols 173–83, vol. 110, fols 297–300, 351–3, 354–62; 1740, vol. 111, fols 2–30, 93; 1741, vol. 111, fols 117–32, and vol. 112, fols 2–27; 1742, vol. 111, fols 135–8.

17 This operation seems to have been variously run by male and female de Ramezays at different times. Mme de Ramezay is mentioned in C11A, 1726, vol. 48, fols 167–77.

18 C11A, 1734, vol. 61, fol. 159.

19 C11A, 1731, vol. 56, fols 178–9; 1732, vol. 58, fols 38–41; 1740, vol. 114, fol. 288; 1745, vol. 115, fol. 207.

20 Some of these sources are discussed in Jacques Ducharme, 'Les revenus des Hospitalières de Montréal au XVIIe siècle,' in Allard, *L'Hôtel-Dieu de Montréal*, 232; see also *L'Hôpital Général de Montréal* (Montreal: n.p., n.d.), 1:204–13; and D'Allaire's *Les Communautés*, vol. 1.

21 C11A, 1669, vol. 3, fols 34–6.

22 C11A, 1740, vol. 73, fol. 414. See also *DCB*, s.v. 'Jérémie, dit Lamontagne, Nicolas.'

23 See E.J. Divine, *Historic Caughnawaga* (Montreal: Messenger, 1992). This may have been another smuggled item, since the letterbook of Albany receiver of illegal furs Robert Sanders indicates he also purchased ginseng.

24 E.J. Benson, *The America of 1750: Peter Kalm's Travels in North America* (New York: Dover, 1966), 540. Could those utensils have been the '*grosses couverts*' colonial officials mentioned as being manufactured in Quebec by the daughter of Agathe Saint-Père?

25 C11A, 1715, vol. 45, fols 213–14; *DCB*, s.v. 'Amiot, Charles,' 'Amiot de Vincelette, Charles-Joseph.'

26 C11A, 1744, vol. 81, fols 277–89; *DCB*, s.v. 'Lupien, dit Baron, Pierre.'

27 C11A, 1741, vol. 75, fols 307–8v; 1742, vol. 78, fols 256–69; 1745, vol. 84, fol. 71v; *DCB*, s.v. 'Sarrazin, Michel.'

28 C11A, 1732, vol. 113, fol. 470 (Dupuy); 1740, vol. 114, fol. 287v (Portneuf and Youville); 1742, vol. 78, fols 243–54, and vol. 79, fols 327–42v; Lamoureux: 1744, vol. 84 fol. 72v; 1747, vol. 89, fols 120–2v, and vol. 115, fol. 171v, vol. 92, fols 202–19v; Sabrevois 1743, vol. 80, fols 62ff.

29 C11A, 1742, vol. 78, fols 137–41, 173–224v; 1743, vol. 80, fols 186–7v, 191–2v, 217–18v; 1744, vol. 82, fols 29–53; 1745, vol. 83, fols 195–250v; 1746, vol. 85, fols 369–74; 1747, vol. 89, fols 120–2v, and vol. 115, fol. 171v; 1749, vol. 93, fols 321–2, 392–8v; *DCB*, s.v. 'Pommereau, J-B.'

30 C11A, 1741, vol. 76, fol. 105; 1742, vol. 78, fols 173–91, 226–41v, 256–69;

1743, vol. 80, fols 62, 186–7v, 217–19; 1745, vol. 83, fols 195–250v; 1746, vol. 85, fols 369–74; 1747, vol. 88, fols 93–107, 117–31, and vol. 89, fols 77–9; 1748, vol. 92, fols 153–7, 160–9, 224–6, and vol. 93, fols 392–8. Raymond's fourteen pieces of cordage were among May–June provisions of hers to the ship *St Laurent* that totalled 2478 *livres* worth. *DCB*, s.v. 'Renaud d'Avene des Meloizes, Nicolas-Marie.'

31 C11A, 1743, vol. 80, fol. 186; 1745, vol. 83, fol. 248, vol. 84, fol. 77; 1748, vol. 92, fol. 201. In some other cases it was specified, as with the Hôpital Général in 1745, that the meals were supplied to crews, carpenters, or other workers who were patients. Money collected by Mother St Geneviève de l'Enfant Jesus for meals for sick seamen between 1733 and 1736 is recorded in C11A, 1736, vol. 68, fol. 46.

32 *Historical Atlas of Canada*, vol. 1, plates 24 and 48. Expenditures rose from about 0.5 million *livres* at the beginning of the 1740s to 2.5 million annually in 1744–8 (*DCB*, s.v. 'Hocquart, Gilles').

33 C11A, 1689, vol. 113, fols 15–19; vol. 30, fols 329–31; 1731, vol. 56, fols 28–9.

34 C11A, 1740, vol. 114, fol. 274.

35 For discussion of this phenomenon, see Catherine Desbarats, 'Les deniers du Roi dans l'économie canadienne du XVIIIe siècle,' in Dépatie et al., *Vingt ans*.

36 LAC, Baby Collection, Correspondence, II, Havy and Lefebvre to Madame Guy, 3 Aug. 1745, 664–5.

37 C11A, 1748, vol. 92, fols 127–30v, 160–9, 256–71. See also R. Boyer, *Les Crimes et les Châtiments au Canada français du 17e au 20e Siècle* (Montreal: Cercle du livre de France, 1966), 114.

38 On the Desauniers, see C11A, 1750, vol. 97, fol. 384. The others are mentioned in 1744, vol. 82, fols 254–5v; 1745, vol. 84, fols 200–5, and vol. 115, fols 162, 192; 1746, vol. 117, fols 49–74; 1747, vol. 88, fols 248–54v, and vol. 89, fols 77v–9, 103v–7v, and vol. 117, fols 68–74, 95–116; 1748, vol. 92, fols 236–55, 256–71.

39 C11A, 1745, vol. 115, fols 159–62.

40 C11A, 1745, vol. 83, fols 195–250v; 1746–7, vol. 117, fols 435–43, 454v, 459–62; 1748, vol. 118, fols 178–85.

41 C11A, 1745, vol. 115, fols 163, 187, 192 (Baby, Lafayette, Magnon); and fols 165–86 (L'Espérance). Many of these economically active women were related; for example, Madame Baby was Louise de Couagne, niece of Thérèse de Couagne (Madame de Francheville). Cloth cornets were part of female headgear.

42 C11A, 1737, vol. 67, note inserted in fols 80–95.

43 C11A, 1740, vol. 114, fol. 288; 1745, vol. 115, fols 187, 194v, 207.

44 The observation of British historian Peter Earle, discussed in chapter 3 above.

45 Brun, *Vie et mort du couple en Nouvelle-France*, 66–7, 94.

46 C11A, 1679–81, vol. 5, fols 32–70, 82–7, 290–305 (report of Duchesneau). In September 1685 Governor Denonville repeated the estimate of five to six hundred men in the woods.

47 Claude de Ramezay's estimate, C11A, 1715–16, vol. 123, fol. 180.

48 C11A, 1717, vol. 106, fols 368v, 446v.

49 Benson, *America of 1750*, 446; for the remarks of St Vallier, Vaudreuil, and Begon on this subject, see C11A, 1717, vol. 37, fols 23–30, and vol. 106, fols 366–72v; 1718, vol. 106, fol. 446v. Ruette d'Auteuil made the same observation in his 1715 Memoir on Canada (vol. 34, fols 176–92).

50 Gauvreau, 'Vingt ans d'études sur la population pendant le Régime français,' in Dépatie et al., *Vingt ans*, 33.

51 The Crown bought some of these, purchasing, for example, in Montreal in 1732 two live steers from Widow Picard and six hundred *livres'* worth of wheat from Widow Bouat. In the regime's later decades, there were even country merchants in some districts who offered the convenience of going door-to-door to buy up any surplus farm produce, wheat, and legumes to load onto vessels bound for Louisbourg and the West Indies. See C11A, 1732, vol. 113, fol. 477v; and 1741, vol. 75, fols 7–10.

52 Marcel Trudel, *Les Débuts du régime seigneurial au Canada* (Montreal: Fides, 1974), 54–6, 62–3; see also his *Les Terres de Saint-Laurent*, 531, cited in Louise Vachon, '"Barbe de Boullougne," ou L'ascension d'une Femme dans la Nouvelle France du XVIIe siècle' (MA thesis, Université de Montréal, 1999), 136–7.

53 Vachon, '"Barbe de Boullougne,"' 136–40, 153.

54 Moogk, *La Nouvelle France*, 184.

55 The names above were those that happened to be mentioned in one series of colonial correspondence, C11A, 1671, vol. 44, fols 120–1; 1717, vol. 37, fol. 316; 1720, vol. 42, fols 35–50; 1741, vol. 75, fol. 70; 1746, vol. 75, fols 70–2; 1754, vol. 99, fols 227–8; 1760, vol. 104, fols 619–24. For Veuve Neuville's intent to attract blacksmiths, carpenters, *menuisiers* to the settlement, see 1754, vol. 99, fol. 227.

56 See Young, '"… sauf les périls,"' for Madeleine Roberge; Saint-Père is discussed in our chapter 6. Her acquisition of a 38,000-livre *terre* is mentioned in C11A, vol. 123, fol. 309.

57 C11A, 1744, vol. 82, fols 59–80.

58 The widowed seigneuresses are discussed in Benoit Grenier, *Seigneurs campagnards de la Nouvelle France* (Rennes: Presses Universitaires de Rennes, 2007),

185–93, while Widow Duchesnay is discussed in his monograph, *Marie-Catherine Peuvret, 1667–1739: Veuve et Seigneuresse en Nouvelle-France* (Sillery: Septentrion, 2005), chaps 4–5.

59 Kalm, cited in Ernest Gagnon, *Le Fort et Chateau de Saint Louis* (Montreal: Beauchemin), 150, recorded prices at Montreal markets in the late 1740s for cows, pigs, chickens, butter, and eggs – goods clearly being sold there along with wheat. For an account of famine strategies, see C11A, 1737, vol. 70, fol. 11v. On peas for Louisbourg, 1738, vol. 69, fols 200–2v; on the salt pork market, 1730, vol. 53, fols 7–10, 113–27. Town families too kept pigs.

60 Simpson, *Marguerite Bourgeoys and Montreal*, 70, 102. See also Colleen Gray, *The Congrégation de Notre-Dame, Superiors, and the Paradox of Power, 1693–1796* (Montreal and Kingston: McGill-Queen's University Press, 2007), esp. chap. 3.

61 C11A, 1730, vol. 53, fol. 379v. They managed to produce a wheat crop, even in the famine year of 1744.

62 *DCB*, s.v. 'Morin, Marie.'

63 C11A, 1734, vol. 61, fols 152, 163, 180.

64 D'Allaire, *Communautés*, 1:76; Ducharme, 'Les revenus des Hospitalières de Montréal,' 232; *L'Hôpital Général de Montréal*, 1:204–13.

65 C11A, 1745, vol. 117, fol. 87v (Quebec Hôtel-Dieu).

66 C11A, 1748, vol. 91, fols 34–5; 1749, vol. 93, fols 17–18. A Crown agent appointed in the 1730s to make an inventory of lands also complained of the 'labyrinthine' records of lots and seigneuries of convents such as the Hôtel-Dieu that had no treasurer or businessman helping them. Still, as historian Micheline D'Allaire has shown, the orders showed astuteness in managing their properties and asserting their claims. Examples of holdings are found in C11A, 1729, vol. 51, fol. 3; 1734, vol. 61, fols 149–53; 1738, vol. 70, fols 202–5. The window question was debated in 1724, vol. 46, fols 328–31v. The Hôtel-Dieu sisters agreed to release some of their property for housing on one condition: houses must be bare of upper story windows that might permit glimpses of nuns in their convents and gardens.

67 Hocquart's remarks are in C11A, 1737, vol. 67, mostly in a note inserted in folio 95, and on subsequent pages. Some wives of officers who were serving at frontier posts received half of the husband's pay, presumably to assist in running the seigneurie or meeting other expenses.

68 Judith Bennett, 'Medieval Women, Modern Women: Across the Great Divide,' in *Culture and History, 1350–1600*, ed. David Aers (Detroit: Wayne State University Press, 1992), 158. Alice Clark, *Working Life of Women in the Seventeenth Century* (London: Cass, 1968), 4.

5. Comparing Laws of Property

1 Dechene, *Habitants and Merchants*, 218.
2 A study by Molly Richter of rural widows and widowers in the Montreal District showed that they often neglected to make formal inventory and selection of *tutelle* after decease of a spouse, relying instead on the terms of the marriage contract. Richter suggests that poverty, distance, and weather all worked against conformity to the strict letters of the law. 'Remarriage in New France: The Influence of Inheritance and Familial Charge in 17th and 18th Century Quebec' (paper delivered to the Organization of American Historians' Conference, Washington DC, April 2006).
3 On the French illegal trade, see Lunn, 'Illegal Fur Trade,' 61–76. See also the discussion in Miquelon, *New France*, 156.
4 Mendelson and Crawford, *Women in Early Modern England*, 48, 177. Along similar lines, David Lemmings traces the disappearance from eighteenth-century ecclesiastical courts of plebeian women desiring judicial separations. See his 'Women's Property, Popular Cultures and the Consistory Court of London in the Eighteenth Century,' in *Women, Property and the Letters of the Law in Early Modern England*, ed. Nancy E. Wright, Margaret Ferguson, and A.R. Buck, 66–94 (Toronto: University of Toronto Press, 2004).
5 Amy Erickson, *Women and Property in Early Modern England* (London: Routledge, 1993), 233; see also 29, 155, 174–86; and Aileen Spring, *Land, Law and the Family: Aristocratic Inheritance in England, 1300 to 1800* (Chapel Hill, NC: University of North Carolina Press, 1993), 185. Spring's study of probate wills showed that the various kinds of strict settlements and jointures developing in this period did prevent the worst-case scenario in which a husband dissipated the whole property; but the sum allocated to the widow generally amounted to less than the traditional third. The equity courts had a less uniformly positive effect on female inheritance than was once assumed. On women and business and on prescriptive literature, see Hunt, *The Middling Sort*, 75, 152–3, and the broader discussion in chaps 5 and 6. Earle, *Making of the English Middle Class*, 187, situates the urban inheritance changes in the early eighteenth century.
6 Erickson, *Women and Property*, 230.
7 Elaine Forman Crane, *Ebb Tide in New England: Women, Seaports and Social Change* (Boston: Northeastern University Press, 1998), 156–73. Karlsen, *Devil in the Shape of a Woman*, 101, linked even the Salem witchcraft persecutions to a growing male sense of entitlement to lands ceded to daughters and widows where there was no immediate male heir.

8 C. Shammas, M. Salmon, and M. Dahlin, *Inheritance in America from Colonial Times to the Present* (New Brunswick, NJ: Rutgers University Press, 1987), 38.

9 Ibid., 53–61. As always, jurisdictional variety complicates the picture. High mortality in the early Chesapeake region and the South, for example, led to a relative concentration of wealth and estate management in female hands. But farther north, Puritan and Quaker dislike of aristocratic arrangements and insistence on 'marital unity' led to a lack of separate marriage settlements in seventeenth-century Massachusetts, Connecticut, and Pennsylvania.

10 The piecemeal studies that have been published are often contradictory. Though the southern system is usually portrayed as more patriarchal, Lebrun thought wives there had more independence, since they retained control of certain 'paraphernalia' they brought into marriage. It has also been pointed out that in the South and other regions of statutory law, men and women alike from various classes had considerable freedom in disposing of their property through wills, gifts, and provisions in the children's marriage contracts.

11 Both customary and statutory law gave all children some rights to shares in property owned by their parents, the child's *légitime*. Women in statutory regions kept paraphernalia along with power to make wills without husbands' permission, while those in customary regions had the protections attendant upon a marital community of property. There was a degree of primogeniture on the coast of Normandy, and the Norman code was relatively harsh. By contrast, in Bareges and Auvergne, patriarchy softened to such an extent that it was customary for a husband to move into a wife's home. For insightful discussion of one northwestern French code, see Locklin, *Women's Work*, chap. 3. Useful background on French law includes Sarah Hanley, 'Engendering the State: Family Formation and State Building in Early Modern France,' *French Historical Studies* 16 (1989): 4–27; and E. Le Roy Ladurie, 'A System of Customary Law: Family Structure and Inheritance Customs in 16th c. France,' in *Family and Inheritance: Rural Society in Western Europe, 1200–1800*, ed. Jack Goody, Joan Thirsk, and E.P. Thompson (Cambridge: Cambridge University Press, 1976), 89. It should be noted that the sixteenth century was a period of compilation of laws that often endured until the end of ancien régime. For a later century, see James Traer, *Marriage and the Family in 18th Century France* (Ithaca: Cornell University Press, 1980), 43–4. There is also some useful discussion in Suzanne Desan and Jeffrey Merrick, eds., *Family, Gender and Law in Early Modern France* (University Park, PA: Pennsylvania State University Press, 2009), and in Michel Puzelat, *La Vie rurale en France: XVIe–XVIIIe siècle* (Paris: Sedes, 1999), 34–5. It was common

for codes to allow nobles to show greater favouritism to an eldest son in order to keep large estates intact.

12 Simonton, *History of European Women's Work*, 27, 55. Students of both North and South have been surprised by the regularity with which wives were given full guardianship (*tutelle* and *cura*) of minor children or made universal heirs, often with responsibility for choosing which child would receive a privileged share of the estate, according to Barbara Diefendorf, 'Women and Property in Ancien Régime France: Theory and Practice in Dauphinée and Paris,' in *Early Modern Conceptions of Property*, ed. John Brewer and Susan Staves (London: Routledge, 1996), 187. Zoe Schneider's examination of local royal and seigneurial courts in upper Normandy where women were excluded from succession demonstrated a seemingly harsh code that was mitigated in practice, with women parties to a quarter of court cases, most often as plaintiffs. They obtained civil separations and rights to act as *femmes libres*, they acquired property with the assistance of colluding widows (who had greater rights), and they even inherited offices. Zoe Schneider, 'Women before the Bench: Female Litigants in Early Modern Normandy,' *French Historical Studies* 23, no. 1 (Winter 2000): 3–32.

13 According to France Parent, there is agreement among commentators that a revised Custom of Paris in 1580 placed increasing restraint not only on a wife's control of goods but also on her person, no longer allowing her to *ester en jugement* without her husband's consent unless so authorized or legally separated. France Parent, *Entre le juridique et le social. Le pouvoir des femmes au Québec au XVIIe siècle*, GREMF Cahier no. 42 (Quebec: Presses de L'Université Laval, 1991), 36.

14 Diefendorf, 'Women and Property,' 175. Evidence of French women's legal responsibility includes their co-signatures on apprenticeship indentures and mercantile legal documents, and their role in many areas of France ... (as) co-fermiers who signed legal undertakings, selling and buying land jointly with their spouses.

15 Diefendorf, 'Women and Property,' 170, 183–5.

16 Traer, *Marriage and the Family*, 45.

17 Hardwick, *Practice of Patriarchy*, 223.

18 Ibid., 68; on 147 Hardwick notes, 'The practice of "preferential partibility" – that is, the favoring of sons and the preservation of real property by assigning it to one or two sons while giving cash or movables to daughters and younger sons – has been noted among peasant communities in nineteenth century Brittany and in other partible inheritance regions. In the sixteenth and seventeenth centuries, this practice was not at all evident.'

19 Diefendorf, 'Women and Property,' 173–4. The wealthiest families in Dauphinée did, however, tend to favour their sons.

20 Grieco, 'Body, Appearance and Sexuality,' 3:74, citing Lebrun.

21 The size of the *augment* was usually one-third to one-half of the dowry.

22 Diefendorf, 'Women and Property,' 177–8.

23 That was the assessment of Jacques Poumarède in 'Le droit des veuves sous l'Ancien Régime (XVIIe–XVIIIe siècles) ou comment gagner son douaire,' in Haase Dubosc and Viennot, *Femmes et pouvoirs*, 72.

24 Until further studies are done, conclusions remain somewhat tentative. Some scholarship suggests there were aspects of deterioration in the period under discussion. For example, Mousnier and Hanley detected erosion of women's stature in royal law and political theory in the sixteenth and seventeenth centuries (Schneider, 'Women before the Bench,' 2n). Traer, *Marriage and the Family*, 40–1, asserted that seventeenth- and eighteenth-century royal courts consistently extended paternal control over marriage of children and countermanded church law with a developing double standard on adultery. In the eighteenth century, the burden of proof for paternity was shifted onto the mother's shoulders, sharply reducing court-ordered marriages. Grieco, 'Body, Appearance and Sexuality,' 80. Weighing against that were a decline in husbands' power of chastisement in the seventeenth century and increasing use of certain kinds of separation, discussed by Jean-Louis Flandrin, *Families in Former Times* (Cambridge: Cambridge University Press, 1979), 126.

25 Traer, *Marriage and the Family*, 138. When the new government decreed freedom of divorce in 1792, legislators soon had to swallow their own taunt of 'Have you ever seen a woman refuse marriage?' More women than men sought divorce. Numbers ran as high as one divorce for every four marriages for a few years in Paris. Divorce could be initiated by either party on equal terms – quite a departure from patriarchal marital traditions. Also revolutionary were abolition of the *lettres de cachet* once used to confine unruly wives and daughters, and the creation of a family court, particularly since the latter afforded mothers with rights over children that were nearly equal to those of fathers.

26 Traer, *Marriage and the Family*, 191, and his discussion 174–91; also Mary Ann Glendon, *The Transformation of Family Law: State, Law and Family in the United States and Western Europe* (Chicago: University of Chicago Press, 1989), 97. Traer writes that although some scholars claim that Napoleonic provisions governing the family reverted to the Roman law tradition of pre-Revolutionary southern France, 'the contention is not completely correct. While the *ancien régime*'s version of Roman law did permit a wide exercise of marital and paternal power, it also guaranteed a wife a measure of separate legal personality and permitted a daughter to bring an action against her father for establishment in marriage – rules that the civil code eliminated.'

On Revolutionary and Napoleonic changes, see also Irene Théry and Christian Biet, eds., *La Famille, La Loi, L'État de la Révolution au Code Civil* (Paris: Imprimerie Nationale, 1989). Especially useful are the contributions of P. Murat, 'La puissance paternelle et la Révolution française: essai de régénération de l'autorité des pères,' 390–411; and J-P Lévy, 'L'évolution du droit familial français de 1789 au Code Napoléon,' 507–14. The latter concurs with Traer on the code's explicit intent to buttress paternal authority and adds that 'presque toujours, quand elle a le choix, elle adopte la solution la plus défavorable a la femme, soit celle de l'Ancien Régime, soit celle de la Révolution.' See also the summary of Napoleonic Code changes in McMillan, *France and Women*, 37–40. Canadian scholar Brian Young concurs that during the ten-year preparation of the Napoleonic Code 'revolutionary principles were subordinated to defense of property and an authoritarian and patriarchal vision of the family.' Young, *The Politics of Codification: The Lower Canadian Civil Code of 1866* (Montreal and Kingston: McGill-Queen's University Press, 1994), 146.

27 Seccombe, *Millennium of Family Change*, 245.

28 After using more than one code in the 1640s and 1650s, the colony in 1664 officially adopted the Custom of Paris (in the same edict that established the *Compagnie des Indes*).

29 France Parent and Geneviève Postelec, 'Quand Thémis rencontre Clio: les femmes et le droit en Nouvelle-France,' *Cahiers de droit* (Québec) 36, no. 1 (1995): 301 (my translation).

30 To that end, widows who remarried lost dower and *preciput*, and widowers lost *preciput*. They were returned to the Community as the legacy for the heirs of the initial marriage.

31 Cited in Yves Zoltvany, 'Esquisse de la Coutume de Paris,' *RHAF* 25, no. 3 (1971): 378–9 (my translation). He discusses limitations on parental favouritism, 379–81. For additional discussion of the different rules affecting transmissions of whole seigneuries, see Parent, *Entre le juridique*, 42.

32 For a sampling of studies on this subject, see Sylvie Dépatie, 'La transmission du patrimoine dans les terroirs en expansion: un exemple canadien au XVIIIe siècle,' *RHAF* 44, no. 2 (1990): 171–87; Béatrice Craig, 'La Transmission des Patrimoines Fonciers dans le Haut-Saint-Jean au XIXe siècle,' *RHAF* 45, no. 2 (1991): 207–28; Louis Lavallée, 'La transmission du patrimoine dans la seigneurie de Laprairie 1667–1760,' in *Évolution et Éclatement du Monde Rural*, ed. Joseph Goy and J-P Wallot (Montreal: Presses de l'Université de Montréal, 1986), 341–51; Louis Michel, 'Héritage et établissement dans des populations rurales en croissance. Premier aperçu de la situation dans les deux paroisses de Varennes et Verchères en 1700, 1720 et

1740,' in *Famille et Marché: XVIe–XX siècles*, ed. C. Dessureault, John Dickinson, and Joseph Goy, 299–322 (Montreal: Septentrion, 2003).

33 For percentages on marriage contracts and acceptance of a community of goods in different settings, see B. Bradbury, P. Gossage, E. Kolish, and A. Stewart, 'Property and Marriage: The Law and the Practice in Early 19th Century Montreal,' *Histoire Sociale / Social History* 26 (1993): 9–40; and also Nathalie Pilon, 'Le destin de veuves et de veufs de la région de Montréal au milieu du XVIIIe siècle. Pour mieux comprendre la monoparentalité dans le Québec préindustriel' (MA thesis, Université de Montréal, 2000). Eighty per cent of couples in New France wrote marriage contracts. Overwhelmingly they indicated their desire to enter a community of goods.

34 Pilon, 'Le destin de veuves,' 77–80. Pilon, like Zoltvany, offers lucid definitions and explanations of relevant provisions of the Custom of Paris.

35 Yves Landry, ed., *Pour le Christ et le roi: La vie au temps des premiers Montréalais* (Montreal: Libre expression, 1992), 145.

36 This latter figure applies to the period after 1716 in Quebec City. The material on widows is drawn from Josette Brun, 'Gender, Family, and Mutual Assistance in New France: Widows, Widowers and Orphans in Eighteenth-Century Quebec,' in *Mapping the Margins: Families and Social Discipline in Canada, 1700–1975*, ed. N. Christie and M. Gauvreau (Montreal and Kingston: McGill-Queen's University Press, 2004), 58n; Danielle Gauvreau, *Québec, une ville et sa population au temps de la Nouvelle-France* (Sillery: Presses de l'Université de Québec, 1991), 115; Serge Lambert, 'Les pauvres de la société de 1681 a 1774' (PhD diss., Université de Laval dissertation, 1990), 225. On the remarriage of widows with young children and the reluctance of older ones to remarry, being said not to want 'a new master,' see Pilon, 'Le destin de veuves,' 47.

37 Zoltvany, 'Esquisse de la Coutume,' 370. See also Pilon's lucid outline of such provisions, 'Le destin de veuves,' 85. On encumbered English dowers, see Hunt, *Middling Sort*, 165.

38 In addition, the widow (and in this case the widower as well) had a right to the *preciput.* Dower and *preciput* were sometimes prefixed in the marriage contract but were more often evaluated according to an inventory of goods taken after the husband's death. Often *preciput* was one-third to half the size of the dower and included goods such as bed, clothes, and livestock, in addition to money.

39 Particularly helpful in clarifying widows rights is Parent, *Entre le juridique,* 40–1.

40 Pilon, 'Le destin de veuves,' 120, notes this trend.

41 As with all such contracts among people who possessed little, these may

have presented a somewhat idealized image of what was actually available. See the discussion in Luce Vermette, 'Les donations: activités domestiques et genre de vie 1800–1820 and 1850–1870,' in *Évolution et éclatement du monde rurale: structures, fonctionnement et évolution différentielle des sociétés rurales françaises et québécoises, XVIIe–XXe siècles*, ed. Joseph Goy and J-P Wallots (Montreal: Presses de l'Université de Montréal, 1986), 512.

42 Lorraine Gadoury, *La Famille dans son intimité* (Montreal: Hurtubise, 1998), 36.

43 This case is cited in Brun, 'Gender, Family, and Mutual Assistance.'

44 Susanna Moodie, *Life in the Clearings versus the Bush* (New York, 1855), 291. For another case, see Katherine McKenna's discussion of the unmarried daughter of the Powell family dependent on her siblings' goodwill and shifting needs for her services. K. McKenna, 'Options for Elite Women in Early Upper Canadian Society: The Case of the Powell Family,' in *Historical Essays on Upper Canada: New Perspectives*, ed. J.K. Johnson and Bruce Wilson, 401–24 (Ottawa: Carleton University Press, 1989).

45 For instances, see Brun, 'Gender, Family and Mutual Assistance.'

46 Parent, *Entre le juridique*, 185.

47 Ibid., 70–86.

48 Ibid., 185; Parent and Postelec, 'Quand Thémis rencontre Clio,' 301. Parent's study found that many of the women had been widows at some point. However, since some had remarried, in the final tally nearly two-thirds of the women were married, so marital judicial incapacity did not seem a great deterrent (311–12). John Dickinson's study *Justice et justiciables: La procédure civile a la Prévoté de Québec, 1667–1759* (Toronto: n.p., 1977) noted the predominance of widows and single women who had reached the age of majority among the women who appeared, which seems to link economic activity to the judicial capacity those groups enjoyed. The status of '*femme marchande*' was apparently seldom invoked in New France (Parent, *Entre le juridique*, 38).

49 Parent, *Entre le juridique*, 87–98, 133–7, 185, 188; Parent and Postelec, 'Quand Thémis rencontre Clio,' 299–313.

50 Josette Brun, thesis summary, *Le veuvage en Nouvelle-France. Genre, dynamique familiale et stratégies de survie dans deux villes coloniales du XVIIIe siècle, Québec et Louisbourg* (PhD diss., Université de Montréal, 2000), iii. For the subsequently published version of these findings, see Brun, *Vie et mort du couple en Nouvelle-France*, 33, 97.

51 Brun, 'Gender,' 37.

52 Preliminary results of the research of Benoit Grenier and Catherine Ferland presented at the French Colonial Historical Society in Paris June 2010 in their paper 'Absence des hommes, pouvoir des femmes: Les procuratrices

a Québec au XVIIIe siècle.' A version also appears in Grenier and Ferland's edited volume, *Femmes, Culture et Pouvoir: Relecture de l'histoire au féminin* (Quebec: Presses de l'Université Laval, 2011).

53 Brun, 'Gender,' 37.

54 Cugnet in 1775 did indicate, without elaborating, that Canada had adopted customs of its own regarding *cura* and *tutelle* that differed from those of France. François-Joseph Cugnet, *Traité abrégé des anciennes loix, coutumes et usages de la colonie du Canada auhourd'huy province de Québec* (Quebec: G. Brown, 1775).

6. Noble Codes, Colonial Translations

1 Miquelon, *New France 1701–1744*, portrays the early colony struggling in the shadow of century-long French economic depression and other difficulties, and failing to repay the investment even when times improved: 'Between 1701 and 1744 Canada remained a frustration, a colony that always fell short of the promise it seemed to hold. Its role in the story of empire ... was to be not so much economic as political' (94). A similarly lacklustre economy is portrayed in Dechene's *Habitants and Merchants*, which stresses the export of fur trade profits. Portrayals of 'backwardness' began with the Enlightenment critique of François Raynal in the 1770s, *A Philosophical and Political History of the Settlements and Trade of the Europeans in the East and West Indies* (London: Cadell, 1777), and were elaborated in nineteenth-century works such as François-Xavier Garneau's *Histoire du Canada depuis sa découverte Jusqu'a no jours*, 3 vols (Quebec: 1845–8), and François-Edme Rameau de Saint-Père's *La France aux colonies* (Paris: Jouby, 1859). Yves Zoltvany discusses the liberal critique of New France in *The Government of New France: Royal, Clerical or Class Rule?* (Scarborough, ON: Prentice Hall, 1971), chap. 2. For a penetrating modern analysis of this ancien regime 'society of orders' that is unburdened by the pejorative overtones of the earlier liberal critique, see Miquelon, *New France*, chap. 11, 'The Old Regime: Linkages.' Louise Dechene added the important notion that the Turner thesis 'mistakes the locale for the cause,' that Canadian colonists did not innovate as they moved further west because, unlike their American contemporaries, they lacked the capital to do so. Dechene, *Habitants and Merchants*, 282. See also Jean Hamelin, *Économie et Société en Nouvelle France* (Quebec: Presses de l'Université Laval, 1970); and Fernand Ouellet, 'Propriété seigneuriale et groupes sociaux dans la vallée du Saint-Laurent (1663–1840),' *Mélanges d'histoire du Canada-français offerts au professeur Marcel Trudel* (Ottawa: Éditions Université d'Ottawa, 1978).

2 These changes are discussed in chapters 1 and 5 of this book. There are

also summaries of them in Anderson and Zinsser, *History of Their Own,*
2:96–9, 112–22; Roland Mousnier, *La famille, l'enfant et l'éducation en France
et en Grande-Bretagne du XVIe au XVIIe siècle* (Paris: centre de documentation
universitaire, 1975), 319–31. While the middle and upper classes assimilated
the new gender attitudes, working-class women found that class could still
outweigh gender in regards to their status and the heavy labour expected
of them. Deborah Simondon, as we saw in chapter 1, argued that after the
French Revolution, 'a clearly articulated and formulated ideology of womankind emerged which was relevant to European women of all classes, was
propagated and diffused on an unprecedented scale' (*History of European
Women's Work*, 69). Autonomy of convents was curtailed too with the destruc-
tion of Port Royal and then more decisively, as chapter 1 indicated, during
the Revolution.

3 At Library and Archives Canada, the MG1, C11A series contains most of the
correspondence from and about Madame de Repentigny. C11A, 1705, vol.
22, fols 343–6; 1705, vol. 23, fol. 193; 1706, vol. 24, fols 167–8; 1707, vol. 27,
fols 142–3; 1708, vol. 29, fols 251–2; and 1717, vol. 27, fols 142–3 outline
key activities, as does Colonial Series F, vol. 22, 348. Some of the relevant
documents on Agathe Saint-Père are printed in *RAPQ*, 1939–40; see also *Collection des manuscrits … relatifs à la Nouvelle France* (Quebec: Cote, 1883–4);
DCB, s.v. 'Legardeur de Repentigny, Pierre,' and 'Saint-Père, Agathe de';
Jean B.A. Ferland, *Cours d'Histoire du Canada* (Quebec, 1865), 2:392; Joseph-
Noel Fauteux, *Essai sur l'Industrie au Canada sous le régime français* (Quebec:
Proulx, 1927), 1:465–7; Marine Leland, 'Madame de Repentigny,' *Bulletin
des recherches historiques* (*BRH*), 1954, 75–7; E.Z. Massicotte, 'Agathe de St
Père,' *BRH*, 1944, 202–7; P-G. Roy, 'La Famille Le Gardeur de Repentigny,'
BRH, 1947, 165–76, 195–216, 227–47.

Was it a mistake when there was an eventual change in the wording of
Saint-Père's longstanding annual 200-*livre* gratifications, that of 1745 (C11A,
vol. 115, fol. 219) mentioning a factory founded at Quebec, when earlier
documents clearly indicate foundation in Montreal? Or was this Quebec
establishment possibly her daughter's work, the award being made to 'Mlle
de Repentigny' for 'manufacture des grosse couverts qu'elle a établi à Québec'? There had been several mistakes in payments (as officials pointed
out), undermining one's faith in the specific details of these documents.
For Saint-Père's request to the Crown for powder for her kinsman Augustin
de Courtemanche, see C11A, 1717, vol. 27, fols 142–3v. For some of her other business dealings, see 1716–17, vol. 123, fol. 309 (and relevant correspondence on 19 oct. 1716, 23 oct. 1716, 3 mars 1717, 29 août 1729). Relevant
too are ANQ-M, Fonds Famille de Repentigny; Musée McCord, Documents,
relating to New France 1638–1759, déc. 1710, janv. 1711.

Although it is always hard to weigh the truthfulness of colonial petitions, it is possible Saint-Père's fortunes declined. By the time of her 1747 death, officials asked for the transfer of her 200 *livre* pension to her unmarried daughter, claiming she needed it. They asserted that Saint-Père, having established some of her manufactures at her own expense, was the main reason 'qu'elle n'avoit pas laissé de bien a sa famille.' C11A, 1747, vol. 87, fol. 161. Another puzzle is that in 1709 Intendant Raudot informed the Crown that Saint-Père (who was fifty-two and would live for another thirty-eight years) as 'a very elderly lady who deserves whatever graces you can bestow.' 1709, vol. 30, fol. 271ff.

4 Early Montreal inventories confirm that settlers possessed little in the way of cloth-making equipment such as spinning wheels, carders, and looms, necessitating the purchase of cloth. In 1707, 120 *aunes* (ells) a day were being produced. An English ell is about 114 centimetres or forty-five inches, with the measure varying somewhat in different countries. On the homespun *surtouts*, see C11A, 1708, vol. 29, fols 251–2. A useful source on colonial clothing is Suzanne and André Gousse, *Costume in New France from 1740 to 1760: A Visual Dictionary* (Chambly, QC: La Fleur de Lyse, 1997).

5 The key primary sources on the Ramezay women are in C11A, vols. 48ff.; and in MG18, H54. There are biographies of members of the Ramezay family in the *DCB*. See also Ovide Lapalice, *Histoire de la Seigneurie Massue* (Montreal: Société historique, 1930); E-Z Massicote, 'Un Femme d'Affaires du Régime Français,' *BRH*, 1931, 530; Victor Morin, 'Les Ramezay et leur Château,' *Cahiers des Dix* 3 (1938): 9–72; Pierre-Georges Roy, *La Famille Ramezay* (Levis: 1910). *DCB* biographer Helen Paré advises when and why these sources should be used with caution. She does not specifically address the claim of Fauteux, *Essai dur l'Industrie au Canada*, 1:159, 204–15, 442–3, who identifies Louise de Ramezay's tannery as one in the couteau Saint-Louis, which she purchased from the Bélair family and was expanding in 1753 along with Montreal tanners to open new *boutiques*.

6 Governor de Ramezay, who began the business, encountered theft and shipping problems. Madame de Ramezay's statement is found in C11A, 1726, vol. 48, fols 207–10. The widow claimed her venture would have succeeded if given the same advantages the Crown offered to Abbé Lepage a few years later.

7 *DCB*, s.v. 'Chartier de Lotbinière, Louis-Théandre.'

8 She is also discussed in A. Cimon, *Les Ursulines de Québec* (Quebec, 1863), 1:484. The governor's biography appears in the *DCB*.

9 Madame would subsequently present her own sons to the King. Three generations of Vaudreuils would continue to seek court favour, tendering 'Canadiana' gifts such as bark canoes and a doe. These gifts seem to have been

part of an early-eighteenth-century court rage for the exotic, which saw Intendant Begon proffering deer, swans, partridges, cranes, *outardes*, bears, and beavers to his masters at Versailles. C11A, 1724, vol. 46, fols 239–40; and 1726, vol. 48, fols 226–7.

10 Zoltvany added that her arrival at the French Court 'paid rich dividends,' for Madame de Vaudreuil 'won the favour of Pontchartrain and used her influence to consolidate her husband's position in Canada.' See his 'Joybert de Soulanges et de Marson, Louise-Élisabeth de,' *DCB*. Zoltvany's entry contains an excellent compilation of sources of Madame Vaudreuil. Particularly useful discussions of the family are found in Francis Hammang, *The Marquis de Vaudreuil* (Bruges: Université Louvain, 1938), 110, and Yves Zoltvany, *Philippe de Rigaud de Vaudreuil* (Toronto: McClelland and Stewart, 1974), 215, which assess Mme Vaudreuil's influence. The key colonial correspondence for Madame Vaudreuil is C11A, vols. 21–49, some of which is printed in *RAPQ*, 1942–3, 1946–7, and *Collection des manuscrits*, vol. 1.

11 For contemporaries' criticisms of Madame Vaudreuil, see 'Mémoire sur l'état présent du Canada,' *RAPQ*, 1922–3, 50; also C11A, 1712, vol. 33, fols 265–81; and 'Joybert de Soulanges,' *DCB*.

12 For examples of Madame de Vaudreuil's advocacy, see C11A, 1696, vol. 120, fols 40–4, 121–2; 1711, vol. 63, fols 233–5; vol. 125, fols 257–8; 1717, vol. 37, fol. 34v; 1727, vol. 49, fols 340–2; 1732–3, vol. 56, fols 35–40v; also *RAPQ*, 1938–9, 123; 1939–40, 377; 1946–7, 373, 386. For some refusals, see C11A, 1717, vol. 37, fols 169–71v. Madame de Frontenac's political advocacy is mentioned in 1681, vol. 5, fols 192–7. On land concessions to Madame de Soulanges, see 1716, vol. 123, fols 300–1. Zoltvany in *DCB*, s.v. 'Rigaud de Vaudreuil, Philippe de,' credits Madame de Vaudreuil with securing a captaincy for their youngest son in St Domingue in 1725. On survivors' benefits, see C11A, 1731, vol. 56, fols 35–40.

13 LAC, Colonial Series B, 1712, vol. 34, fol. 147; also in *RAPQ*, 1947–8, 192.

14 Elisabeth Begon, *Lettres au cher fils* (Montreal: Hurtubise, 1972), 204. In the 1740s Madame Vaudreuil's daughters were still collecting rent on the Montreal house she built, and the Ramezay children were collecting rent on their parental home too. C11A, 1741, vol. 115, fols 24, 218v. On the advantageously placed seigneuries, see 1712, vol. 33, fols 122–36.

15 *DCB*, s.v. 'Joybert de Soulanges.'

16 C11A, vol. 36, fols 308–9, 315–16; *DCB*, s.v. 'Joybert de Soulanges.' See C11A, 1710, vol. 31, fols 230–1, on the infanticide.

17 The term is Zoltvany's. On Cadillac and Duplessis, see C11A, 1705, vol. 23, fol. 181, and vol. 24, fols 191–5.

18 Lorraine Gadoury, *La Noblesse de Nouvelle France* (Montreal: Hurtubise, 1991), 156.

19 For a discussion of the permission accorded nobles to trade in New France without fear of derogation, see Sophie White, '"A Baser Commerce": Retailing, Class and Gender in French Colonial New Orleans,' *William and Mary Quarterly*, 3rd ser., 63, no. 3 (2006): 517–50.

20 Leslie Choquette's study of a large number of immigrants (sixteen thousand of an estimated thirty to sixty thousand who embarked) suggested that military personnel made up nearly a quarter. Leslie Choquette, *Frenchmen into Peasants: Modernity and Tradition in the Peopling of French Canada* (Cambridge, MA: Harvard University Press, 1997), 2, 112.

21 There are allusions to this substitution in Moogk, *La Nouvelle France*, 146; and in Philippe Panneton's novel *Thirty Acres* (Toronto: Macmillan, 1960), chap. 2. For a critical analysis of William Eccles's contentions about the role of military spending in the colonial budget, see C. Desbarats, 'Les deniers du Roi dans l'économie canadienne du XVIIIe siècle,' in Dépatie et al., *Vingt ans*, 189–207. On colonial expenditures as percentage of French budget, see Mathieu, *La Nouvelle France*, 165.

22 C11A, 1716, vol. 36, fols 97–9. On the numbers in Canada and in New France, as well as consideration of troops and of migrating Acadians, see Robert Larin, *Brève histoire du peuplement européen en Nouvelle-France* (Sillery: Septentrion, 2000), 161–4. See also Robert Lehaise, *Nouvelle France, English Colonies: Impossible Co-existence, 1606–1712* (Sillery: Septentrion, 2006), which stresses the imbalance between the two colonial groupings.

23 Gadoury, *La Noblesse*, 51. See also Moogk, *La Nouvelle France*, 168–73, for discussion of the varying noble identity of Canadian officials, his definition of nobility, and his inclusion of wholesale merchants as Canada's 'effective nobility.' That is broader than Gadoury's definition, which we follow here. Bougainville reported that the most illustrious colonial military families were a distinct group, which chose its marriage partners very carefully to reinforce its bloodlines. Frégault, *Le XVIIIe siècle canadien*, 292–3.

24 C11A, 1727, vol. 49, fols 43–4. For a list of two dozen noble families with written pedigrees compiled around 1743, see vol. 120, fols 407–9. Military engineer Louis Franquet would echo Hocquart's criticisms, for he judged officers poorly educated, though bright enough. Franquet, *Voyages et mémoires*, 56.

25 These included that of Madame Vaudreuil in the early eighteenth century and, around mid-century, Ramezay and Verchères relatives in the Lanaudière, Renaud d'Avène Des Méloizes/Péan and Beaubassin families who were attached to the circles of Intendant Bigot and General Montcalm. Their wit is noted in P-G Roy, *La Famille Tarieu de Lanaudière* (Levis, 1922), 84–5. See also Sophie Imbeault, *Les Tarieu de Lanaudière: une famille noble après la Conquête, 1760–1791* (Sillery: Septentrion, 2004); and *DCB*, s.v. 'Re-

naud D'Avene Des Méloizes, Angélique.' P-G Roy, *La Famille des Champs de Boishebert* (Levis, 1906), 25, describes two Quebec City salons of the 1750s that were renowned for their elegance and wit, hosted by Louise-Geneviève des Champs de Boishebert (granddaughter of Governor and Madame de Ramezay), and by Madame de Beaubassin.

26 Bacqueville de la Potherie, *Histoire de l'Amérique septentrionale*, 3rd ed. (Paris: Nyon, 1753), 1:279, 366. Martial ardour appears to have cooled towards the end of the regime, when thirst for profits at the posts may have come to preoccupy some of the officers, according to Louis Franquet and others. See also Moogk, *La Nouvelle France*, 190–1. For comments of Hocquart and Beauharnois on noble education and inclinations for travel and trade rather than for studying jurisprudence, see C11A, 1737, vol. 67, fols 95–144.

27 F-X de Charlevoix, *Histoire et description générale de la Nouvelle-France* (Montreal, 1976), 1:399. Intendant Gilles Hocquart too spoke of the universal desire of gentlemen and children of officers to enter the service. C11A, 1737, vol. 67, fols 95–107. On officers' enthusiasm for making their name in military raids, see Evan Haefeli and Kevin Sweeney, *Captors and Captives: The 1704 French and Indian Raid on Deerfield* (Boston: University of Massachusetts Press, 2003), chap. 2. Colonial officials included the caste-like criteria for choosing cadets: 'la naissance, l'ancienneté' in addition to 'leurs services et ceux de leurs pères.' C11A, 1731, vol. 54, fols 97–99v. See also 1729, vol. 51, fols 145v, 276–85.

28 *DCB*, s.v. 'Legardeur de Repentigny, Pierre.' On their twelve-year-old son's service, see C11A, 1717, vol. 27, fols 142–3; for subsequent family military history, 1738, vol. 69, fols 132–3.

29 There is a memorandum of Nicolas-Roch's service in C11A, 1748, vol. 97, fol. 180. For a family military saga in the same vein, see the description of Crevier family service, which included eight-year-old cadets and fourteen-year-old warriors. 1722, vol. 124, fol. 444.

30 'The Social, Economic and Political Significance of the Military Establishment in New France,' in Eccles, *Essays on New France*, 115–16. Historians such as Dale Miquelon, Peter Moogk and Donald Horton have followed Eccles in employing this term. Louise Dechene's *Habitants and Merchants of Montreal* works in a somewhat similar vein in showing how closely the social categories in New France came to resemble those in France. Such interpretations have tended to undermine Cameron Nish's portrayal of the *bourgeois gentilhomme* as a central figure in colonial history, stressing instead the continuing hierarchical nature of the society and exclusiveness of nobles and officers. Categories were not watertight in either metropolis or colony, and

there were intermarriages, particularly of noblemen to bourgeois women, which did not result in derogation.

31 Merriam-Webster, *Third International Dictionary*. On caste, see also David Sills, ed., *International Encyclopedia of the Social Sciences* (New York: Macmillan, 1968), 2:334.

32 Franquet, *Voyages et mémoires*, 148.

33 Gadoury, *La Noblesse*, 57–68, 124, 140–9.

34 Nobles had a rate of vocations five to ten times higher than commoners. Gadoury, *La Noblesse*, 62–8, female vocations far outnumbering male ones.

35 Ibid., 20. The ascetic governor was Jean de Lauson in the 1650s, cited in Moogk, *La Nouvelle France*, 159.

36 Various transgressions of nobles are retailed in Boyer, *Les Crimes et les Châtiments au Canada Français*, and in R-L Seguin, *La Vie Libertine en Nouvelle-France au XVIIe siècle* (Ottawa: Lemeac, 1972). For other cases, such as the Saint-Ours-Blainville trial, see C11A, 1705, vol. 22, fols 326–42; and 1711, vol. 32, fols 10–22. For the storied Repentigny murder of his landlord, see *DCB*, s.v. 'Jacquin, *dit* Philibert, Nicolas' (and C11A, 1748 for appeals of officials and bishops for leniency).

37 The significance of physical grace is discussed in M. Motley, *Becoming a French Aristocrat* (New Jersey: Princeton University Press), 57–8, 140–9. La Potherie noted, as did many other observers, that Canadian elites were passionately fond of dancing (*Histoire de l'Amérique septentrionale*, 1:279). He also noted their refinement.

38 Governor Vaudreuil, for example, surrounded himself with a company of guards others saw as useless. C11A, 1724, vol. 46, fols 324–7v. In Quebec City the members of the noblesse were reported to attend dinner parties separate from those of other elites. La Potherie, *Histoire de l'Amérique septentrionale*, 1:278. One wonders whether colonial onlookers admired this showy group. When Madame Elisabeth Begon returned to mid-eighteenth-century France after many years in the colony, she observed less respect for rank there than in Canada; and officers arriving from France were surprised how highly St Louis Cross–holders were regarded. Nobles considered it a birthright to strike or cane inferiors, and instead of hitting back, the inferior might be heard to say, 'Why are you beating me? I did nothing wrong.' Likewise merchants would swallow losses and go on extending credit to profligate nobles (Moogk, *La Nouvelle France*, 149–70). But commoners were known to resist young nobles who tried to get foot soldiers to carry their packs, who got too light a sentence for harming a non-noble. Gadoury's fine study of the noblesse in New France contains much demographic information, and we await scholarship that will investigate popular views of this

group's pretensions. Zoltvany, *Vaudreuil*, mentions the baggage incident. *DCB*, s.v. 'Legardeur de Repentigny, Pierre-Jean-Baptiste-François-Xavier,' notes public opinion against noble exemption for his killing. Governor Vaudreuil was among those said to physically assault an inferior who displeased him (*DCB*, s.v. 'Ramezay, Claude de').

39 C11A, 1667, vol. 2, fols 355–9; and 1669, vol. 3, fols 149–53.

40 Franquet, *Voyages et mémoires*, 56; La Potherie, *Histoire de l'Amérique septentrionale*, 1:366–8. See also Eccles, 'Military Establishment.' As we have noted, some French observers felt trade concerns were supplanting this martial spirit late in the regime.

41 *DCB*, s.v. 'Ramezay, Claude de.'

42 C11A, 1705, vol. 22 (12 Oct. 1705, Ramezay to the minister).

43 J. Peristiany makes this point in *Honour and Shame: The Values of Mediterranean Society* (Chicago: University of Chicago Press, 1996), 11.

44 Roy, *Famille Ramezay*, 7.

45 See, for example, inventory of the Chateau St Louis, *RAPQ*, 1921–2, 238–61. Other works casting light on aristocratic material culture include the catalogue *Chateau Ramezay* (Montreal: Société d'Archéologie et de Numismatique, section féminine, 1984); Ernest Gagnon, *Le Fort et le Chateau St Louis* (Quebec: Beauchemin, 1908); John Hare, Marc Lafrance, and D-T Ruddel, *Histoire de la ville de Québec* (Quebec: Boreal, 1987); Yves Landry, ed., *Pour le Christ et le Roi* (Montreal: Libre Expression, 1992); Monique Eleb-Vidal with Anne Debarre-Blanchard, *Architectures de la vie privée: Maisons et mentalités XVIIe–XIX siècles* (Brussels: Archives d'architecture moderne, 1994).

46 Franquet, *Voyages et mémoires*, 134–5, 140.

47 C11A, 1724, vol. 46, fols 117–22. About a third of servants in Quebec City were male, indicating the colony may have resisted French and English trends towards feminization of service. The history of service in New France remains to be written, though Francine Barry made a start with 'Familles et domesticité féminine au milieu du 18e siècle,' in *Maîtresses de Maison, Maîtresses d'école*, ed. N. Fahmy-Eid, M. Dumont, and F. Barry (Montreal: Boréal, 1983), 223–35. For references to various kinds of servants accompanying the nobility, see C11A, 1713, vol. 123, fols 12–13 (a fire in the intendant's palace killed Begon's secretary and *valet de chambre* plus two *'femmes de Madame Begon'*). C11A, 1716, vol. 123, fol. 317 indicates the governor's sea crossing with sixteen domestics; the next year Madame de Vaudreuil was granted new staff for the Chateau St Louis: a lackey and a *maître d'hôtel*. Governor and intendant each sailed in 1732 with a *valet de chambre*, among other servants. A *Lieutenant du roi* sailing for Trois-Rivières with wife and child brought four domestics in 1717 (C11A, 1717, vol. 37, fol. 215; 1732,

vol. 58, fol. 57). Often orphans were pressed into service, suggesting that Charlevoix's assertion that adult Canadians spurned work as servants held some truth (cited in Moogk, *La Nouvelle France*, 218). On gender trends, see Yvon Desloges, *A Tenant's Town: Quebec in the Eighteenth Century* (Ottawa: Parks Canada, 1991), 60–1, which discusses the censuses of 1716 and 1744: along with 7–8 of unknown sex, there were 35 male servants and 77 female ones in 1716; 77 males and 161 females in 1744, an immaterial decline in females, from 68.75 to 67.64 per cent. Claudette Lacelle's *Urban Domestic Servants in Nineteenth Century Canada* (Ottawa: Parks Canada, 1987), pointed to a feminizing trend that made for noticeable differences between the early and the late nineteenth century. Servant numbers overall were modest in New France, representing only 5–6 per cent of the Quebec City populace between 1716 and 1744, whereas in many eighteenth-century towns in France they constituted a tenth of the urban population. See Sarah Maza, *Servants and Masters in Eighteenth Century France: The Uses of Loyalty* (Princeton: Princeton University Press, 1983), 25, 314. Fewer than 30 per cent of households had servants, and on average they employed fewer than two. Over the course of the eighteenth century, smaller rooms connected by halls were appearing in French patrician homes, and domestics became more confined to kitchen, hall, and antechamber, with bells and pulleys introduced in order to summon them from a distance. Maza, *Servants*, 253–4. On spatial considerations, see also Peter Ward, *A History of Domestic Space, Privacy and the Canadian Home* (Vancouver: UBC Press, 1999).

48 C11A, 1724, vol. 46 (Madame de Vaudreuil to Maurepas, 29 oct. 1724). Madame Vaudreuil was appalled by the rudeness of the Quebec to which she returned in 1724, thefts and illicit brandy sales to natives common in the town, and the courtyard of her Chateau St Louis residence turned into a dangerous gunpowder manufactory. She also found the cost of living appallingly high.

49 Franquet, *Voyages et mémoires*, 142.

50 C11A, 1704, vol. 22, fols 71–81; 1706, vol. 24, fols 205v–7. In 1718 Madame de la Forest reported she had six children (she had married in 1680, so some were likely adults by then). She had a share of the Tadoussac fur trade and later purchased the county of the Isle de Orléans – which made her (until the purchase was rescinded for non-payment) a countess. Colonial records indicate she was able to persuade the metropolitan government to give considerable deliberation over many years to her many, mostly unsuccessful, land claims. Some combination of her aristocratic pretensions, forceful personality, and factional partisanship caused a number of colonial officials, including the Vaudreuil family, to deem her a detestable character.

51 C11A, 1723, vol. 45, fols 312–13v. The Beaujeus were a noble family whose
   progenitor, having access to the French court, kept his court ties after
   migrating to the colony. In 1706 he married Thérèse Migeon, widow of
   Charles Juchereau de St Denys, who had been lieutenant-general of Montreal and a prominent fur trader. His wife's role in the trade is discussed in
   chapter 4. She was now apparently following Madame de Vaudreuil's trajectory and becoming a courtier, as *remueuse* for the *enfants du roi*. On the family. see *DCB*, s.v. 'Lienard de Beaujeu, Louis.' (It seems more likely that the
   remueuse position related to looking after baby linen rather than champagne
   supplies, though my dictionaries propose both possibilities).
52 See the governor's *Inventaire après décès* in *RAPQ*, 1921–2, 237.
53 Gadoury, *La Noblesse*, 76, found a nine-year gap for nobles.
54 Ibid., 146–51. On infancy and childhood, see also Denise Lemieux, *Les petits
   innocents: L'Enfance en Nouvelle France* (Québec: L'Institut québécois de re-
   cherche sur la culture, 1985).
55 C11A, 1705, vol. 22, C. Ramezay to the minister, 12 oct. 1705; Lapalice,
   Histoire de la Seigneurie Massue, 30. Some noble mothers such as Madame
   Begon and Madame Denys instructed one or more children in their homes
   (Magnuson, *Education in New France*, 84). Boys could study navigation and
   fortifications in the colony with the Jesuits and the Charron Brothers. The
   Denonville family took school friends of their daughters into their home,
   the gubernatorial mansion.
56 C11A, 1729, vol. 51 (Hocquart to Maurepas, 25 oct. 1729); *RAPQ*, 1946–7,
   409; Eccles, 'Military,' 116. On Hertel's death, see C11A, 1748, vol. 91, fols
   245–6, in which Hertel Sr petitioned that 'my poor child' be replaced in the
   army by one of the younger children; see also Moogk, *La Nouvelle France*,
   181.
57 John Bosher, 'The Family in New France,' in *In Search of the Visible Past*, ed.
   Barry Gough, 1–13 (Waterloo, ON: Wilfrid Laurier University Press, 1975).
   On occasion a noblewoman such as sixteen-year-old orphan Marie Jeanne
   Renaud D'Avène Desmeloizes braved the fury of an elder by resisting his
   choice of groom for her; her grandfather gave the rejected suitor part of
   the property to which she was entitled. A correction of Bosher's figures, the
   age of majority is taken from Mathieu, *La Nouvelle France*, 187.
58 For an overview and bibliography see Lenard Berlanstein, 'The French in
   Love and Lust,' *French Historical Studies* 27, no. 2 (2004): 465–79. Various
   colonial scandals discussed in C11A include 1731, vol. 56, fols 203–4; 1735,
   vol. 61, fols 225, 259–60; vol. 63, fols 27–42; vol. 64, fols 109–16; 1736, vol.
   65, fols 10–14; 1740, vol. 73, fols 15–16; 1742, vol. 78, fols 429–30; on sexual
   insults see Moogk, *La Nouvelle France*, 140.

59 Nicole Deschamps, ed., *Lettres au cher fils: correspondance d'Élisabeth Bégon avec son gendre (1748–1753)* (Montreal: Hurtubise, 1972).

60 C11A, 1722, vol. 44, fols 356–63; 1724, vol. 46, fols 73–4v, 232–8v.

61 Cliché, 'Unwed Mothers,' 39–52.

62 On the La Durantayes, see C11A, 1717, vol. 38, fols 226–7; 1720, vol. 41, fols 257–61; 1721, vol. 43, fols 320–31v; 1722, vol. 45, fols. 291–8. Gadoury, *La Noblesse*, discusses illegitimacy rates among the noblesse. For the wider population, see Cliché, 'Unwed Mothers,' 41–52, which also discusses the La Durantayes and Pierre St Ours. On foundlings, see also *DCB*, s.v. 'Martin de Lino, Jean-François.' On colonial illegitimacy up to 1730, see Lyne Paquette and Réal Bates, 'Les naissances illégitimes sur les rives de Saint-Laurent avant 1730,' *Revue d'histoire de l'Amérique française* 40 (1986): 239–52.

63 See, for example, Moogk, *La Nouvelle France*, 140. Historian of New Netherlands Dennis Sullivan and I both take issue with such an interpretation of crude epithets, which may be more a reflection of the lack of imagination of the often-inebriated slanderers than a reliable indicator of social norms. Sullivan found the same two everyday slanders (men as crooks and women as whores) in Dutch New York, but explained that in a sense 'there was little difference between the two terms,' because they both suggested their victims were 'shiftless rabble, untrustworthy to do an honest day's work or to oversee a well-managed, steady, godly household.' Dennis Sullivan, *The Punishment of Crime in Colonial New York: The Dutch Experience in Albany during the Seventeenth Century* (New York: Peter Lang, 1997), 120–7. See also Jan Noel, '"Fertile with Fine Talk": Ungoverned Tongues among Haudenosaunee Women and Their Neighbors,' *Ethnohistory* 57, no. 2 (2010): 201–23. For additional evidence that feminine honour was not based entirely on sexuality but 'included piety as a Christian, skill as a household manager, and devotion to one's children' and being 'an honest worker,' see Nancy Locklin, *Women's Work and Identity in Eighteenth-Century Brittany* (Burlington, VT: Ashgate, 2007), chap. 4.

64 McMillan, *France and Women 1789–1914*, 3. Gadoury calculates that use of contraception appeared among the Canadian noblesse in the eighteenth century, affecting perhaps 20 to 25 per cent of couples (*La Noblesse*, 135).

65 Gadoury, *La Noblesse*, 130; on France, see McMillan, *France and Women 1789–1914*, 3.

66 Dispatches of Oct. 1734 include several commentaries on this affair. See also C11A, 1735, vol. 64, fol. 109; 1736, vol. 65, fols 10–14. Mlle de Leigne later married René Ovide Hertel de Rouville (to his mother's despair), a man who became a perfectly respectable judicial officer.

67 Bishop Saint-Vallier, who was not known for judiciousness, levelled the

charge against Montreal Governor Louis-Hector Callières and Madame
de Ramezay, according to Robert Lahaise and Noel Vallerand, *La Nouvelle-
France* (Montreal: Lanctot, 1999), 175.

68 John Lambert, *Travels through Canada, and the United States of North America,
in the Years 1806, 1807 and 1808* (London, 1816), 1:291–2.

69 Seguin, *La Vie Libertine*, 326, provides the evidence to identify the assailant
as Pierre and not some other member of the Repentigny clan. When a child
resulted from these assaults, Marie Delugré appealed to the governor general. The lack of a resultant enquiry or trial suggests an informal settlement
was made. See Gadoury, *La Noblesse*, 132–5, on this and another case of a
servant violated by a noble master. On the wild conduct a few years earlier
of young Legardeur and d'Ailleboust who 'ran about the streets of Montreal
and the surrounding countryside in the middle of the night disguised as
Indians, carrying guns and knives and stealing money from the purses of
those they encountered ... while threatening to kill and burn anyone who
denounced them,' see Dechene, *Habitants and Merchants*, 217.

70 Hocquart stalled Raimbault's promotion, despite his incredulity about the
liaison, since the alleged paramour was 'ugly and nearly fifty' and Raimbault
about sixty. On Raimbault, see C11A, 1729, vol. 51, fol. 291; 1730, vol. 53,
fol. 16; 1731, vol. 55, fols 71–2, and vol. 56, fols 40, 287–93; 1735, vol. 64,
fols 26–33; 1740, vol. 73, fols 16, 40; and his biography in *DCB*. Ladies dared
to quarrel even with Governor Vaudreuil himself about who should marry
whom. A misstep that displeased the governor could land an officer in punishment as severe as banishment from the colony (C11A, 1708, vol. 28, fol.
297).

71 La Potherie, *Histoire de l'Amérique septentrionale*, 367–8; see also Franquet,
Voyages et mémoires, 56. Governor Beauharnois and Intendant Dupuy observed, 'L'habitant est ici le plus à son aise mais l'officier n'a que ce qu'il lui
faut pour vivre ... sa famille, communément nombreuse, perd tout quand
il cesse d'être' (C11A, vol. 48, fols 90–105). The problem persisted in 1747,
when La Galissoniere reported Canada's surplus of 'braves gens privés de
récompenses' and the large, poor families in the officer class (1747, vol. 87,
fols 276–9). Rations for needy wives at Ft Fréderic were sought in 1742, vol.
77, fols 344–51. See also 1716, vol. 123, fol. 399; and 1750–1, vol. 119, fols
364–70, 400–4, regarding Crown expenditures to support widows, veterans,
and orphaned daughters of officers. Non-noble widows also received occasional help (1737, vol. 69, fol. 72; 1742, vol. 78, fol. 39). If a nobleman *had*
money but neglected his children, his income might be garnisheed in their
favour (1727, vol. 44, fols 114–15). The St Ours family fieldwork is cited in
Greer, *Peasant, Lord and Merchant)*, 10. As Greer points out, noble 'poverty'

was relative. The comparison group would have been the minor or *campagnard* nobility of France, not destitute commoners.

72 See C11A, vols 52–8, for a rich sampling of petitions. Fur trading licences or *congés* were usually resold to a trader.

73 Cited in Guy Frégault, 'Un Cadet de Gascogne: Philippe de Rigaud de Vaudreuil,' *Revue d'histoire de l'Amérique française* 5 (1951–2): 21.

74 *RAPQ,* 1926–7, 111–31; C11A, 1690, vol. 11, fols 159–63; 1699, vol. 17, fols 66–75.

75 C11A, 1724 (Vaudreuil and Beauharnois to Maurepas, 2 oct. 1724); *DCB,* s.v. 'Rigaud de Vaudreuil, Philippe de'; Morin, 'Les Ramezay,' 43.

76 C11A, vol. 50 (24 mai 1728, and correspondence of Madame de Ramezay to Maurepas, 8 oct. 1728); vol. 56 (Mme Ramezay to Maurepas, 25 août 1731); vol. 58 (Hocquart to Maurepas, 7 oct. 1731 and 15 oct. 1732). Estate business was handled in 1719; see MG18, H54, De Ramezay Family Documents, p. 1578. The family won support from Governor Beauharnois, who felt the old enmity between the more successful Vaudreuils and the de Ramezays left the latter in need of his protection. C11A, 1732, vol. 57, fol. 339. Gedeon de Catalogne in 1712 indicated how frequently men were away from their seigneuries. See also Moogk, *La Nouvelle France,* 184, 212.

77 For deeds and correspondence outlining the land transactions of the Ramezay siblings, see MG18, H54, particularly 28 fév.–17 août 1752, 5 mai 1761, 10 sept. 1763. The whole series between 1759 and 1769 sheds fascinating light on the impact of the conquest on this family. Lapalice, *Histoire de la Seigneurie Massue,* 25–36, outlines many of the transactions and disputes regarding the family land claims. Another trading single woman, who appeared in our chapter 3 was Mlle D'Allonne. She is documented in C11A, 1700, vol. 18, fols 220–7; 1717, vol. 37, fols 140–3; 1717, vol. 38, fols 119–20; 1718, vol. 124, fols 29–30, as well as in her biography in *DCB.*

78 On Marie-Louise Denys de la Ronde and the D'Ailleboust family, see Gadoury, 'Une famille noble en Nouvelle France,' 74–154; and Young, '"… sauf les périls,"' 34–46, which also discusses the de Ramezay women; see also Young's *Kin, Commerce and Community,* 28, 39–42.

79 Madame de Ramezay inherited a problematic enterprise. Governor de Ramezay claimed that a number of the 3,000 planks he milled in 1709 were stolen, and there were shipping problems. Though in 1726 his widow declared herself in a position to fill the hold of the King's ship with planks of oak and pine, she was not very successful either (C11A, 1726, vol. 48, fols 207–10). On the seigneurial front she secured an ordinance fining Sorel inhabitants for taking wheat to other mills. P.G. Roy, *Inventaire des Ordonnances*

des Intendants de la Nouvelle-France conservées aux Archives Provinciales de Québec (Beauceville: L'Eclaireur, 1919), 2:76.

80 Gadoury, 'Une famille noble en Nouvelle France,' 74–5, 93, 117, 127, discusses Madame D'Argenteuil and also Françoise Denys. See also Young, '"... sauf les périls,"' 39. On the Denys-Lanouguères, see *DCB*, s.v. 'Lanouguère, Thomas de.' This family became the Lanaudières, who were still producing witty and forceful women long after the conquest, characters described with relish in the memoirs of Philippe Aubert de Gaspé.

81 See C11A, 1688, vol. 10, fols 147–62; 1691, vol. 11, fols 531–42 on the seventeenth-century boutiques; see Moogk, *La Nouvelle France*, 154–60 on Lotbinière.

82 ANQ-M, Pinguet de Vaucour, J-N, 29 avril et 4 mai, *procurations*; 5 oct. 1746, *inventaire*; 17 oct. 1746, *renonciation*; 21 oct. 1734, *obligation*; C11A, 1747, vol. 87, fols 171–2v; 1748, vol. 91, fols 24–5v; 1751, vol. 97, fol. 201v.

83 During the second Governor Vaudreuil's rule in Louisiana his wife was said to have strong interests in the posts, requiring the governor to manage in servile fashion the officer corps and many other people. It was said she had a shop from which she and her *maître d'hôtel* profited by selling all kinds of goods. See the two 1751 letters of Michel de la Rouville to the minister cited in P-G Roy, *La Famille Rigaud de Vaudreuil* (Lévis: n.p., 1938), 127–8. C11A, 1757, vol. 102, fols 43–5, contains Jeanne-Charlotte's appeal to the minister. See also White, 'A Baser Commerce,' 538–42, who notes that a high-ranking official accused her of running 'a storehouse at her house of all sorts of drugs, which her steward sells; and when he is not there she takes up the ell and measuring rods herself. Her husband ... gets a good revenue from it.' Selling dry goods through an agent as well as fur trade goods also numbered among her activities. On the younger Madame Vaudreuil, see also Guy Frequault's *Le Grand Marquis: Pierre de Rigaud de Vaudreuil et la Louisiane* (Montreal: IHAF, 1952).

84 For example, documents from 1725 show her variously contracting to build a house in Montreal in her husband's absence, arranging and paying for merchandise to be sent to him at Kiministiquia, and administering the St Ours seigneurie by granting one piece of land and seizing another for un-paid rent. Later she sold land, acting as her husband's procuratrice, even though he was back in Montreal. ANQ-M, Lepailleur, M., 5 fév. 1725, 26 juin 1725; Adhémar, J-B, 13 juin 1725; Raimbault, 20 juin 1725; Danré de Blanzy, L-C, 12 juin 1740. For Mlle de Repentigny's fur transaction, see C11A, 1717, vol. 37, fols 439–43.

85 C11A, 1731, vol. 55, fol. 100; 1747, vol. 89, fols 73, 84–103.

86 The most accessible archival source for Hocquart's remark on women having a disposition for business is in the transcribed version, C11A, 1737, vol.
67, C-2393, 40–62.

87 LAC, Baby Collection, Correspondence 2, Havy and Lefebvre to Mme Guy,
3 août 1745, 664–5.

88 On favouring officers' families, see C11A, 1740, vol. 74, fols 119–20; on
transfer of business powers, see LAC, Baby Collection, Correspondence,
2, Havy and Lefebvre to Mme Guy (3 août 1745), 664–5. On Roberge, see
Young, '"… sauf les périls,"' 38.

89 Massicotte, 'Agathe St Père,' 202–7.

90 Signed Agatte de St Père de Repentigny, this letter was written to the colonial minister 13 October 1705. Under Jean Talon's regime in the 1670s
there had been efforts to establish manufacture of linen and cloth. For
habitants re-spinning old wool, see C11A, 1706, vol. 24, fols 137–44, 331–52.
For Saint-Père's report of the twenty-eight Montrealers who now knew how
to weave, see 1706, vol. 24, fols 331–52; on the Montreal Hôpital Général as
a site for some of this work, 1706, vol. 25, fols 261–4. For the series of letters
describing her work, see 1705, vol. 22, fols 343–6, and vol. 23, fol. 193; 1706,
vol. 24, fols 167–8; 1707, vol. 27, fols 142–3; 1708, vol. 29, fols 251–2.

91 Ibid. Saint-Père does not allude to her husband in her series of letters beginning in 1705, which described her enterprise to the minister. But he
does make a seemingly pro forma appearance in various contracts signed by
her and including the phrase 'authorized by Pierre LeGardeur de Repentigny.' See, for example, LAC, Baby Collection, deeds of 26 fév. 1717, 3 mars
1717, 29 août 1729.

92 C11A, 1731, vol. 55, fols. 377–7v; 1733, vol. 60, fols 410–13.

93 Louise was respectfully addressed by the bishop (who gave her a small piece
of land she coveted) as a 'most noble lady.' Governor Beauharnois made a
special point of extending his protection to the family long after its head
had died.

94 This dictum found in the work of the early Victorian writer Mrs Ellis is
quoted in Davidoff and Hall, *Family Fortunes*, 287 (see chapter 1 above).
Davidoff and Hall exaggerate somewhat in saying she expressed the view
with 'chilling finality,' since in her text Mrs Ellis added that she herself did
not agree with this dogmatic maxim. The shame that Upper Canada's Family Compact would feel about antecedents in trade is discussed by Katherine
McKenna, *A Life of Propriety: Anne Murray Powell and Her Family, 1755–1849*
(Montreal and Kingston: McGill-Queen's University Press, 1994). This represented a view changed from that of the early eighteenth century. In his
sample from London 1695–1725, for example, Peter Earle found that

almost half of female informants (fifteen of thirty-two) who were married to 'gentlemen' nonetheless worked for pay. For analysis of Earle's findings, see Hunt, *Middling Sort*, 129.

95 This is discussed in chapter 1 above. There was a decline in persecution of English 'scolds' after 1650. Pontchartrain, despite warning Vaudreuil against women's talk, himself often listened to Vaudreuil's wife, as well as referring patronage requests to his own wife. On the ministerial response to Agathe Saint-Père's request for an employment for her younger son (then in the colonial troops), for example, is the minister's comment 'recommended to Madame de Pontchartrain.' C11A, 1706, vol. 24, fols 167–8.

96 C11A, 1723, vol. 45, fols 344–6. Raudot's complaint appears in his *DCB* biography.

97 Abbé A. Daniel, *Histoire des grandes familles françaises du Canada* (Montreal: Senecal, 1867), 438–40.

98 Both the nuns and the governor turned down the sisters' offer as too likely to kill them. On this and other charitable and seigneurial activities, see Daniel, ibid., 440; Grenier, *Seigneurs campagnards*, 440; M-H Lapalice, *Histoire de la seigneurie Massue* (n.p.: n.p., 1930), 31.

99 Duke of Saint Simon, *Memoirs of Louis XIV and the Regency* (Washington: Dunne, 1901), vol. 2, chaps 16–28; vol. 3, chap. 6.

100 Begon, *Lettres au cher fils*, 177.

101 Her demeanour is mentioned by the bishop of Quebec. He reported, but seemed somewhat resigned to, the Vaudreuils' determination to destroy the hospice in Montreal, suggesting compensation if it happened. See C11A, 1721, vol. 124, fol. 469; 1722, vol. 24, fols 466ff.; 1725, vol. 47, fol. 452. See also *DCB*, s.v. 'Chaussegros de Léry, Gaspard-Joseph.' On religious encroachments, see *RAPQ*, 1941–2, 239, and Hammang, *Marquis de Vaudreuil*, 78.

102 *Collection des manuscrits contenant lettres, mémoires et autres documents historiques relatifs a la Nouvelle France* (Québec: 1884), 2:511–12.

103 The *badinage* is discussed in Frégault, 'Un Cadet de Gascogne,' 31. The manoeuvring is well described in *DCB*, s.v. 'Raudot, Jacques.' For deliberation on her nominee Lotbinière, see C11A, 1717, vol. 37, fol. 34. In 1723 Governor de Ramezay was filled with trepidation, and he composed his own lengthy self-defence, when Madame de Vaudreuil sailed off to the court to retail her husband's stinging rebuke of Ramezay in front of a group of officers (C11A, 1723, vol. 45, fols 231–7).

104 C11A, 1731, vol. 31, fols 67–70, has the reference to killing horses. See also her 'Mémoire' of 1710 in *Collection des manuscrits*, 2:511–13; and *RAPQ*, 1947–8, 186–8. Maurepas repeated the admonition in 1731, vol. 56, fols

124–6. The minister perhaps went overboard. In 1731 Beauharnois and Hocquart wrote of the difficulty in collecting the tax of a minot of wheat or peas per horse that had been levied, since Canadians were little accustomed to taxes and asserted that horses were, after all, useful (C11A, 1731, vol. 54, fols 70–6v). On appointments, 1717, vol. 37, fol. 34; on garrisons, 1711, vol. 120, fols 121–2, 154–7; 1711, vol. 125, fols 257–8; on d'Auteuil's dismissal, 1717, vol. 123, fols 388–93. The regent (the duc d'Orléans) and Marine Council also supported a request for approval of her husband's controversial handling of a habitant revolt in Montreal, 1718, vol. 124, fols 26–8. De Ramezay's comments appear in 1723, vol. 45, fols 326–31.

105 Gagnon, *Le Fort et le Chateau*, 129. For her appeal to court, see C11A, 1757, vol. 102, fols 43–5.

106 For the extension of Madame de Maintenon's long arm to help the Quebec Seminary, see C11A, 1702, vol. 20, fols 88–9.

107 Jane Brierley, ed. and trans., *A Man of Sentiment: The Memoirs of Philippe-Joseph Aubert de Gaspé* (Montreal: Véhicule Press, 1988), 123.

108 In Janice Potter-Mckinnon's *While the Women Only Wept: Loyalist Refugee Women in Eastern Ontario* (Montreal and Kingston: McGill-Queen's University Press, 1993), chap. 4, documents the tendency of Loyalist women petitioning the British authorities for compensation to play down any heroism of their own and stress that of male relatives. McKenna, *Life of Propriety*, shows an individual family adopting the 'cult of true womanhood' after her migration to Upper Canada and rejecting her past 'in trade.'

109 C11A, 1727, vol. 49, fol. 339.

7. Decoding the Eighteenth-Century Convent

1 Terrence Crowley, 'Women, Religion and Freedom in New France,' in *Women and Freedom in Early America*, ed. Larry Eldridge (New York: New York University Press, 1997), 110–11.

2 Jean, *Evolution des Communautés*, 199.

3 These and other imbroglios will be discussed in this chapter. Some of the richest documentation on this is found in the outburst of Intendant Dupuy on 20 Nov 1727 (C11A 1727, vol. 49, fols 124–55); see also 1730, vol. 52, fols 156–7. One official dispatch of 1665 suggested that at that point the bishop reviewed their accounts yearly (vol. 7, fol. 63), but the colony subsequently experienced quite a few years of absentee bishops.

4 For a book that interweaves spiritual and secular dimensions more artfully than I have been able to do here, see Gray, *The Congrégation de Notre-Dame*. For an attempt to integrate the spiritual and material dimensions, see

my 'Stone Walls Do Not a Prison Make: French America's Cosmopolitan Cloisters,' in *Religion and Space in the Transatlantic World*, ed. John Corrigan (Bloomington: University of Indiana Press, forthcoming). See also the excellent chapter on spirituality in Dinet-Lecomte, *Les soeurs hospitalières.*

5 Laywomen's activities are signalled in Guy Frégault, 'Politique et Politiciens,' in his *Le XVIIIe siècle canadien*, 159–241; and are the focus of Anka Muhlstein's *La Femme soleil: Les femmes et le pouvoir* (Paris: Denoel/Gonthier, 1976); and my 'Women of the New France Noblesse,' in Eldridge, *Women and Freedom*, 26–43. Roland Mousnier noted the need to study the role of both sexes in client networks (Mousnier, 'Enquête internationale sur les fidélités,' *Hommage à Roland Mousnier: Clientèles et fidélités en Europe à l'Epoque moderne*, ed. Yves Durand (Paris: Presses universitaires de France, 1981), xxiii.

6 On convents and parlements, see Mita Choudhury, 'Despotic Habits: The Critique of Power and Its Abuses in an Eighteenth Century Convent,' *French Historical Studies* 23, no. 1 (Winter 2000): 35, 50.

7 Even religious vocations were related to caste. Nobility passed down from father to son, but daughters would lose noble status if they married non-nobles. Unfortunately there were not enough noble grooms to go around. Colonial officers often died young, and those who joined the French army often married abroad. Eighteen per cent of noblewomen entered religion, compared to 6 per cent of noblemen. Nearly half the Hôpital nuns entered the convent at sixteen or younger, still quite nubile. Judging by the many accounts of aspirants renouncing beaus and dancing, to go out and care for the poor, and who had to overcome parental objections, many who took the vow were truly devout. But the move could also serve family interests by forestalling marriage to a commoner.

8 The state did not acquire 'its celebrated modern impersonality' until the eighteenth century,' according to Julius Kirshner, 'Introduction: The State Is "Back In,"' *Journal of Modern History* 67 (Dec. 1995): S1. Giorgio Chittolini, in 'The "Private," the "Public," the State,' *Journal of Modern History* 67 (Dec. 1995): S42–3, asserted there is 'a growing conviction that a history of the state conceived as a history of public structures of governance, tidily planned institutions, hierarchies of power, and actions of magistrates and officials cannot adequately describe the … dynamics' at work. A state functioning in the name of abstract sovereignty and public interest above any 'private' purposes and forces, Chittolini observes, 'simply did not exist.' Well before this wave of writing on the modern state, Canadian scholar John Bosher drew attention to the phenomenon in New France. See 'Government and Private Interests in New France,' *Canadian Public Administration* 10 (1967), 246.

9 Moogk, *Nouvelle France*, 184.

10 S.J.R. Noel, *Patrons, Clients, Brokers: Ontario Society and Politics 1791–1896* (Toronto: University of Toronto Press, 1990), 14.

11 Sharon Kettering, *Patrons, Brokers, and Clients in Seventeenth-Century France* (Oxford: Oxford University Press, 1986), 11.

12 LAC, MG18, H54, Ramezay Family Papers, Documents, 1709ff., 1 juin 1701, Jean Phélypeaux to Claude Ramezay, Certification of Nobility.

13 Guy Chaussinand-Nogaret, *La Noblesse au XVIIIe siècle* (Paris: Hachette, 1976), 53, 70. These racial notions are also discussed in Jonathan Dewald, *Aristocratic Experience and the Origins of Modern Culture: France 1570–1715* (Berkeley: University of California Press, 1993), 127, 206. Pride in lineage was seen in the tendency of noble nuns to select the name of a parent as a name in religion. Mother St Claude assumed her father's first name.

14 *DCB*, s.v. 'Ramezay, Claude de'.

15 The significance of physical grace is discussed in Motley, *Becoming a French Aristocrat*, 57–8, 140–9. La Potherie noted, as did many other observers, that Canadian elites were passionately fond of dancing. A contemporary indication of the rigid social segregation of the military noblesse is that in Quebec City this group was reported to attend dinner parties separate from those of administrators and bourgeoisie. La Potherie, *Histoire de l'Amérique septentrionale*, 1:278–9.

16 Kettering, *Patrons, Brokers, and Clients*, 38. She fills out her definition on pages 3–15.

17 Ibid., 9. Noel, *Patrons, Clients, Brokers*, 71, notes the importance of brokers in the pioneer province of Upper Canada in attaching local leaders to the centre.

18 Sharon Kettering, 'The Historical Development of Political Clientelism,' *Journal of Interdisciplinary History* 18, no. 3 (Winter 1988): 425–6. Kettering also asserts that both she and Mousnier share the view of the French government 'retaining clientelist characteristics until the Revolution.' On the intendants of New France, see Jean-Claude Dubé, 'Clients des Colbert et des Pontchartrain à l'Intendance de Québec,' in *Hommage à Roland Mousnier: Clientèles et fidélités en Europe à l'Epoque moderne*, ed. Yves Durand, 205–12 (Paris: Presses universitaires de France, 1981).

19 *DCB*, s.v. 'Beauharnois de la Chaussaye, François de.'

20 See, for example, Bishop St Vallier's assertion of this in C11A, 1718, vol. 106, fol. 447. For an example of Madame Vaudreuil's intervention, see C11A, 1711, vol. 32, fol. 255.

21 Kettering, *Patrons, Brokers, and Clients*, 34.

22 Vaudreuil and Beauharnois to Maurepas, 2 oct. 1724; *DCB*, s.v. 'Ramezay, Claude de'; V. Morin, 'Les Ramezay et leur château,' *Cahiers des Dix* 3 (1938): 43. For La Potherie's comment, see *RAPQ*, 1926–7, 111–31.

23 Mother St Claude informed nuns in France about colonial military strategy, including the size of the forces and the strengths of various forts. Her letter is printed in [Helena O'Reilly], *Mgr de Saint-Vallier et l'Hôpital Général de Québec* (Quebec: Darveau, 1882), 331–3. Madame de Vaudreuil informed the colonial minister on the different strategies and equipment needed for summer and winter raids in the colony. General Montcalm chastised the wife of the second Governor Vaudreuil for interfering in military councils, both incidents discussed in chapter 6 of this book.

24 Micheline D'Allaire's *L'Hôpital Général de Québec 1692–1764* (Montreal: Fides, 1977) is the definitive history, based on exhaustive combing and sophisticated qualitative and quantitative analysis of the seventeenth- and eighteenth-century records in the Hôpital archives. Unless otherwise attributed, most details on Hôpital possessions, procedures, and personnel are drawn from D'Allaire's book, and D'Allaire attributions in this chapter, unless another title is named, refer to *L'Hôpital Général de Québec*. D'Allaire, *Hôpital Général*, 93, 114; and also her *Les dots des religieuses au Canada français 1639–1800* (Montreal: Hurtubise, 1986), 167. D'Allaire's time frames vary. Her 37.2 per cent figure applies to the period 1693–1800, while her 45.9 per cent appears to relate to 1700–60. Is it possible Gadoury, *La Noblesse*, 68, based her lower 22 per cent figure on converses and choir nuns, D'Allaire on the latter alone?

25 Pierre-François-Xavier de Charlevoix, *Journal d'un Voyage Fait Par Ordre du Roi dans l'Amérique Septentrionale* (Paris: Nyon, 1744), t. 3, 78; Kalm, *Travels*, 454; P-G Roy, *La ville de Québec sous le régime français* (Quebec: Redempti Paradis, 1930), 2:265; see also 'Mémoire sur l'état de la Nouvelle-France,' *RAPQ*, 1923–4, 6.

26 Charlevoix, *Journal d'un Voyage*, t. 3, 77–8: 'C'est la plus belle Maison du Canada, & elle ne depareroit point nos plus grandes villes de France.' On the Hôpital building, see also Kalm, *Travels*, 454–5; Roy, *La ville de Québec sous le régime français*, 2:265; 'Mémoire sur l'état de la Nouvelle-France,' 6; Captain John Knox, *An Historical Journal of the Campaign in North America for the Years 1757, 1758, 1759 and 1760*, ed. A.G. Doughty (Toronto: Champlain Society, 1914), 2:214–15; *Mgr St-Vallier*, 331.

27 Kalm, *Travels*, 2:455. They also had stables, various carriages and sleighs, and boats large and small. D'Allaire, *Hôpital Général*, 160–2.

28 For sketches of the superiors, see Joseph Trudelle, *Les jubilés et les églises et chapelles de la ville et de la banlieue de Québec, 1608–1901* (Quebec: Le Soleil, 1904), 116–19.

29 The Juchereau Duchesnays are an example. Drawn from a line of warriors so illustrious one writer remarked that their history after their 1692 enoble-

ment 'resembled a novel,' the family included many women who took the veil. Mother Geneviève de St Augustine ruled as superior for a decade. Her younger sister, Mother Marie-Joseph de l'Enfant-Jesus, became her assistant superior at twenty-one. She officiated nearly twenty years as superior, another twenty in such offices as hospital director, despositary, *discrète*. Their niece Mother Marie-Catherine de St Ignace wrote the annals. P-G Roy, *La famille Juchereau Duchesnay* (Levis: 1903), 1:178–86, 221.

30 *DCB*, s.v. 'Ramezay, Marie Charlotte de.'

31 D'Allaire, *Hôpital Général*, 168–9, has a fascinating hour-by-hour description of their routine, which brings out the spiritual side of their existence – a subject that deserves fuller study than we give it here.

32 There was one exception: converses were allowed to vote on whether the term of the community's confessor should be extended. D'Allaire, *Hôpital Général*, 152–3. 'Cinderellas of the convents' is Dale Miquelon's felicitous phrase.

33 For discussion of the cloister in France (and some relaxation of the rules there), see Rapley, *Social History of the Cloister*, 111–18.

34 *Mgr Saint-Vallier*, 253, discusses godparenting. D'Allaire, *Hôpital Général*, 120–1, lists the population of domestics, pensioners and ecclesiastics. The convent made active efforts to acquire and work more land. See, for example, the efforts on the Islets seigneurie (C11A, 1719, vol. 40, fols 81–2).

35 D'Allaire, *Hôpital Général*, 19, 128. For insightful discussion of the economic enterprises and socio-political strategies of a group that falls outside our immediate purview in this chapter, the Ursulines of New Orleans, see Emily Clark, *Masterless Mistresses: The New Orleans Ursulines and the Development of a New World Society, 1727–1834* (Chapel Hill: University of North Carolina Press, 2007).

36 C11A, 1708, vol. 29, 137 (mother superior to Pontchartrain). D'Allaire discusses revenue in *Hôpital Général*, 39–49.

37 For the couple without heirs, see P-G Roy, *Le Vieux Québec* (Quebec: n.p., 1922), 1:109. On alms, see D'Allaire, *Hôpital Général*, 41.

38 There is reference to this in C11A, 1744, vol. 107, fols 65–6, which mentions the Quebec Ursulines' two seigneuries of Portneuf and St Croix. They acquired Rivière-du-Loup seigneurie in connection with a dowry payment. Gedeon de Catalogne gives a good indication of the extensive holdings of female religious orders in 1714. See also the detailed accounting of Hôtel-Dieu de Montréal in 1741, vol. 107, fols 276–81, and the list of the Montreal Hôtel-Dieu's holdings in Jacques Ducharme, 'Les revenues des Hospitalières de Montréal au XVIIIe siècle,' in Allard, *L'Hôtel-Dieu de Montréal*, 230–33. Ducharme notes the importance of lobbying to secure government grants.

39 That is the assessment of M-C Dinet-Lecompte, who – besides her deeply researched survey *Soeurs hospitalières en France* – examined Canadian orders in 'Les hospitalières françaises en Amérique aux XVIIe et XVIIIé siècles,' *Revue d'Histoire de l'Eglise de France* 84, no. 213 (1998): 261–82. On sources of revenue, see also D'Allaire, *Les Communautés religieuses de Montréal*, 1:84.

40 C11A, 1715, vol. 113, fol. 272v.

41 Enlightening on this topic are Amy Froide, *Never Married: Singlewomen in Early Modern England* (Oxford: Oxford University Press, 2005); and Hill, *Women Alone*.

42 François Rousseau, *La Croix et Le Scalpel: Histoire des Augustines de l'Hotel-Dieu de Québec I: 1639–1892* (Sillery, QC: Septentrion, 1989), chap. 9, elucidates the Augustinian Rule and routines.

43 Notarized documents survive of seigneurial purchases signed by several sisters listing their official positions such as superior, assistant superior, director of novices, *Discrète*, or *Dépositaire*; or the signatures of numerous members of the community who gathered under the convent bell to sign formal agreements of dowries, some even specifying how those several thousand *livres* would be invested in a mill or other communal project. For a sample Hôpital Général contract, see C11A, 1720, vol. 107, fols 423–5.

44 These were said to amount to 200,000 *livres* (C11A, 1738, vol. 70, fols 225–6). The Trois-Rivières Ursulines, short of both lands and Crown subsidies, seem to have been the most desperate case, noted by the authorities in 1732 as so absurdly poor they could not even afford surgical instruments, requiring surgical patients to be sent to Quebec and Montreal. For more information on holdings of the Ursulines, Congrégation of Notre-Dame and Hôpital Général (and his complaints about their recordkeeping), see Verrier's report in C11A, 1737, vol. 70, fols 204–7v, 400.

45 For an overview of the literature and the controversies regarding hôpitaux and poor relief in Europe, see M.H.D. van Leeuwen, 'Logic of Charity: Poor Relief in Preindustrial Europe,' *Journal of Interdisciplinary History* 14, no. 4 (Spring 1994): 589–613. See also our discussion in chapter 1 of this book. Historian Jacques Mathieu, *La Nouvelle France*, 189, writes that the Quebec Hôpital 'contrairement aux organismes de la métropole ... n'est pas considérée comme une maison d'enfermement mais comme une institution de charité.' Certain hard years produced a remarkable number of urban mendicants, nearly 300 in a population of 1,200 in 1676. (Cited in D'Allaire, *Les communautés religieuses de Montréal*, 1:21, based on *Jugements et délibérations du Conseil souverain de la Nouvelle France* (Quebec: Coté, 1886), 2:30.

46 See also D'Allaire's figures, *Hôpital Général*, 120–2. Mother St Joseph claimed in 1716 they cared for more than sixty – higher than any of the

figures on D'Allaire's chart. Mother St Joseph to Conseil de la Marine, 12/14 nov. 1716, is found in C11A, vol. 36; see also 1748, vol. 91, fol. 33. In 1717 (vol. 36, fol. 212) Mother St Joseph, superior of the Quebec Hôtel-Dieu, recorded more than sixty *pauvres*.

47 In an earlier case, a smallpox epidemic arrived with a mission Indian who had visited New England in 1733. It spread like wildfire among a populace already enduring a crop failure, and some two thousand people jammed the hospitals.

48 Mgr Saint-Vallier, 327–32. The Ursulines who ran the hospital at Trois-Rivières lost six nuns to an epidemic in the winter of 1749–50, leaving only nine. C11A, 1750, vol. 107, fols 39–40.

49 D'Allaire attributes the upsurge of postulants in the 1750s to desire for a safe haven in wartime, a theory also expressed by Bishop Briand. See also Crowley, 'Women, Religion and Freedom,' 121. On the manufactory, see C11A, 1717, vol. 106, fol. 446; on the renown of the school, P-G Roy, *La Ville de Québec sous le régime français* (Quebec: Redempti Paradis, 1930), 1:528.

50 C11A, 1731, vol. 54, fols 93–6.

51 C11A, 1740, vol. 73, fols 40–1. See also the Report of the Congregation of Notre Dame in C11A, 1731, vol. 106, fols 67–8.

52 C11A, 1734, vol. 61, fols 135, 147. In a similar vein, Baron de Longeueil obtained seventy-seven signatures of well-placed Montrealers in a petition in support of Madame de Youville's attempt to reincarnate the Montreal Hôpital Général (1751, vol. 97, fols 124–6v). On Trois-Rivières, see 1733, vol. 60, fols 348–9.

53 On points of contention between the Vaudreuils and the bishop, see C11A, 1721, vol. 124, fol. 469; 1722, vol. 24, fols 466–70; 1725, vol. 47, fol. 452. On various encroachments, see also *RAPQ*, 1941–2, 239; and Hammang, *Marquis de Vaudreuil*, 78.

54 On ecclesiastical infighting and its negative effect on convents, see Henri Tetu, *Les Evêques de Québec* (Quebec: N. Hardy, 1889), 175–6. On the burial controversy, see also Miquelon, *New France*, 253–4; and Dale Standen, 'Politics, Patronage and the Imperial Interest: Charles Beauharnois's Disputes with Gilles Hocquart,' *Canadian Historical Review* 60, no. 1 (1979): 19–40.

55 Dosquet to Maurepas, C11A, 1730, vol. 53, fols 379–80. He also requested that they be returned to the control of the Hôtel-Dieu. The governor and intendant observed that Dosquet's absolutism alienated most Canadian religious communities, adding that it did not help that he was neither French nor noble. C11A, 1725, vol. 107, fols 231–2; see also 1731, vol. 56, fols 186–7.

56 D'Allaire, *Hôpital Général*, 135. Fortunately for the convent, its letters patent

required concurrence of the governor and intendant with the bishop on major changes. On the relatively large powers of the state, see Jean, *Évolution des communautés*, 201–2, 208. Guy Frégault elucidates the complex relations between church and state in *Le XVIIIe siècle canadien*, 86–158.

57 C11A, 1728, vol. 50 (Geneviève St Augustin Supérieur à Votre Grandeur, 4 oct. 1728).

58 The false pretences were that legal proceedings might be taken against the party that had offended them, and that they would be shunned.

59 C11A, 1728, vol. 50 (Soeur Agnes to the minister, 19 oct. 1728).

60 C11A, 1731, vol. 54, fols 36–9 (15 janv. and 3–6 oct.). D'Allaire too identifies a spirit of independence as the nuns' foremost trait, in *Hôpital Général*, 173.

61 This information comes from a letter from the Quebec Hôpital that survived in the Augustinian archives at Rennes, cited in D'Allaire, *Hôpital Général*, 176.

62 Jean, *Évolution des communautés*, 199, 295, provides context, showing cases in which nuns sometimes won, sometimes lost disputes with ecclesiastics. In this case the nuns seem to have lost the battle but won the war. For instances of intendant and governor siding with the nuns during this dispute, see C11A, 1731, vol. 56, fols 175–88.

63 D'Allaire, *Hôpital Général*, 217 (see also 50 and 117).

64 C11A, 1737, vol. 107 (Mother Marie-Joseph Duchesnay to the minister, 24 oct. 1737).

65 C11A, 1737, vol. 107 (Beauharnois and Hocquart to the minister, 24 oct. 1737).

66 Hocquart's remark is in C11A, 1744, vol. 81, fol. 401v. The nuns also benefited from protectors in France. A generous procurer represented them at Versailles and looked after their financial interests, sometimes paying their debts from his own pocket. He also shopped around for the fancy fabrics they loved. Advice and assistance came too, from the Augustinian convents in France. It appears the nuns largely controlled their own finances. Bishop Saint-Vallier replaced the lay administrators in 1698; but he was abroad for some fifteen years of his reign. Major initiatives required approval of court or colonial authorities (see, for example, C11A, 1721, vol. 43, fols 411–12, and vol. 44, fols 6–28); but day-to-day decisions, such as increases in the number of poor, were made by the nuns. Mother St Claude's dowry contract (for which I am indebted to Hôpital archivist Soeur Juliette Cloutier for supplying a copy) was signed by not only her father, the bishop, and the mother superior, but all the choir nuns, indicating their collective involvement. Choir sisters would vote on use of dowry capital too.

67 D'Allaire, *Hôpital Général*, 135. For supportive letters from the governor

and intendant, see C11A, 1732, vol. 57 (1 oct. 1732); 1735–6, vol. 107 (26 oct. 1735, and 6 oct. 1736). For signs of favouritism, see 1750, vol. 119, fols 369ff. For the plan to absorb the Montreal Hôpital Général, 1750, vol. 95, fol. 72.

68 C11A, 1727, vol. 49, fols 124ff. There was disagreement, too, about whether the nuns were required to accept as patients gentlewomen and servants as well as soldiers and the poor.

69 C11A, 1730, vol. 52, fols 156–7. The officials mused that the sisters' independence may have sprung from the fact that the Quebec communities pre-dated the establishment of either bishop or royal government. One official dispatch of 1665 suggested that at that point the bishop reviewed their accounts yearly (vol. 7, fol. 63), but the colony subsequently experienced quite a few years of absentee bishops.

70 C11A, 1750, vol. 95, fol. 72; 1751, vol. 98, fols 3–5. The nuns insisted such funds were supposed to come from the separate hospital treasury. For Dr Benoist's complaints against the Montreal Hôtel-Dieu, see 1740, vol. 74, fols 223–4. Other imbroglios with the authorities included the Quebec Hôtel-Dieu's five-year resistance in 1737–42 to returning soldier-patients' uniforms to the government as well as its attempts to restrict building in the neighbourhood that might disturb its privacy (see, for example, 1724, vol. 46, fols 328–31v).

71 Ducharme, 'Les revenus,' 238–43. See also Robert Lehaise, *Les édifices conventuels du Vieux Montréal* (Montreal: Hurtubise, 1980), 45.

72 Letters from both ecclesiastics are printed in A. Gosselin, *Mgr de Saint-Vallier et son temps* (Evreux: Imprimerie de l'Eure, 1898), 97–102. Governor Philippe Rigaud de Vaudreuil and his wife expressed great affection for the Hôpital's first superior, Madame de Vaudreuil bringing French medicines to her bedside.

73 C11A, 1731, vol. 56 (Dosquet to Maurepas, 4 Sept. 1731); see also 1737, vol. 107, fol. 242v.

74 She was one of two Hôpital nuns reporting personal funds (215 *livres* in paper money) in 1762. Trudel, *L'église canadienne sous le régime militaire 1759–1754* (Montreal: Institut de l'histoire de l'Amérique française, 1957), 2:307. Trudel, 302, also quotes Brooke's letter. Briand's 1766 letter (now at the Archives of the Archdiocese of Quebec) is partially reproduced in D'Allaire, *Hôpital Général*, 184–5.

75 *Mgr Saint-Vallier*, 393. Sister St Claude attempted to extend convent rights on the La Durantaye seigneurie (C11A, 1720, vol. 107, fols 421–2).

76 On links with the Soumandes, Duchesnays, and Hazeurs, see D'Allaire, *Hôpital Général*, 18, 28, 49, 95, as well as her other study, *Les dots*, 23–4;

and O'Reilly, *Mgr Saint-Vallier*, 370n. On the Levasseur family as a source of sculptors, craftsmen, and craftswomen, postulants, and pensioners, see *Journal of the Royal Architectural Institute of Canada* 7, no. 2 (1931): 69. Trudel, *L'église*, 309, notes Conquest-era loans from kin such as Mme Boishebert (Mother St Claude's sister) and M. de Lanaudière.

77 C11A, 1734, vol. 62, fols 296–7.

78 P-G Roy, *La famille Adhémar de Lantagnac* (Levis, 1908), 21.

79 See D'Allaire, *Hôpital Général*, 32–3; and O'Reilly, *Mgr Saint-Vallier*, 350ff.

80 A month later the Hôpital cemetery was full of French dead. And 183 battle victims were still being cared for by the nuns, according to H.R. Casgrain, ed., *Lettres de divers particuliers au Chevalier de Lévis* (Quebec: Demers, 1895), 16–17. See also J-Y Bronze, *Les morts de la Guerre de Sept ans au Cimetière de l'Hôpital Général de Québec* (St Foy: Presses Universitaires Laval, 2001).

81 Mother Saint-Henri unbound and hid a British officer about to be tortured by one of France's native allies. *Mgr Saint-Vallier*, 615.

82 A. Doughty and G.W. Parmelee, *The Siege of Quebec and the Battle of the Plains of Abraham* (Quebec: Dussault and Proulx, 1901), 2:164. Of Wolfe's successor General Murray, the French commissary Bernier wrote to chevalier de Lévis in October 1759, 'Il paroit vouloir protéger toutes les Maisons des Dames religieuses' (*Lettres de Divers Particuliers au Chevalier de Lévis*, 28).

83 Captain John Knox, *An Historical Journal of the Campaign in North America for the Years 1757, 1758, 1759 and 1760*, ed. A.G. Doughty (Toronto: Champlain Society, 1914), 2:213. Regarding sources, the chief primary documents for this study are the official colonial correspondence at LAC, MG1, C11A, and also MG18, H54, Ramezay Family Papers. Also invaluable are the annals of the Hôpital Général, much of them printed verbatim in the nineteenth-century edition of [Hélena O'Reilly], *Monseigneur de Saint-Vallier et l'Hôpital Général de Québec* (Quebec: C. Darveau, 1882). My thanks to Soeur Juliette Cloutier, the archivist of the Hôpital Général, who supplied me with documents relating specifically to Mother St Claude de la Croix.

84 Knox, *Historical Journal*, 237.

85 Ibid., 368.

86 Ibid. This story is repeated, with additional details of Mother St Claude's rumours, in *Mgr de Saint-Vallier*, 393–4. Editor Doughty's note in Knox's journal remarks on Murray's subsequent goodwill to the Hôpital, which makes the editor 'unwilling to believe that Murray had any knowledge of the letter attributed to him by the author. Possibly it was mere gossip circulated in the camp' (Knox, *Historical Journal*, 367–8 note). D'Allaire, writing Mother St Claude's biography, treats the story as true. *DCB*, s.v. 'Ramezay, Marie-Charlotte de.' Marcel Trudel, without dismissing Doughty's doubts,

notes on the other hand that the officer Malartic reported in June 1760, without specifying the reason, that Murray was annoyed with the nuns. Trudel, *L'église canadienne*, 2:294. Though Knox identified Mother St Claude as superior that autumn, another superior had been elected to replace her in May 1759.

87 *Mgr Saint-Vallier*, 360. Bishop Briand's estimate of the number of wounded treated at the Hôpital in its aftermath of the battle of St Foy was 1,100 (C11A, 1766, vol. 107, fol. 2).

88 Trudel, *L'église canadienne*, 2:202. The order with the next highest proportion (6.7 per cent) was the Ursulines.

89 O'Reilly, *Mgr Saint-Vallier*, 355–8.

90 The French original is quoted in Trudel, *L'église canadienne*, 2:312. Mother St Claude's letter to France also expressed concern that there would be no new postulants. D'Allaire, 132.

91 Another nice example of the gentlemanly ethos was General Murray's volunteering to supply the French officers, encamped some distance from the town, with their customary coffee, sugar, wine, and liquors. This eased the dilemma of the officer Malartic, in charge at the Hôpital, of needing to buy from the British 'sans témoigner beaucoup d'empressement ni avoir l'air d'un acheteur, ce qui ne convient pas à un officier de garde.' *Lettres de divers particuliers au Lévis*, 220–2.

92 A. Shortt and A. Doughty, eds., *Constitutional Documents Relating to the History of Canada*, 2:54 (cited in Trudel, *L'église canadienne*, 2:305).

93 Figures available for the period 1800–23 indicated government aid amounting to about a thousand British pounds per annum. *Journal of the Legislative Council of Lower Canada*, 1824, app. 1, 'Report of the Special Committee ... for ... Insane ... Foundlings ... Sick and Infirm Poor,' 2–3. It is indicative of the post-Conquest elite mindset that Murray informed the British government that nothing would be more popular with the inhabitants of the colony than assisting the Hôpital, since the nuns came from the best Canadian families. LAC, MG1, series Q, 2:367.

94 *DCB*, s.v. 'Curot, Marie-Louise.'

95 Allard, *L'Hôtel-Dieu de Montréal*, esp. 40–5, 238–9. This institution experienced severe overcrowding during the war, accommodating a hundred patients in buildings designed for forty by co-opting the chapel and even some of the sisters' own dormitory space. On relations with General Amherst, see also Soeur Jeanne Bernier, *Trois siècles de charité a l'Hôtel-Dieu de Montréal, 1642–1692* (Montreal: Therien, 1949), 85.

96 At the urging of their families, two of the Hôpital nuns did emigrate to France. O'Reilly, *Mgr Saint-Vallier*, 385.

97 LAC, MG18, H54, Ramezay Family Papers, 11 mar. 1766, Thouron et frères at La Rochelle to J-B-N Roch de Ramezay at Blaye; 19 avr. 1774, M. Latuilière at Bordeaux to J-B-N Roch de Ramezay at Blaye.

98 Philippe-Joseph Aubert de Gaspé, *A Man of Sentiment: Memoirs 1786–1871*, trans. Jane Brierley (Montreal: Véhicule, 1988), 96.

99 Even before Mother St Claude was chastised by Knox and Murray, the wife of the second Governor Vaudreuil (daughter-in-law of the powerful Elisabeth de Vaudreuil), who expressed her views on military matters all the way to the French court, had been chastised for it by General Montcalm, who held up to her as a model his wife in France, who would never dream of speaking out on such matters.

100 Gadoury, *La Noblesse*, 68, gives the figures: Quebec Ursulines 20.7 per cent, Quebec Hôtel-Dieu 17.2 per cent, Quebec Hôpital Général 22.4 per cent; in Montreal, the Hôtel-Dieu had 19 per cent and Congrégation de Notre Dame, 14.6 per cent.

101 Trudel, *L'église*, 1:76ff., documents the difficulties among parish priests and members of orders. On the declining noblesse, see Murray's remark above and Gadoury's figures, 156. From a peak of 3.5 per cent of the Canadian population in 1695–1704, nobles declined steadily. They were 1.3 per cent of population in 1754, 0.8 per cent in 1764. In absolute terms, their numbers dropped from 809 in 1745–9 to 474 in 1765.

8. Continuities in British Quebec

1 More general interpretations of the impact of the British conquest on French Canadians have varied tremendously. Writers such as Francis Parkman and A.L. Burt would have us believe it was a 'happy conquest,' with benevolent British governors favouring the polite and courageous *habitants* over the grasping merchants of their own nationality. The Catholic nationalist Abbé Lionel Groulx deemed the Conquest happy for a different reason, since it distanced French Canadians from the toxic atheism of the French Revolution. Later the Montreal school of historians that included Guy Frégault and Michel Brunet, writing at the time Quebec nationalism burgeoned after 1950, repudiated such sanguine views, asserting that displacement of leaders, especially the economic ones, amounted to virtual decapitation. Subsequently Jean Hamelin and Fernand Ouellet countered that the conquerors did not so much decapitate the conquered as invigorate them with new markets. Louise Dechene suggested the Conquest made no great difference to local economies because the profitable export trade under both regimes was controlled by metropolitan merchants, not

colonial ones. Christian Dessureault on the other hand stressed growing economic development and differentiation within habitant society.

2 Micheline Dumont, M. Jean, M. Lavigne, and J. Stoddart, *Quebec Women: A History* (Toronto: Women's Press, 1987), 58.

3 Ruth White, *Louis-Joseph Papineau et Lamennais* (Montreal: Hurtubise, 1983), 23.

4 On the switch to tea, see David-Thiery Ruddel, 'Consumer Trends, Clothing, Textiles and Equipment in the Montreal Area, 1792–1835,' *Material History Bulletin* (Fall 1990): 56. Ruddel and Adrienne Hood also documented British adaptations in textiles in 'Artifacts and Documents in the History of Quebec Textiles,' in *Living in a Material World*, ed. G. Pocius, 55–91 (St John's: Institute of Social and Economic Research, 1991). John Lambert, *Travels through Canada, and the United States of North America in the Years 1806, 1807 and 1808* (London, 1816), 1:155, observed the use of skillets to boil water in the first decade of the nineteenth century. In terms of population, the 1759 population of about 70,000 had already reached 561,051 in 1831.

5 Lambert, *Travels through Canada*, 164. He discusses housing, 136, 151–4.

6 For example, see Christian Dessureault, 'L'inventaire après décès et l'agriculture bas-canadienne,' *Material History Bulletin* 17 (Spring 1983): 127–37. The author's initial study of late-eighteenth and early-nineteenth-century St Hyacinthe had led him to challenge earlier historians' views that the rural French-Canadian population was largely homogenous in wealth, debt, possession of consumer goods, and so on, or that differences related to 'life cycle' stages. Notable among his St Hyacinthe findings was the lack of even a plow on some farms, while others were well equipped. Since women were the traditional dairy workers, it is significant that 85 per cent of the families studied had at least one cow. Dessureault's comparison of the two seigneuries of Lac-des-Deux-Montagnes and St Hyacinthe presents the argument that most Lac households 1795–1824, with an average of four cattle, two horses, five sheep, two or three pigs, and a few poultry, were largely oriented towards their own needs. The horses and cattle tended to be worth two or three times the value of all the agricultural instruments, and 'le peu de valeur des biens de production, comparativement au cheptel vif, témoigne du niveau technique de l'agriculture ancienne' (136). See also the assessment by R.C. Harris of the lacklustre growth of towns and trade in the forty years after the Conquest in *Historical Atlas of Canada* 1:117 and plate 68. For a useful overview of changes and continuities, see Serge Courville, *Quebec: A Historical Geography* (Vancouver: UBC Press, 2008).

7 Maurice Seguin, *La Nation canadienne et l'agriculture, 1760–1850* (Trois-Rivières: Boréal, 1970).

8 The context of these remarks is discussed in P.B. Waite, ed., *Canadian Historical Documents Series: Pre-Confederation* (Scarborough, ON: Prentice Hall, 1965), 2:50–3.

9 When civil courts were established in 1764, it became the practice that French law was administered in courts of common pleas, in which most litigants were French Canadians. English-speaking appellants could have their civil cases tried in the court of King's Bench, which applied English law. The situation led, however, to challenges and confusion. See Hilda Neatby, *The Administration of Justice under the Quebec Act* (Minneapolis: University of Minnesota Press, 1937), 3–4.

10 The most important change was allowing the right to make wills, though it continued to be a matter of debate to what extent wills could override traditional principles of division of land among children. It remained uncommon for French Canadians to embrace this right, until further clarification was made at the beginning of the nineteenth century. François-Joseph Cugnet's 1775 summary of the Customary Law, *Traité abrégé des anciennes loix, coutumes et usages de la colonie du Canada ajuourd'huy province de Quebec* (Quebec: G. Brown, 1775), which gave a good idea of practice at the time, offers the best evidence that the Custom of Paris principle of balancing the interests of all family members was alive and well, following passage of the Quebec Act. New provisions for making wills were bounded with traditional restrictions. Regarding dower, Cugnet observed that *Coutume* provisions 'diffère beaucoup des loix Anglaises qui n'accordent a la femme que la jouissance du tiers' (Cugnet, *Traité abrégé*, 163–8, 180–1). The 1801 Act clarified the extent of testamentary freedom, which made it possible to will most of the property outside the family, or to a spouse or a favoured child. Judge Panet and Judge Sewell each perceived different implications of testamentary freedom. Sewell thought it would lead wives to leave their shares to men, while Panet stressed wives' free choice in such matters. See also Jacques Boucher, 'L'histoire de la condition juridique et sociale de la femme au Canada français,' in *Le Droit dans la Vie Familiale*, ed. J. Boucher and A. Morel (Montreal: Presses de l'Université de Montréal, 1970), 160; B. Bradbury, 'Itineraries of Marriage and Widowhood in Nineteenth-Century Montreal,' in *Mapping the Margins: Families and Social Discipline in Canada, 1700–1975*, ed. Nancy Christie and Michael Gauvreau (Montreal and Kingston: McGill-Queen's University Press, 2004), 107, 133n; and B. Bradbury, P. Gossage, E. Kolish, and A. Stewart, 'Property and Marriage: The Law and the Practice in Early 19th Century Montreal,' *Histoire Sociale / Social History* 26 (1993): 30. Cugnet maintained that Canadian practice regarding guardianship of minors differed from the practice in France – a subject that will not detain us here but warrants investigation by legal scholars of this period.

11 *RAPQ*, 1933–4, 212.

12 Hocquart's remarks are in C11A, 1737, vol. 67, mostly in a note inserted in fol. 95, and on subsequent pages.

13 Lambert's unusual access to various classes and his reliability is discussed in a recent French translation of his account. For his assessment of female influence, see *Travels*, 165. Supporting female literacy in this period was the continuing opening of new rural schools by the Congregation of Notre Dame. See *DCB*, s.v. 'Baudry, Marie-Victoire.' Literacy studies of the first half of the nineteenth century suggest very low rural literacy of both sexes, but it is true that methods of determining 'literacy' tend to overlook the fact that women were often taught to read without being taught to write.

14 Cited in R-L Seguin, 'La Canadienne au XVIIe et XVIIIe siècles,' *Revue d'histoire de l'Amérique française* 13 (1960): 502. Seguin's article contains a number of instructive comments by post-Conquest and early-nineteenth-century observers.

15 Lebrun, *Tableau statistique*, 248. In the same decade John Wenham informed the Society for the Propagation of the Gospel that a great proportion of French-Canadian males were 'ignorant of letters, the females only being instructed to read and write in Canada.' LAC, MG24, J49, Society for the Propagation of the Gospel History, handwritten ms.

16 Quoted in Dumont et al., *Quebec Women*, 123.

17 Bradbury, 'Itineraries of Marriage,' 120. British dower applied to use or revenues of only one-third of the husband's inherited real property, and the practice of conveyancing simplified the process of alienating dower rights if the wife formally agreed to sale. By contrast the right was inalienable in Lower Canada, unless alternate arrangements had been made in the marriage contract.

18 One strategy adopted by some was to advertise in newspapers for all who had dower or other customary claims or inheritances to appear within the month at the office of a certain lawyer or other official to stake their claim. For examples, see *Gazette du commerce* (Montreal), 10 juin 1778; and 7 oct. 1778.

19 Cugnet, *Traité abrégé*, 99, 109; Joseph-François Perrault, *Abrégé des lois*, 1810, 111.

20 Henry Desrivières Beaubien's 1832 *Traite sur les lois civiles du Bas-Canada*, with its fifty-page chapter on dower, contrasts with the eight pages that the diminished dower rights received in the Civil Code of 1866. Josette Brun, who noted that New France merchants seemed to accept dower claims as part of the cost of doing business, pointed out that we need a serial study of dower implementation in New France, and the same is true for the Lower Canadian period. Perceptions of inconveniences and frauds relating to dow-

er, and attempted remedies, were discussed by Lambert, *Travels through Canada*, 197–8. Noting that community of property and dower did mean that 'married women's property interests were far better protected against their husbands than in England,' Murray Greenwood concluded that regarding English complaints about dower clogging up land transactions 'there was some justification, but also some prejudice and definite insensitivity to the high value Canadiens tended to place on protecting the vulnerable, whether debtors or family members ... the Coutume de Paris reflected humane values appropriate to a pre-industrial society imbued with feudal concepts, Christian notions of equity, and paternalistic ideals that vulnerable members of society deserved legal protection against the avaricious.' See F. Murray Greenwood, *Legacies of Fear: Law and Politics in Quebec in the Era of the French Revolution* (Toronto: University of Toronto Press, 1993), 10, 13. These values may have even had a salubrious effect on British newcomers. Arthur Davidson explained to a British correspondent that 'laws are different here' when he decided to place a larger-than-usual settlement on his deserving wife. McCord Museum Archives, McCord Family Papers, no. 1448, Arthur Davidson to James Tod, 8 Oct. 1800.

21　D-B Viger, *Mémoire de Denis Benjamin Viger, écuyer, et de Marie Amable Fortier, son épouse, appellans, contre Toussaint Poitier et autres* (Montréal: Lane, 1827), v–vi.

22　In Montreal in the 1820s, about 40 per cent of English marriage contracts rejected dower, while only 5 per cent of French-language contracts did. On marriage contracts and the campaign against dower, see Bettina Bradbury, 'Debating Dower: Patriarchy, Capitalism, and Widows' Rights in Lower Canada,' in *Power, Place, and Identity: Historical Studies of Social and Legal Regulation in Quebec*, ed. T. Meyers, K. Boyer, M.A. Poutanen, and S. Watt, (Montreal: Montreal History Group, 1998), 62. Bradbury's 'Itineraries of Marriage and Widowhood' supplies the additional point that of the Montreal marriage contracts studied, 80 per cent of those written in French versus 25 per cent of those written in English appointed the widow the sole executor. In terms of community of goods; 90 per cent of the French contracts stipulated this in the 1820s and 70 per cent in the 1840s, as indicated in Bradbury et al., 'Property and Marriage,' 31. That article also raises the possibility of some advantage accruing to women from separation of goods, since they protected each spouse's goods against the other's creditors in what was a period of frequent bankruptcy. The separation gave a wife some freedom to administer her property; but the ensuing discussion suggests that courts in fact usually demanded husbandly authorization for anything beyond household necessities (22–3).

23 For a catalogue of these, see chapter 3 of this book.

24 She is mentioned in Neatby, *Quebec*, 72–3. Madame Baby was another post-Conquest trader, one who operated under the name of male relatives, as others may have done. Even newcomers such as the family of John Howard, Governor Carleton's appointee as vendue-master of Montreal, let it be known that all those wishing to dispose of houses, lands, and other holdings when he was out of town should 'apply to Mrs Howard, who will dispose of the same in the absence of her husband' (*Gazette du Commerce* [Montreal], 8 juillet 1778). Some post-Conquest female merchants, including Madame Baby, operated under the names of male relatives, which adds to historians' difficulties in getting a sense of the numbers involved.

25 In 1809 Lambert, *Travels through Canada*, 516, noted that two or three of the NWC-owned ships annually shipped Canadian cargoes. That British nationals brought their views with them is perhaps the most plausible explanation of the seeming disappearance of women from the trade and shipment of furs. Many of the Scottish and American traders who gradually took over the upper reaches of the trade seem to have immigrated without wives, and a number of them took country wives. In contrast to the situation in British Quebec, Jay Gitlin's *Bourgeois Frontier: French Towns and Traders and American Expansion* (New Haven: Yale University Press, 2010) suggests that women traders remained important among the Franco-Metis trading families in the Mississippi Valley considerably longer, until these families began to be displaced by American traders around 1840.

26 See, for example, McKenna's description of the dishonour Loyalist Anne Murray Powell felt in regard to her earlier career in a millinery shop in *A Life of Propriety*. Similar shame was felt by Loyalist John Beverley Robinson about his mercantile mother. On the Lower Canadian front, worth investigating is the long legal imbroglio that saw the valuable Lemoine-Leber house, Lachine staging point for outfitting western traders, transferred out of the hands of the heirs of Marie-Madeline Lepailleur and into the hands of Donald Grant of the North-West Company. For Wollenstonecraft's comment, see Miriam Brody Kramnick, ed., *Vindication of the Rights of Woman* (Hammondsworth: Penguin, 1975), 261.

27 Thomas Doige, *An Alphabetical List of the Merchants, Traders and Housekeepers Residing in Montreal* (Montreal: Lane, 1819), 48–183. Margaret R. Hunt, *The Middling Sort: Commerce, Gender and the Family in England 1680–1780* (Berkeley: University of California Press, 1996), chap. 5, points out that women's presence was hidden because legal and insurance documents were often placed under a male name, and the same applied to urban directories (which also tended to omit smaller concerns). Among examples of unlisted

occupations were female furriers Nathalie Pilon found in her studies of
Lower Canadian pollbooks, in 'Le destin de veuves,' 83. Information on the
market stalls appears in Brian Young, 'Getting Around Legal Incapacity:
The Legal Status of Married Women in Trade in Mid-Nineteenth Century
Lower Canada,' in *Canadian Papers in Business History* 1, ed. P. Baskerville
(1989): 2. V. Robichaux's biography appears in *DCB*.

28 Shoemaker, *Gender in English Society*, 116–22. Even in the mid-nineteenth
   century, Henry David Thoreau reported female traders, including old
   women presiding over tables of merchandise at riverside in Quebec (their
   age perhaps reflecting a dying practice?), *Yankee in Canada*, 30, 109. Even
   in Lambert's much earlier day, local customs apparently differed, for he
   reported ladies did not attend the market at Trois-Rivières. On funerals, see
   Montreal Herald, 15 Mar. 1817.

29 See Thoreau, *Yankee in Canada*, 30, 51, 109. Evidence from later periods
   indeed suggests country wives never ceased venturing into town with produce, and some townswomen would continue to run groceries, taverns, and
   boarding houses. On women and gendered drinking patterns at Quebec
   markets, see Lambert, *Travels through Canada*, 71, 109, 156. See also Joseph
   Sansom, *Travels in Lower Canada* (London: R. Phillips, 1820), 15.

30 That census reported about 27 per cent of Montreal's women as members
   of the workforce, an under-representation. Viger missed about half of the
   women involved in dressmaking, according to Mary Anne Poutanen's study
   of apprenticeship contracts, 'For the Benefit of the Master: The Montreal
   Needle Trades during the Transition 1820–42' (MA thesis, McGill University, 1986), 34, 71, 159. Poutanen discusses their under-representation in legal
   documents as well.

31 That is the assessment of Poutanen, 'Benefit of the Master,' 4–5.

32 See, for example, the St Paul's Church, Montreal, baptismal records, where
   until the 1840s the child's parents are usually recorded as 'John Brown
   and his wife Mary Jones.' This usage is also to be found in many early-nineteenth-century anglophone court cases and newspaper reports in Lower
   Canada. In the French-Canadian community the usage was customary, then
   as now.

33 See McCord Museum Archives (Montreal), McCord Family Papers, Diary
   of Anne Ross McCord, entries for 4–5 and 26–7 June 1821. The Robertsons
   chose an old woman who promised a cure while the McCords chose the
   physician. Another medical matter warranting further research is the proclivity of Lower Canadian women to a form of goitre, discussed in Lambert's
   discussion of Trois-Rivières and also in 1816 correspondence of Rosalie-Pap-
   ineau Dessaulles. On servants, see Claudette Lacelle, *Urban Domestic Servants*

in 19th Century Canada (Ottawa: Parks Canada, 1987), 19, 31–2. The 1825 census indicated about one-third of Montreal servants were male.

34 Poutanen, 'Benefit of the Master,' 4–5, 38–47, 54, 72–6. (Between 1833 and 1842 Major engaged thirty-three apprentices.) Census figures, which tend to under-represent female production and other economic activity, are unreliable. But even the sketchy data on female labour force participation that historians have been able to extrapolate from the Viger census of 1825 (27 per cent) bear comparison with later, more complete figures for female workers cited by Cross (33 per cent in 1871, 28 per cent in 1891). See J-P Bernard, P-A Linteau, and J-C Robert, 'La Structure Professionnelle de Montréal en 1825,' *Revue d'Histoire de l'Amérique française* 30, no. 3 (1976): 397–9; and Suzanne Cross, 'The Neglected Majority,' in *The Neglected Majority*, ed. A. Prentice and S. Trofimenkoff (Toronto: McClelland and Stewart, 1977), 1:74. More revealing are the apprentice contracts, which allowed Poutanen to uncover women owner-directors of five of Montreal's largest dressmaking firms between 1820 and 1842. It may be a sign that there was greater resistance to change among French Canadians that the smaller-scale operators known as *couturières* continued to eschew job segmentation and piecework, to create whole outfits and even whole wardrobes for their clients. The term *couturière* continued to have this broader meaning in Canada after it had come to refer to mere sewing in France itself (Poutanen, 10, 31–3).

35 This was in 1830, the year the Montreal Court of Special Sessions began to restrict merchandisers who cluttered the streets with tables and handcarts in favour of 'the respectable class of traders who offer merchandise in their shops.' Cited in Young, *Politics of Codification*, 142–3, citing Special Sessional Papers, AJQM 25 Jan. 1830.

36 Basil Hall, *Travels in Canada and the United States in 1816 and 1817* (London: Longman, 1818), 61–4, 83–8, 93, 126. Lambert too commented on the lack of ornamental trees, and on cleanliness. On the latter question he said that, in contrast to Kalm's day, some wives now had higher standards. On the non-specific payments, see Sansom, *Travels in Lower Canada*, 32–3. A useful compendium that contrasts the slow pace of change in the country with the innovations in towns in areas such as housing, heating, and hygiene, is Jean-Pierre Hardy, *La vie quotidienne dans la vallée du Saint-Laurent 1790–1835* (Montreal: Septentrion, 2001). For a neighbouring region that stood in contrast to Lower Canada, one can note New England's commercialization of daily life, with a growth in literacy, circulating libraries, local newspapers, general stores, and advertising all tending to supplant barter and open-air markets. See William J. Gilmore, *Reading Becomes a Necessity of*

Life in Rural New England, 1780–1835 (Knoxville: University of Tennessee Press, 1989).

37 George Heriot, *Travels through the Canadas* (London, 1804), 255. Female fieldwork was especially prevalent in areas where the men worked seasonally for the fur or timber trades. In her classic study of women workers, Ivy Pinchbeck. *Women Workers and the Industrial Revolution, 1750–1850* (London: Routledge, 1930), noted both the persistence and the criticism of female agrarian labourers in certain pockets of England into the nineteenth century.

38 Lambert, *Travels through Canada*, 1:163, 509.

39 Lebrun, *Tableau statistique*, 283. See also D. Dainville, *Beauté de l'histoire du Canada* (Paris, 1821), 483. For a useful summary of travellers' observations, see Seguin, 'La canadienne.' See also Le Duc de La Rochefoucault Liancourt, *Travels through the United States of North America and the Country of the Iroquois and Upper Canada, in the Years 1795, 1796 and 1797; with an Authentic Account of Lower Canada* (London: R. Phillips, 1799), 1:318; N.P. Willis, *Canadian Scenery Illustrated* (London: G. Virtue, 1842), 1:97; *Canada Temperance Advocate*, 15 Aug. 1853.

40 Thoreau, *Yankee in Canada*, 48–9.

41 Lebrun, *Tableau statistique*, 228–9.

42 Discussion of farm products in Quebec market and elsewhere appears in Lambert, *Travels through Canada*, 71–4, 90, 102, 139, 159–60. Much male effort went into constructing housing, vehicles, and equipment. Lambert noted that the *habitants* 'build their own houses, barns, stables and ovens, make their own carts, wheels, ploughs, harrows and canoes.' On feminine farm production, see also Lebrun, *Tableau statistique*, 282–3; and Willis, *Canadian Scenery*, 97.

43 Ruddel, 'Consumer Trends ... Montreal,' 52. See also his 'The Domestic Textile Industry in the Region and City of Quebec, 1792–1835,' *Material History Bulletin* 17 (1983): 95–126; and his 'Domestic Textile Production in Colonial Quebec, 1608–1840,' *Material History Bulletin* 31 (Spring 1990): 39–49; Luce Vermette, 'L'habillement traditionnel au début du XIXe siècle,' *Material History Bulletin* 20 (Fall 1984): 44–7; Pierre Sales Laterrière, *A Political and Historical Account of Lower Canada* (London, 1830), 131; Lebrun, 232, 281–3.

44 Lambert, *Travels through Canada*, 1:153, cited in Seguin, 'La canadienne,' 507.

45 Ruddel, 'Consumer Trends ... Montreal,' esp. 53–5, also his 'Domestic Textile Production,' 39–49; and C. Dessureault, 'Y-eut-il une "révolution industrieuse" en Amérique du nord?' in *Famille et Marché, XVIe–XXe siècles*, ed.

C. Dessureault, John Dickinson, and Joseph Goy (Sillery, QC: Septentrion, 2003), 37. The latter article also discusses the meaning of the feminization of weaving. It raises the possibility that Laurel Ulrich's New England findings that part-time, feminine cloth-making was connected to freeing men to focus on more profitable commercialized agriculture may be applicable to Lower Canada. See L. Ulrich, 'Wheels, Looms and the Gender Division of Labour in Eighteenth Century New England,' *William and Mary Quarterly*, 3rd ser., 55, no. 1 (1998): 3–38. Another mystery revolves around whether the looms typified the more affluent farm families, as Dessureault found for rural St Hyacinthe, or the less affluent ones, as Ruddel found for farms around Quebec. An instructive discussion of the economic significance of homespun is found in Beatrice Craig, *Backwoods Consumers and Homespun Capitalists: The Rise of a Market Culture in Eastern Canada* (Toronto: University of Toronto Press, 2009).

46 Lebrun, *Tableau statistique*, 389–90, supplies the count; Ruddel too discusses feminization of weaving. In his data for the village of St Eustache, Serge Courville found a decline from three male weavers in 1831 to one in 1851. Serge Courville, *Entre Ville et Campagne: L'essor du village dans les seigneuries du Bas-Canada* (Quebec: Presses Universitaires Laval, 1990), 127. Hardy observes that from the 1770s British troops wore Canadian coats (as well as moccasins). This may have provided a market for local weaving, tanning, and tailoring, and perhaps was connected with the few textile operations that appeared in and around Montreal. See also Dessureault, 'L'inventaires,' 135, which reports spinning and carding equipment in most early-nineteenth-century inventories found for Lac-des-Deux-Montagnes and St Hyacinthe.

47 Ruddel, 'Domestic Textile … Quebec, 1608–1840,' 42–3. It was largely for rural consumption. Few advertisements for homespun are found in town newspapers from the period, and it is known that even the artisanal class tended to dress in cheap imported cloth, though some of their bed and table linen was homespun. With the possible exception of 1837 when wearing *étoffe du pays* briefly became a badge of patriotism, historians doubt that much of this homespun material reached urban markets. On female production of linen, flannel, stockings, socks, and mittens, see also *Lower Canada Agricultural Society Journal* 3 (Feb. 1850): 52–3.

48 E-Z Massicotte, *Moeurs, Coutumes et Industries canadienne-françaises* (Montreal: Beauchemin, 1924), citing L-P Lemay, 47.

49 See ANQ-M list of tavern- and ferry-keepers, carters, pilots, peddlers, and hawkers, Montreal and District 1817, p.1000/46-937, reel 2592. On provision for both sexes on pedlar licence forms of the 1790s, see Marc Lebel,

'Pedlars and Peddling in the St Lawrence Valley,' *Archivist* 20, no. 2 (1994): 2–4.

50 For Courville's findings, *Entre Ville et Campagne*, 128–9. At mid-century about 100 of the village's 415 women still did paid work. Courville points out that even the more complete enumeration of 1851 yielded this more limited occupational range. D.T. Ruddel discussed home production in 'Consumer Trends, Clothing, Textiles and Equipage in the Montreal Area, 1792–1835,' *Material History Bulletin* 32 (Fall 1990): 63–94. Lambert mentioned Trois-Rivières craftswomen, *Travels through Canada*, 489. He does not mention the race or gender of canoe-builders there, whom Franquet in the 1750s identified as female. For additional discussion of home production, see Vermette, 'L'habillement traditionnel.' While we have focused on *habitant* women, a seigneuresse such as Rosalie Papineau Dessaulles was also at work planting or having planted gardens and orchards, serving as an employment agent for live-in seamstresses, cooks, and servants, and running the seigneurie during her husband's absences and after his death. She was conversant with the details of farm prices, and the varied activities with which she was concerned included care of fowl and bees, crops, laundering, dairy production, herbs, and other garden produce. See Georges Aubin and Renée Blanchet, eds., *Rosalie Papineau-Dessaulles: Correspondance 1805–1845* (Montreal: Editions Varia, 2001).

51 *Journal des Campagnes du Chevalier de Lévis en Canada de 1756 à 1760* (Montreal: C.O. Beauchemin, 1889), 117–19; Louise Dechene, *Habitants and Merchants in Seventeenth Century Montreal* (Montreal and Kingston: McGill-Queen's University Press, 1992), 269. The Prince Edward Island Escheat riots, in which women physically assaulted officials, is interpreted as flowing naturally enough from their heavy work on the farm – an interpretation also relevant for New France. See Rusty Bittermann, 'Women and the Escheat Movement: The Politics of Everyday Life on Prince Edward Island,' in Strong-Boag, Gleason, and Perry, *Rethinking Canada*, 47–58.

52 *Rapport de l'Archiviste de la Province du Québec*, 1927–8, 447, 450, 480, contains this and the other remarks regarding the invasion of 1775–6. Also published as Aegidius Fauteux, *Journal of Mssrs Baby, Taschereau et Williams* (Quebec: n.p., 1929).

53 Greenwood, *Legacies of Fear*, 89, citing Osgoode Correspondence, 1796.

54 Nathalie Picard, 'Les femmes et le vote au Bas-Canada de 1792 à 1849' (MA thesis, Université de Montréal, 1992), 857, is an incomplete figure because a number of pollbooks are missing. The 1834 bill was abrogated in 1836, not because there was outcry against removing the vote from women, but because another section of the bill allowed committees to sit after the Cham-

ber was prorogued. The 1791 Act established that voters needed to possess land or other real estate with an annual yield of forty shillings or more on country property, or five pounds sterling in town.

55 See Picard, 'Les femmes et le vote,' esp. 69–78; and Bettina Bradbury, 'Women at the Hustings: Gender, Citizenship and the Montreal By-Elections of 1832,' in *Rethinking Canada: The Promise of Women's History*, ed. Mona Gleason and Adele Perry (Toronto: Oxford University Press, 2006), 82.

56 See Mary Ryan, *Women in Public: Between Banners and Ballots, 1825–1880* (Baltimore: Johns Hopkins University Press, 1990). Catherine Clinton, *The Other Civil War: American Women in the Nineteenth Century* (New York: Hill and Wang, 1984), 15–16, traces the elimination of female franchise in New Jersey, where it was practised until 1807, then eliminated after an unruly election for 'the safety, quiet, good order and dignity of the state' (without any direct allusion to Rousseau's notion of female impropriety).

57 Picard's study overturned myths about female voters. Contrary to notions that they were major property-holders, they came from diverse backgrounds. After all, only a small property qualification was required, leading to enfranchised women from many walks of life that included teacher, farmer, milliner, furrier, laundress, and tavern-keeper. Moreover, their ranks included women of French, English, Jewish, and Italian background, as well as some twenty-five from First Nations. Also overturned is the notion that they voted conservatively and thereby incurred the enmity of the Patriot-dominated assembly, since 60 per cent voted for Patriot candidates.

58 On dress of the new bourgeoisie, see J-H Hardy, 'Niveaux de richesse et intérieurs domestiques dans le quartier Saint-Roch à Québec, 1820–1850,' *Material History Bulletin* (hereafter *MHB*) 17 (1983): 63–94; also Craig, *Backwoods Consumers*; Jan Noel, 'Defrocking Dad: Masculinity and Dress in Montreal, 1700–1867,' in *Fashion: A Canadian Perspective*, ed. Alexandra Palmer, 68–89 (Toronto: University of Toronto Press, 2004); and D-T Ruddel, 'Costume Trends, Textiles and Equipment in the Montreal Area, 1792–1835,' *MHB* 32 (Fall 1990): 45–64.

59 For a wet nurse ad, see *Montreal Gazette*, 5 Mar. 1789. Benoit Grenier found an interesting example of a seigneuresse, Catherine Duprès Juchereau Duchesnay of Beaupré, who in appealing for separation from her husband in 1795, made repeated reference to the fact that she had nursed her own infants to buttress her claims for custody, seeming to suggest she perceived nursing as exceptional for members of her class. See Benoit Grenier, *Marie-Catherine Peuvret, 1668–1739: Veuve et seigneuresse en Nouvelle-France* (Sillery: Septentrion, 2005).

60 Jean-Jacques Rousseau, *Politics and the Arts: Letters to M. D'Alembert on the*

Theatre, trans. Allan Bloom (Glencoe, IL: Free Press, 1960), 82–3. See also Shojiro Kuwase, *Les Confessions de Jean-Jacques Rousseau en France (1770–1794)* (Paris: Honoré Champion, 2003), 220–5. Carol Blum, *Strength in Numbers: Population, Reproduction, and Power in Eighteenth-Century France* (Baltimore: John Hopkins University Press, 2002), 114–31, notes the fate of Rousseau's children and shares more of the master's observations, including the one that 'the real mother of a family, far from being a woman of the world, is scarcely less reclusive at home than a nun in her cloister.' Women were to have at least four children each to keep the 'species from perishing,' modelling themselves on the Greeks who 'as soon as [they] were married ... were no longer seen in public, shut up in their houses, they limited their activities to the household and the family. This is the way of life that nature and reason prescribe to the sex; from mothers like this are born the healthiest, the most robust, the most well-built men on earth.'

61 Cited in Bradbury, 'Women at the Hustings,' 79.

62 See Louis-Joseph Papineau, *Lettres à Julie,* ed. Georges Aubin et Renée Blanchet (Sillery: Septentrion, 2000); and also Julie Papineau, *Une femme patriote,* ed. Renée Blanchet (Sillery: Septentrion, 1997).

63 'Quant a l'usage de faire voter les femmes, il est juste de le détruire. Il est ridicule, il est odieux de voir traîner aux hustings des femmes par leurs mari, des filles par leur père, souvent même contre leur volonté. L'intérêt public, la décence, la modestie du sexe exigent que ces scandales ne se répètent plus. Une simple résolution de la Chambre, qui exclurait ces personnes-là du droit de voter, sauverait bien des inconvenances.' Papineau's intervention in the discussion of the amendment of the election law appears in *La Minerve,* 3 fév. 1834. The explicit exclusion of women had begun to appear in Lower Canada in 1831, both in the Act to Incorporate the City of Montreal, which specified that property-holding males were members of the Corporation (and therefore voters), and in a document of the Legislature of Lower Canada that year calling for civil and political rights, 'les femmes exceptées.' See Picard, 'Les femmes et le vote,' 66, who also cites a legislative interchange in which Papineau did not refute a charge that he had personally welcomed female supporters at the polls (appendix, xii).

64 That Papineau came from a clan of formidable females who did not yield readily to his opinions may have heightened his relish for Rousseau's thesis that they had no business expressing political views. As we have seen, Papineau's cousin Rosalie Cherrier was a fierce anti-Patriot. His views were contested closer to home, too. Women needed to absorb, Papineau informed his wife Julie, in an ironic invocation of scripture, St Paul's stricture, 'Wives be subject your husbands.' However, Julie's protest that Papineau

functioned as a 'domestic tyrant' while trying to secure liberty for others suggests the power struggle continued at home. Indeed the correspondence between Papineau and his wife echoes the famous exchange between Abigail Adams and her husband John Adams. In 1776 Abigail exhorted him to 'remember the Ladies' when he and colleagues in Philadelphia theorized the new republic, since 'men would be tyrants if they could.' For the exchange and analysis of it, see Elaine Forman Crane, 'Political Dialogue and the Spring of Abigail's Discontent,' *William and Mary Quarterly,* 3rd ser., 56, no. 4 (1999): 744–60. John Adams treated this advice jocularly, in the same way that Papineau treated that of Julie Bruneau Papineau. Bradbury, 'Women at the Hustings,' provides details about female voting in Montreal.

65 The 1849 provision that specifically excluded women from voting was *An Act ... for the regulation of Elections of Members to represent the People of this Province in the Legislative Assembly thereof* (12 Vict, c. 27, s. 46, Province of Canada).

66 Bradbury, 'Women at the Hustings,' 83.

67 Prior to that time, some propertied Frenchwomen had cast votes in elections of the Estates Généraux.

68 Cited in Greer, *Patriots and the People*, 191.

69 *Vindicator and Commercial Advertiser*, 4 July 1837.

70 See DCB, s.v. 'Beaubien, Marguerite.' M. Darsigny, F. Descarries, L. Kurtzman, and E. Tardy, *Ces femmes qui ont bâti Montréal* (Montreal: Les Éditions du remue-ménage, 1994), 598, mentions the 1833 foundation of a club of Patriot women that held its meetings on rue Bonsecours.

71 Greer, in his *Patriots and the People*, chap. 7, discusses the apparently unorthodox sex life of Rosalie Cherrier (though we have little information about context and one wonders how to separate the reality from the insults). On Cherrier, see also Renée Blanchet, *La Chouayenne: Récits de 1837–1838* (Montreal: Les Éditions Varia, 2000), 11–25. Perhaps reflecting a more traditional acceptance of female political activity was the silver teapot Montreal Constitutionalists presented to Hortense Globensky. However, the lack of outcry by either Loyalists or Patriots to the removal of female franchise in 1834 suggests a lack of any real conviction on that score. For additional discussion of women during 1837–8, see Marcelle Reeves-Morache, *Les Québécoises de 1837–37* (Montreal: Les Éditions Albert St-Martin); and Dumont et al., *Quebec Women*, 118–24.

72 While one should note that women did not tend to be arrested even when they did participate in uprisings in that era, leadership would likely have been at least mentioned in the press. Rosalie Cherrier (Madame St Jacques) could perhaps be seen as a political prisoner, for when she or someone else in her house fired at a crowd of Patriots holding a politically driven chari-

vari at her door and wounded two of them, she was apprehended by a magistrate and committed to Montreal goal. LAC, Colborne Papers, MG24, A40, Gosford Correspondence, 12 oct. 1837.

73 Greer, *Patriots and the People*, 216. Women in political crowds on both sides of the Atlantic sometimes took advantage of the reluctance of authorities to arrest women, by marching at the forefront or initiating the riskiest tactics. For a Canadian case, see Bittermann, 'Escheat Movement.' Female rioters did not disappear altogether. At the time of the 1849 Montreal Rebellion Losses riot and torching of Parliament, 'it was remarked that a great number of females accompanied the men who were present' (*Stanstead Journal*, 3 May 1849).

74 See, for example, *L'Aurore des Canadas*, 18 déc. 1840, cited in Bradbury, 'Debating Dower,' 73. The resolutions during that period as well as a defence of dower are also cited in Greer, *Patriots and the People*, 208–10; *Montreal Gazette*, 2 Feb. 1837; *La Minerve*, 14 août 1837; and *Le Populaire*, 21 août 1837. L-H Lafontaine criticized the 1841 Special Council legislation as being an ill-drafted hodgepodge, but in his 1843 pamphlet stated that he agreed with the basic idea of registry of contracts. His 1843 *Analyse de l'ordonnance du Conseil spécial dur les bureaux d'hypothèques* focused on the 1841 document's drafting inconsistencies and expense, not on the protection of women. Beaubien's fifty pages on dower in his 1832 legal manual contrasts with the eight pages the by-then restricted rights received in the Civil Code of 1866. On the code, see Young, *Politics of Codification*. In terms of pre-Code practices, Young noted that many *habitants* did not bother going to Registry offices, even after changes made dower rights dependent on doing so. Brun, in *Vie et mort du couple en Nouvelle-France*, noted that New France merchants seemed to accept dower claims as part of the cost of doing business, pointing out that we need a serial study of dower implementation in New France, and that the same is true for the Lower Canadian period. Our discussion leaves for other scholars the question of wives with special status to manage their own business affairs, the status of *marchande publique* or (in common law) femme sole trader, which seem to have been of limited significance. Pilon and Parent estimated their numbers were limited in New France. In Lower Canada, the term apparently usually applied to smaller traders from the popular classes. Moreover, judicial decisions kept a fairly strict rule of requiring explicit husbandly consent, even for transactions relating to the wife's own business (Young, *Codification*, 155).

75 Bradbury, 'Debating Dower,' 70, 76–7. Sara Sundberg's paper 'Under Her Authority: Women and Property in Early Louisiana,' delivered at the Canadian Historical Association, Saskatoon, May 2007, set out to test the convic-

tion of a number of historians of early America that women possessed more property and more autonomy in the civilian tradition, and her comparison of Louisiana with neighbouring Mississippi (a common-law jurisdiction) confirmed the point. For an overview of the Canadian situation, one can consult William Bennet Munro, who believed that Roman law began seeping into post-Conquest rulings in Quebec as early as the 1770s, when the Committee of Gentlemen that Governor Carleton appointed to make a digest of pre-Conquest laws turned for guidance of difficult questions to French commentators of their own period, who were increasingly influenced by Roman law. Over the ensuing eighty years 'a considerable development of law took place' in which 'the judges of the province constantly turned for enlightenment to the recognized commentators, to the French courts, and above all, to the provisions of the Code Napoleon after that compilation had been prepared,' thereby departing from the older Custom of Paris while purporting to uphold it. This trend culminated in slavish adoption of many provisions of the Napoleonic code in the recodification of 1866 in Lower Canada (Canada East). W.B. Munro, *The Custom of Paris in the New World* (Stuttgart: Enke), 146–8.

76 This theme appears in Constance Backhouse, *Petticoats and Prejudice* (Toronto: University of Toronto Press, 1991), and Lori Chambers, *Married Women and Property Law in Victorian Ontario* (Toronto: University of Toronto Press, 1997).

77 The battle of the Assembly to control funds that flowed from the government to institutions was an additional motive for seeking change. The attacks on the nuns' abilities are cited in Jean-Marie Fecteau, *Un nouvel ordre des choses: La pauvreté, le crime, l'état au Québec de la fin du XVIIIe siècle a 1840* (Montreal: VLB, 1989), 157–8.

78 Doige, *Alphabetical List*, 17; *Annuaire de Ville-Marie, Première Année, 1863: Origines, Utilité et Progrès des Institutions Catholiques de Montréal* (Montreal: Senecal, 1864), 144–5.

79 F. Rousseau, 'Hôpital et société en Nouvelle-France: l'Hôtel-Dieu de Quebec à la fin du XVIIe siècle,' *RHAF* 31 (juin 1977): 47; Noel, 'New France: Les Femmes favorisées,' 87–8. While Canadian female literacy was relatively low, the gap between the sexes was smaller than that existing in contemporary France, England, and New England; see Allan Greer, 'The Pattern of Literacy in Quebec 1745–1899,' *Histoire social / Social History* 11, no. 22 (Nov. 1978): 332.

80 *Journal of the Legislative Assembly of Lower Canada* (*JLALC*) 1824, App. 1. Our material on the Hôtel-Dieu and the Hôpital Général is drawn largely from this document. The Legislative Committee reported grants of nearly five

thousand pounds to the Montreal Hôtel-Dieu in the first twenty-three years of the nineteenth century, with the rest supplied by 'Providence and Industry,' which would have included products from the sisters' seigneuries, gardens, kitchens, and workshops. During that period the Assembly made grants for the care of foundlings, the ill, and the inform poor, amounting to nearly 50,000 pounds at Quebec, with lesser amounts to Montreal and Trois-Rivières. The figure for 1823 for the sick and infirm poor was 6,500 pounds to Quebec, 2,350 to Montreal, and 450 to Trois-Rivières. In terms of personnel, in the first decade of the nineteenth century at Montreal there were about twenty sisters at the Hôpital Général, forty at the Hôtel-Dieu, and upwards of forty members of the Congregation of Notre Dame (over sixty by 1840). Lambert, *Travels through Canada*, 519–20, and Newton Bosworth, *Hochelaga Depicta* (Montreal: William Grieg, 1839), 143. For a discussion of Quebec convents' varied production and income, see Joseph Bouchette, *The British Dominions of North America* (London: Longman, 1832), 1:248–9.

81 William L. Stone, *Maria Monk Show-up, or the Awful Disclosures a Humbug* (New York: Go-Ahead Press, 1836), 9.

82 Also helpful on the Hotel-Dieu nuns is the museum and archival collection at the Hôtel-Dieu de Montréal, including its 'Tableau de bois' of patient and physician information; see also Robert Lahaise, 'L'Hôtel-Dieu de Vieux Montréal (1642–1861),' in Allard, *L'Hôtel-Dieu de Montréal*, 11–56.

83 *JLALC*, 1824 app. 1; *Annuaire*, 1864, 70. On pioneering daily visits to the poor, see D'Allaire, *Communautés*, 1:76. See also Bosworth, *Hochelaga Depicta*, 143. Another useful overview of Montreal benevolence in this period is Huguette Lapointe-Roy, *Charité bien ordonnée: le premier réseau de lutte contre la pauvreté à Montréal au 19e siècle* (Montreal: Boreal, 1987).

84 *DCB*, s.v. 'Coutlee, Therese-Genevieve,' and 'Lemaire, Marie-Marguerite.'

85 For the governor's special permit to import the machine, see McCord Family Papers, no. 1617, D. Ross Correspondence, 29 July 1820.

86 The figures the Hôpital reported to the 1824 Legislative Committee were seventeen foundlings in 1760, twenty-eight in 1761, thirty-seven in 1762; averaging in the twenties for the rest of the eighteenth century; jumping to thirty-nine in 1800, then escalating fairly steadily from 1807 (forty-five) to 1823 (eighty-six). By the late 1730s the government of New France had ceased paying nursemaids to care for foundlings, and their needs were one of the reasons d'Youville founded the group that became the Grey Nuns. Foundling homes became widespread in the eighteenth century, appearing in Dublin in 1704, London in 1741, Moscow and St Petersburg in the 1760s. See also Peter Gossage, 'Les enfants abandonnées a Montréal au 19e siècle:

La crèche d'Youville des Soeurs Grises, 1820–1871,' *Revue d'histoire de L'Amérique française* 40, no. 4 (1987): 537–59.

87 *JLALC*, 1824, app. 1.

88 Mrs C.A. Pearce, *A History of the Montreal Ladies' Benevolent Society* (Montreal: Lovell, 1820), 18; Alfred Sandham, *Ville-Marie* (Montreal: G. Bishop, 1870), 289–90. There is also a good outline of the Benevolent Society's history in LAC, Finding Aid 1504, 'Summerhill Homes.' Mrs Beniah Gibb, *née* Eleanor Praetorius, was the society's first president. Prominent in the society was Marie-Catherine Fleury Deschambault, who in 1770 married William Grant, owner of Longueuil seigneurie.

89 Pearce, *History of the Montreal Ladies' Benevolent Society*, 14.

90 *Montreal Almanack of Lower Canada Register for 1831* (Montreal: Rbt Armour, 1831), 144–6. The society fostered practical skills. Its Minute Books (in possession of the LAC) recorded that in March 1824 that the children under its care were all learning how to knit.

91 See Denise Robillard, *Emilie Tavernier-Gamelin* (Montreal: Méridien, 1988), and the insightful chapter on Tavernier in Bettina Bradbury, *Wife to Widow: Lives, Laws and Politics in Nineteenth Century Montreal* (Vancouver: UBC Press, 2011). On Catholic activism, see also Claire Daveluy, *L'Orphelinat Catholique de Montréal (1832–1932)* (Montreal: Levesque, 1933); H. Lapointe-Roy, *Charité bien ordonnée*, 82–3; *Annuaire*, 1864, 77–8. Both Lebrun and Lady Aylmer were impressed with the proceeds of the Montreal Bazaar.

92 Lebrun, *Tableau statistique*, 72–3; and Pearce, *History of the Montreal Ladies' Benevolent Society*, 23.

93 Pearce, *History of the Montreal Ladies' Benevolent Society*, 7.

94 Jean-Marie Fecteau, *Un nouvel ordre des choses: La pauvreté, le crime et l'État au Québec, de la fin du XVIIIe siècle à 1840* (Montreal: VLB, 1989), 193–4; see also his *La liberté du pauvre: sur la régulation du crime et de la pauvreté au XIXe siècle québécois* (Montreal: VLB, 2004). On Montreal relief efforts, see also Bradbury, *Wife to Widow*; M-C Daveluy, *L'Orphelinat catholique de Montréal (1832–1932)* (Montreal: Levesque, 1933); and Robillard, *Emilie Tavernier-Gamelin*. See also D'Allaire, *Communautés*, 1:34, 153; and Huguette Lapointe-Roy, *La Charité bien ordonnée* (Montreal: Boreal, 1987).

95 On the prominence of voters among *benevolés* from families such as the Forestier-Vigers, Tavernier-Gamelins and Longueuil-Grants see Picard, 94–7.

96 While we have not focused on education here, women seem to have led the way there too in early nineteenth-century Montreal. In Micheline D'Allaire's assessment, 'dans la région de Montréal, le système d'écoles le plus stable durant le premier quart du XIXe siècle est celui des soeurs de la Congrégation.' The order typically numbered fifty to sixty members during the

seventy-year period after the Conquest. At the beginning of the nineteenth century the order's fifty-eight members had three schools in Montreal and seven in the countryside of that district. They opened several new schools in the 1830s, so that by 1841 the sixty-eight sisters were educating two thousand girls a year in the Montreal District. At their boarding schools, they taught not just literacy and ladylike attainments but meaty subjects such as history, geography, rhetoric, chemistry, and philosophy. On this growth and on the window of opportunity for women, see M. D'Allaire, *Les Communautés religieuses de Montréal*, 2:16, 21–53, and 149. The Sulpician Order helped fund some of these efforts (even paying for the sisters' transport by horse and cart) as well as a number of little schools conducted by lay schoolmistresses and masters. Lebrun reported the findings of an 1831 Lower Canada Education Committee: the province had 45,000 male pupils, 20,500 female; the Committee inspected 186 boys' schools and 183 girls' schools, 884 mixed ones. Of these, 872 were syndical, 66 Royal Institute, the others run by *fabriques* or individuals. The Committee calculated there were 670 schoolmasters and 635 schoolmistresses in the colony. Lebrun, *Tableau statistique*, 191–2 discusses education; and bazaars, 247 which were also regularly reported in Lower Canadian newspapers. Lady Aylmer's handwritten *Recollections* at Library and Archives Canada give further detail on bazaars as well as describing Montreal nuns' attempts to entertain her. On men's monopoly of civic leadership in England by the eighteenth century, see Smail, *Origins of Middle-Class Culture*, and Hunt, *Middling Sort*, 131–2.

97 Bosworth, *Hochelaga Depicta*, 210–11. For some examples, see 124–46, 188–93, 205. Montreal gentlemen in the late 1820s were serving as weekly 'visiting governors' to the General Hospital and National School. *Canadian Courant*, 13 June 1829.

98 This occurred in the 1840s for the Montreal Lying-In Hospital and Orphan Asylum. Young, *Politics of Codification*, 144.

99 Post-Conquest bishops, like legislators, made occasional attempts to exert more control over convent finances and administration, but without the consistency and energy characteristic of Bishop Bourget and his successors. As two Montreal historians observed, 'Catholic Church … officials would secure neither sufficient religious recruits nor political power before the 1840s to ensure a steady hold over their flocks or broader policy.' B. Bradbury and T. Myers, 'Introduction' in their edited collection, *Negotiating Identities in 19th and 20th Century Montreal* (Vancouver: UBC Press, 2005), 9. For examples of tightening ecclesiastical control after 1840 reining in the independence of an outstanding female activist, see Robillard, *Emilie Tavernier-Gamelin*. For another instance of Bishop Bourget tightening the reins

in the 1840s (over the Congregation of Notre Dame), see *DCB*, s.v. 'Huot, Marie-Françoise.' There is fascinating documentation of another case, the overruling of the nuns of the Hôtel-Dieu de Montréal by the combined will of the bishop and the doctors of Laval medical school after a three-decade battle (LAC, MG24, L3, vol. 49, 'Education 1803–1883,' correspondence beginning 15 Nov. 1849). Such change was relative rather than absolute. Even under this more organized and gendered hierarchy, convents did continue to supply opportunities for female managerial talent and unorthodox occupations, as is shown in M. Danylewicz, *Taking the Veil* (Toronto: McClelland and Stewart, 1987).